15.00
dir

DEBUSSY
MUSICIAN OF FRANCE

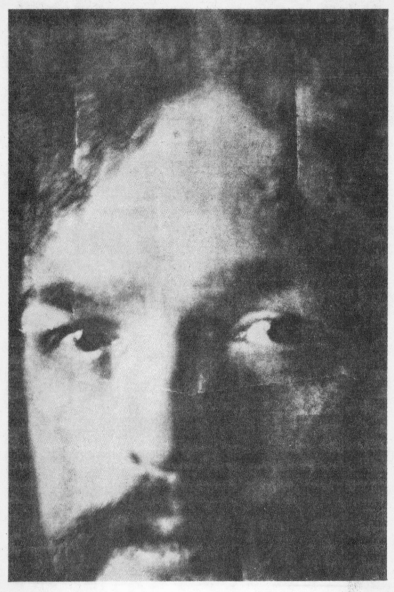

Photo of Debussy taken by Pierre Louÿs and later torn up by Debussy in a moment of anger against his friend. *Collection of Mme. Gaston de Tinan.*

Debussy

MUSICIAN OF FRANCE

*

VICTOR I. SEROFF

Biography Index Reprint Series

BOOKS FOR LIBRARIES PRESS

FREEPORT, NEW YORK

73-313

INTERNATIONAL STANDARD BOOK NUMBER:
0-8369-8032-8

LIBRARY OF CONGRESS CATALOG CARD NUMBER:
73-126326

PRINTED IN THE UNITED STATES OF AMERICA

"It is well, amid pressing occupations, to think of the great musicians and, above all, to bring them into the thoughts of others."

CLAUDE DEBUSSY

FOREWORD

A GREAT MANY BOOKS have been written about Debussy and his
music—mostly about his music—but none as detailed as Léon
Vallas' *Claude Debussy et son temps* published in 1932. This
volume, long out of print and available only in libraries, served
as the basis for all subsequently written biographies, including a
second Debussy biography by Vallas published during the German
occupation and therefore a slightly altered portrayal of the man;
otherwise, it was distinguished only by its smaller size. All these
works *d'après* the first Vallas, although more readable, suffer from
some of its inaccuracies as well as incompleteness.

This is easily explained. The three volumes of Debussy correspondence (with Robert Godet and Jean Aubry, with Pierre Louÿs,
and with d'Annunzio), René Peter's revised and more complete
Claude Debussy, Eugène Ysaÿe's biography, Valléry-Radot's
Souvenirs de Claude Debussy, Mary Garden's Story, and many
articles in newspapers and periodicals which throw a new light on
the life of the composer, were not published until the last war
and even later. If nothing new has been added to the analysis of
his music—nothing was "discovered"—the complete picture of
Debussy's personal life became available only with the newly
published material.

My portrait, I admit, differs from the accepted Debussy legend.
But I hope that my readers will judge the man for what he has
given the world as much as for what he took from it.

V. I. S.

*Illustrations will be found
following page 192.*

CONTENTS

DEBUSSY

MUSICIAN OF FRANCE

CHAPTER I

BACKGROUND

DURING WORLD WAR I when France was struggling against her most formidable foe, when heroic deeds on the battlefield and civilian contributions to the war effort were being rewarded with medals, citations and patriotic acclaim, Debussy, too old and ill to take part in the national defense, proudly signed his compositions "Claude Debussy, *musicien français.*" This he maintained was the highest honor he could claim. But the name of *Claude de France,* as Gabriel d'Annunzio, the Italian poet, called him, was more appropriate to the outward splendor in which the composer lived at this time.

12 Square de Bois de Boulogne in Paris is an exquisite private house with a beautifully kept lawn, guarded by a high iron fence. No street noises of the busy metropolis reach this spot, well sheltered by the mansions of "the rich and mighty" along the Avenue Général Foch leading from the Étoile into the Bois de Boulogne. Here was the home of Claude Debussy during the last thirteen years of his life. It was not, however, a family estate. The composer's genealogy does not intertwine with that of the Counts de Bussy of Burgundy who once lived at Bussy-le-Grand in the famous wine province, although it has been related that, like the composer, a twelfth century Count de Bussy had a prominent forehead. Madame de Sevigné's cousin, he was known as Roger Bussy-Rabutin, a warrior and writer whose escapades with women were his other principal distinction.

Claude Debussy never spoke of possible ties with this family, not even in his youth when for a while he took to spelling his name de Bussy, thus implying noble blood, and he certainly did not credit his success with women to his ancestry. What would be the advantage in that? He did well enough on his own. But Manuel Debussy, his father, when given to reveries, often added a romantic touch and claimed lineage with the Counts of Burgundy. He completely disregarded the short distance of five miles separating the château—the seat of the noble family—from Courcelles-sous-Grignon, the little village his ancestors actually came from.

It has been ascertained that Debussy's forebears were plain people: artisans, farm workers and small businessmen, none of them distinguished enough to have their lives recorded; that during the French Revolution one of them, Pierre Debussy (the composer's great-grandfather, the first in the family to write his name in one word) came to Montrouge; that his son Claude worked as a carpenter and cabinetmaker in Paris; that Marianne-Françoise Blondeau, a fringe maker, became his wife; and that on May 10, 1836 they had a son, Manuel-Achille, the composer's father.

Twenty-five years later, on November 30, 1861 at Levallois, near Paris, Manuel-Achille married Victorine-Joséphine-Sophie Manoury, a girl in humble circumstances, a few months his junior, and the day after the ceremony went with her to Saint-Germain-en-Laye, where they started a china shop.

In dealing with their subjects biographers usually explore all the traits of their ancestors for clues. But as Cervantes' Sancho Panza would have said, in this case there was one extraordinary thing— there was nothing extraordinary about the ancestors of the extraordinary subject of this study. Except that, on August 22 of the following year, 1862 (those with a flair for mathematical accuracy point at the date with a significant *sic*), a boy was born at Saint-Germain-en-Laye who was not christened Achille-Claude until July 31, 1864—that is, almost two years later, an unusual occurrence in a Catholic lower-class family, especially for a first-born son; thus adding another *sic* to the mystery created by no less a man than Léon Vallas, the well-known Debussy biographer, whose information has served as a basis for all the subsequently written works on the composer.

In his preface Vallas said: "In this book on Claude Debussy I have avoided all biographical details the publication of which might be deemed premature and indiscreet. The secrets of his private life belong to those who shared it and who bear his name. For the purpose of this book I have made use only of such documents as were originally intended for publication or which have by chance become public property." [1]

This provocative preamble is followed on the second page of the same volume with: "Debussy never spoke of his childhood, except for occasional allusions to his sojourn on the Côte d'Azur. The secrecy he maintained on this subject was deliberate. It is not for us to elucidate the mystery. Future historians may attribute it to the fact that the remembrance of the china shop where he was born was not a source of vanity to him; but those who wish to ascertain the real reason for Debussy's silence regarding his childhood at Saint Germain and Paris must base their investigations on a public document. His baptismal certificate," M. Vallas goes on, "bears two names which he declared later were unknown to him: those of his godfather, Achille-Antoine Arosa, and his godmother, Octavie de la Ferronnière. The identity of the financier, Arosa, will be disclosed some day, and Octavie de la Ferronnière will be despoiled of the high-sounding name she assumed; we shall ascertain what relationship, legal or otherwise, united the two people who held Achille-Claude at the baptismal font: then only shall we know the exact circumstances of his childhood. We do not propose to reveal here any further particulars on the subject."

Having thrown this firebrand, Vallas—whether intentionally or by oversight—revealed on the following page that Debussy's godmother was his aunt, Manuel-Achille's sister, Madame Roustan. The book created an uproar among admirers of Debussy. Two years later, in 1934, in a long and detailed article published in *La Revue Musicale*, Henri Prunières brought the controversy to a boil. Accus-

[1] Leon Vallas, *Claude Debussy et son temps* (Paris, 1932).

ing Vallas of flagrant inaccuracies throughout the work, Prunières referred to the slanderous insinuations concerning Debussy's birth. Vallas rebutted, answering Prunières point for point, mostly blaming his accuser for not understanding the French language.

The polemic, drawn out in several issues from May till October, was complicated by arguments about correct and false construction of the sentences, and did not prove anything; but it brought a few additional suppositions to light.

"Some of us, like Godet [1] and myself," Prunières wrote, "understood [from Vallas' book] that there is a doubt of the legitimacy of Debussy's birth. Madame Debussy (the composer's widow) asked me if I ever heard it said that Debussy could have been the son of this Arosa of whom she had never heard him speak. . . . Others have supposed that Debussy was the product of the love affair between Arosa and Octavie de la Ferronnière and that the Debussys agreed to bring up their child."

Having reached this impasse, no one up to the present time has "elucidated the mystery." It seems to me that there are only two solutions to the problem: either to accept the official record of his birth and close one's eyes to some of the unaccountable aspects of Debussy's character, as well as to some episodes in his life and, once and for all, discard Vallas' insinuations as valueless, or to accept Vallas' challenge, leave false respectability aside and face the simple fact that this extraordinary being may have been a product of an extraordinary union.

If this is another "Wagneriana," who was this man Arosa—the Ludwig Geyer in the Debussy case? He was a banker, that much is known, and most probably of Spanish extraction. His name does not appear in any records connected with music, but on May 6, 1891, at the Drouot Gallery, a *Collection de Monsieur A . . . A. Tableaux moderne, aquarelles, dessins et bronzes* was offered for sale at an auction. Among sixty-one items there were works signed by men like Corot, Delacroix, Harpignies, Jongkind, Sisley, Daubigny, Gavarni, and Pissarro, to name a few, and as the art judges

---

[1] Robert Godet, a Swiss journalist, Debussy's lifelong intimate friend.

said: "The collector made a noble and severe choice, excluding the less important ones." Some of the canvases, according to Charles Yriarte's short article for the catalogue, Arosa had acquired "at a good time when amateurs at the beginning of their careers were not overburdened with money, while he [Arosa] had faith in their genius."

One can easily imagine the refined taste of the owner: there were no large canvases, nothing to cause a sensation. These were of a more intimate character and showed his preference for Corot and "the modern," the impressionists. Among them were Pissarro's now famous "Four Seasons"—four door panels—commissioned after the Franco-Prussian War when Arosa was rebuilding his home in St. Cloud, pillaged and burned by the victorious Germans. If Paul Gauguin's works were conspicuously missing at this sale it was most probably because they belonged to Gustave, Arosa's brother, the photo-engraver, who lived with him—the man who was referred to as Gauguin's godfather because he took care of the young Paul after his return from sea duty. Through his son-in-law, the director of the Bertin agency, Gustave was instrumental in arranging for Gauguin a job on the Paris stock exchange, but it was due to Achille-Antoine that Gauguin eventually became a painter. More than from the evening classes at the Académie Collarossi, Gauguin learned much from the week ends spent at the Arosas, where "the talk was all of painting," where he met Pissarro, who used to bring his latest canvases there.

There is no sense in speculating as to how a man of Achille Arosa's social position and artistic interest happened to associate with Madame Roustan, obviously out of the circle of his acquaintants. In France, "high-sounding" names like Octavie de la Ferronnière were sported by *cocottes*, but as there is no proof for such an allegation, it is possible that at first she worked for Arosa in one capacity or other and later, when she became his mistress (this has been firmly established), took this name to fit in the banker's *ambiance*.

It is most unlikely that if Claude Debussy were the son of Arosa and Octavie de la Ferronnière, or even Victorine herself, that throughout his life he would have remained the son of his official parents, refusing to admit even the knowledge of Arosa's name. Yet this supposition could be based on the theory that, in either case, Arosa had arranged for Manuel Debussy to marry Victorine and the small china shop may have closed the bargain. Judging by the scant information on Manuel, he had neither the education nor workmen's skill to earn his livelihood either before or after his marriage, and the proximity of Saint-Germain-en-Laye to Saint Cloud (five miles) may have added extra weight to the argument.

Victorine's behavior and the relationship between the members of the Debussy family is no less puzzling in the whole mystery. A highly emotional woman, domineering and given to violent outbursts of temper, she did not make her boy's childhood a happy one. She slapped his face regularly and was reported to have said: "I would rather have given birth to a bunch of vipers than to bring up this child of shame." Yet she kept him to herself, while her four younger children she turned over to her sister-in-law (Octavie de la Ferronnière) to nurse and to bring up because, it was said, she did not like children.

She taught Achille-Claude to read, write and count, and with this his formal education came to an end. Young Debussy was never sent to school, "presumably because the Debussys were too poor," and the composer's writings even in the later years of his life suffered from a lack of grammar and poor spelling.

Thus the meager official data on Debussy's background show that there is no obvious hereditary explanation for the genius of the great French composer, but that at least one thing was certain: the Debussy family conformed to few rules and agreed with little of of the personal etiquette imposed upon them by the civilization in which they lived.

After his fourth or sixth year (the dates concerning his childhood and adolescence are mysteriously conflicting) the young Debussy was taken by his aunt to Arosa's homes at Saint Cloud or at Cannes, where he spent many months during the following years, being spoiled by all the things his parents could not afford. These "vacations" were the only bright days in the boy's otherwise gloomy childhood.

It is interesting (if not significant) that in all the voluminous writings about the composer there is no information about his playmates nor even his brothers and his sister, except for a laconic statement that his sister Adèle was born in Saint Germain, while the three brothers Alfred, Emmanuel and Eugène were born in Paris, and that Eugène died of meningitis in infancy. The only vague mention of them as grown-up men is that Emmanuel lived somewhere in the south of France, Alfred either in Le Havre or in Cardiff in Wales, and Adèle in Paris. Debussy, it was said, did not care to talk about them and one gathers from his few remarks that they were not artistically endowed.

If to this information is added the fact that Arosa's son Paul (by his later marriage) was not merely "artistically endowed" but was a poet (his works were used for the Prix de Rome contests), and that to my inquiries he flatly denied any blood relation with the composer—it will confuse the already complex issue even more.

Eight years before Vallas raised this question, Gabriel Pierné, the conductor, had given an illuminating glimpse of the teen-aged Debussy which certainly furnishes additional material for thought: "He was a gourmet, but not a gourmand. He adored good things to eat and the quantity mattered little. I remember well the way he savored a cup of chocolate which my mother invited him to take at the Café Prévost, or how, at Bourbonneux's famous pastry shop, he used to choose a tiny sandwich or a little *timbale aux macaronis*, or some delicate pastry from the show-window specially marked as the *produit de luxe* while his friends were more likely to be content with something more substantial.[1] This poor boy, who had come from a coarse class of society, had in everything the taste of an aristocrat. He was particularly attracted to minute objects and delicate and sensitive things. My father had a beautifully bound set of *Le Monde Illustré*. When Achille (at that time this was his first name, and Debussy's mother to the end of her life never called him by any other) came to the house, we used to look at the pic-

[1] This is also mentioned in Alma Mahler's *Gustav Mahler* as having been reported to her by Paul Dukas.

tures with delight. He preferred those which took up little space and were surrounded by a large margin. One day he persuaded me to help him cut out these pictures to adorn the walls of my room. The crime was soon committed and I remember that Debussy went off with reproductions of famous pictures, some by Meissonier in particular, surrounded by those large margins."

Would this sketch of the young Debussy lead us to Manuel Debussy, who wished his son to become a sailor, or to Arosa, the connoisseur in arts and collector of rare pictures? Who could have taught him such discrimination?

As far as I know there are no documents in existence proving Arosa's parentship to Debussy, but from my study of Debussy's character I have come to the conclusion that Arosa, if he was not physically his father, was as good as one, and his early influence was as great as if it were hereditary. I believe that a true nobleman needs no ancestors, but it is fortunate that there was such a man as Arosa during Debussy's formative years. In Arosa's home the boy learned a different way of living and from then on consciously or subconsciously he longed for the beautiful, the refined, so much, that as a grown-up man he often said: "At the sight of something ugly I become positively ill."

"See how easily they are mistaken," Debussy once said to a journalist in Vienna. "Some think I am a melancholy northerner, others that I am from the south, from Provence, the country of Daudet —*tireli, tirela!* Well, I am only a native of Saint Germain, half an hour from Paris."

Indeed, Debussy was born at Saint-Germain-en-Laye; for the police record—on the second floor in a modest house at 38, Rue au Pain, and for astrologers—at four-thirty in the morning on August 22, 1862. There, where today hangs a large sign *Teinturerie Rogier, fondée en 1887,* Manuel Debussy had his china shop, nine feet wide and fifteen feet long. A narrow, dark, long corridor leads from the street into a small rectangular court and a heavy wooden staircase to the apartment above the store once occupied by the Debussys. Although there are not one, but two commemorating plates on the wall of the house facing the street:

Ici est né
le 22 août 1862
Claude Debussy
compositeur de musique

À Claude Debussy
un groupe d'admirateurs anglais
1er juillet 1923

the concierge does not seem to know much about *le musicien*, probably because only a rare visitor comes to inquire.

Saint Germain attracts tourists by reason of far more imposing historical monuments. But the fact that *Le Roi Soleil* came from the same town, that the Château de Saint Germain can rival those at Fontainebleau and Versailles, that it has a mile-long terrace along a beautiful park with one of the most magnificent views of Paris, has really nothing to do with the boy's first impressions, which should be traced in his compositions. For the Debussys had to give up their business and move to Paris to seek a better existence soon after Claude's second birthday. The seeds of this extraordinary nature were sown neither in Saint Germain, nor in Montmartre or Clichy in Paris, where he lived with his family, but in Saint Cloud and in Cannes, where "uncommunicative and closed in upon himself, liking neither his lessons nor his games, he would spend whole days sitting on a chair thinking no one knew what." Perhaps his thoughts were akin to those Debussy, many years later, expressed to his publisher: "I remember the railway passing in front of the house and the sea stretching out to the horizon. Sometimes you had the impression that the railway came out of the sea or went into it— whichever you like. Then there was the route d'Antibes, where there were so many roses. I never saw so many all together in all my life." It was with his recollections of Cannes that the world of sound, which eventually he made his own, was connected with "a Norwegian carpenter, who used to sing—Grieg, perhaps—from morning till night."

In Arosa's house Debussy knew laughter, joy and happiness, and kind gestures of care and love, and it was Arosa who talked to him for the first time of art and music. Little did Arosa know that a hostile fate would give his pet the yoke of an ox to bear and the instinct of a lion, to become one of the immortals.

CHAPTER II

AT THE PARIS CONSERVATORY

It would not have been surprising had Debussy become a painter. There were more artists in Arosa's circle than there were musicians. Unfortunately, because of the "mystery of his childhood," no records are left of his studies—not even, perhaps, with one of the great masters of the impressionist school, except that he kept a palette zealously, like a sacred relic. But while he did not become a painter, he certainly thought of himself as one in his own art. He added to this illusion not only by calling his compositions "pictures," "sketches," "engravings," "arabesques" and "studies in black and white," but by his own physical appearance and way of living.

However, at Cannes, at the age of seven Debussy was given his first piano lessons. His teacher, an old Italian, Cerutti—no one seems to have remembered his first name—was not impressed with him and Debussy never mentioned how long he studied under him. Nothing is known of what happened to the Debussys during the Franco-Prussian War. Most probably the family remained in Paris but the eight-year-old boy stayed with Arosa in Cannes, and either then or upon their return his *pianoter* was heard by Madame Marie Mauté de Fleurville, a former pupil of Chopin.

As a French poet put it, if a book were written in memory of unknown women of importance, a page should be dedicated to her for the role she played in French poetry and French music at the end of the last century. Madame Mauté de Fleurville was the first to recognize genius in the dissipated, ugly-looking clerk at the Paris town hall, Paul Verlaine, and later welcomed him as her son-in-law. "She was a charming person, an artist by instinct and by talent, an excellent musician with exquisite taste, intelligent, and devoted to those she loved," Paul Verlaine said of her.

According to the accepted story, after hearing Achille play a few popular tunes and fragments of military marches by ear, she told Manuel Debussy that his son should become a musician and offered to teach him. Actually Madame Mauté probably spoke not to Manuel but to Arosa, whom she knew socially and who paid for the lessons. Thus the career of painter was discarded, but the new plans received a severe blow. A year or two later Arosa left Madame Roustan to marry another woman and was supposed to have severed all his connections with the Debussys. If Debussy refused to admit any knowledge of Arosa it may have been because of this "affront" to his family, where the name of Arosa became anathema. Manuel still wanted his son to go to sea. Fortunately for Debussy Madame de Fleurville offered to continue the lessons free of charge.

"I owe her the little I know about the piano," Debussy used to say about Madame Mauté when he was already an accomplished pianist and a famous composer. "She knew a great deal about Chopin." And indeed Madame Mauté must have been an excellent teacher, for in 1872, after only two years of study, she presented her pupil for the examinations at the Paris Conservatory and he was accepted into Albert Lavignac's *solfeggio* class.

Achille's success awakened an unusual interest in his parents. Manuel Debussy, at first not too eager for a musical career for his son, suddenly was struck by the vision of Achille as a great concert pianist, easily gathering fame and fortune. It was a seductive picture for a man still engaged in small odd jobs and without a permanent occupation. An artist's career seemed far more lucrative than that of a seaman, and Manuel took a stern attitude toward his son's piano practice. His endeavor was well rewarded: a year later Achille was admitted to Antoine Marmontel's advanced piano class.

But Achille-Claude Debussy was more of a problem child than a child prodigy. His parents' stern discipline may well have contributed to his progress, but it also drove the boy into himself. Unusually sensitive, he was quick to react to different shades of treatment. Such children resent autocratic parental behavior. They have their own sense of right and wrong, order, time and duty. They are timid and there is a certain dignity in their stubbornness. Later, when they mature, they express boldly the revolt which must have been slumbering in their minds.

The following six years in his new teacher's class proved that Achille's pianism would not reach the standards of virtuosity necessary for a concert career. It is hard to say who was responsible for this failure.

Antoine Marmontel *père*, as the sixty-year-old professor was called, had been teaching at the Conservatory for thirty years, was well respected, and had no patience with anyone doubting his authority, when the eleven-year-old Achille entered his class as an awkward, shy boy, but already with a mind of his own. Where Marmontel expected obedience, his new pupil was argumentative; where Marmontel's experienced advice bore fruit with other students, little Achille neglected to pay the necessary attention. Their two temperaments clashed more often than they harmonized.

The record of this unfortunate association shows both progress and regress in Debussy's pianistic accomplishments. In July 1874, after only eight months at the Conservatory, Achille made his debut in the old hall of the music school playing Chopin's Concerto in F minor at a competition. He won a second honorable mention and the newspaper reviewers spoke of "this little boy of eleven, who exhibited a degree of assurance and vigor that were quite remarkable in a child of his age."

There was good reason for the Debussys to rejoice. Fortune at last was kind to them: Manuel was starting on his second year as a clerk in an industrial concern with the Fives-Lille railroad, his first permanent job, and Achille was off to a good start. The critical remark of *Le Temps* that "he obtained the second honorable mention because to youth much must be forgiven" did not dampen their high hopes.

Achille did even better the following year with Chopin's Ballade in F major. This time he received first honorable mention and the reporters hailed him as "a boy of twelve destined to become a first-class virtuoso."

But a year later (1876) Debussy's playing the first movement from Beethoven's Sonata Opus 111 disappointed them. He received no prize and there was no mention of his name in the newspapers. One more year went by and in 1887 he won a second prize for his playing of the first movement of Schumann's Sonata in G minor, and this time the editor of the *Journal de Musique* predicted that Debussy would surely carry off the first prize at the next competition. Achille competed twice again in the following years, in 1887 playing the *Allegro* from Weber's Sonata in A flat major and in 1879 Chopin's Allegro de Concert. He failed both times and *La Revue et Gazette Musicale* mercilessly nailed down his hope for a brilliant future as a concert pianist with the cryptic remark that Debussy "seemed to be progressing backwards."

Unfortunately there is no record of exactly why Debussy's playing failed to please the jury and one has to judge it from general impressions of him as a piano student told some fifty years later in reminiscences by his fellow students Gabriel Pierné, Paul Vidal and Camille Bellaigue. The consensus of opinion of these musicians (all three well known in the musical field—a conductor, a composer, and a critic) was that Debussy's playing was technically far from perfect: he played trills with difficulty, breathed raucously when performing difficult passages, had a nervous habit of emphasizing the strong beat by a kind of panting, and exaggerated the marking of the rhythm and every effect. He appeared to be in a violent rage with the instrument, ready to ill-treat it with his impulsive gestures. Yet they agreed that at times he was capable of such delicate effects that they had never forgotten them.

These characteristics of Debussy's playing between the ages of twelve and seventeen, taken in connection with such a taxing repertoire as is shown by the list of compositions he played at the competitions, lead me to believe in the lack of psychological perception not only of his teacher Marmontel, but of his fellow students as well. The shy, awkward Achille obviously was a musician first and a pianist second. In the first year of his studies with Lavignac, Debussy must have impressed him not only with his inquisitiveness (at times, probably he was just as argumentative as with Marmontel) but with a sort of musical intuition and good taste.

Not an old man like Marmontel, Lavignac, only twenty-six but already respected for his musical erudition, was too young to wear a *perruque sale et usée* and to guide his pupil according to the established routine of teaching of the Conservatory. Lavignac said that their relationship almost from the start grew into a friendship, that he himself benefited by Achille's "indiscreet" questioning of the "sacred" rules of composition, and that he found it necessary to introduce to Debussy music far too advanced for the curriculum prescribed for his class. Many a time Lavignac kept Achille after school, and it was on one of these occasions that Achille for the first time heard Wagner's *Tannhäuser*. It was also due to Lavignac's influence that the young Debussy read Haydn and Mozart quartets when he should have been "practicing scales" for his lessons with Marmontel.

It is hard to imagine that Achille, stimulated by his analytical work and general discussions with Lavignac, would leave his musical knowledge and inspiration outside, like a pair of old galoshes, before he entered Marmontel's class. He was far more advanced as a musician than as a pianist, and his "panting, his raucous breathing and exaggerations of every effect" stemmed from his feeling, his "musical vision," "musical emotion," and the enthusiasm for music of a musician who as yet was restrained by lack of the technical skill to express it fully. Marmontel is said to have remarked that "Debussy is more fond of music than he is of the piano," but apparently he never bothered to look into the reasons.

I am inclined to believe that Debussy may already have had a far deeper understanding (if only intuitive) of Beethoven's Opus 111 than Marmontel and was incapable of playing it as a well-drilled Czerny étude. Was not Debussy severely reprimanded by Ambroise Thomas, the veteran composer of *Mignon*, then the director of the Conservatory, for the subtle shades of expression in his playing the F minor Prelude from the second volume of Bach's Well-tempered Clavier, because it was in the tradition of the school to consider this work as a collection of dry exercises in polyphony? And did not Debussy say that his early antipathy to Beethoven was caused by Marmontel's adding *"O mère, douleur amère"* in Beethoven's Sonata Pathetique to passages which made his teacher's feeling vibrate with sentimentality? Nor did Marmontel take into consideration that young Debussy already showed a decided preference for certain composers, felt closer to the romantics than to the classicists, to Chopin and Schumann rather than Weber and Beethoven, as his performances at the competitions showed. Many pianists have made a career playing one type of music, either romantic or classic or modern.

It was unfair that the decisive judgment of a student's capacity was based on the results of competitions open to the public. When, later, Debussy expressed his distaste for competitions he said nothing original, but he spoke from his own experience—the whole career of a student should not depend on such performances.

By nature Debussy lacked all the qualities necessary for competition. Where a mediocrity would get ahead by sheer boldness and exhibitionism, Debussy's self-consciousness would strip the last vestige of his self-assurance. Obviously not a born performer, he might have developed into one had he been given an opportunity to acquire the necessary experience, but facing the footlights once a year is hardly sufficient. Had Debussy had a winning personality perhaps all these drawbacks would have been taken into account, but in the eyes of his teachers as well as his schoolmates he was almost an exceptional case among the rank and file at the Conservatory. Short, thick-set, with pale complexion and a mop of black hair, dressed in a belted corduroy jacket, carrying in his hands some sort of cap edged with braid, with a red tassel in the center like a sailor's hat, he gave the impression of a workman's child. Nothing in him suggested the artist, present or future: neither his looks nor his speech. His teachers had few illusions about him, and his comrades had many but none too flattering, for he was an introverted, rather sullen boy and not popular with his schoolmates. And there was no one who particularly cared about him; in his childhood he had no childhood and his adolescence was dragging from year to year in the drab and coarse atmosphere of his parents' home without any diversions normal for a growing boy, let alone pleasures and happiness.

"Oh, how well I remember you slapping my face," Debussy used to say with gentle reproach to his mother, when as a grown-up man he thought of those far-gone days.

He had no elementary education, no easy manners, and did not know how to make friends, but was intelligent enough to be conscious of his shortcomings, as he was of his family's social standing in comparison with his more fortunate schoolmates. Perhaps it was because of this that he made a pitiful gesture in self-defense when he suddenly bestowed upon himself a title of nobility—he signed his name *Ach. de Bussy*—which six years later he relinquished just as suddenly without apparent loss of prestige or property.

Eventually Debussy became a very fine pianist with qualities exactly opposite to those described by his fellow students. He was a *charmeur*, with such an exquisite touch that the listener forgot that the instrument had hammers. His three-dimensional way of treating the instrument, now as an orchestra, now as a solo instrument, his finesse in nuances—*"Laissez parler le piano"*—and mastery of pedaling effects knew no rival. He had a most remarkable way of playing often completely unrelated chords legato. He avoided exaggerations and brought out the melodic lines without accentuating them, but rather enveloping them in rich sonorities with subtleties that seemed limitless. "Lord! how well this man played the piano," Stravinsky said of Debussy in his memoirs. Yet his career as a concert pianist was doomed by the results of the school competitions, for such were the rules of the entire educational system in the old Paris Conservatory. It was a blow to his parents' plans and the worst of it was that he could not comfort them with good reports from his harmony class. This was both distressing and inexcusable.

After winning all the available prizes in Lavignac's class, in the three years of studying harmony under Émile Durand young Achille did not achieve a single favorable mention. True, like Marmontel, Durand saw nothing unusual in his pupil, but with Durand it was for another reason. He neither liked music, nor teaching, nor his pupils. Having been awarded the second Prix de Rome at the age of twenty and having written a few songs and two operas which were performed in some small theaters in Paris, Durand was given the post of professor of harmony at the Conservatory. He carried out his duties to the letter, according to the old rules of the institution, like an old clerk.

In his harmony exercises Debussy exasperated his teacher with countless mistakes in musical syntax, although on more than one occasion, after blue-pencilling his paper, Durand would remark that as unorthodox as his harmony was, he had to admit that some of it was ingenious. Some twenty-five years later, when Debussy was a famous composer, a critic and a member of the jury at the Conservatory, he remarked, "I did not do very much in my harmony class. In my time, it was almost a habit for the professors to train pupils in the foolish little game of guessing the harmony of the author. I humbly confess that I never succeeded in guessing it. . . ." And Debussy's exercise books, which are kept among his other manuscripts at the Conservatory library, show by what a wide margin Debussy missed the mark. But it did not bother him in the least, for, as he said, neither in his schooldays nor later had he been able to discover any key to those conventional, automatic formulas that constitute the composer's "stock in trade."

Yet no one could have accused Achille of not being interested in harmony. It was even then the quintessence of his musical thinking and he searched for his own, personal harmony, free from all the rules written in text books. He searched for it by improvising on the piano; a few such improvisations he wrote down and showed to his classmates: a *Rapsodie* in the style of Liszt; a song, *Madrid, princesse des Espagnes;* and a *Ballade à la lune* after a poem by Alfred de Musset. These were lost, but they must have been in the same genre as a set of songs he often played to his friends, and even made Paul Vidal learn by heart, since he refused to put them down on paper. A year later, purely by chance, Vidal discovered these songs in Debussy's home. They were *Les Joyeusetés de bonne com-*

pagnie by Emile Pessard, which Achille was introducing to his friends as his own.[1]

There was one field where Achille did excel and did not need to indulge in adolescent pranks. One of his professors was Auguste Bazille, an unknown but able musician. In his class on the "art of accompaniment" the student had to display all his previously acquired knowledge. He had to read music at sight, transpose, read orchestral scores at the piano, and improvise extemporaneously an accompaniment to a given song or ensemble work. Despite his "insufficient" marks in the harmony class and failure with Marmontel, Debussy not only passed the examination at the end of his first year with Bazille, but to the great surprise of everyone won first prize. This was fortunate for him and in the nick of time. No student at the Conservatory was allowed to join the composition class unless he had been awarded first prize in one of the three classes—harmony, piano or accompaniment—and for a while Achille's whole future musical education hung in the air.

The final triumph bolstered his spirit—he was in the midst of choosing his future teacher when an unexpected event took place in his life which not only influenced him as a musician, but was a most decisive factor in his development into manhood.

[1] *Chanson d'un fou* (Alphonse Daudet), published under Debussy's name, is a song from this set by Pessard.

CHAPTER III

FIRST AMOROUS ADVENTURE

MARMONTEL *père* was certainly the last person at the Paris Conservatory Debussy would have suspected of having any interest in his future. Yet it was the old professor who suggested Achille when he received a request for a good pianist from a foreigner living in Switzerland. For years the name of the *grande dame* was guessed wrongly and misspelled. She was referred to as *Madame Meitch*, the wife of a rich industrialist, or as *Madame la baronne de Metch*, or even as *Madame Meuch*. Debussy never spoke of this early adventure and few in France knew anything of the intimate lives of foreign musicians. Eventually, sentimental biographies of Peter Tchaikovsky have disclosed the name of the *grande dame*, the "beloved friend" of the Russian composer. But not until some twelve hundred of the two thousand letters they wrote each other were published in the U.S.S.R.[1] during 1934-1936 was it possible to have a true picture of the woman and the young Debussy's connection with her.

Madame Nadejda von Meck was a Russian of middle class who acquired her titled German name through her marriage to Karl von Meck, a railroad engineer, originally from the Baltic region in the old Russian Empire. During the first few years of this union the von Mecks were poor, living at times on "ten cents a day," but this did not deter them from having eleven children.

An opportunity for a better life came in the early 1860's when,

---

[1] *Tchaikovsky's Correspondence with N. F. von Meck (Perepiska s N.F. von Mekk)*, 3 vols. (Vol. I, 1876-8; Vol. II, 1879-81; Vol. III, 1882-90).

prodded by his wife's ambitions, Karl von Meck, in association with a certain Peter G. von Dervis, managed to get from the Imperial Government (mostly through bribery and court intrigue) a concession for the construction of three important railroads. Having invested a relatively small sum of money in the preliminary investigations and construction plans, they raised a large amount of capital from shares chiefly sold abroad, way beyond the actual cost of the construction. To this was later added a handsome yearly income from the high tariffs they imposed on the transportation of goods, plus the profits made by paying sub-standard wages to the workers. Thus, fifteen years later, when Karl von Meck died in 1876 he left his widow an estate worth several million roubles and Madame von Meck became a patroness of the arts, music in particular.

Although she helped many musicians, she treated no one as generously as Peter Tchaikovsky, and her sole claim to fame in musical history rests on this financial help to the composer and on the record of their strange relationship for fourteen years. Madame von Meck was passionately in love with Tchaikovsky,[1] but the two never met. Since, *faute de mieux*, she derived a vicarious satisfaction from his music, her pride in "owning" him and their constant correspondence (ranging from "dear sir" to "my precious one," "my beloved," "my Lord and Master," echoed by her correspondent's "my dear one" and "true to the grave"), it mattered little whether she lived in her mansion in Moscow, on one of her estates in the country, or betook herself on the *Grand Tour de Grand Duc* across Europe. Perhaps she thought there might be a better chance to run her protegé to ground outside their native soil—she always invited him to join her and hoped in vain.

Madame von Meck was fifty, with three of her eldest children already married, when in 1880 she came to spend the summer in Switzerland, France and Italy. She traveled in grand style, taking

---

[1] In their correspondence, I have read one letter to Tchaikovsky which dispels the legend of purely platonic feeling on Mme von Meck's side. Barbara von Meck, the co-author of *Beloved Friend, The Story of Tchaikovsky and Nadejda von Meck,* (New York, 1937) told me that this was the only such letter that she and her sister-in-law were able to save for publication. Other letters of the same import were either destroyed or kept from publication by the men in von Meck's family. V.S.

along her two sons (Nicholas and Alexander), three daughters (Julia, Sonia and Ludmila), a whole retinue of nurses, governesses, tutors, private maids and valets, and two or sometimes three musicians as part of her personal entourage. It was then, in Interlaken in the middle of July, that young Debussy became a part of her household.

His duties were to teach her children piano, to accompany their violin playing and singing, to play duets with Madame herself and to play any music she wished to hear, either solo or with her other musicians. Madame von Meck once wrote to Tchaikovsky that she wished she were Ludwig, King of Bavaria so that she too could have an opera performed for her alone. This she never achieved. "But why shouldn't I have a trio of my own?" she thought. "In Nice Monsieur de Dervis [1] has his own orchestra, in Florence they have Becker's quartet [2] and in Vienna—Hemesberger's quartet." [3]

Debussy became the pianist in this "Trio de Madame von Meck." His partners, Vladislav Pakhulsky, violin, and Peter Danilchenko, cello, were permanently attached to their patroness. The former eventually became her son-in-law (he married Julia), acted as her private secretary and on the side, composed inoffensive music, while the latter gambled away every penny at the roulette wheel—both natural consequences of a long association with Madame.

In her youth Madame von Meck learned to play the piano, and while her taste and judgment were far from infallible it is certain that she had an insatiable desire to hear and to know everything worth while in music. She knew baroque music as well as she did the classics and the romantics, but she preferred the contemporary, and as soon as a piece appeared in print she would have it sent to her and either play it herself or have one of the musicians read it to her.

"Everything I read [in music] is new to me and certainly it is new to 'my Frenchman'," she said. Thus Debussy's remarkable ap-

---

[1] Peter G. von Dervis, Karl von Meck's associate.

[2] Jean Becker (1833-1881) German violinist. In 1866 founded the famous quartet of Florence.

[3] Josef Hemesberger, from 1849 the head of Vienna String Quartet.

titude for sight-reading stood him in good stead. In fact, it so impressed Madame von Meck that her enthusiasm rose to a pitch usually reserved for a few chosen occasions. She declared it was miraculous. "He even read your manuscript at first sight," she wrote to Tchaikovsky and hastened to add that his second virtue, "a reflective virtue, so to speak," was that he was delighted with Tchaikovsky's music. She described to the composer how Debussy, after playing his suite, exclaimed: "Among all the modern fugues I never found anything as beautiful. Monsieur Massenet could never have equaled it." And Jules Massenet, Madame von Meck explained, was Debussy's guiding star.

Actually this was the only time that Debussy expressed such a glowing opinion of Tchaikovsky's music, but considering how the Tchaikovsky cult saturated the atmosphere at Madame von Meck's it is not surprising that her quick conclusions were a bit premature and exaggerated. She liked Debussy for it and that was a good thing, for otherwise Achille's efforts to impress her did not succeed.

To give himself more pedagogical authority (Sonia was five and Ludmila ten years younger than he but the boys were about his own age, and Julia was nine years older) Debussy told Madame that he was twenty. Her experienced eye saw that the beardless youth was younger. She said he looked sixteen—Debussy was eighteen. He told her that he was Massenet's pupil and this she believed. Debussy never was Massenet's pupil, neither in the past nor in the future, but Massenet was a good name, better known than those of his professors.

He also implied that he had already graduated from the Conservatory with a first prize in the piano class. "God help those who study at the Paris Conservatory," was Madame von Meck's reaction. She thought that technically Debussy played well, but without personality, and on the whole that he demonstrated the superiority of the Russian music schools. "And to think of it," she went on, "here is a young musician, crowned with laurels, the first prize, and already working for the Prix de Rome—all nonsense, those prizes, not worth a rap." Debussy must have been talking out of turn, he was three years ahead of himself.

Nevertheless Madame von Meck commissioned Debussy to make a four-hand arrangement of the three dances from Tchaikovsky's *Swan Lake* ballet and busied herself with trying to get them published by Jurgenson, Tchaikovsky's publisher. "Only," she cautioned her friend, "do not use Debussy's name because if it fell into the hands of Jules Massenet, my young man might be scolded." [1]

Madame von Meck referred to Debussy as "my little Frenchman," and either called him just Bussy or by a Russified endearing nickname, *Bussyk*. Obviously the young man won her favor and she drew him into her orbit. Even if all the stars revolved around her "Lord and Master," this was not the worst thing that could have happened to Achille, who did not have as yet a wide knowledge of music. She was pleased to hear Debussy praise the works of Édouard Lalo, for she herself admired them for their individuality, daring and brilliance. She showed Debussy works by Max Bruch, who after having written a good violin concerto annoyed her by trying to imitate Lalo in his second, and Karl Goldmark's symphony, *Ländliche Hochzeit*, and his violin concerto, which she thought achieved a happy medium between the classical style and modern innovation. She let him browse through a large collection of songs she had bought during her travels in Spain, the Basque country and Italy. But above all Debussy heard, thanks to her, the works of the Russian contemporary musicians of both schools: that of Moscow, associated with Tchaikovsky, and of St. Petersburg, associated with "The Mighty Five." In discussing all the various composers and their works, Madame von Meck was happy to hear that Debussy did not care for the Germans—"*Ils ne sont pas de notre tempérament, ils sont si lourds, pas clair.*"

Whether in Interlaken, where they stayed less than a month, or in Arcachon, where their sojourn was cut short because Madame von Meck found the living quarters, the two large villas they occupied, too inadequate for her taste, or in Florence, where they finally settled down after a trip via Paris, Nice and Naples, Debussy for the first time lived in a whirl of musical and social activities.

[1] The arrangements were published in Russia, but the name of the publisher is unknown.

Wherever they travelled they attended theater, concert and opera performances, or the local musicians were invited to join them in their own musicales. But that was not all. The luxury of their accommodations was such as he never dreamed of. Not since his childhood when he was with Arosa and his aunt had he been treated to all the amenities of life. His salary must have been more than adequate, judging by the generous amounts Madame von Meck paid her other musicians—usually equal to a professor's fee at the Conservatory. Teaching her children was a pleasure—they all soon became fast friends, and when his employer and hostess discovered that he composed he found in her a most encouraging patroness.

"I am sending you for your appreciation a little composition— one of many—by my little pianist, Bussy. This youth intends to become a composer and writes nice things, but they are all echoes of his professor, Massenet," Madame von Meck wrote Tchaikovsky as she dispatched to him Debussy's *Danse bohémienne*. Tchaikovsky's prompt verdict was: "A very nice little thing, but altogether too short. Not a single thought is developed to the end, the form is bungled and there is no unity." Debussy swallowed the pill, but saw to it that no other "nice little things" were sent to Tchaikovsky, for with at least one of these "little things" he abused his friends' confidence in him. Gambling on their ignorance of the true identity of the composers of *Ici bas tous les lilas meurent*, a song written by the brothers Paul and Lucien Hillemacher after Sully-Prudhomme's poem, Debussy not only coached Julia von Meck in singing it, but must have written it down as his own composition, for years later it was found among Alexander von Meck's collection of Debussy manuscripts and eventually was published posthumously under Debussy's name.

But in all his relations with the von Mecks Debussy's honesty and sincerity were never doubted. They were devoted to *le bouillant Achille*, and this had a remarkable effect on his character and behavior. Although to Madame von Meck he was still only a Frenchman and a product of the Parisian boulevards, no one in her family thought he was awkward, or shy, or illiterate. On the contrary, they and their friends found him delightful, even witty, always in a good humor, always ready to help around the house, and they were more amused than impressed when, because of his friendship with one of the Russian tutors, who without any foundation claimed to be an aristocrat, young Achille also began to give himself airs. But the tutor soon was sent back to the university where he was a student, and Achille became "his old self again" to the great satisfaction of the whole family, the same *gamin* whose French pronunciation of Russian words was a source of endless merriment. Also, the von Mecks liked Debussy's looks. At that time he wore his hair in waves brushed up from his forehead and, indeed, there was something in his face that resembled Anton Rubinstein. Tchaikovsky, after receiving his photograph, confirmed this impression and the von Mecks echoed the "Master's" wish that Debussy "might become as great a musician as the Czar of all pianists."

The three happiest months of his life flew by before Achille realized that he should be back at the Conservatory. He did not want to go and Madame von Meck wrote to Paris and asked for another two weeks leave for him. This gave him time to complete the trio on which he was working, in G major, in three movements: *Andantino con moto, allegro; Intermezzo;* and *Finale appassionata.* It was promptly performed by the "Trio de Madame von Meck" and although Massenet-ish was enthusiastically applauded.

But there was no time to make a copy to send to Tchaikovsky and on November 15, 1880, Madame von Meck wrote to him: "My little Frenchman has left, and it is very annoying that I can no longer hear your Piano Sonata and other charming compositions I adore, especially the F sharp minor Waltz which Debussy played very well. My trios are ended too. Imagine, the boy wept when he left! It truly touched me deeply; he has such a loving heart. He would not have gone at all, but the directors of the Conservatory were already annoyed because he had postponed his return."

Were *Bussyk's* tears genuine? At the Conservatory he used to show his friends how well he could cry real tears at any given time and then burst into peals of laughter. But I think on this occasion one should give him the benefit of the doubt. He was saying goodbye to everything that he really loved—true, not his own, still as much his own as he had ever had. With this ended the first, but not the last chapter in his relationship with Madame von Meck.

In Paris at the Conservatory Debussy surprised everyone by dedicating his Trio not to Marmontel, who had sent him to von Meck, but to his harmony teacher—"An offering of many notes and much friendship from the composer to his professor, Monsieur Émile Durand." Nor did he join Jules Massenet's class in composition, as might have been expected, but that of Ernest Guiraud, a newly appointed member of the faculty.

Debussy made this choice because of the newcomer's personality, far more congenial to his own. A winner of the second Prix de Rome and the author of short operas performed at the Opéra Comique, Guiraud was popular among the students for his informal classes and his comradeship outside the Conservatory walls, playing billiards, occasionally having a glass of beer and sharing packs of cigarettes with them while discussing all sorts of subjects far into the night.

Debussy, never of a nature to submit to discipline, was even less pliable now that he had breathed the "free artist" air at the von Mecks. No other teacher would have been willing to discuss his often paradoxical opinions and audacious declarations against the accepted rules of harmony and composition. For a short while Debussy did, however, attend César Franck's class in "free improvisation." But soon he discovered that the esteemed pedagogue was an apostle of traditional rules. He constantly drove his pupils into a set frame quite against Debussy's instinctive feeling for "free improvisation," and Debussy only irritated his teacher. "*Modulez, modulez,*" Franck kept prodding his pupil. "Why should I modulate," Debussy rebelled, shocking the whole class, "if I feel perfectly happy in the tonality I am in?"—"César Franck is a modulating machine," Debussy said afterwards and never returned to the class.

Thus, had it not been for Guiraud's lenience with this insubordinate pupil, Debussy's studies at the Conservatory might have come to an end. For there was no one else sufficiently interested in him who could have influenced him.

After his "artistic journey" with the von Mecks, his own home with its *petit bourgeois* life, its domestic squabbles, his father whom he thought a mere windbag and his despotic mother, narrow-minded and mean, was more depressing than restful, let alone in-spiring. Achille was constantly reminded that it was high time for him to earn his own living and get on with some kind of profession. Without much enthusiasm he gave piano lessons and was rather happy when Vidal arranged for him the position of accompanist at the Madame Moreau-Santi school of singing.

He enjoyed working with the singers and particularly with one Madame Pierre Vasnier, who had a small but exceptionally beauti-ful, silver-like soprano. Besides her musical attributes she was a strikingly good-looking woman in her thirties. She was the mother of two small children, a boy and a girl, and she had a husband—twice her age, some said—Pierre Vasnier, a well-known architect, a sensitive man of culture, interested in the arts. It was not long be-fore Achille became almost a daily visitor at their fifth floor apart-ment on Rue Constantinople—a pleasant change from his parents' home.

M. Vasnier gradually took charge of Achille's education, discuss-ing literature with him, giving him books to read and introducing him to works by Paul Bourget, Théodore de Banville and Paul Verlaine, while Madame Vasnier inspired him to write songs for her. At last Debussy found the right environment for his work and one might think that he could now devote himself to his studies at the Conservatory and perhaps work toward winning the Prix de Rome.

But with the coming of spring Achille's thoughts turned again to Madame von Meck and he wrote to Russia and asked if he could join her. Madame von Meck had already made her plans for the summer: she was going to spend it either on her estate in Brai-lov in the Ukraine, or in Moscow, and she had engaged a pianist, Pakhulsky's elder brother Henrich, but, as she said, she did not have the heart to refuse her little Bussyk. Early in July 1881 he arrived in Russia.

Once again Debussy was in his element—an artistic musical life with no prescribed hours for work, no imposed discipline—everything happening as though it were all done in fun. For, indeed, everything appeared as if by magic: music, books, theater, opera and concert tickets were to be had for the asking. The von Mecks received him with open arms. He became Monsieur Bussykoff. He was treated as one of the family.

The von Mecks were a large family but only where Nadejda von Meck presided was music all absorbing. However, whenever any doubts arose among the absent members of the von Meck clan, sometimes hundreds of miles away, as to the merits of Tchaikovsky's music, Debussy and his pupil Alexander, score in hand, would be at once dispatched to prove Madame's points in the argument and to crush any dissension in the ranks. Thus Debussy had a chance to see more than just Moscow, but nothing could have surpassed his impressions when he was taken by the von Mecks to Brailov, their three-million-rouble estate. Never before had Debussy seen or heard of such a place. Far away from the railroad, this "kingdom in itself," as some Russians called it, was lost among the gentle hills and dark oak forests of the Ukraine, offering its wealth to all known pleasures.

The main house was a smaller version of Madame von Meck's fifty-three-room mansion in Moscow, also a palace with a multitude of rooms with high ceilings, richly furnished and containing collections of valuable paintings, works of art, books and manuscripts, as well as an extraordinary assortment of musical instruments ready to serve any musical performance.

It was summer, the time to relax and play, to try one's skill in shooting, horseback riding, sailing, to take long walks through the forests and down to the river to fish, to go bathing, to row by moonlight, or to drive to picnics lasting way past bedtime, and to listen to weird stories—particularly to one favorite legend about "the subterranean passage which led to an old forgotten Catholic monastery, and further on to a grave with a white cross where two brothers were buried—they were rivals in love and no one knew any more about them"—all this to the accompaniment of nightingales . . . . These may well have been magnetic, miraculous hours that begat love and romance and could never be forgotten.

Debussy spent four months with the von Mecks in Brailov and in Moscow and then, after a trip with them to Rome, returned to Paris at the end of November. He seems to have been perfectly happy to remain one of Madame von Meck's "animate objects," as she often described the people in her service, for in the summer of the following year he came again, this time to her new estate near Moscow. Although she did not then suspect anything, this last visit brought the dénouement.

In August 1882 Debussy arrived in Plescheyevo to find Madame von Meck in an unusual turmoil. She had been suffering from a cold and rheumatic pains in her right arm. She said she could hardly hold a pen and for her this must have been a real calamity. Her doctors advised a warmer climate, Italy or the South of France, and perhaps a consultation with specialists in Paris or Amsterdam. Alexander was also rheumatic and could not continue his studies in St. Petersburg, and she decided to go to Vienna for the winter, where he could enter the University and the two girls, Sonia and Ludmila, could continue their studies of languages and music as well as anywhere else. Since the von Mecks moved about Russia and Europe with the ease of crossing the street, this otherwise not extraordinary turn of affairs was merely a nuisance to her, for it complicated and conflicted with her main preoccupation at the time: to arrange the future matrimonial ties of her adolescent children.

Madame von Meck, the archenemy of marriage, as she claimed, had learned from bitter experience that all her preaching was not heeded, "because nowadays it is society and not the parents who bring up the children." Although the three elder children had married "very well," Madame declared that from now on it would be she who would personally attend to the matchmaking, and as she was getting old there was not much time left, even if matchmaking for children in their early teens might seem a bit premature—something more Oriental than Russian.

Without ever seeing Tchaikovsky's sister, Madame Davidov, or her children, she managed through her correspondence with the composer to arrange an engagement between her son Nicholas, with whom Debussy played piano-violin sonatas, and the composer's niece Anna. Now she was hard at work to marry her even younger son Alexander to Anna Davidov's younger sister Natasha. This, Madame von Meck maintained, would bring her even closer to the composer, and she explained "there was no real mixing of the blood, against which she was firmly opposed both for moral and biological reasons."

Whatever Madame von Meck's virtues were, she was confused on more than one subject. A staunch supporter of an absolute monarchy, she bluntly declared herself a socialist and in the same breath she delighted in "the hanging of all these so-called idealistic socialists" and spoke of Émile Zola as a cheap charlatan. Like many another *parvenue*, she was a snob and a ruthless despot with her children's personal lives. All this would belong to a book on Tchaikovsky and his "beloved friend" had Debussy not planned to marry into the von Meck family.

Sonia was "the apple of her mother's eye" and the next in line in Madame's matrimonial projects. When Debussy first came to them in Switzerland in 1880, she was thirteen, a giddy and spoiled youngster. Speaking of her, her mother (in the manner of Leo Tolstoy) used French, although what she said would have sounded just as well in Russian: "*Sonia c'est l'enfant terrible de la famille, volontaire et emportée jusqu'a l'excès et il faut un grand savoir-faire pour réprimer.*" At home in Russia Anatol Gally, Tchaikovsky's former pupil, a professor at the Moscow Conservatory, had succeeded with this task to her satisfaction. During Debussy's first summer with the von Mecks it was up to his *savoir-faire* to make his pupil behave.

Sonia was then a delicate, pale child with blond hair with a slight reddish tint. Her eyes were brown and according to her doting mother her eyelashes were so thick and long they threw a shadow when she lowered them. Every one expected her to grow into a great beauty and Sonia had been aware of it since she was eleven, when she was cared for by her French and German governesses. Sonia learned the art of coquetry at the same time as the declension of regular and irregular verbs. In all fairness, however, one must admit that nature did not deprive her of a certain amount of intelligence, even if she did not always use it wisely. She spoke both French and German equally well, like a native. In fact she spoke foreign languages better than her own. In R·· sian she had difficulty in pronouncing the hard "l," which added a certain charm in her compatriots' ears. On the whole, everyone was pleased with how she said it, if not always with what she said. Wrapped in many shawls in accordance with the latest vogue, with her pale complexion fitting the pose of *La Dame aux camélias*, she threw "wicked glances" at men who observed her blossoming figure. But Achille at eighteen was not yet a man, and boys of eighteen take no notice of girls of thirteen. Or was he more of a man than he betrayed, already following a far-sighted plan?

A year later, at Brailov, Sonia was going through a period when she studied poetry, wrote and recited verse, and wanted to die to the strains of Tchaikovsky's "Serbian March." Like Paolo and Francesca, Sonia and Achille read poetry together and her gentle dilettantism almost passed for the highest intellectual attainment. And now in 1882 at Plescheyevo Debussy was well aware of the rapid change in Sonia. She had grown into a lovely young lady— she looked twenty, had gained poise, knew when to speak and how much and when to listen. And if all this were not enough to show Debussy that his little pupil was ready any day to step into society and take her place in the world, he must have heard all the plans for her future—according to Russian law in one year she would be eligible for marriage. He certainly had heard that Xavier Gretener, the Swiss *doctor de juris*, the tutor at the von Mecks when Debussy first met them, had fallen in love with Sonia and asked Madame for her hand. According to von Meck herself he was a charming man, from a good family and very good looking, but ... she had to let him go, as she would one of her drunken coachmen.

"I am not interested in just getting Sonia married—this she can manage without me," Madame von Meck used to say. "But I am concerned with the choice: it has to be the right one. Any man would choose Sonia—she is young, beautiful and, as women go, well educated, but most important she is an heiress. If I were willing to open my doors to her suitors, there would be so many of them I would not know how to get rid of them. I don't even want a man of Sonia's choice. I want the one whom I am going to appoint, and Sonia will like him."

Whether this dictum was uttered only in confidence or proclaimed as a manifesto, Debussy was biding his time: it was almost more important for the aspiring lover to get Madame to say "I do" than Sonia.

After Plescheyevo Debussy moved with them to Moscow, where they stayed for a month before they finally went to Austria. In Vienna they were busy helping Madame furnish her apartment and getting down to the schedule of lessons, concerts and opera. Just when and where the budding Don Juan and *La Dame aux camélias* met in their decisive hour has never been disclosed, but it must have been in Vienna when Madame von Meck began to call Debussy "her dear little Bussyk" that he decided the time had come to tell *Maman* of his honorable intentions. The interview was short and to the point. Madame Nadejda von Meck had to let him go.

"Sonia has a new piano teacher, because Debussy went back to Paris," was all that she wrote about it to Tchaikovsky.

This thwarted love affair left the von Mecks with sketches and unfinished manuscripts Debussy forgot in his hasty departure, and Debussy with a souvenir he kept to himself—the painful awakening into manhood.

And what happened to Sonia? A year later she married Alexei Rimsky-Korsakoff, a distant relative of the composer. Later she divorced him to marry Prince Golizin. But she was unhappy again and divorced him too. Barbara von Meck told me that in their family they used to tease Sonia about Debussy. Sonia blushed, but said nothing.

During the years following his departure from Vienna, Debussy appealed to Nadejda several times for financial help. She always responded generously. Then, when in 1885 von Meck read a notice concerning Debussy, she wrote to Tchaikovsky: ". . . In the whole French nation I love only two men: Georges Bizet and Alphonse

Daudet. Did you by any chance happen to read in *Figaro* that that little Frenchman, Achille Debussy, who spent several seasons with me, had received the Prix de Rome for his composition *Enfant prodigue,* which they praise highly? This is not surprising. He is a talented youngster and while he was with me he had an opportunity to widen his musical knowledge and develop his taste through learning the works of composers from other lands. He knew how to make good use of it." This was the last time she ever mentioned Debussy's name in her correspondence with Tchaikovsky. It sounds distant and detached.

Seven years later Madame von Meck died and twenty-five years after her death Debussy went again to Russia—Serge Koussevitzky invited him for a concert in Moscow. Debussy was fêted by the Russian musicians and honored as the greatest French composer. During the short visit there he saw no one of Madame von Meck's children except Sonia. Neither Debussy nor Sonia disclosed what happened at this meeting, but I imagine that both of them realized how similar their situation was to that in the last scene in Tchaikovsky's opera *Eugene Onegin*—the von Mecks' favorite opera— only with the fate of Tatiana and Onegin in reverse: it was Debussy who must have said, "I belong to someone else, and I will remain true."

CHAPTER IV

INFLUENCES AND FIRST LOVE AFFAIR

A GREAT DEAL has been written by musicologists and Debussy's other biographers about the influence Russian music may have had on him. But among the compositions that are mentioned, Tchaikovsky's music is conspicuously absent. One might well imagine—not without malice, I admit—that the nation-wide French dislike for Tchaikovsky was caused by the amount of his music France's most illustrious composer had to endure in his youth: he had heard enough to suffice the whole nation.

The references to Russian influence are concerned with the then-revolutionary group "The Mighty Five" (Balakirev, Borodin, Cui, Moussorgsky and Rimsky-Korsakoff) and in some instances it has been implied that Debussy met members of this group. Actually he never did. First of all, one must bear in mind that "The Mighty Five" lived in St. Petersburg and only occasionally visited Moscow, and Debussy did not go to St. Petersburg; and second, the St. Petersburg musicians were opposed to Tchaikovsky and his followers and it is certain that not one member of the group ever had any personal connections with Madame von Meck, Debussy's only possible link with them.

Lacking correct data on Debussy's journeys to Russia, it was assumed that he had met Moussorgsky and it was taken for granted that he had become acquainted with Balakirev, Borodin and Rimsky. Cui was left out, probably because his music was the least important (although it was Cui's *La musique en Russie* that was to supply Debussy with many aesthetic concepts). This error resulted from the false belief that Debussy met Madame von Meck as early as 1879 and went with her to Russia during the winter of the same year after their stay in Florence. Debussy went to Madame von Meck in 1880, returned to Paris after his sojourn in Florence, and did not go to Russia until the summer of the following year. When he arrived there at the beginning of July 1881, Moussorgsky had already been dead for three months.

Borodin spent the summer of 1881 in Germany, in Magdeburg and, later, visiting Franz Liszt in Weimar. By the time he returned home, Debussy had left Russia. Rimsky-Korsakoff, during the summer of 1881, was sent by the Navy Department to Nikolaev to review the Black Sea port naval band, which he had transformed from brass into a mixed band seven years earlier. He was in Yalta and Sebastopol and, after a trip to Constantinople, returned via Odessa and Kiev to his summer place at Tyitsy. Later he went back to St. Petersburg to prepare the first performance of *Snegourochka*.

Balakirev, who about that time had emerged from his self-imposed exile from the musical world because of his religious obsession, was living in St. Petersburg seeing no one except his new group of disciples, with whom he met once a week at his apartment. No women were allowed at these gatherings and any association with Tchaikovsky or his patroness would have closed his door to a stranger, rather than open it.

The chances of Debussy's meeting Borodin or Rimsky during the following summer in 1882 were just as slight. Rimsky spent the summer at Tyitsy and although he did go to Moscow to conduct two concerts at the All-Russian Exposition, there is no reference anywhere in his memoirs to a meeting with a young Frenchman, whose name he knew well when years later he was writing the *Chronicle of My Life*. And as for Borodin, even if he had received a letter introducing young Debussy, he would probably have said "What of it?", gone on nursing his old and sick cat Vaska, and then forgotten all about it.

Madame von Meck was not in Moscow when the Exposition opened. She deliberately missed all the concerts, including the one entirely devoted to Tchaikovsky's music. She said she did not want to be seen there for fear she would be asked for money; and besides (it was true), she did not feel well and was getting ready for her trip abroad. But although Debussy did not meet any of them (the composers) personally, there is every reason to believe that he either stopped in Moscow on his way to Plescheyevo, only twenty miles away, or went there with Pakhulsky, who acted in the capacity of an observer and a reporter for Madame von Meck, and attended the concerts at the Exposition. Thus, Debussy then had the opportunity of hearing a great deal of Russian music, of which only a small portion was presented in Paris several years later at the Exposition in 1889. At these ten concerts he must have heard most of the works of "The Mighty Five," as well as those of Mikhael Glinka and Alexander Dargomijsky. He may have had the opportunity, also, to hear Dargomijsky's opera *The Stone Guest*—a perfect example of the modern opera, without additional choruses, ballet or dances, with only two arias, written to fit the exact words of Pushkin's original songs. As early as 1857 Dargomijsky spoke of "expressing the spoken word in music" and conceived (in 1868) a new principle for an opera, that of writing the music to a literary work without altering a single word of the original text. His *Stone Guest* was the prototype of the "parlando" opera and in this work one may find the seeds of Debussy's *Pelléas et Mélisande*, even if harmonic influence obviously leads to Moussorgsky's *Boris Godunov*, a work he studied much later in Paris.

From his association with Madame von Meck Debussy came away with an intimate knowledge of a great deal of Russian music: orchestral—through playing it four-handed with Madame von Meck; chamber—through her "Trio"; and vocal—through working on songs with Julia and later with Sonia. It has also been suggested that Debussy's fascination with the music of the gypsies —their spontaneous improvisations, their free, supple rhythms and languishing melodies—dates from his visits to Russia. When I spoke of this to Barbara von Meck she said that his acquaintance with the gypsies was not only possible, but most probable.

Gypsies and gypsyism formed a special chapter in Russian life, for it is undeniable that tastes of all Russians—regardless of what social stratum they came from, regardless of their professions—met at this focal point: vodka, champagne and gypsies; these formed one harmonious Russian chord. Some found inspiration in gypsyism; others found their ruin. Pushkin and Apoukhtin, Leo Tolstoy and Alexander Block, Tchaikovsky, the two Rubinstein brothers, Chaliapin, Rachmaninoff and a score of others admired the singing of the gypsies and spent many a night in their company. The qualities of every gypsy singer were seriously discussed, for a good singer had to have a "sob" in his or her voice and the listeners had to be "moved to tears"—usually they wept, and this was expected. A number of restaurants and night clubs had gypsies on their programs, but many preferred more intimate contact and often went directly to the gypsies' homes on the city outskirts. Only a few, however, visited with them for purely artistic enjoyment—the young gypsy women were notably successful with their admirers, and many even became mistresses of aristocrats and wealthy industrialists. The interest of Vladimir, Madame von Meck's eldest son, lay rather with women than with music, and Barbara von Meck told me that he was well known for squandering his own and part of his mother's fortune on his escapades with the gypsies, sometimes lasting for weeks. Although ten years Achille's senior, he may have taken Debussy along "to listen to their music"—provided *Maman* was not looking.

Influence is an elastic term which can cover a wide range from direct quotations and "borrowed themes" to technical devices and harmonic innovations; it can stem from one impression or a whole gamut of emotions; it can be theoretical or practical, positive or negative, and it can be completely intangible. The musicologists are still debating whether Borodin's "Queen of the Sea" and "Sleeping Beauty," to mention just these two songs, have found an echo in Debussy's *Paysage sentimental, Voici que le printemps* and *La Belle au bois dormant*—all composed by him in 1880. Debussy did not bring many scores back with him, but a few years after his return to Paris he gave his friend Paul Poujaud several of Borodin's songs with French translations written by him under the Russian text. Either Madame von Meck or her children must have helped him, as they did with the works of Tchaikovsky, Balakirev and Moussorgsky.

The only symphony Debussy ever wrote was composed in Russia, but it was not discovered in Moscow till the early 1930's when K. S. Bogouchevsky, a mathematician, bought a collection of symphonic works arranged for piano duets. An undated manuscript dedicated to Madame von Meck and signed Ach. Debussy was included in the folder. The first page also carried the following, written in French: "Symphony en Si—Andante, Air de ballet, Finale." Judging by the date when N. Gilayev presumably edited the work and wrote a preface (1933) and that of actual publication (1936), it took three years for experts to establish the authenticity of the work. Only a part of the symphony, marked *Le double plus lent,* most probably of the last movement (a sort of apotheosis), was published in a piano duet version. Some point to the main theme as reminiscent of Brahms and fragments resembling Schumann, while others speak of Rimsky-Korsakoff, basing their assumption on the "shorthand" marks for the orchestration of the piece.

This "material evidence"—a progression of unrelated chords, unresolved dissonances and "borrowed themes"—attributed to the time when Debussy was unscrupulous enough to give as his own someone else's compositions, only serves a further proof that he liked certain things in Russian music well enough to adopt them as his own.

The influence of the spirit and the original ideas of the Russian composers was to manifest itself later, when a more mature Debussy had digested and assimilated them and was ready to formulate his own esthetics. Meanwhile, although he traveled to France by the same Smolensky road as did Napoleon and other would-be conquerors, he returned home a better educated musician and with a knowledge of foreign compositions far superior to that of most of his compatriots.

At the Conservatory he continued his studies under Guiraud, but adolescent argumentativeness for the sake of an argument gave way to a more mature and better expressed point of view. By now he had heard enough of music to know that what yesterday was considered dissonance is consonance today. He saw no reason to resolve every dissonance into a consonance, particularly since he felt a certain intoxication (*le régal de l'ouïe*—a feast for the ear, as he put it) in hearing the sound *per se,* be it dissonance or consonance. The great discovery, the basis of Debussy's revolutionary idea, the one which divided music into "before and after Debussy," was expressed by him in simple words long before he could convince his listeners of the validity of this idea through his music.

"Look at them!" He would turn a mocking smile on his classmates bewildered by the cascades of dissonant chords with which he imitated the groaning of the buses going down the street. *"Foule ahurie!* Are you incapable of listening to chords without demanding to see their identity cards and travel orders? Where do they come from? Where are they going? Do you have to know? Listen to it: that should be enough. If you hear nothing, then run to the director and tell him that I ruin your ears. . . ." And when he was asked, "But what rules do you follow?" Debussy defiantly said: *"Mon plaisir"*—my pleasure, my whim. He was aware of being considered an eccentric, a revolutionary. It not only flattered his ego, but supported a conscious feeling of his own personality, the lack of which Madame von Meck often pointed out. It gave him courage to be bold, and he was growing audacious in more than one way.

If the rude setback of his first emotional adventure with Sonia von Meck did not leave a deep scar in his heart, it certainly made him behave with less regard for conventional proprieties. While Debussy's thoughts were concentrated on Sonia, he remained a musician-friend in the Vasnier family and the accompanist of the singer Madame Vasnier, but upon his return from Russia he reappraised the situation and its obvious virtues. Though he still lived with his parents, he had a room of his own in the Vasniers' apartment where he could "work undisturbed" at any time. M. Vasnier resumed their *causeries* on literature and art, and Madame Vasnier by her close presence stimulated him to write songs for her: he serenaded her more than he coached her in the songs she prepared for her appearances at various society musicales. On the *Romance* written at about this time to words by Paul Bourget, he wrote this dedication: "All that is any good in my mind is here; judge for yourself." He also wrote the *Chanson espagnole* for two voices, to sing with her at a fancy dress ball. And when the Vasniers moved for the summer to a small villa they rented at Ville d'Avray, Debussy spent more time there than in Paris.

It would be doing an injustice to the artistic temperaments of Madame Vasnier and the young Achille to infer that they did not make the best use of these opportunities. Madame Vasnier, besides having found the fulfillment of her ambitions as a singer in a devoted composer who wrote especially for her, was well aware of his ardent youth. Under her influence he changed his hair-do, wearing the thick, black curls flat on his forehead, and "in the evening when his hair had become untidy—which suited him much better—he looked like a mediaeval Florentine painting." And Debussy, still hazy from the recent wound to his ego and more than a little muddled by the miscellaneous reading of poetry and novels he was doing, was doomed to his fate—he was ripe and ready to become her lover.

But at twenty-one Debussy was not like Franz Liszt, who at the same age and in a similar situation with the Countess d'Agoult had taken the onerous responsibility in a love affair with a married woman with two children and had faced the consequences of such a liaison. It is true, nonetheless, that Liszt's Countess had a fortune of her own and Liszt if need be could earn his living, while Debussy had little to offer except his talent and his youth. Madame Vasnier was dependent on her husband and as matters stood so was Debussy. Thus he let things take their own course, except that he never missed an opportunity to tell M. Vasnier how indebted he was for all the financial help the old architect provided. It is not known whether Pierre Vasnier realized how generously Debussy was already repaying him, yet it would be a little naïve to suspect M. Vasnier of complete ignorance.

The lack of a clear-cut understanding in this *ménage à trois*, however, must have caused Debussy's unusually temperamental behavior at the home of his benevolent friends. Men with more experience in such cases have difficulty in concealing their uneasiness, and young Achille was only a novice in this role. His nervous state is understandable and explains his moodiness and supersensitivity. The slightest thing would irritate him, just as something utterly unimportant would make him hilariously happy. Still far from being a man of the world, he had no manners at his command to cover his embarrassment at meeting strangers at the Vasniers. He gave the impression of a morose and boorish individual, though in the company of his close friends he was just as engaging and entertaining as he had been at Madame von Meck's. Then he would accompany Madame Vasnier, improvise, play and sing selections from Wagner operas, or do imitations of Italian street singers, using his cane for a guitar.

Debussy loved card games, but he was both a poor player and a bad loser, and it was Madame Vasnier who saw to it that on leaving them he would find in his coat pocket enough change to get him home and a pack of cigarettes to console him. He smoked a great deal. He preferred to roll his own and already had developed the habit of flipping the ashes with his index finger so characteristic of him in later years.

Smoking, pacing up and down the room and humming were the prerequisites of his composing. Not until he had the musical sentence completely formed in his mind would he go to his desk to put it down on paper. Even his homework for the composition classes shows very little correction and rewriting.

But Debussy did better in writing for Madame Vasnier than he did for his professor at the Conservatory. The first set of the *Fêtes galantes: Mandoline, Pantomime, En sourdine, Clair de lune,* and *Fantoches* on Verlaine's poems were the fruits of her suggestion and his devotion. In the most elaborate handwriting the "eternally grateful author" dedicated to Madame Vasnier "these songs which she alone made live and which would lose their enchanting grace if they were never again to come from her singing fairy lips." These ecstatic lines were the only outburst (in print) of his passion not censored by Achille's regard for Madame Vasnier's reputation; the rest, his and the fairy lips kept to themselves. Debussy's happiness was complete. Even if it was based on a dissonant chord, he did not see any need to resolve it. Who knows how long and how far he would have let himself be carried by this all-engulfing wave of feeling if M. Vasnier had not stood by as the only one with a practical sense of reality.

While the happy lover showed no particular urge for further accomplishments at the Conservatory, M. Vasnier tried as best he could to impress on him the value of the Prix de Rome: official recognition as well as material advantages; three years in Rome free of financial worries were nothing to sniff at for a penniless beginner. Debussy listened to M. Vasnier but did not betray his own thoughts: three years away from Madame Vasnier certainly was not his idea of happiness, and he pretended not to see through M. Vasnier's pathetic argument that only interest in Achille's career dictated his concern.

Debussy also listened to Guiraud who, after a careful reading of his score *Diane au bois* after Théodore de Banville's poem, said: "It is all very interesting, but you must keep that sort of thing for later on, or else you will never get the Prix de Rome."

What both men meant was clear and simple: it was too early for Debussy to live and to compose as the "free artist" he fancied himself to be, and he had better conform to the established utilitarian rules of the old school and get on with his work as a student. "To have or not to have the Prix de Rome decides whether one has or does not have talent," Debussy sulked, but there was nothing for him to do but to obey.

During the following two school years (1883 and 1884) Debussy was docile enough to take part in "this national sport—the Prix de Rome," as he said. "They expect you to be full of ideas and inspiration at a given time of the year. If you are not in form that particular month, so much the worse for you. It is a purely arbitrary affair, without any significance as regards the future," he protested against the procedure of the Prix de Rome contests, as he had earlier against the yearly competitions in the piano classes at the Conservatory. He criticized the members of the jury "who adjudicate the various matches indiscriminately, whether the games are played in music, painting, sculpture, or engraving." And added: "It has not occurred to anyone to include a dancer on the committee, though this would be logical, for Terpsichore was not the least among the nine Muses."

Debussy was still bitter over his unfortunate experience when, in the spring of 1882, just before he went with great hopes to Russia, he had gone for the preliminary examination for the Prix de Rome. He had failed. The fugue written on a theme supplied by Charles Gounod and the chorus for female voices and orchestra entitled *Printemps* (when published in 1929 rechristened *Salut, Printemps!*) to the poem by Comte de Ségur showed his originality only in the way he misspelled words in copying the text.

As hateful as such experiences were to him, he entered for the final competition in 1883 after passing the preliminary examination, and was awarded the second prize for his cantata *Le Gladiateur*, by Émile Moreau. The works which won the prizes were performed in public and the critics were kinder than usual to Debussy. In comparing him to Vidal, the first-prize winner, they said that although he was less expert in the technique of his art, he had more originality and had the temperament of a real musician. This did not bring him any closer to Rome, except that he did become Roman enough to say *"Basta"*—he was not going to compete any more. He said that he was against these cantatas—"a hybrid form, that partakes clumsily of all that is commonplace in the opera, or in the choral symphony;" that it was purely an invention of the Institut, and that he had none of the religious feeling required for the type of text to which they were to be written. It took all M. Vasnier's eloquence and Guiraud's persuasion to bring him to the competition the following year.

This time Debussy was shrewd enough to write his cantata keeping his eye on the judges' ears, so to speak, restraining himself from his usual desire for innovation, and adorning his score with melodies à la Massenet and Delibes, the jury's favorites at the time. It was a clever hoax. By comparison with a song, *L'ombre des arbres dans la rivière*, in the group of *Ariettes oubliées* written with true Debussy spirit some four years earlier, the airs of Azrael and Lia strike a note of the commonplace, musically devoid of real emotion.

Twenty-two of the twenty-eight members of the jury voted for Debussy's *L'Enfant prodigue*. In an article in *Le Figaro* (July 1, 1884) Charles Darcours wrote somewhat prophetically:

This year's competition brought to light a young musician of talent, a student who does not surpass his colleagues in actual attainments, but who proves in the first bars of his composition that he is not one of the common herd. This is worth something in an age when everyone has talent and no one individuality.... M. Debussy is a musician who is destined to meet with a great deal of praise ... and plenty of abuse. At any rate he is the most alive of the candidates this year and for many years past. We find nearly all the faults that characterize the work of the musical dreamer. The tonality is often indefinite, the parts are written without much attention to practical vocal range, there are frequent and unaccountable outbursts of violence, and confusion would seem to be the guiding principle. Yet, in spite of all this, M. Debussy's cantata is an exceedingly interesting work, by reason of its coloring, the expressive quality of the occasionally over-emphasized declamation, and above all the exuberant individuality it reveals.... It is up to the young musician now to find his own path, amidst the enthusiasms and the antagonisms he is certain to arouse.

This was more than a favorable review of a composition. It was the first recognition of that individuality, that "personality of his own"—the root of his artistic creation. And as if to give him his blessing for a long and a twisted road to success, Charles Gounod took Debussy aside and whispered into his ear: "*Toi, mon petit, tu as du génie.*"

CHAPTER V

PRIX DE ROME (PART I)

WHILE, at the *Institut des Beaux Arts*, the jury was debating the fate of the contestants for the Prix de Rome, Debussy was not far away—on the Pont des Arts, one of the bridges that span the river Seine. He stood there among the other idlers watching the *bateaux-mouches* scurrying up and down the stream. Fascinated by the reflection of the sunlight on the water, he almost forgot about the decisive hour when some one tapped him on the shoulder: "You have won the Prix de Rome."

Far from feeling proud and exuberant, Debussy looked as though a severe blow had been dealt him. The one thing he dreaded most came to pass: for three years of material independence he would have to give up his own "free" way of life, his freedom to compose when and how he pleased. But worst of all, it meant that he would have to live in Rome, to part from Madame Vasnier. Many thoughts and plans must have passed through his mind following the first shock, but none offered an acceptable solution to his problem. The least he could do in the face of this calamity was to shorten the imposed years of "exile" by postponing his departure, arriving as late as possible in Rome and then . . . there must be a way of escaping the ordeal and returning to Paris.

Seven months went by before, feeling utterly miserable, Debussy finally took a train to Italy. Torn away from his love and helpless in what was to him an unbearable situation, he hated everything that was connected with the Prix de Rome long before he reached his destination. At Marseille in the last hour before he left France he wrote a short note to M. Vasnier:

DEAR M. VASNIER,

I have little to tell you, particularly because I am afraid I will annoy you with my *ennui* and I assure you that I am doing everything I can to have courage. I even try to forget you. It is not ingratitude—come, you know better—besides, rest assured I wouldn't be able to. I shall write you at greater length from Rome. Believe me to be your sincere friend,

ACH. DEBUSSY

P.S.

Please give my regards to Madame Vasnier and kiss Marguerite and Maurice for me.

This was the first of many letters he wrote M. Vasnier, some of them with almost filial devotion. Only a few of them survive. But those he wrote Madame Vasnier were too intimate for anyone else to appreciate them properly and must have been destroyed.

Apparently in abandoning everything dear to him in Paris he also included his titled name. From now on he signed his name "Debussy," as if to emphasize his feeling of degradation and that he was being sent to "forced labor," as he said. Nothing about the journey to Italy pleased him. When he arrived it rained and there was a strong wind. "You must admit," he mocked, "that it wasn't necessary to come all the way to Rome to find the same bad weather we have in Paris—especially for some one who is as full of rancor for everything Roman as I am."

His fellow Prix de Rome students, among them his old friends from the Conservatory, Gabriel Pierné, Paul Vidal and Georges Marty, came to meet him at Monte-Rotondo. But what was a friendly gesture on their part only annoyed him, because they had to spend the night, all six of them, in a dirty little room and Debussy already abhorred the communal life. "And if you but knew," he cried later in his reports to M. Vasnier, "how they have changed! There is nothing left of the old friendship in Paris. They are stiff, they have the air of men convinced of their own importance—there is too much Prix de Rome about them."

At the first sight of the Villa Medici he took a violent dislike to the whole institution. Louis-Nicolas Cabat, the director in charge, an elderly landscape painter, was merely "a head jailer" to him, for Debussy's impression was that he did not care for the students but was only interested in administration. And Debussy did not like the administration any more than he did the building itself—its dining-hall walls covered up to the ceiling with portraits of the winners of the Prix de Rome since its inauguration, all with the same look stamped on them: Prix de Rome.

Debussy's relationship with his fellow students got off to a bad start from the first night of his arrival. He played his cantata to them. It had a moderate success among the laureates in painting, sculpture and literature, but none with the musicians. "But I don't care," Debussy said, and this I-don't-care attitude which he adopted at the age of twenty-three was to remain with him for the rest of his life.

In a short time he came to the conclusion that with one or two exceptions it would be difficult for him to find anyone with whom he could enjoy a conversation. He thought their topics were banal, mostly concentrated on the *table d'hôte* and petty gossip about life at the Villa. He called them all egotists who, it seemed to him, indulged with delight in a malicious sport: they talked against each other behind their backs. Marty with Pierné tore apart Vidal, Pierné and Vidal "demolished" Marty, and so on. It made him nostalgic for the charming and instructive *causeries* he had had at the Vasniers, which, he said, had opened his mind to so many things. And when he finally was alone in his room, nicknamed by the students the "Etruscan tomb"—so immense that its green walls seemed to recede as he walked toward them, where he had to "travel" from one piece of furniture to another—he felt so utterly forlorn that he wept like a child and wrote M. Vasnier imploring for sympathy.

I have been accustomed to your intelligent friendship, too used to your interest in me and what I was doing—and I will never forget, sir, all you have done for me, the place you gave me in your family. I will do everything I can to prove to you that I am not ungrateful. I beg you again not to forget me, and to keep my place in your friendship, because I feel I will need it.

Only those who knew Debussy superficially might have said that he was an aloof and whimsical young man. On the contrary, he was sentimental and capable of the most faithful devotion. He needed friends, or at least one (and obviously not M. Vasnier) in whom he could confide, for he was going through an emotional state he did not know how to master—his first love affair, too absorbing for him to think rationally. He would have taken the first train to Paris had he not been afraid that this would be against M. Vasnier's wishes and would only complicate an already entangled situation. Paving the way for a decisive step, he wrote M. Vasnier:

Yes, and I repeat this, I fear I shall have to return to Paris earlier than you think. It will be silly, perhaps, but what is there to do? I am afraid to argue with you and make you cross, for I should be very sorry for trying your friendship. But if you have a little sympathy with me you will not accuse me of lacking courage. Also, I don't feel well—always for the same reason—my devil of a heart is restive against the Roman air. I rack my brain for work, but nothing comes of it, except a fever which knocks me down, leaving me without any strength.

Had Debussy in desperation lost control of discretion? For obviously he was not suffering from any kind of fever but love fever. Later on, when the Roman summer set in with its unbearable heat, he did contract a fever and then he was wretched indeed, but in the first two months of his stay at the Villa Medici he only heard of the dreaded disease.

Fortunately for all concerned, at about this time he attached himself to an older member of the community, M. Popelin, not a musician but apparently congenial to his temperament. At any rate, although of short duration (for the man soon left the Villa) their friendship was powerful enough to keep Debussy from resigning the Prix de Rome, and intimate enough for him to confide his most personal thoughts.

.... Do I have to tell you [he wrote M. Popelin on June 24, 1885] that these two months have changed nothing in me, that they have done nothing but to aggravate certain feelings in me? I have to admit their force, because in the absence of what inspires them I am unable to live —for when your imagination refuses to obey you, you might as well not be alive. As I have told you before, I have been too accustomed only to want things and to conceive them *through her*.[1] And I say this to you with a certain fear. For I am far from doing what you advised me to try, to reduce to a durable friendship this love which is mad, I know it, but its madness prevents me from reasoning. Not only would my thinking about it tend to further madness, but it makes me feel as though I have not sacrificed enough for this love.

Little wonder that he could not concentrate on anything else, that he tried to do some work "but nothing came of it." "You know how much I love music," Debussy wrote M. Vasnier, for whom he had a different version, "and you can imagine how this state of mind upsets me." He said that he could not live the life of the Villa Medici students, that he could not share their happiness, and that it was not his arrogance that should be blamed for his hating it—he simply could not adjust himself, because, as he said, he lacked the "special adeptness" and the "necessary indifference" which one had to have.

But while he was engaged in these futile arguments with Vasnier, he nevertheless realized that there was no escape from the one obligation of every winner of the Prix de Rome: each year the student at the Villa Medici had to submit to the Institut des Beaux Arts in Paris his *envoi*—that is, a sample of his work.

For a while Debussy worked on some sketches for a composition for chorus and orchestra, *Zuléïma*, to Georges Boyer's libretto, adapted from Heinrich Heine's "Almansor." Not knowing the German language he had to use a translation, but before he completed the first of the planned three parts he condemned it as "too old-fashioned and fusty."—"Those great silly verses, great only in their length, bore me," he said, "and my music surely will sink beneath their weight ... and besides, there is something even more serious: I believe I shall never be able to enclose my music in a strict mold. I am not speaking of the musical form, of course," he

[1] Madame Vasnier.

explained, "but simply from the literary point of view. I shall always prefer a subject, where, somehow, action is sacrificed to expression of the feeling of the soul. It seems to me that then music might become human, more alive, and one could then discover and refine upon a means of expression."

Obviously lacking a new idea, Debussy turned again to his old composition *Diane au bois,* the one that his teacher Guiraud had advised him to leave alone "if he wanted to win the Prix de Rome." Debussy argued that his *Diane* in no way resembled the poems generally used for the *envois,* which, he said, were only highly polished cantatas. "Thank God!" he exclaimed, "I had enough with one of them and it seems to me that I should take advantage of at least one good thing that the Villa offers—the complete liberty to work in order to do something original and not to fall into the same old path.

"It is certain that the Institut will not be of my opinion, arguing naturally that their way, of course, is the only right one. Well, too bad! I love my liberty and what is my own too much. At least, if I am denied the choice of the *milieu,* I can revenge myself through my spirit. In this, of course, I am only joking, the truth is that I can write only this kind of music. Now, whether I will be capable of doing it, this I don't know. But at any rate I will do everything I can so that at least a few will be satisfied. As for the rest, I don't care."

Debussy signed this declaration of independence on June 4, 1885, but, as all manifestoes go, it took some time before he could live up to it. He talked, argued and complained, but could not bring himself to work. This time, however, he had a legitimate excuse. As I mentioned earlier, he caught the fever and even when he was getting better the unbearable heat left him limp with exhaustion. He was, indeed, a sorry sight. When he tried to play the piano "it sweated like a human being," he said, and at night swarms of mosquitoes and what he called "nocturnal beasts" invaded his room and kept him awake. All his protestations led to nothing. Ernest Hébert, the new director who succeeded Cabat, also a painter, was so enamored with everything Roman that he told Debussy that there was nothing wrong with his room, that an artist could sleep in the Coliseum "where grandeur and awe would amply atone for any inconvenience," and as for the mosquitoes and the heat, it was all exaggerated, a pure invention of his imagination. *He* did not feel it, Hébert said.

Fortunately Count Joseph Primoli, a wealthy dilettante whom Debussy met by chance, took pity on him and invited him to his place at Fiumicine. Originally the invitation was for a week, but Debussy stayed at the Count's villa much longer because Primoli had to go to Paris and Debussy was given free run of the place in the Count's absence.

For the first time since he had left Paris Debussy enjoyed his environment. "Fiumicine is a charming spot, where the Romans come to bathe in the sea. There is a little harbor with the most picturesque small boats," Debussy reported to M. Vasnier, saying that he lacked the talent to describe its beauty in words; he did not forget to mention, however, that the Count's villa was a "delightful cottage" where everything was done for his comfort, and that he could fully enjoy his solitude—never to speak to anyone, except when ordering his meals. There was no "casino" and no "society" and he took great pleasure in his walks and even did a little work.

But no sooner did he return to Rome to "that abominable villa," to that combination of "a cosmopolitan hotel, a private college, and a compulsory civilian barracks," and to that existence where nothing happened except the *ennui*, than he began again to plead with Vasnier to let him return to Paris.

"Let us say, if you like, that it is forbidden to be bored in the midst of the most marvelous, inspiring to the imagination. That might be so, but one can not make oneself over," he declared with defiance.

The trouble was that Debussy came to Rome in adverse circumstances, too early in life to appreciate its beauty and treasures. He was, outside of music, an ignorant young man. To him, Roman history was a *tabula rasa* and Rome was one large graveyard with tombstones and monuments—a painful reminder of his lack of education. The magnificence of Rome, the splendor of its architecture only oppressed him—*"Saint Pierre est une salle pour géants raison-nables et sans goût."* He preferred San Severino or the Villa Pia in the Vatican gardens. He took refuge in the little streets of the old Rome, where he could browse in the antique shops as he would in Paris. He behaved as a stranger, yet there was no need for it. This was not his first visit to Rome, he had been in Italy three times before. Of course, then he had been traveling with Madame von Meck and this made all the difference. He had ridden in lovely carriages and had lived like those who owned the beautiful villas he now could only admire. Young Debussy was a poor man who once had tasted the life of luxury. He was a poor boy with little hope for a bright future when chance brought him into Madame von Meck's entourage. During his visits with her he lived like a patrician. He even aspired to make this sort of life his own by marrying into her family, and his failure brought him once again face to face with reality. The Vasniers' home was a godsend, for while it could hardly have been mentioned in the same breath with that of the von Mecks, it was certainly better than anything his own family could offer him.

After his return from Russia he readjusted, but it would be naïve to assume that he ever lost sight of the life of the rich and that he did not feel it beckoning him. He came to Rome on a scholarship providing him with food and board and a little pocket money. Except for what Vasnier gave him and some money he occasionally received from Madame von Meck, he had none to spare. It is hard to get used to poverty, it is so easy to live like a rich man. No wonder he enjoyed living at Count Primoli's villa, catered to by the servants as if he were a count himself. It was only natural that in reference to Villa Medici he spoke of "the indescribable discomfort of feeling out of his proper atmosphere." His superior taste in food and wines and his "lordly manner" estranged him from his fellow students. He complained of the poor comradeship among the students but his own condescending behavior did little to foster his popularity. His attitude of a man who is used to "better things," used to caviar, *foie gras* and choice wines, but who would be satisfied with two fried eggs and a cup of tea [1] rather than partake of their student meals—and this is literally what he did—was a constant irritant to them.

Debussy's friends noticed how "he delighted in all that was refined, delicate and unusual—and that in every domain." His taste made him extravagant, for he rarely could resist temptation. It showed in his choice of ornaments, small *objets d'art* he would collect, *de luxe* bindings of books and special perfumes. And as most of the time his meager means did not permit him a wide variety of indulgence, he used his cunning to gain the objects of his desire. Vidal has related at least one such case when Debussy, obviously much perturbed, came to see him one morning and told him that his father was seriously ill, needed an operation, and that he should go at once to Paris but he had no money. Vidal was going to help him in his distress. Count Primoli was away, but the Hochons, wealthy Parisians, were staying at the Villa, and Vidal managed to get from them one thousand francs for Debussy. That day Achille was absent at lunch and when Vidal did not see him at dinner he thought he should tell the director of Debussy's sad news and sudden departure. On his way to Hébert he saw the light in Achille's room. To his surprise he found Achille sitting at the table, looking in ecstasy at several small ivory statuettes he had been longing to acquire for some time. Vidal told the story many years later when Debussy was a famous musician to whom in retrospect a great deal was forgiven. He did not say how he had felt at the time nor whether Debussy was forced to return the coveted bibelots to the antique dealer. In his letters to Vasnier Debussy spoke only of things on a higher plane.

You speak of the tranquillity which the Villa offers. Oh! Lord knows what I would give for a little less of it and at any price, for this tranquillity depresses me and deprives me of a real life. Let's say again that this is not serious, but the most important thing is that my work suffers from it a great deal. I cannot see much good in every day that makes me fall into a deeper mediocrity. You must admit that this gives me the right

---

[1] Debussy was later known for the precise and punctilious ritual of tea-making à l'Anglais he went through whenever anyone called at his home.

to pause and to think of my future. Thus I feel that the experience of one year is sufficient to prove that I shall do nothing worthwhile here and that the year was completely lost for me and only made me regress.

I sincerely believe that to force me to start on the second year would be a rather poor service to me—it would only make me struggle and strip me of the old easy way of composing which I once had. No one can say that I did not try. This lost year proves it sufficiently. Therefore I have decided to resign at the end of the year, and it is you, dear sir, whose affection I know, whom I ask not to consider it wrong on my part, for I am no longer speaking of myself, but of my future.

But these were the words of a mere boy who wanted to be a brave man, who wanted to lead his own life and be with the woman he loved, but who was financially dependent on the woman's husband's good graces. While fancying himself an apostle on the new, untrodden path in art, Debussy was deep in a banal and old-fashioned *ménage à trois* and he had to contrive and lie about himself both to his paramour as a faithful lover and to her husband as a grateful sort of adopted son. He could wish, but he could not decide—and Vasnier knew this.

That Vasnier's disapproval of his intentions, reminding him that his unreasonable behavior might strain his friendship (including the occasional financial help) had a sobering effect on Debussy is clear from his sudden change of tactics in the "softening process" of Vasnier. He followed Vasnier's advice to be less critical of Rome and to profit by every available opportunity. He discovered the small church of Santa Maria dell' Anima "stuck away among the horrible little streets." He liked the church because of its pure style and because it was so unlike the others "with their array of sculptures, pictures and mosaics, all so theatrical." There he attended two Masses: one of Palestrina, the other of Orlando di Lasso. He was impressed by these sixteenth-century masters of counterpoint, particularly by di Lasso, who, he thought, was more decorative and human than Palestrina.

The only other occasion when Debussy's musical feelings "were at all awakened" was when he heard Franz Liszt. At the end of 1885 Liszt came to Rome and was a frequent visitor at the Villa. At Hébert's, Debussy and Vidal played Chabrier's *Valses romantiques* for him and later on, at Giovanni Sgambati's home, Debussy had the pleasure of hearing Liszt and Sgamabati play Saint-Saëns' "Variations on a theme of Beethoven" for two pianos. This was the last time Liszt played in Italy. He died six months later. Liszt was seventy-five and no longer the Mephisto of the old days. He was tired and there was not much left of the bravura of his *Glanzperiode,* but still it was a great master's playing and Debussy never forgot one particular detail—his pedaling. "It was as if he were breathing," Debussy said.[1]

And should these reports of his "musical activities" not be sufficient to appease Vasnier, Debussy also wrote him that he was working hard, because he said, he felt he must make sure of quantity, since he could not count on the quality of his *Diane.* He complained that he had a "lot of trouble" with it. He could not find the right way to express her personality as he saw it. She must have a cold beauty, he said, that suggests no idea of passion. But after eight months in Rome he made little progress. He blamed it again on the state of his mind. He may have accepted the inevitable—that is, that if he returned to Paris he would lose his "second home" at the Vasniers and therefore he might as well "serve his term" at the Villa. He resigned himself "to live the life of a noncommissioned officer on full pay," but not without sulking.

After two months' silence, he told Vasnier in a letter:

My negligence in writing comes from the life I lead, in which my *sauvagerie* only increases. At times I am so completely run down that when I feel I should write a letter, I say to myself: 'What for? No one can get me out of it.' It is much better for me to remain quietly in my corner and suffer the *ennui* apparently incomprehensible to many people. What can I say? I shall die in impenitence in regard to the prodigious benefits offered by the Villa Medici to the artists, and all the beautiful sermons (please forgive me for saying this) like your affectionate remonstrations will do no good.

---

[1] For technical analysis of Liszt's art of pedaling, see my article "Look into your piano," published in *Etude,* May, 1946.—V.S.

But according to his fellow students Debussy was neither dying of boredom nor "quietly remaining alone in his corner," as he pretended to the Vasniers. He had been going into the city to look for diversion more often than he would admit, and while in his letters to Vasnier he claimed that he was not interested in the "gatherings" at M. Hébert's and his society friends, actually he was the heart of these parties—the *serpent noir* who coiled and exhibited his rings and not "Prince of Darkness," as he was at first nicknamed by the students. Debussy wrote Vasnier:

At the present moment Villa Medici is very busy. Hébert has invited many friends, a certain M. Hochon and his wife, society people ... but I have found a way to escape them. I have told Hébert that I had to sell my evening clothes and that my finances don't allow me to have new ones made. He called me a fool, but I don't care. I have succeeded in what I wanted, for Hébert is too fanatically devoted to decorum to introduce a miserable-looking business suit into the splendor of décolleté gowns and white ties.

But the truth was that not only did he not sell his evening clothes, but on all the picnics arranged by Hébert and his "society friends" Debussy sported an "irresistible white flannel suit," to the envy of his fellow students.

And if his occasional amorous escapades in the dark streets of Rome did not count, there was at least one episode that remained in his memory for a long time. It seems that after one of these evenings at Hébert's, where Debussy played and sang his compositions and generally was a great success, a beautiful young Parisian woman carefully tiptoed through the dark corridors of the Villa and came to his room. She was naked under her long overcoat.

Fifteen years later, when Debussy held a long discourse about love with another "beautiful young Parisian woman," he must still have remembered that night at the Villa Medici. On that occasion, according to René Peter,[1] he maintained that love, of supernatural essence, has forever been belittled, disfigured, by reason of the fateful and total incomprehension which is the fundamental char-

---

[1] René Peter, French dramatist, writer, Debussy's intimate friend.

acteristic of human beings; that a source of infinite happiness is stolen from us by the fact that instead of uniting at once in all simplicity, man and woman believe they must first go through a kind of furtive cross-fire battle, according to artificial ancient rites.

Thus, he said, one sees in the old *bourrées* of Auvergne the lover abounding in graces, in tricks, parading like a rooster, trying to win the loved female, then, disappointed, brusquely turning away. What happens? A sudden reversal of the roles. It is now she who is going to play the suitor, so much so that at the third and last figure a double joy manifests itself.

"Wouldn't it have been infinitely better for them," concluded Debussy (nonetheless amused by these dances), "to begin where it had to end?"

"There is however a minimum . . ." the young lady interrupted.

"A minimum of what?"

"But . . . of decency, to observe. The woman, at least—"

"Where do you see any need of decency for the practice of the one thing which in essence is the one which demands none?"

"All the same, one must know how to make oneself a little bit desired, to heighten one's value."

"What makes you think, my dear, that there is a real difference in values between you and us in these matters? What magnifies love, makes it divine, is to be a creator of beauty, to put beauty in everything everywhere without distinction of sex or caste."

"If one were to let you go on," the young lady smiled, "it would be up to women to do the courting."

"Here we are, the big word has come out! For, in the end, it is much more the word which shocks you. All that could be so much simpler!"

"How?"

"Well . . . couldn't one, for instance, imagine a woman who, feeling herself loved by a man whom she finds attractive—you all have such an amazing instinct for these things—would come to him without all the superfluous talks, insipid compliments which are only a waste of time, even often a weakening of true love, and would tell him: "Take me, you big stupid!" "

"What a flattering opinion he would have of her!"

"As flattering as the one she would have of him, my pretty lady," Debussy concluded.

But to return to the Villa Medici at the beginning of February, 1886. No sooner had Hébert's friends the Hochons departed for France than Debussy concocted a new scheme—to get permission for a short leave to go to Paris. Through his participation at Hébert's musicales and his successful entertainment of his friends he had achieved a closer association with the director. Hébert was an amateur violinist and a worshiper of Mozart. He liked to play "all the Mozart sontatas" and Debussy was ready to oblige. And while he carefully accompanied the amateur's poor playing, often quickly transposing passages to keep in harmony with his partner, he never forgot to press his plea for a leave to Paris. The old director remained adamant, until one night Debussy threw himself at his feet and, crying hysterically, threatened to commit suicide unless the director let him go. Whether, at this melodramatic scene, Debussy actually brandished a revolver, as has been reported, is doubtful, for all his life Debussy had a mortal fear of firearms and besides, it was not necessary: his tears appeared so genuine that the frightened man at once granted him his request.

On the following day Debussy was on his way to Paris. He had no intention of returning to Rome. But after a cool reception by M. Vasnier and four weeks of calming his overheated imagination in the arms of his paramour, he again obeyed her husband's advice and went back to the Villa.

CHAPTER VI

PRIX DE ROME (PART II)

THE SHORT EXCURSION to Paris did not affect Debussy's feeling toward the Villa Medici. Upon his return he hated it just as much as before. And his letters to Vasnier were replicas of those he had already written him many times—all of them as if according to the formula he contrived when he first came to Rome. He usually said that he was not going to complain and then did nothing else for the rest of the letter. But as time went on his irritation with Vasnier's sermons became more apparent, although it was always expressed in the most careful terms.

To please Vasnier he let himself "be dragged to the Sistine Chapel, as if to the gallows," and to the museums; he would have appreciated the masterpieces more if they were in Paris, he said. He preferred Raphael's *Loggias* to the large compositions of the School of Athens, and Signorelli's "La Résurrection des morts" amazed him, "not merely because the angels in it play trumpets." But he stubbornly maintained that the seduction that the contemplation of a masterpiece produces on the imagination demands an entirely different state of mind than was his at that time.

It was Debussy's nature to be influenced by his surroundings—he said that Rome crushed him, annihilated him, that he suffocated and was absolutely incapable of shaking off the horrible "numbness" which made him see things in a detestable light. He had worked himself up into such an emotional state that he was afraid he would lose all sense of beauty, and he believed (or at least he said so) that already he did not love the beautiful in the way he should—all this because he was in Rome under duress.

I feel the weight of the shadow of the Academy! Ah! the Villa Medici, filled with academic legends, from the doorman in the green frock coat to the director who lifts his eyes up to the skies with an ecstatic air each time he speaks—and all those eulogies to Michelangelo—like speeches at a reception! I am sure that Michelangelo would laugh if he could hear. I might be mistaken, but it seems to me that Michelangelo—this is the most modern art in its extreme. He had daring bordering on folly, but I think that if one were to follow his path it would not lead directly to the Institut. Of course, we are only small fry, much too young to be allowed to go adventuring on this road.

After his return from Paris Debussy made friends with several laureates in painting, sculpture, and literature—they were not musicians, but knew enough about music to be interested in discussing the correlation of the arts. Among them were Gaston Redon, the architect, who played the flute, Marcel Baschet, the painter of a famous portrait of Debussy, Xavier Leroux, and Ernest Chausson's friend, Lombard.

Always conscious of his lack of education outside the purely musical domain, Debussy was an enthusiastic listener in this new circle, where they read together and discussed the works of Baudelaire, Verlaine, and even Schopenhauer and Spinoza. They read Shakespeare and they introduced Debussy to Rossetti's poems, and when they visited the galleries he shared with them their fascination with the new style of the pre-Raphaelites. Whistler's "Nocturnes" held Debussy spellbound.

During his short visit to Paris Debussy had become acquainted with Émile Baron, the wealthy owner of a stationery-bookstore on the rue de Rome. Baron was interested in the liberal arts and a whole coterie of young artists; he spoiled them with his extravagant dinner parties at which *"le corps était si à l'étroit, mais où l'esprit était si à l'aise."* They first met when Debussy, poor as he was, insisted on minute details in the execution of his orders for supplies of writing paper: there were to be two different sizes with the initials A.D. engraved in the left corner, set off in vermilion on the large size and in pale silver on the small. He also bought the latest issues of the literary reviews and started a sort of charge account with the understanding that Baron would supply him with books while he was in Rome. As the months went by, the bookstore in Paris filled Debussy's orders for complete sets of *La Revue Independante*, *Vogue*, a symbolist publication, the complete works of Shelley (in translation), and various other journals and books. Nonchalantly referring to the mounting bills, Debussy would ask: "Don't you have anything else by Verlaine, or *Rose-Croix* by Albert Jounet, or ... ah! what about *Les Croquis Parisiens*, by J. K. Huysmans?" and stipulated that he wanted *l'edition sur japon* (de luxe edition).

Debussy had progressed a long way from Bourget's poems. Like so many other musicians he did not escape the fascination of Flaubert's *Salammbô* and even seriously considered it as a subject for his *envoi*, but after making a few sketches he laid it aside. An avid reader, Debussy was rapidly filling the gaps in his general education, and the search for the direction of his own art kept him restless. With Paul Vidal he read scores of both classical and contemporary music, and played two-piano arrangements of Bach's organ works and Beethoven's Ninth Symphony. He spent weeks studying *Tristan und Isolde* for "at that time he was Wagnerian to the point of forgetting the most elementary principles of courtesy." As a rule, works that were on a grand scale astonished him rather than aroused either his admiration or enthusiasm, and his sensitive nature rebelled against Wagnerian grandiloquence and long-winded argumentativeness, but contradictory as it may seem, he was impressed with *Tristan*. On the other hand, he enjoyed the performances of typical Neapolitan *Polichinelle* given at the small popular theater, and while he did not care for Italian operas like Donizetti's *La Favorita* and the early works of Verdi, he made an effort unusual for him to meet the old master.

Prompted by Vasnier, in the hope of gaining some valuable advice, or, perhaps, out of plain curiosity, he visited several Italian musicians. For some unaccounted reason Debussy would not speak of these visits, except that many years later he related them to Andrew de Ternant, an English journalist, making him promise not to disclose the secret while he was alive.

Debussy knew Ruggiero Leoncavallo casually as a music and drama critic, long before his *Pagliacci* brought him world fame. It was he who suggested a way to meet Verdi, through Arrigo Boïto, Verdi's librettist.

Achille was more impressed with the way Boïto lived than with what he said about contemporary music. The study in Boïto's Milan apartment resembled the library of a literary man more than a musician's studio. Books and magazines in Italian, French and German were strewn all over the room. There was not a single piece of music, printed or manuscript—in fact, nothing to indicate that the owner was also a composer except, perhaps, for the piano, old and dilapidated, which looked as if no one had touched it for years. And indeed no one had. Boïto had been disappointed with the fate of his own music. Gounod's *Faust* had delayed the production of his *Méfistofèle*, and knowing the difficulties caused by the production of Anton Rubinstein's *Nero* he was too discouraged to continue with his own *Nerone*. He told Debussy that he thought that the works of both Shakespeare and Goethe provided excellent material for librettos, but that on the whole he would not advise anyone to compose either for the theater or the church. The future belonged to the concert hall, Boïto said. Then he wrote a letter of introduction to Verdi and Debussy went off to Sant' Agata.

"So you have come to bother an old man." Verdi, puttering in his vegetable garden, smiled as he greeted Debussy. "I suppose you will soon be sending the newspapers an account of how Verdi plants salads. Well, he does it very much like any other old man, but I shall have to take precautions and protect my vegetables, or some English or American tourist may run away with my greenstuff as souvenirs." Debussy explained who he was. "Ah, so you are not an iniquitous journalist, you are the French musician Boïto wrote me about," Verdi said. "You won the Prix de Rome at the Paris Conservatory. Well, you are lucky. I didn't get anything at the Milan

Conservatory, except much sorrow and many enemies. But I am still alive, and planting salads in my garden."

Debussy stayed for lunch with Verdi, but the old man was not too anxious to talk about music and even less about contemporary musicians, since he did not want to be charged with professional jealousy. A composer was not necessarily a good music critic, he said. He knew that such qualifications were sometimes combined, but it was not always beneficial to musical art. To illustrate this point of view, he spoke of Vasari,[1] a painter of merit, but who had rendered more service to art and posterity by his *Lives of the Painters, Sculptors and Architects.*

Verdi had one word of advice to give to all prospective composers—to write simply, to make their scores easy to perform. But he shook his head and added that it was of no use preaching to young people, they would go their way and follow impractical methods. No matter why Debussy would never discuss the visit: it is clear that he did not follow the old maestro's counsel—he behaved exactly as Verdi had predicted.

After eighteen months at the Villa, Debussy finally put *Diane au bois* aside with only one act completed, and turned back again to *Zuléïma.* Having little time left before his *envoi* should reach the Institut, he did "a lot of darning" on this composition which he felt was dead—Meyerbeer-and-Verdi-like, and not at all the kind of music he really wanted to compose. Calling it a "symphonic ode," he sent it on to Paris. The Academy was even less pleased with the work than the composer. Its verdict appeared in the *Journal Officiel* on December 31, 1886:

The work which earned the first prize in musical composition for M. Debussy in 1884 gave the Academy reason to expect that this remarkably talented young artist would give further evidence of the melodic and dramatic qualities which he exhibited in the competition piece. The Academy must regretfully record the exact contrary. At present, M. Debussy seems to be afflicted with a desire to write music that is bizzare, incomprehensible, and impossible to execute.

[1] Giorgio Vasari, 1511–1574.

With the exception of a few passages that show individuality, the vocal part of his work is uninteresting, both as regards the melody and the declamation. The Academy hopes that time and experience will bring salutary modifications to M. Debussy's ideas and compositions.

By the time this sermon reached Debussy he had been given a new room at the Villa, and he could enjoy a beautiful view of Rome outside his windows and dream about his new work—*Printemps*. At last he had the esthetic pleasure of watching the Roman men and women, and the long, black and red processions of priests, "like fantastic black radishes and roguish pimentos. It is just like certain pictures of fairyland in which chimeric vegetables of all sizes stretch out into the infinite."

The winter of 1886-1887 was unusually severe in Rome. Covered with snow, the city of eternal spring resembled Moscow, Debussy said. The cold was bitter and the Romans did not know what to make of it. But the snow, he thought, gave a beautiful color to the ruins, restoring their original cold and pure lines. "It's a thousand times better than this annoying blue sky and the usual clay-colored earth."

Debussy thought of spring when he was determined to leave Rome, no matter what happened. It gave him an idea for a composition: *Printemps*—"perhaps something like Botticelli's 'Primavera,' not Spring in its descriptive sense, but rather from the human point of view," he reflected. It was not going to be a program piece based on some kind of literary work. In his composition he wanted "to express the slow, painful birth of everything in nature, then the ascending fruition ending in an outburst of joy, of rebirth into a new life, whatever it might be."

However, he was still uncertain about the choice of a subject for his next *envoi*. Influenced by the enthusiasm of his friends for the pre-Raphaelite school, he thought of Dante Gabriel Rossetti's "The Blessed Damozel." It is impossible to say how well Debussy knew the English poet-painter's tragic story: his love for the golden-haired Elisabeth Siddal, the poor, illiterate "fairy creature from the shoddy garishness of the cheap London shop" who had nothing but a willingness to learn and the wisdom to listen in silence when the conversation floated far above her head, but whom the poet loved and made unhappy and who died of consumption.

A prophetic story, almost as if a page from Debussy's own biography of later years was placed before him. Or was he acquainted only with Rossetti's romantic gesture at the end of the story: Rossetti had buried the sole manuscript of his poems in the coffin of the woman who inspired them and for whom they were written?

Debussy's *La Damoiselle élue* after Rossetti's "The Blessed Damozel" (in Sarrazin's translation) was still in embryo, like another composition, the *Fantaisie* for piano and orchestra, actually not completed until two years later, when he announced that he was through with the "hardest" part of the *Printemps* and that all there was left for him to do was to orchestrate it.

It is interesting that he wrote nothing about these compositions to Vasnier—"the only man with whom he could discuss his work and be sure to be understood," as he used to say. Their long-distance relationship had been strained for some time and now in his letters to Émile Baron, Debussy assured his new friend that *he* was the only man in whom he could confide, and that it was *his* bookstore on the rue de Rome and everyone connected with it that had his affection and that he missed most. Debussy wrote Baron that he had been a whole eternity in the Eternal City, but that it would not be long now: "I want to see some Manet and hear Offenbach! This may seem paradoxical, but I assure you that breathing the art of the factory of spleen, you begin to have the most fantastic ideas."

And sure enough, two months later, after he had sent *Printemps* off to Paris, Debussy wrote Vasnier:

Forgive me, now I will need not only your friendship, but your indulgence. I cannot stay here, I have tried everything, I have followed your advice. I swear to you that I have used all possible good will on my part. All this proved only one thing: I could never live and work here.

You probably are going to say that I have taken my decision in haste and did not think about it carefully. I assure you that I did. Here is what will happen to me if I stay—I will annihilate myself completely. I feel that ever since I came here my spirit has been dead, and I want so much to work, to do something of my own. And then there is another thing: you know how constantly I doubt myself while I work. I need someone to encourage me. I have found this so often in you, sir, and I assure you it was only you who gave me courage. When something pleased you I felt much stronger. Here I will never find it. My comrades laugh at my *tristesse* and I cannot expect any encouragement from them. Naturally, if things do not work out, I know too well that many people will abandon me. But I would rather work twice as hard in Paris than lead this life —a ready-made one, but so monotonous that—and I repeat this to you —one either goes to sleep or is irritated by it, as in my case. Well, go try to do something worth while under such circumstances!

I am leaving on Saturday and will arrive in Paris on Monday morning. I beg you, sir, do not be too severe with me. I will have nothing left except your friendship, please keep it for me. I will need it so much.

Believe me sincerely yours,

A. DEBUSSY

This was his last letter from Rome. Debussy was on his way to Paris before the letter reached Vasnier. He traveled in a sleeping compartment of an express train—a luxury for a student, but appropriate to the occasion: as in his latest composition, he was going with *éclat* to a new life, to his *Printemps*, although the period of fruition was not over.

At the Vasniers' he was received with anything but a hearty welcome. Soon after his return the Vasniers moved to new quarters and there did not seem to be a room reserved for him "to work undisturbed." The Vasniers had made new friends and Achille Debussy was no longer the center of their interest. But he did go to see them, to play for them what he had composed in Rome, or to get some of the manuscripts which he had left with them before he went to Italy. He did not compose for Madame Vasnier any more nor accompany her singing at concerts. Their relationship was friendly but no longer what it had been.

Debussy realized that he was on his own. He could not bear staying with his parents and he had no money to live by himself. He had to make his way by giving piano lessons. He offered to teach the Vasniers' daughter Marguerite, but Debussy was a poor teacher. He had no patience, nor the ability to explain a problem to his young pupil. They had to give it up.

Afterwards his visits became less frequent. He came for advice, or to ask them for money. Then they never saw him again. If this was the end of his passionate love affair with Madame Vasnier, then it was the only instance of its kind in his life, for Debussy's future love affairs were to overlap each other—he would not give one up until he was safely in the arms of the next.

CHAPTER VII

BOHEMIAN PERIOD—GABY

THE SIX YEARS following Debussy's return from Rome have been called his Bohemian period. In fact it was so Bohemian that during the first two years no one knew where or how he lived, let alone the details of his personal life. Except for a few musicians, fellow students, no one spoke of him, and among the literati and the painters with whom he preferred to visit not much notice was taken of him. His official address, 27 rue de Berlin (today rue de Liége), was that of his parents, but it had become even less of a home to him after a few years of being away from it.

Debussy never spoke of his brothers and sister who must have lived there, nor did any of his friends mention them in their recollections. Yet this was the only period in his life (short as it was) when Debussy was forced by circumstance to live in close quarters with his family. He did not like it. "The atmosphere" was far from congenial and perhaps he was self-conscious about it, for he avoided having his friends visit him there. His mother had not changed, except that she grew a bit heavier and even more brusque in her manner. His father held on to the same job and otherwise remained a great enthusiast of *Le Pré aux clercs* and *La Fille du régiment* as played at the Opéra Comique—"masterpieces," in his opinion. The couple were not happy about their son. They had to give up their ambitions and dreams, and to console themselves with their *popote* and sedate existence. Debussy, on the other hand, felt that he had no common interests with them, he knew that his ideas were above their heads, and he frankly spoke of his father as a "presumptuous windbag." This attitude, however, need not be interpreted except as a reflection of his general state of mind. He was irritable and was going through a crisis commonly experienced by a rejected lover— he needed affection, to love and to be loved, and, searching aimlessly "without sails and rudder," he took it where he could find it. His parents' home was merely a place where he stayed when there was nowhere else to go.

For a while a society woman, flattered by the role of Muse to a genius, was supposed to have been unusually generous with her charms with this young man free-lancing in the field of love. Some thought it might have been Madame Hochon whom Debussy knew when, with her husband, she was visiting Hébert at the Villa Medici. So secret was their attachment that nothing more is known than this. His emotions were not seriously involved in the affair, for he seems to have extricated himself without much damage to his feelings. The liaison was of much shorter duration than that with Madame Vasnier, leaving him to a wider scope of amorous activities among the habituées of the cafés and night clubs he frequented.

Then, one day in 1888, Debussy moved to a room on the third floor of an old dilapidated house at 42 rue de Londres at the foot of Montmartre, a few blocks away from his family's home. It was an attic where plain boards served as walls and ceiling. A low table with a washbasin and an inkpot, three straw chairs, something that resembled a bed, and a splendid borrowed Pleyel piano completed the furnishings of this garret otherwise distinguished by its disorder. Debussy lived there, but not alone. The new abode and its master were zealously guarded, as if by a sentinel, by a well-built, pretty young blonde with a forceful chin, who would open the door to a visitor and look at him as resolutely as a cat. The color of her eyes was green and there was nothing vague in her attitude.

No one knew where Debussy met her. The gossips claimed that he had picked her up in some frivolous place on one of his routine visits there, but René Peter was less harsh on the girl. She certainly was the least frivolous blonde he had ever met, he said, and he thought that while she may have followed a path that does not claim virtue, that it was not for a long time, and that it might have been more of an impasse into which such poor and pretty girls often were driven, but that once her little love adventures brought her to Debussy, her flighty heart felt something strange had happened and that from then on it became permanently settled on her last choice. Her name was Gabrielle Dupont, but to Debussy's friends she was known as Gaby Lehry or simply as Gaby, and was remembered by them as the one who for ten meager years kept the roof over their heads—ten years of Gaby's reign over what one would not exactly call a faithful subject.

Living with Debussy she learned of beautiful things, yet the arts remained to her both unknown and inaccessible. She watched her lover's devotion to the "great mysteries" and she knew how to be patient and how to wait for the promised rewards of his labor. Meanwhile she took charge of their domestic affairs and that was not a simple task, for even when their lunches (if they had any at all) were made of a small chocolate bar and a piece of bread, Debussy remained an *enfant gaté* and would empty his purse for a bibelot or a statuette that caught his fancy, without giving a moment's thought to how they would eat on the following day. It was up to Gaby's ingenuity and her charm to keep the creditors away and, if everything else failed, to take the object of yesterday's fancy to a pawnshop, while the musician's mind was wandering in the heights of his artistic creations.

What Gaby did to earn a living has never been reported, except for one reference: "... at about seven thirty, after having finished her hard labors, Gaby would join Debussy with his friends, bringing them bonbons which they divided not too fraternally." She may have worked in a store, or done washing or scrubbed floors. She was not the kind to shy away from any work, no matter how hard. And it must have been incomprehensible to her that Debussy would refuse to give a piano lesson for twenty francs, an immense fee, in Gaby's estimation, for that sort of hour's pastime, simply because the pupil had no real talent; or would sell for the same price a piece of music on which he had worked for days, and sell it to whom?—a dilettante who was going to claim the authorship as his own! It made far more sense to her to exchange a piece of Japanese silk with trees and fish swimming in the water painted on it, a perfectly useless object as far as she could see, for an umbrella they really needed.

Gaby, however, could not complain, for Debussy was not always the loser. As one of his friends philosophically remarked, "it was all according to the rules of the game." Debussy had more luck with M. Hugo (not the writer), a little tailor on the rue de Vivienne to whom he was already in debt for his clothes. When, after Debussy's return from Rome, Hugo heard that he had "nothing to wear," the tailor went to see him and told him that a great artist like him should not go about looking like a beggar. Thereupon he made him an evening dress, a dinner jacket, a raincoat, an overcoat and a couple of suits, saying that Debussy could pay him later on ... when he became famous. Later on, "when he became famous," Debussy forgot about M. Hugo—it was all according to the rules of the game.

Not all their life was spent in misery and dreams of better days. Often at the end of the day Gaby would discover that they had a little money left over and then they would go out to a café, or circus, or to watch a billiards match. Debussy was very fond of the game. At the circus he loved the clowns and was as excited by the childish amusements as if he were a child himself. He also liked the popular singer Jeanne Bloch, intended "for adults only," who more undressed than dressed, but with a small cap cocked over one ear "threw at her audience her drunken voice, her big stomach, her large breasts and her fat behind." The audience roared and Debussy enjoyed both the act and the public.

And when Vital Hocquet, an old friend, would call on them, they would give themselves up to a regular celebration. Under the name of Narcisse Lebeau, Hocquet worked as a humorist and a writer of spicy verse at the Chat Noire. He was a celebrity in Montmartre, but also (and this was far more important) he earned five hundred francs a month in a plumbing business and could afford to take his friends to dine at Chez Boilesve on the rue Monthyon, or to a show at the Guignol on the Champs Elysées, or to the Folies Bergère, if Gaby preferred, and then to a late supper at the Cabaret du Clou on the rue Trudaine or at one of the restaurants on the boulevards where the chic people took their women.

Gaby and Debussy were young, if not always gay, and in one of those tender moments when they were alone and after everything was said and done, Gaby felt happy enough to promise her lover: "If ever you ... you know what ... with anybody else, I will shoot you like a rabbit." Debussy gave his word, but never kept it. And as the years went by Gaby accepted as inevitable, though never wholeheartedly, a partial victory. Debussy roamed like a cat, but like a cat he always returned home.

But at this point in my story I will let Debussy interrupt me as he did a friend on a similar occasion: "My dear lady, among the occupations which you assign to my activities you have forgotten ... the music!"

In all fairness, Debussy could have blamed no one but himself. Did not he pretend at that time that nothing gave him greater offense than to be taken for a professional musician and that the title filled him with such horror that, on one occasion, when as witness at a friend's wedding he had to fill out the register, he put down *jardinier* (gardener) as his profession? And did not Debussy, as if purposely avoiding musicians, except for a few, frequent literary circles almost exclusively? How many of his close friends then knew that not all his nocturnal wanderings in various quarters of the city were in pursuit of amorous adventures?

Upon his return from Rome Debussy joined the poets, painters and sculptors in their debates over impressionism, poetic realism, mysticism and symbolism. The pre-Raphaelites were as popular in France as they were in England. The young enthusiasts were in search of their dream: to correlate the arts in the kinship to which Baudelaire pointed in his essay on Wagner: "It would be truly surprising if sound were not capable of suggesting color, if colors could not give the idea of a melody, and if sound and color were inadequate to express ideas, for things have ever found expression in reciprocal analogies since that day when God put forth the world as a complex and indivisible whole."

It was the time when Chabrier was collecting paintings by Cézanne, Monet, Manet; Degas was painting his "Les danseuses se baissant"; Berthe Morisot her "Au bain"; and Verlaine had just published his *Jadis et Naguère.*

The French poets conceived their poetry like musicians, they sought to express their ideas in corresponding sounds. *"De la musique avant toute chose, de la musique encore et toujours,"* Verlaine wrote. Of all the literary groups the esthetic theories of the symbolists were the most satisfying to Debussy. Although at that time Paul Bourget was his favorite poet, he did not find his real conception of modern melody until he read more of Baudelaire, Verlaine and Mallarmé.

Debussy liked particularly to visit a small bookstore at 9 rue de la Chaussée d'Antin and to browse there among the rare books and engravings. Some of these books carried on the front page the emblem of the publishing house: an oval medallion which framed the figure of a siren with a slogan *"Non hic piscis omnium."* And indeed, they were not everybody's fish. They were published by the owner of the store, Édmond Bailly, a gnome of a man, with a little goatee, gold-rimmed glasses, and a black skullcap. It was said that he was a poet and that he composed little melodies, but for his personal satisfaction he brought out the works of the symbolists and made his store their favorite meeting place. No one would have believed that this was what was left of the revolutionary spirit which in his youth, when Bailly was an officer in the artillery, led him to take a part in the Commune, particularly since at his store he presided over occultists' séances. He claimed to be on just as good terms with the poets already departed from this world as he was with his own authors and painters, and he edited the *Revue de séance ésotérique.*

The little store also had its own literary past. Before Bailly it had belonged to Édouard Dujardin, the director of the *Revue Independante,* on which Stéphane Mallarmé, Villiers de l'Isle Adam, Paul Verlaine and Jules Laforge collaborated. In 1885 Dujardin established the *Revue Wagnérienne* which a year later, in January 1886, dealt a "symbolist grand slam" by publishing Mallarmé's and Verlaine's odes to Wagner.

Whether Debussy met these poets at Dujardin's or later on at Bailly's, actually he never became close friends with them, although he was seen at some of Mallarmé's famous Tuesdays. The poets, on the other hand, paid little attention to him, since Debussy did not speak much about himself, his work or his projects. While they talked Debussy would listen, turning over the leaves of a book or examining an engraving. But he studied their works and in the course of the first years after his return from Rome composed two sets of songs: *Cinq Poèmes de Baudelaire* (1887-1889) and six *Ariettes* after Verlaine (1888). In these compositions he showed himself an equal of Schumann and Schubert in expressing the intimate nuances of the poems, the atmosphere and *arrière-pensée*. He brought into display all his diversity and subtleness in evoking images. The *Ariettes* were published by *veuve* Girod (1888) but no one would publish the set of Baudelaire poems until Bailly became a great Debussy enthusiast. Thus Debussy's early work was brought out not by a music, but a literary publisher. This, however, was in 1890, and meanwhile Debussy was far from idle.

After his return from Rome Debussy ceased to be a student—he had no intention of returning to the Villa Medici, although he did not officially resign and the Academicians still hoped to bring him to the right path. Their criticisms of his *envoi*, however, were hardly encouraging in that direction. The Academie des Beaux-Arts' official report, published at the end of 1887, runs:

Debussy has sent in, as his second year's work, a symphonic piece in two parts, entitled *Printemps*. As the orchestral score of this work was burnt at the bookbinder's to whom the composer had sent his manuscript, it was only possible to judge the young student's work from the point of view of general musical tendencies, and the intrinsic value of his ideas— except in the case of some portions which he had hastily rescored.

(Debussy never mentioned this accident at the bookbinder's and some musicians, who knew how anxious he was to leave Rome and how sudden was his departure, were led to doubt the authenticity of his story.)

Certainly, M. Debussy does not transgress through dullness or triteness. On the contrary he shows a rather overpronounced taste for the unusual. His feeling for musical color is so strong that he is apt to forget the importance of accuracy of line and form. He should beware of this vague impressionism which is one of the most dangerous enemies of artistic truth.

The first movement of M. Debussy's symphonic work is a kind of a prelude—an *adagio*. Its dreamy atmosphere and its studied effects result in confusion. The second movement is a bizarre, incoherent transformation of the first, but the rhythmical combinations make it somewhat clearer and more comprehensible. The Academy awaits and expects something better from such a gifted musician as M. Debussy.

This lack of understanding of his first effort to express "his own art" certainly failed to induce him to return to Rome and only reminded him once again that there was no need to "await and expect something better" from the Academy. Pierre Vasnier had lost his power of persuasion and there was no one else to take his place. Debussy was independent at last and he was going to do what any other composer would who was not attached to the apron strings of the Academy tutelage. He was going to by-pass official recognition and find himself a publisher. With this practical aim in view he undertook two trips, to London and to Vienna, but he never spoke about them to anyone except Andrew de Ternant, whom he swore to secrecy as he did about his previous visits with Verdi and Boïto.

With a few scores from the meager stock of his compositions, including the unfinished *La Damoiselle élue,* in his briefcase and a letter of introduction to Franz Hueffer, the music critic on The Times, Debussy arrived in London with high hopes in search of a publisher. Hueffer took him to Berthold Tours, a Dutch musician whose opinion carried great weight in London, and there Debussy's venture reached an impasse. After examining Debussy's compositions, Tours told him that since they had no commercial value he did not know of anyone who would bring them out at his own risk. After a week's visit Debussy returned to Paris.

His trip to Vienna was just as unsuccessful, but there, at least, he eventually met Brahms. Brahms did not make it easy for Debussy to see him: he left Debussy's letter unanswered and twice, when Debussy ventured to call on him, he was turned away. And Brahms was not particularly gracious when through a mutual friend Debussy was invited to lunch. "Are you the young Frenchman who wrote me and called twice at my home? Well, I will forgive you this time, but don't do it again." Perhaps this was German humor. During the lunch Brahms ate and did not utter a single word, but at the end of the repast, after drinking several glasses of French champagne, he commented on "the most glorious wine in the world" by quoting from Goethe's *Faust* Brander's lines in Auerbach's cellar:

> *Man kann nicht stets das Fremde meiden,*
> *Das Gute liegt uns oft so fern.*
> *Ein echter Deutscher Mann mag keinen Franzen leiden,*
> *Doch ihre Weine trinkt er gern.*[1]

Having made this poetic announcement Brahms proceeded with his thesis: Franco-German wars were inevitable, but French and German art would always flourish and would be, until the Day of Judgment, the glory and wonder of the world. He said he was aware that the French considered him as the most German of contemporary composers. He was proud to be a German composer—a musician who abandoned his nationality in art would never leave any permanent mark on the history of the music of his own country. He saw no excuse for the imitation of foreign music and that was why he admired French culture, art, and music. Auber's music was French through and through, although the scenes of his operas take place in Italy, Spain and Portugal. In Brahms' opinion the greatest opera produced in Europe since the Franco-German war was Bizet's *Carmen*. He had seen twenty performances of it at the

---

[1] One cannot always do without the foreigner,
The good things are often so far from us.
A true-born German cannot bear Frenchmen
But he likes to drink their wines.

Vienna State Opera house. Bismarck, said Brahms to give more weight to his contention, "who was certainly the best amateur judge of music I ever met, told me he had seen *Carmen* twenty-seven times." Brahms would have "gone to the end of the earth to embrace Bizet," and on the following day invited Debussy to dinner and a performance of *Carmen.*

Thereafter Brahms felt kindlier toward Debussy, showed him the Vienna Conservatory, and visited Beethoven's and Schubert's graves with him. But except for this report and the fact that Brahms embraced him, wishing him *bon voyage,* what Debussy sought or gained from this journey remains a mystery.

The authenticity of de Ternant's reports (to whom Debussy told this) has been questioned by musicians because of lack of corroboration from any other sources, including Brahms' and Verdi's biographies. It seems improbable that de Ternant invented them, and it is just as inconceivable that Debussy made them up. Debussy's extensive correspondence with Alexander von Meck, his former pupil, could perhaps have thrown light on these projects, but unfortunately it was lost during the Russian Revolution.

Thus the only clue is the "circumstantial evidence" offered by Edward Lockspeiser, who discovered, in a letter from Sir Charles Stanford to W. S. Hannam [1] recommending the works for the 1910 Leeds Festival, this reference to *La Damoiselle élue:* "A lovely thing which curiously enough much delighted Brahms himself." If, as Mr. Lockspeiser suggests, it is unlikely that Brahms had obtained a copy of it when it was published in a limited edition in 1893—when he could have seen it? The only performance before Brahms' death took place in Paris at a time when Brahms was in Vienna.

I think, since it is all matter of conjecture, it is possible that Debussy was advised to seek Brahms' help or had heard of the kindness hidden beneath his gruff manner. I happen to know of at least one instance of Brahms' generosity to a younger composer. [2]

[1] October 21, 1909, published in Plunket Greene's book on Stanford.
[2] "Dr. Dvořák as I knew him" by Joseph J. Kovarik (*Fiddlestrings,* 1918.)

Brahms had asked Antonín Dvořák to move to Vienna and when the latter explained that with his large family he could not afford living there, Brahms said: "Well, I have no children and no one to care for, so consider my funds as yours, and it will be one of the happiest days of my life when I go marketing with madame." Dvořák did not accept his offer. Later on Brahms not only arranged Dvořák's works to be published by Simrock, but did all the proofreading for the composer, who was not aware of it.

When Debussy, in closing his story, told de Ternant that Brahms, wishing him *bon voyage* and a successful career, embraced him like a son—"the crusty old bachelor had quite as much fatherly feeling as a more fortunate man"—perhaps he betrayed his earlier hope of gaining Brahms' affection and assistance.

His failure in Vienna and London did not discourage Debussy. In December 1887 he wrote *La mort des amants*, the first composition after his return from Rome, and a month later *Le Balcon*, for which he used a theme from *La Damoiselle élue*. During the first half of 1888 he finally completed the score of *La Damoiselle élue* and sent it to the Academy as his Roman *envoi*, although technically speaking it was an *envoi* from Paris. Not a work of major importance, it certainly was the first to reflect Debussy's esthetic tendencies, his inclination toward the pictorial nourished by poetry, and his traits in handling material. Rossetti's innocent poem did not call for a large orchestra and Debussy showed that with a careful choice of instruments he could create the atmosphere of the unspoken characteristic of his subject, despite the old form of the cantata—his score was a sort of oratorio.

The Academy's reaction [1] toward this composition was more favorable than to his previous one:

The text chosen by M. Debussy is in prose, and rather obscure; but the music which he has adapted to it is not deficient either in poetry or charm, although it still bears the marks of that systematic tendency toward vagueness of expression and form of which the Academy has already com-

[1] January 29, 1889.

plained. In the present instance, however, these propensities and processes are much less noticeable and seem to some extent justified by the very nature of the subject and its indefinite character.

A few months later, when he heard that the Academy was planning a concert of his works, for the first time Debussy's spirit rose. In keeping with the tradition of performing the works of the Prix de Rome laureates at the end of their sojourn at the Villa Medici, the Academy had announced a Debussy program for December 1889. Then it had to be postponed to the following year because the date should have been reserved for Paul Vidal (Debussy's predecessor), but this delay did not destroy the effect of the original announcement on Debussy's sudden verve for work.

He wrote *Harmonie du soir, Jet d'eau* and *Recueillement*. These, with the already composed *Le Balcon* and *La mort des amante*, formed his *Cinq Poèmes de Baudelaire* opus. He completed the *Fantaisie* for piano and orchestra he had started on during his last weeks in Rome, made a first draft of *La Suite bergamasque* for piano and wrote, for piano duet, the *Petite Suite: En bateau, Cortège, Menuet* and *Ballet*. Durand published the *Suite* in 1889 and Debussy and Jacques Durand, the son of the publisher, played it at a private musicale. It made no particular impression on the audience. But this was of minor importance to Debussy.

For months he had been talking about the forthcoming "Festival Debussy." He had been announcing it to everyone he knew and inviting them to attend the great event. Then he heard that his *Printemps* was going to be excluded from the program because it had not been approved by the Academy three years previously. This threw him into a rage. "Either all or nothing," he fumed, and refused to alter his condition.

Actually it was not "this condition" that "killed his festival," but Debussy's stubborn unwillingness to supply the traditional overture for the prize-distribution ceremony—a part of every laureate's duty. Thus, because of a whim, he deprived himself of a public presentation of his works with all the honors provided under the auspices of the Academy, and all possible future advantages resulting from such an occasion. With this defiant gesture he cut the last link with the Institut. Had Debussy cared sufficiently for this official recognition he would have made the concession, but by 1890 his esthetic problems could not be solved by the Academy, which seemed to him senile, and all he said was: "I don't care."

CHAPTER VIII

BOHEMIAN PERIOD—DEBUSSY'S ESTHETICS

EVER SINCE THE Wagnerian wave had engulfed France, French musicians had made yearly pilgrimages to Bayreuth. Some of them were very emotional. It has been reported that Chabrier, one of the most joyful French composers, burst into tears while listening to the prelude to *Tristan,* and that Guillaume Lekeu fainted and had to be carried out of the theater. Some listened with excessive admiration and others as if in a state of delirium, some returned home resigned to experimenting in the old art of love, while others looked for new mistresses. At twenty-six Debussy was strong and brave enough to face the ordeal, and he was curious and anxious enough to declare that if need be he would go there on foot. This, however, was dictated more by his financial status than his ardor. Luckily his wealthy friend Étienne Dupin invited Debussy to join him as his guest on the journey to the Wagnerian Mecca, thus making it less of a heroic feat.

Debussy neither burst into tears nor fainted, although he behaved like a pious monk. He heard *Die Meistersinger* and *Parsifal* and came away as devout as a communicant. During the following year he returned to Bayreuth and besides these operas heard *Tristan.* This time he was completely disillusioned. The sudden change in his feeling toward Wagner, which became final, has always been attributed to his enthusiasm for Moussorgsky's *Boris Godunov* (meanwhile he was supposed to have read the score). In my opinion only lack of information about his trips to Russia could have led to such a supposition. Actually the Russian influence, although important, was only a background and not the primary factor in Debussy's apostasy. He did not see the score of *Boris Godunov* till three years later. But while he did not know the score of this particular opera, he must have been well acquainted with the principles of the new Russian school—The Mighty Five—as opposed to Wagner's opera reform, long before it was brought to the attention of the French by Téodor de Wizewa's report published on February 8, 1886 in the *Revue Wagnérienne*. The French musicians had an exaggerated notion of the lack of knowledge in Russia of Moussorgsky or other members of his group. The Tchaikovsky–von Meck camp, although antagonistic to The Mighty Five, was a well informed one, to be sure, and Debussy's early connections with Russian music came through that channel. While with Madame von Meck Debussy could not have missed either the discussions of their works and aims, or Cui's book on Russian music with its complete exposé of his group's ideas. In general agreeing with the Wagnerian reform of the opera, the Russians laid down the following principles:

1 Dramatic music should have an intrinsic value as absolute music.
2 Nothing should stand in the way of the true and beautiful.
3 The vocal music should match the meaning of the words.
4 The music as well as the libretto—i.e. the structure of the themes—should depend on the individual character and function of each actor as well as on the general sense of the piece.

These principles were very like those underlying the Wagnerian reform; it was the means of implementing them that differentiated the two schools. To begin with the Russians maintained that the subjects of Wagner's operas had nothing *human* in them; they were personified abstract ideas which, like puppets, were incapable of inspiring real interest. The Mighty Five believed themselves to be concerned with the human passions that charm and trouble, stir and confuse the lives of men. Wagner, they charged, concentrated all his interest in the orchestra, giving the vocal parts a secondary role only. He stated his themes through the orchestra, while the actors had only fragments of recitative which, if taken separately, had neither intrinsic value nor any precise meaning. They believed that the actors in the opera are not there merely to complement the orchestra but to create the action. The public watches them, listens to them, and it is therefore they in whom the principal interest should center. The vocal parts in Wagner's operas, they said, battle with the orchestra, only to be killed by it. In short, they believed opera should be essentially vocal—Wagner's was symphonic.

As for the Wagnerian *leitmotiv*, every character is tagged with one and must wear it like a coat wherever he goes, no matter what happens to him, and all his entrances must be announced by it. Wagner gives *leitmotivs* even to vengeance, or to objects—a sword, for instance. It is sufficient merely to mention the idea or the object for the motif to pop up, as though a spring had been pressed. This childish device does not honor Wagner's heroes and why, they asked, is each of them condemned to one perpetual *leitmotiv*, without the slightest development and almost without the slightest alteration, which constitutes still another element of monotony and boredom?

One of the basic principles of the Russian school was variety of form. They were not satisfied with giving a hero one musical idea only, but instead insisted that the themes should be multiplied and developed as the action demanded, with different rhythm, harmony, color; in short, that the characters be painted with all the means at the composer's disposal.

They also rejected the very essence of dramatic plot: the progressive development of conflict, as it was known on the Western European stage. They believed that the real essence of an opera lies in the *idea* of the presented work. Whether this idea was expressed in a series of pictures (dramatic or not in themselves) was not important so long as the presentation as a whole was vital and vivid. Generally speaking, and duly acknowledging Wagner's talent and strong individuality, they thought that his doctrine was false, that he had written more annoying music than good, and that the mad Wagnerian cult was more fanatical than sincere.

That much Debussy must have known, even if he did not agree with all of it wholeheartedly when he went to Bayreuth in 1888. Later on some of these ideas would be put forth as his own without acknowledging the source. But before he left for his second trip there, in 1889, he had learned something that in his search for his own credo was far closer to him and more important than the point of view of the group of Russian Nationalists.

In April, 1889, La Grande Exposition Universelle commemorating the centennial of the French Revolution, for which the famous Eiffel Tower was built, opened its gates. Singers, dancers, actors and musicians from the European countries as well as from the Near and the Far East came to represent their respective peoples. At the Trocadéro hall two concerts devoted to Russian music (June 22 and 29, 1889), mostly compositions of The Mighty Five conducted by Rimsky-Korsakoff, created a sensation with the French, who were not familiar with the works of the contemporary Russians except, perhaps, for Anton Rubinstein and Tchaikovsky.

That Debussy was not among the enthusiasts of the Oriental sumptuousness of their brilliant orchestra coloring is a further proof that these compositions were not new to him—he most probably had heard them at the Moscow Exposition when he was there in 1882 and, still better, read them at Madame von Meck's. His interest, instead, was caught by the natives from the Near and the Far East, by the Arabs, and especially the Javanese and Annamese, who, transplanted from the Indian Ocean to the Esplanade des Invalides right in the heart of Paris, bivouacked in the midst of their bazaars and palm-roofed huts as if they were at home. There for the first time in his life Debussy heard the *gamelang,* a weird orchestra made up of percussion instruments, drums, clappers and gongs which supported a lone player who improvised on the only string instrument, a kind of a two-stringed viola. This music, the performances of the Bedayas, the native dancers—either voluptuously swaying or emphasizing their stiff, hieratical gestures—and the natives' theatrical spectacles not only left an indelible impression on Debussy, but were a major factor in his development as a composer.

Many years later, when speaking of the evolution of modern music, Debussy referred to the magic which kindled his imagination in those days before he went for his last visit to Bayreuth:

Despite the destruction brought by civilization, there have been, and there still are even now, charming little peoples who learn music as simply as they do breathing. Their music schools are the eternal rhythm of the sea, the wind in the trees, and a thousand little noises around them. Their traditions exist only in the very old songs, mixed with dances, where each one of them, century after century, brings his respective contribution.

Javanese music, for instance, observes a counterpoint in comparison to which that of Palestrina is nothing but a childish game. And if one would listen, without European prejudice, to the charm of their 'percussion' one would have to admit that ours is nothing but the barbarous noise of an outlandish circus.

The Annamites present a sort of embryo of a lyrical drama, influenced by the Chinese, where one recognizes the forms of tetralogy; only they have more God and less decor.... A small clarinet passionately directs the emotion, a tam-tam creates a terror... and that is all! They do not need a special theater, nor the hidden orchestra [a reference to Bayreuth]. Nothing but an instinctive necessity for art, ingenious to satisfy, not a single trace of bad taste! And to say that these people never thought to look for their 'forms' at a school in Munich, now what they could be thinking of?

No wonder, then, that three months later Debussy listened to Wagner's operas (at a special theater with the hidden orchestra) with different ears and saw them with different eyes, so to speak. He returned to Paris with a philosophical censuring of his own early worship of Wagner—"You should, while very young, love beautiful things. That way you have more time to be disgusted with them later."

If the Russians had found a national basis for their music, why could not he as a Frenchman do the same? He believed that his compatriots, including the symbolists and Mallarmé, had committed a fundamental error in choosing Wagner as their idol. Wagner was a German. "The French," Debussy said, "easily forget their own qualities of clarity and elegance, to be influenced by the length and the heaviness which are the German characteristics." He did not doubt Wagner's genius, but, he said, Wagner created an art of his own and he held no brief for him as a dramatist. "Four evenings for one drama! Does this seem to you really admissible?" Debussy asked. "And mind you, during these four evenings you always hear the same things. The cast and the orchestra exchange in succession the same melodies and you arrive at the *Götterdämmerung* —once more a resumé of everything that you have just heard! Well, I repeat, all this is inadmissible for those who love clarity and conciseness."

Debussy explained that in his judgment of Wagner's theater he simply let his nature and his temperament speak for him. He was trying to become once again a Frenchman, he said. Intelligence had never been known to be a hindrance to anything. To know the good measure, to be conscious of one's own capacity as well as that of one's listener—these are the natural qualities of a Frenchman. The Frenchman is bored by lengthy arguments as he is by repetitions of statements already made. Do not insist—a Frenchman's pleasure is to guess, to read between the lines, to imagine what has only been suggested. To him music, as any other form of art, must first of all give pleasure. He expects an artist to use self-control—a saturation of emotions produced by piling up sonorities with an inevitable discharge of cymbals and percussion batteries leave him unsatisfied, for it becomes too plain, too commonplace, and does not belong to the domain of art, as he feels it. To a Frenchman finesse and nuance are the daughters of intelligence. "They don't flirt in the opera," Debussy said, "they scream the incomprehensible words and when they exchange solemn promises they do it with the approval of trombones." And Debussy could have added that the most delicate, intimate situations are performed as if in public, and that lovers make their avowals to the galleries and not to their partners.

He had long technical discussions with his former teacher Ernest Guiraud. Debussy maintained that in the realm of harmony Wagner was less of innovator than Berlioz; that although in his vocal parts Wagner tried to approach the spoken word, actually he had neither *recitative à l'italienne* nor *l'air lyrique;* that on the whole

Wagner's operas "sang too much," where one should sing only occasionally; and that Wagner leaves no place for the *sous-entendue* —the unspoken.

"You are then a sort of a liberal Wagnerian," Guiraud remarked.

"I certainly have no intentions of imitating what I admire in Wagner," Debussy replied. "I imagine an entirely different form for a dramatic composition: the music will begin where the words are impotent; music is made for this 'inexpressible.' I would like it to appear as though it came from a shadow and that from time to time it will return there. The music must always remain a *'discrète personne.'* "

And when Guiraud asked him what poet would provide him with a suitable libretto, Debussy said: "One who will only hint at things (*disant les choses è demi*) and will thus enable me to insert my dream into his; one who will not despotically impose set scenes on me, but will let me be free, here and there, to outdo him in his artistry and to perfect his work. And he need have no fear! I shall not follow the usual plan of the lyrical drama, in which the music predominates insolently and where the poetry is relegated to the background and suffocated by elaborate music trappings. There is too much singing in the music dramas. The characters should sing only when it is worth while, and the pathetic note should be held in reserve. The intensity of expression should vary in degrees. At times it is necessary to paint in monochrome and limit oneself to gray tones. . . . Nothing should retard the progress of the dramatic action; all musical development that is not essential to the text is wrong. Apart from the fact that any musical development which is at all protracted cannot possibly correspond to the mobile words . . . I am dreaming of poems which would not condemn me to contrive long and heavy acts, poems which would offer me the scenes which move in their locality and character, and where the actors do not argue but submit to life and their fate."

Fortunately this prophetic statement was taken down almost verbatim by Maurice Emmanuel, who was present during their talks. It is a valuable document dated October, 1889, not to be brushed aside by those who insist on certain influences on Debussy such as Erik Satie and Pierre Louÿs, whom Debussy did not know at that time.

And it is an even more valuable document because it contains the very kernel of Debussy's esthetics. It is a product of long, instinctive search, of enthusiasm and disappointment, of study and experiment. The year 1889 may mark the date when Debussy attained a clear vision of what he wanted to do, but years were to go by, years of further studies and experiments, before his own creative forces would give birth to a true product of this vision. Curiously enough, it was not through his association with a man whose ideas were erroneously presumed to have influenced Debussy while he was still in the process of digesting various trends, but through the practical test of these ideas that Debussy was liberated from the Wagnerian shackles, as no theoretical discussions succeeded in doing. I am speaking of Catulle Mendès and *Rodrigue et Chimène*, the first opera Debussy ever wrote.

Catulle Mendès was a writer and journalist. A native of Portugal, he became French by naturalization and was more of a French nationalist than many a Frenchman. His enthusiasm for music led him to visits with Richard Wagner at Bayreuth and Triebchen, and these to writing a libretto for Chabrier's *Gwendoline*, an opera so Wagnerian that it had to have its first success in Germany before it could be accepted in France.

In 1885, however, Mendès wrote a long article in the *Revue Wagnérienne*, "Le jeune Prix de Rome et le vieux Wagnériste." Because Debussy won the Prix de Rome in 1885 and because later on Debussy's views on Wagner seemed to have been influenced by this article, it has been attributed *post factum* by some musicians as Mendès' hint to Debussy. Calling on composers to listen to folk songs and "seek in them the characteristics of our own music, and thus achieve—aided by inspiration and individual labor—a perfect artistic expression of the unconscious musical soul of our country," Mendès wrote:

.... A new glory is in store for the first musician of genius in France who will steep himself in the musical and poetical atmosphere that fills our legends and songs while adopting all the Wagnerian theories that are compatible with the spirit of our race. Such a man will succeed—either alone or with the aid of some poet—in freeing our opera from the ridiculous, old-fashioned conventions that fetter it. Let him bring poetry and music into intimate union, not with the object of making the one heighten the effect of the other, but for the sake of the drama alone. Let the poet in him sternly repress all literary embellishments, and let the musician in him reject all such vocal and orchestral effects as would interrupt the dramatic emotion. Let him forego all recitatives, arias, *strettos*, and even ensembles, unless the dramatic action—to which everything must be sacrificed—requires the union of several voices. Let him break the framework of the old symmetrical melody. Without Germanizing his melody, let him prolong it indefinitely to suit the rhythm of the poetry. In a word, let his music become speech, but a speech that is all music. In particular, let the orchestra use all the resources of science and inspiration, so as to blend and develop the themes which represent the various emotions and personages, until it becomes like a great vat, in which all the molten elements of the drama may be heard seething together. Meanwhile, enveloped in the emanating atmosphere of tragedy, the lofty heroic action —which, in spite of its complexity, is the logical outcome of one single idea—will hasten onwards, amidst violent passions and unexpected incidents, amidst smiles and tears, toward some great final emotion. Whoever creates such a work will be a great man and he will earn our love. For, even though he borrow his forms from Germany, he will modify them and, in his inspiration, he will remain a Frenchman. Then when the Germans extol the great name of Richard Wagner, we shall proudly acclaim this name—as yet, unknown—but which we shall soon hear greeted with cries of applause and welcome.

This manifesto, a hodge-podge of ideas in part lifted directly from Cui's *La Musique en Russie* published in 1881, and here presented in true Valhallian style, plus the fate of Chabrier's *Gwendoline,* should have served Debussy as a warning rather than as an inspiration when the two men met some five years later. Mendès, then forty-nine, was a familiar figure in artistic circles and particularly at the apéritif hour or "after the theater" at one of Debussy's favorite cafés, the Brasserie Chez Pousset, famous for its Munich beer and "the best hard-boiled eggs in Paris."

Situated between the Grands Boulevards and Montmartre, the

Brasseries Chez Pousset was an ideal spot for sessions held after the day's work or before the night shift by journalists, writers or theater people, not to speak of hopeful painters accompanied by gracious models who forgave them a great deal. With half-finished reviews protruding from his green overcoat pockets, Mendès was pointed out as an influential man with good connections at these gatherings where *le monde* used to come to get the wind of this "élite's" opinion for their directions in the good life. For the élite changed according to the vogue, so that those elected in one season were dethroned during the following one and *l'homme d'aujourd-hui* succeeded the lion of yesterday. But Mendès' reputation remained intact, whether as a handsome and dapper young man he propagandized Wagner or as an aging, slovenly vagabond, "a perfect target for an accident or a suicide," as Alphonse Daudet said about him, he would buttonhole his neighbor and talk to him about God or the future of French art in a most conspiratory manner. Debussy must have met Mendès at Chez Pousset, although there is another version of their meeting, which Debussy neither denied nor confirmed.

This is set in a different café where Mendès used to come to play dominoes to the accompaniment of many rounds of apéritifs. Mendès is supposed to have asked a man at a neighboring table if he cared to play. His partner turned out to be a genius at losing every game and most generous about paying for all the drinks. He introduced himself as M. Debussy and said that he had a son, a composer who had won the Prix de Rome. Perhaps under the influence of drink, or of his new acquaintance's charming attitude toward the bill, or possibly flushed by his victory at dominoes, Mendès at once offered to write an opera libretto for his new friend's son. At any rate, however Debussy met Mendès, he accepted his proposition, no doubt because he hoped that through Mendès he would be able to publish his other works and have them performed as well. It is fair to presume that Mendès even promised him as much.

For the opera entitled *Rodrigue et Chimène* Mendès based his libretto on Guillem de Castro's [1] famous *Las Mocedades del Cid*,

---

[1] Guillem de Castro y Bellvis (1569-1631), Spanish dramatist.

to the first part of which Corneille was largely indebted for the material of his tragedy. For two years Debussy worked on the score. At times, after he had finished the first two acts, he was ready to play them for his friends and then again would complain that he was kept in a state of feverish anxiety by this opera in which everything was against him, and that he was afraid that he had perhaps been victorious over himself, meaning that it was the exact opposite of everything he would have liked to express—"The traditional nature of the subject demands a type of music that I can no longer write," he explained.

But he did plow to the end, that is to the end of the third, last act up to the final scene, before he gave up the whole project. Debussy said that when Mendès came for the score, he played and sang some part of it for him, but after screaming at the top of his voice the words of the victorious warriors *"Et la croix de Jésus luira sur les mosqué-é-é-es!"* he said *"Non, ah non! Ce n'est pas mon affaire!"*, tore up the score and threw it into the fireplace.

The dramatic gesture was a pure invention of Debussy's fantasy. Actually he did not destroy the score, unless he had two copies, which seems unlikely. The manuscript eventually turned up as a collectors' item and now belongs to Alfred Cortot, the French pianist. The few musicians who have seen the score say that in his minuscule handwriting Debussy wrote about one hundred pages, some of it on three, some on four staves, adding notes regarding the instrumentation. The work shows a predominantly Wagnerian influence, although some parts are reminiscent of Moussorgsky and of Borodin's *On the Steppes of Asia*. Cortot and Debussy's heirs have acted in accordance with the composer's wish; the work will never be made public. Thus Debussy's first opera will remain on the shelves in a collector's library or a museum, and is destined to be seen but not heard.

As alluring as Mendès' proposition was to a poor and utterly unknown musician, Debussy preferred to forego his chance for fame and money and to accept the reproaches and criticism of well-meaning friends rather than to "diminish myself to the status of a popular composer," as he said. "One may die or suffer, but one must stay pure and eurythmic," [1] he repeated one of his favorite quotations. This remark, however, was more than merely a reference to his failure with the opera. Debussy's mind was not entirely on this work. During his sporadic occupation with the score his heart was torn by a frustrated love affair. And how pure and eurythmic he had to remain can be seen from the following.

In April 1890, when he started on the opera, Debussy dedicated *Rodrigue et Chimène* to Gaby, but he was either already in the throes of a passionate love affair with another woman or met her soon afterwards. For a while he was happy and then at the close of the year came "the sadly unexpected end of the story, a banal end with silly little stories and words that should never have been spoken!" he confessed to a friend, although he never disclosed the name of his latest choice. "I realized the strange change in her tone, that at the very moment when such harsh words fell from her lips I heard within me everything that she had said before—so adorable! And these false sounds (real, alas!) came clashing against those which sang in me, tearing me to pieces so that I could hardly understand. But I had to understand; I have left a great deal of myself caught on those thorns and it will be a long time before I will be able to put myself to the personal culture of the art that heals everything. This is a beautiful irony, this art which contains all one's sufferings, and then one knows those who are healed by it. Ah! I really loved her very much and with even more sad ardor because I felt from the obvious signs that she would never take the steps that would engage her whole soul and that she would keep herself inviolable against the question of the stability of her heart. ... Now it remains to be seen if she has what I was looking for! If it was not all a *néant!* Despite everything, I am crying over the disappearance of the Dream of this dream! After all, this perhaps is the least upsetting! Ah! those days when I felt I should die and when I myself was the one who watched this death and oh! that I shall never relive them!"

Perhaps Debussy really believed that he loved as people love no

[1] Apparently Debussy's own free version of the last words of Ernest Renan addressed to his son: *"Sois bon, sois beau, mais surtout sois eurythmique."*

longer ... and that his was the love of poets, stronger than other men are doomed to feel. The mysterious woman makes no further appearance in his story.

At twenty-nine Debussy certainly was a very impressionable young man. A great deal has been said and in some cases much has been made of the fact that Debussy, never a man alone, even while very happy with his feminine companions, was always in need of men as close friends. It is true that his "women" were not his intellectual equals and that he made a better choice among men, and this was the chief reason for many devoted friendships—still one should not dismiss a rather feminine trait in him, that need of confiding his feelings. Sometimes he suffered more from not having "a sympathetic ear, while he had the thirst to tell all," than from what actually pained him. Naturally he could not speak of his latest episode to Gaby and even took good care that letters which may have had any reference to the affair should be sent in care of his parents.

Not to speak of remaining pure, he was far from eurythmic: after the unfortunate love affair, he said that some streets in Paris were like Mount Calvary to him, the pavement resounding with nothing but the sad echo of steps once so lovely. He wanted to flee from Paris and stay in London with Robert Godet, whose acquaintance he recently had made—an acquaintance which grew into a lifelong friendship.

"Do you think that by scraping together a few pennies I could join you in London? It would be pleasant to live for a while near you. I need it to cure me, to put myself back on my feet, and you are one of the rare human beings who does not look at life from the hard utilitarian point of view—I have had enough of their programs, already made."

Always in need of money, Debussy at that time sold many of his compositions (*Rêverie, Ballade slave, Tarantelle Styrienne, Valse romantique* and *Nocturne*) to various publishers, and either intentionally or absent-mindedly sold *Rêverie* to two different firms. But either his harvest was too meager or Gaby pulled in the reins—Debussy did not go to London.

Debussy seemed to be content to live with Gaby, yet he was constantly on the look-out for "the dream of his dreams," someone he would marry; meanwhile his experiments in this sphere (and there were many) disturbed his equilibrium. That in this state of mind he did so much work is more surprising than the indifferent attitude he showed to the ultimate fate of his compositions, for although the publishers bought some of them they remained on their shelves for years before they actually were printed. Yet his early works contained more than mere "promise," they had the embryo of those qualities which gave his important scores their value. If they escaped recognition it was only because the large public was still fascinated by Wagner's grandiloquent art.

Never an opportunist in his musical career, early in life Debussy developed that complete disdain for popular acclaim which justified his living in what is commonly known as an ivory tower. "I am afraid of publishers," he said, as if he were speaking of an allergy. His music he claimed had a different purpose. "Such music as mine has no other aim than to become part of things and people," he wrote Godet. "That you have accepted it is a more lovely glory than any approval from the elegant people who kow-tow to the Wagnerian Monsieur Lamoureux with his eyeglasses and hieratic forefinger...." Feeling as he did, he was perfectly content to have his *Cinq Poèmes de Baudelaire* brought out by Bailly in a limited de luxe edition of one hundred fifty-eight copies. He dedicated them to his friend Étienne Dupin, who had helped to finance the publication. The copies were sold by subscription at the rather exorbitant price of twelve francs at a time when the piano score of an opera twenty times as voluminous sold for twenty.

The publication had at least one immediate valuable effect—it caught the attention of Georges Hartmann, the music publisher, who was known for discovering such men as Saint-Saëns, Massenet, Charpentier, Franck, Lalo and Bizet, and launching them on their careers. It must have been particularly embarrassing to Debussy that *Rêverie*, which he wrote to oblige Hartmann, the man he hoped would become his patron, was among those sold to two different publishers. When, fifteen years later, Hartmann bought the piece for his firm and published it, Debussy said he thought it was a mistake to bring out a composition that was written in a hurry and therefore was bad.

Usually shrewd in his judgment of a situation, Debussy often behaved irrationally under the influence of emotional stress. I spoke earlier of how he "cut off his nose to spite his face" when he severed his connections with the Academy. About the same time his *Fantaisie* for piano and orchestra became a victim of his lack of cool judgement. It was accepted by the Société Nationale for a performance on April 20, 1890, with Vincent d'Indy conducting. But after the first rehearsal Debussy suddenly realized that this work was far from representing "his art," that in fact it was contradictory to his own theories against the use of classical forms. He was dissatisfied with the *Finale*, there were too many variations—"an easy means of getting a great deal out of very little," as he told his friends—and on the whole too reminiscent of d'Indy's *Symphonie sur un thème montagnard Français* (1886). Moreover, he was annoyed by the little time given for rehearsal of the piece because of the unusually lengthy program. Without a word to anyone, after the last rehearsal Debussy gathered the orchestral parts from the music stands and went home, leaving a note for d'Indy as his only conciliatory gesture.

And despite the fact that Choudens, the publisher, had already engraved the score and printed the proofs on a luxurious paper (which pleased Debussy, who always insisted that his work should be attractively presented), he forbade both the further printing of the score and all public performances. Only in December 1919, twenty months after his death, and against his wishes, did the work become known to the public.

His temperamental behavior most probably was another manifestation of his hurt ego and "I-don't-care" attitude.

CHAPTER IX

BOHEMIAN PERIOD—ERIK SATIE

DEBUSSY, as I have said before, preferred the company of literary men to that of musicians, yet his meeting with Erik Satie at about this time (1891) led to a lifelong friendship. Four years younger than Debussy, Erik Satie was then better known for what he said about music than for what he actually put down on paper. And there was good reason for this, for, as a close friend put it, after suddenly interrupting his studies at the Paris Conservatory at the age of nineteen, he found himself in the situation of "a man who knew only thirteen letters of the alphabet and decided to create a new literature." But his bantering spirit, his wit and practical jokes were an inexhaustible source of merriment for a small group of Bohemian comrades-in-arms and he won their acclaim as a prominent composer.

In defiance of the established rules, Satie left the Conservatory and the respectable bourgeois home of his parents—his father was a music publisher—to "live a life of his own," as young girls would say. He moved to 6 rue Cortot at the top of Montmartre to a room the size of a wall closet, but with a superb view "all the way to the Belgian border." There he "worked in peace" and, with a few manuscripts under his arm, he would majestically descend to daily rounds of publishers and nocturnal visits in cafés with his friends. He had already composed his *Sarabandes* and *Gymnopédies* on which, even his severest critics admit, rest his reputation as a pioneer in modern music.

Debussy must have heard about him from their mutual friend

Vital Hocquet, who was instrumental in getting Satie his first job as a pianist at the Chat Noir when Satie had reached the bottom of his resources. *"Erik Satie, gymnopédiste!"* Hocquet gravely announced as he presented his protégé to Rudolphe Salis, the proprietor of the night club. Bowing low, Salis acknowledged the pleasure of meeting him with *"C'est une belle profession, Monsieur,"* and from then on Satie, when not playing the piano for the guests, held court in a room filled with tobacco smoke where around the tables covered with bottles of wine and beer furious discussions of art were carried on. Everyone tried to outdo his neighbor in appearing "more advanced" and all of them declared their horror of everything banal, conventional, "already seen." The most audacious doctrines were proclaimed and there was no place for trivialities or vulgarity. The spirit of these gatherings was spontaneous and caustic, but it never exceeded certain limits: if they gave crushing blows to the pontiffs, it was done in the name of the independence of art and individuality. One might say that Satie's originality, at first contested and later accepted, had its roots in the Chat Noir.

In this sphere so different from that where he grew up, Satie, until then timid and reserved, gave vent to all the treasures of humor and irony that must have slumbered for years within him. The contrast of this independent and disorderly life with that of the bourgeois milieu of his parents showed him the absurdity of certain prejudices and hypocrisy of many conventions, and stimulated in him an utter disdain for the commonplace, for habits produced by false vanity and artificial reputation. He repudiated everything that he had loved according to tradition and became an enthusiast of the beauty of an effort—free, bold and uncontrolled—not encumbered by rules or accepted methods—recognizing no censor but himself. He admired and joined those who without worries over today or the difficulties of tomorrow, with utter contempt for the bourgeois, their souls in delirium, lived joyfully in their pursuit of an ideal.

Rudolphe Salis was one of the first to arouse this uncompromising spirit. When, after several years of perfectly harmonious association, Satie decided that Salis had abused his authority as his employer and shown a lack of respect for him as a prominent composer, Satie walked out of the Chat Noir slamming the door so hard that it was heard for years afterwards. Whereupon, he took a job as a pianist at L'Auberge du Clou on the Avenue Trudaine. There, followed by his admirers from the Chat Noir, he established his headquarters in a large room in the basement—a setting quite similar to his previous one. By that time Satie had announced that in collaboration with his old friend J. P. Contamine de Latour, he had written *Uspud*, a ballet in three acts. Latour said that actually Satie had composed half a dozen musical phrases to his libretto, but Satie declared it to be his "orchestral score." All Montmartre "intellectuals" knew about it, for Satie's "talking" stirred passionate discussions of this new work of art: some called it a masterpiece, while others labeled it abominable humbug. Finally, one evening at L'Auberge du Clou, Satie played "his orchestral score." It produced the effect he was anticipating: enthusiastic approval and violent condemnation.

To those who did not understand his masterpiece Satie "explained" that they were ignorant and "bourgeois," that he was going to force the Paris Opéra to produce it and that he alone was right even if against the opinion of the whole world. "And besides," he added seriously, "I am far superior to all of you, but my well-known modesty prevents me from telling it to you." In the midst of the tumult of noises and babel of voices this declaration provoked, one man remained impassive, his arms crossed over his chest, smiling quietly into his beard. This man was Debussy. He had grasped right from the start everything that was audacious, sensitive and even serious in Satie's humor and understood the qualities of Satie's mind, anxious like his own for the "new" and the "unheard of."

"From the moment I saw him," Satie said later, "I was drawn to him and wished always to live by his side. I had the pleasure of realizing this wish during the following thirty years."

Different versions of their first meeting and various comments on their friendship have caused a controversy over the extent of Satie's influence on Debussy. This has never been resolved—both sides remain firm in their convictions, those for Debussy respecting his originality and those for Satie insisting on his generosity in sharing his ideas with his new friend. A great many years later, at a lecture on Debussy, Satie said:

"... Debussy's esthetics are symbolist in some of his works and impressionist in most. Please forgive me—for am I not a little responsible? That's what people say. Here is the explanation. When I first met him ... he was full of Moussorgsky, and conscientiously was seeking a path which he had difficulty in finding. In that respect I was much better off than he, for my progress was not slowed down by any *Prizes*, whether from Rome or any other town—I don't carry that sort of thing on my back, because I'm a type rather like Adam, the "Paradise" Adam, who never won a prize—a lazy type, no doubt. At that time I was writing music for *Le Fils des étoiles* on a text by Joseph Péladan, and I explained to Debussy the necessity for a Frenchman to free himself from the Wagnerian adventure which in no way corresponded to our national aspirations. I told him that I was not anti-Wagner in any way, but that we ought to have our own music—if possible without *choucroute*. Why shouldn't we make use of the methods employed by Claude Monet, Cézanne, Toulouse-Lautrec, etc.....? Nothing simpler. Aren't they just expressions? That would have been the origin of a new beginning and would have led to results almost bound to be successful—and profitable too.... Who could have provided him with examples? Shown him new discoveries? Pointed out to him the ground to be explored? Given him benefit of one's experience? Who? I don't wish to answer: I am no longer interested."

Should this claim be ascribed to Satie's "well-known" modesty? Those who had the opportunity to be eyewitness to Debussy's friendship with Satie said that there often were violent outbursts of temper, yet they did not mar the relationship. They might have been two brothers placed by circumstances in different positions, the one rich and the other poor; the former gracious and open-hearted, but conscious of his superiority and always ready to make it felt, the latter hiding his humiliation and paying his share by cracking jokes for the entertainment of his host. They were always on their guard, but they could not help being fond of each other.

Satie made his audacious statement about his influence on Debussy when some thirty years later he was hailed as the head of a new esthetic movement that damned the recognized contemporary composers, including Debussy. "... And you too, Satie...." Debussy murmured, bed-ridden by a disease that took his life.

But one certainly must grant that Satie did deal the *coup de grâce* to Debussy's Wagnerism, and Debussy may have renounced Mendès' project under his influence, although he made his final decision after he became interested in *Pelléas et Mélisande*.

Jean Cocteau, the French poet and the most ardent champion of Satie, insists that Debussy's friendship with Satie had far more importance—it was "the door through which Debussy ascended to his glory." According to Cocteau, at their first meeting Satie told Debussy that he contemplated making an opera out of Maeterlinck's *La Princesse Maleine* and only wished he knew how to obtain permission from the Belgian writer. Thereupon, says Cocteau, "a few days later" Debussy received Maeterlinck's authorization, but for another play: *Pelléas et Mélisande*, and immediately started to work on it. Actually it did not happen as simply as all that. It is true that in 1891 Debussy did ask for and received the rights for *La Princesse Maleine*, but at that time there was no question of *Pelléas et Mélisande*. Therefore the "few days later, Debussy...." etc. in Cocteau's version of the tale should be granted "poetic license"— the dates and documents tell a different story.

Maeterlinck's *Pelléas et Mélisande* was published by Lacomblez in Brussels on May 4, 1892, one year after Debussy and Satie met; and its first performance by the Théâtre de l'Œuvre at the Bouffes Parisiens in Paris was not given until May 17, of the following year, 1893. It was then that Debussy wrote to M. Lugné-Poë, the director of the theater, and subscribed for a seat. In his letter Debussy said that he did not know the play. This remark, incidentally, opens to question a rather fatuous story originated by Léon Vallas and since repeated by other biographers, that Debussy purely by chance discovered the play on the bookstands as he was sauntering along the boulevards on a hot summer day in 1892.

Maeterlinck's play was more of a failure than a success, but the general criticism did not affect Debussy—he felt that at last he had found the material for the lyrical work he had been dreaming of. Two months later he asked Henri de Régnier to help him obtain Maeterlinck's consent and on August 8, 1893, Maeterlinck wrote to de Régnier that "with all his heart he grants Debussy all the necessary authorization for *Pelléas*."

Thus Debussy received the rights for the play three months before he called on Maeterlinck at Ghent in November of the same year—a courtesy call and not for the purpose of obtaining authorization, as has often been stated. To complete the clarification of the events leading to the birth of Debussy's masterpiece, I must point out an important factor: in 1893 Debussy was not the obscure musician of 1891 and de Régnier by this time had a substantial basis for his intervention with Maeterlinck on Debussy's behalf; added to which there were other important events in his life.

After five long years of hoping and waiting, Debussy's *La Damoiselle élue* was given its first performance by the Société Nationale on April 8, 1893, at the Salle Érard, with Gabriel Marie conducting. In a program of contemporary compositions (Paul Dukas' Ouverture to *Polyeucte*, Paul Fournier's *Iris*, Ernest Chausson's *Poème de l'Amour et de la Mer*, Pierre Bréville's *Medeia* and Henri Duparc's *Phidylé*), *La Damoiselle élue* received most of the comments of both the public and the critics. Far from unanimously praising the work as the most interesting, the criticisms were controversial enough to bring Debussy's name for the first time to general attention and to stir up discussions of his merits as a composer among the wider circle of musicians.

Julien Tiersot in his article in the *Ménestrel* described the piece as "artistically wrought in concise and delicate forms with a rare and subtle skill." He thought that the whole first part was exquisite, with its alternating verses of dialogue between the female chorus and the solo recitative and that, although toward the end the length of the solo part rather dampened the ardor of the general public, the work was nevertheless received with rapturous applause by the more enthusiastic of the audience.

Another critic, Charles Darcours, who five years earlier, speaking of Debussy's *L'Enfant prodigue*, had predicted that the young composer "was destined to meet with a great deal of praise ... and plenty of abuse," wrote in *Le Figaro*: "*La Damoiselle élue* is an original work. It is very insinuating and extremely modern. After listening only a few days ago, with such heartfelt admiration, to the lofty beauty of Palestrina's music, we experienced an almost guilty delight on hearing this composition. For it is very sensual and decadent, rather corrupt in fact, but it has pages of exquisite beauty. How refreshing is a touch of youth!" And as if to justify Darcours' former prediction, Colette's husband, Gautier-Villard, known as Willy, said in his usually ironical and provocative column in *L'Écho de Paris* that *La Damoiselle élue* is "a symphonic painting on a stained glass window by Fra Angelico Debussy, contrived not without a certain amount of perversity."

This sudden interest in Debussy the composer was further spurred by the Librairie de l'Art Indépendant's limited de luxe publication of one hundred and sixty copies of his score. "He is the greatest, the most noble, and is going to be the most illustrious of all," the publisher Édmond Bailly declared in his store on the rue de la Chaussée d'Antin, the seat of the symbolists. "You will see, you who have plenty of time to live: as we have been speaking of the Piccinists and the Gluckists of the past century, one day they will speak of the d'Indysts and the Debussysts!"

This prophetic linking of Debussy's and d'Indy's names was not accidental, for d'Indy—indeed, more than any other musician at that time—was championing Debussy's music. It was due to d'Indy that the Société Nationale had accepted his *Fantaisie* for piano and orchestra. It was also due to d'Indy's insistence that *La Damoiselle élue* was presented by the same organization, despite its coolness toward Debussy after his high-handed behavior in connection with the performance of his *Fantaisie*. When, after the performance of *La Damoiselle élue*, La Libre Esthétique, an "advanced" artistic society at Brussels, decided to give a whole concert devoted to Debussy's works, it was, once again, d'Indy who urged Octave Maus, the director of the society, to include *La Damoiselle élue* in the program. Maus wrote Debussy in such ecstatic terms that, as Debussy said, it would make the lilies which lie asleep between the fingers of *La Damoiselle élue* blush—the date was set for March 1st of the following year.

There was still one more significant announcement in the program of the planned concert: it was going to have the first performance of a still unpublished work, *Prélude, Interlude et Paraphrase Finale pour l'Après-midi d'un Faune.* This was a surprise even to Debussy's closest friends, for until the announcement of the forthcoming publication of this work appeared on the cover of the select edition of *La Damoiselle élue,* Debussy never mentioned the composition. The score carries the dates 1892-1894, yet it has never been established when Debussy actually began to work on it. A copy of Mallarmé's eclogue given by Debussy to one of his friends with the following dedication: *"Amitiés, Esthétique.... Toute la lyre*—A. Debussy—25.5.87." shows that he had been acquainted with it as early as 1887, if not earlier, and it would be fair to assume that if he did not start on the composition at that date, at least he had been thinking about it much earlier than the date marked on the score. His first impression may also have stemmed from the Boucher picture, the original source of Mallarmé's inspiration, which Debussy could have seen at the National Gallery in London during his short visit there in 1887.

Debussy must have written more than one version of this symphonic poem—one of them completed some time during the year 1893—for according to Debussy's own recollections [1] Mallarmé had come to see him at what Debussy called " a little furnished flat on the rue de Londres" where he was living with Gaby. "Mallarmé came in with his prophetic air, wrapped up in a Scottish plaid. After listening to it, he remained silent for a long time; then he said to me: 'I didn't expect anything like that. This music evokes the emotion of my poem and fixes the background much more vividly than color could have done.' "

Mallarmé's reference to the background points up the nature of Debussy's composition. When in 1876 Mallarmé "composed" his

---

[1] A letter to G. Jean Aubry, March 25, 1910.

poem, he wrote it for Coquelin *aîné*, the actor, to be recited as a monologue on the stage. It is probable that Debussy's first version was conceived as incidental music to accompany such a performance. And when Debussy asked Henri de Régnier for his help in obtaining Maeterlinck's authorization for *Pelléas et Mélisande*, he must have played for him the original version. "It has the heat of an oven and sends chills up the spine" was de Régnier's way of expressing his approval. But Debussy himself was not satisfied with the piece. "Here I am, just turned thirty-one and not quite sure of my esthetics," he wrote Ernest Chausson shortly after de Régnier's visit. "There are still things that I am not able to do—create masterpieces, for instance. . . ."

When the time came for the announced performance at Brussels, Debussy said it was not ready. He worked on it, cut and revised it for another sixteen months. Instead he offered his latest work, *Proses lyriques: De Rêve, De Grève, De Fleurs* and *De Soir*, the last dated August, 1893. The lyrics to these four songs Debussy wrote himself and he planned to write five others in the same vein and unite them all under the title of *Nuits Blanches*. And finally Debussy disclosed that he had written a string quartet. "I cannot succeed in making it what I want it to be," he wrote in 1893 to Chausson, "and here I am starting it all over again for the third time. . . ." These revelations in regard to his work spoke of an extraordinary productive capacity on a scale of energy that had never come to him before. Furthermore, whether he felt he had written masterpieces or not, at last he was ready to put his "own art" to the test of public performance, and his one concern was to have it presented in the best possible way. This was why he was so anxious to go to Belgium.

When in November, 1893 he went there to call on Maeterlinck, he stopped at Brussels for a visit with Eugène Ysaÿe, for the famous violinist was going to conduct a "Debussy Festival" during the following spring. Their friendship dated back to Debussy's Prix de Rome days when the two musicians used to meet at Émile Baron's bookstore on rue de Rome. Only four years older than Debussy, Ysaÿe treated his friend as if he were his younger brother, and both his faith in him and the prestige Ysaÿe already enjoyed were great assets to Debussy's first steps in his public career. Debussy dedicated the quartet to him and Ysaÿe patiently studied the score and just as patiently worked on it with his partners (Crickboom, Van Hout, and J. Jacob), who time and again refused to play it because they failed to understand it.

If such was the attitude of the musicians who performed the work in Paris at the Société Nationale on December 29, 1893, it is easy to imagine the complete bewilderment of the public who heard the piece for the first time. "The mandarins of our class," as Debussy nicknamed the musical élite of the audience, were used to classical quartets—Haydn, Mozart, Beethoven—some of them were emancipated enough to accept Wagner and Franck, and, as Chausson said, "to win their approval was equal to passing an examination for the Doctor's degree." And Debussy's thesis, though written in the traditional form, i.e. divided into four parts, was just another *"Non hic piscis omnium."*

The critics were just as disconcerted by the quartet as were the "mandarins." Almost a decade later they were still saying "it would be difficult to be more vague without being incoherent." [1] It is not surprising, then, that after the first hearing of the piece they either said nothing at all, or extricated themselves from an embarrassing situation by using the generalities and stock-in-trade phrases every critic has in reserve for just such occasions. They—J. Guy Ropartz, a young composer of the Franck school, in the *Guide Musical*, January 7, 1894 and Willy in *L'Écho de Paris*—spoke of "a very interesting work," of "poetical themes and rare tone-coloring," of "the diabolical difficulty of the piece which was bewildering, full of originality and charm . . . with two first movements particularly noteworthy and a finale rather abrupt. . . ." In short it would have been difficult for these critics to be more vague without being incoherent.

This reaction did not seem particularly to trouble Debussy, but

[1] *La Revue Bleue*, April 26, 1902.

Ernest Chausson's disappointment was a different matter, for both Chausson and his wealthy brother-in-law Henri Lerolle, the painter, were more than mere acquaintances. During the previous year they had taken an unusual interest in Debussy's work and often came to him with financial assistance.

"Should I tell you that I have really been hurt by what you have told me about my quartet?" Debussy wrote Chausson. "For I have felt that, after all, it made you love certain things, while I hoped it would make you forget them. Well, I am going to write another one for you, and I mean seriously, for you, and I will try to put it in a more noble form."

Debussy hoped that Chausson would come to Brussels for his concert—he had a peculiar belief that his music would have more success abroad than in France. He spoke of Paris as a city of exile where he was condemned to live, where there was nothing for him to hope for and where he was destined to lead a petty, melancholy existence.

But, despite Ysaÿe's efforts to make it a success, the concert at Brussels turned out to be another setback for Debussy. The public reaction was similar to that of the Parisian audience. The guest of honor, F. A. Gevaert, director of the Brussels Conservatory and the author of a widely known treatise on instrumentation, whose favorable opinion Ysaÿe was particularly anxious to gain, said that he "understood nothing at all." Only Octave Maus, the organizer of the concert, was ecstatic in L'Art Moderne and praised Debussy's "torrent of youthfulness and harmonic audacity." Lucien Solvay, the Brussels correspondent of the Paris Ménestrel and L'Indépendance Belge, singled out Debussy's quartet and spoke of it as "reminiscent of Borodin, Grieg and Wagner." But the final word came from Maurice Kufferath, the well-known Wagnerian musicologist (later the director of the Théâtre de la Monnaie in Brussels) in a long article in Guide Musical on March 4, 1894.

Kufferath confessed that he had been listening to the new work with feelings of surprise and alarm. The quartet struck him as bizarre. Its Oriental quality reminded him of the *gamelang* at the Paris Exhibition of 1889 with "bounding rhythms, violent harmonic jerks, alternating with languid melodies and pizzicato effects suggestive of guitars and mandolins."

Still, he thought that Debussy's music had unusual qualities, wonderful refinement, great richness, and here and there a very effective pathetic note, and concluded his verdict by saying that "our grandchildren will perhaps call us old fogies for not understanding Debussy, just as we did our predecessors because they did not appreciate Wagner."

Kufferath took the words out of Debussy's mouth, but this was hardly a consolation. The concert at Brussels was more than an artistic fiasco, for there was another shock in store for Debussy's susceptibilities—in a different realm, I admit, but a far more important one to him than the criticisms of his art.

The years of Bohemian life, not of his own choice but forced on him by lack of money, had a wearing effect on him. Debussy may have brushed aside the fate of his compositions with his "I-don't-care" attitude, but as the years went by he became more and more impatient with his hand-to-mouth existence until his determination to put an end to it reached a point similar to that when he decided to escape from the Villa Medici. After his return from Rome he had earned a miserable living by occasionally giving piano lessons, occasionally coaching or accompanying, occasionally doing arrangements of scores for publishers or composing a few pieces, among which only the *Marche Écossaise* made a substantial contribution to Debussy's purse and the catalogue of his works.

From the flowery dedication of the piece one gathers that Debussy was commissioned to write this *"Marche des Anciens Comtes de Ross"* by their descendant, a certain General Meredith Read. To give the piece a glamorous send-off, an explanatory note was attached to the score: "The origin of the Earls of Ross, Chieftains of Clan Ross of Rosshire, Scotland, dates back to the remotest times. The Chieftain's Band of Pipers used to play this March for their Laird before and during battle, as well as on festival days."

Apparently Debussy had been given the primitive march air, which he skillfully used as a sort of *thème populaire* for his composition, originally a piano duet. Years later, in 1908, he orchestrated this version and it has been reported that when in 1913 he heard it for the first time, conducted by D. E. Inghelbrecht at the Théâtre des Champs-Élysées, Debussy said, *"Mais c'est joli."* But whatever he received for the March at the time did not change his situation.

Men around Debussy with less intelligence and talent had their families, children, were independent, but Debussy had passed his thirty-first birthday and still did not succeed in "being responsible," as he put it. "I see reality only when it is forced upon me, and then unsurmountable." He admitted that it may have been because he had been too preoccupied with himself, with "making himself into a somebody," as he said, hoping, apparently that this accomplishment would solve all his problems. During this process he gradually dropped his mythological name, first reversing the order of his two Christian names to Claude Achille and eventually, from the beginning of 1893, omitting Achille altogether. But these were the external signs of making his name as a composer.

Far more serious was his desire to have a "settled" life that befitted a successful artist. Debussy longed to have his own home, he wanted to marry. In his quest for material security and his planned matrimonial life he even considered taking a permanent job at Royan. But after discussing it with Léon Jehin, the conductor who offered him this position, he realized that instead of "playing about with an orchestra," as he first understood the appointment, his job would have been the work of an accompanist, taking up most of the time during the day and evenings in return for a meager salary of three hundred and fifty francs a month. With "thoughts very gray, and melancholy bats flying around the belfry" of his dreams, Debussy resigned himself to carrying on his drab existence and improving his finances by occasionally conducting amateur choruses.

"I hardly recognize myself," he wrote Chausson, in February, 1894. "I am to be seen in drawing rooms, bowing and smiling, or conducting choruses at Countess X's. . . . Yes, sir! and I am so impressed by the beauty of the choir that I tell myself it is a fitting punishment for such wretched music to be murdered by intrepid society ladies. . . ."

Debussy was brooding over his fate while the years were passing with little change in his life. The wallpaper, or what there was of it, in his furnished apartment on rue de Londres was still the same, "representing, by the singular imagination of its creator, President Carnot surrounded by little birds. Can one imagine where contemplation of such a sight may lead? . . . the necessity never to stay at home, among other things," Debussy said. The atmosphere of squalor and poverty depressed him, and while he dedicated the first sketch of *L'Après-midi d'un Faune* to Gaby, he was far from dedicating many more years of his life to her.

Then came the first performance of *La Damoiselle élue* and its relative success. Georges Hartmann, the music publisher, granted him an income of five hundred francs a month as an advance for his future compositions, and Chausson's and Lerolle's financial help set in motion a high fermentation of his scheming. He began to look for new living quarters and lost no time in becoming officially engaged to a young singer, Thérèse Roger, the daughter of a well-known pianist. It is hard to imagine that Gaby, if not consulted, was ignorant of the procedure, since Thérèse Roger suddenly was the chosen performer of Debussy's songs, and in the main role of *La Damoiselle élue* had appeared with Debussy as her accompanist at both performances in Paris and in Brussels—thus giving Debussy a legitimate excuse for spending a great deal of time in her company. It is much more probable that Gaby knew her lover too well to be prematurely worried.

At the Brussels concert Debussy made his last appearance as Thérèse Roger's partner either on stage or in plans for their future lives. To what seemed to have been an harmonious chord in their relationship Debussy carelessly introduced a dissonant note—*volage* in a lighter vein, a bit out of time and convention, which Mlle. Roger failed to appreciate. Their engagement was broken, and Debussy, not exactly what one would call a happy bridegroom, returned to Paris, to Gaby, who was used to the affectionate but faithful infidelity of his nature, and to his work on *Pelléas*—"my only hope," as he said, thus concluding a chapter in his life of which, as yet, I have told but one part.

CHAPTER X

BOHEMIAN PERIOD—PIERRE LOUŸS

"WHEN WILL THEY sing poems that are real poems, when will they write real cavatinas and duets worthy to be included in the anthologies among the sonnets and who will be our Quinaults,[1] who will be our Hérédias [2] and our new Mallarmés? And who, above all, will be the first to know how to rhyme a song in such a way that a composer would need to do nothing else than to transcribe and orchestrate it, as if it were made to order; who will write poems so perfect that music written for them will have the appearance of a discreet and servile partner and the work could, with pride, be called a lyric drama?"

This was written in a diary on October 17, 1890 "after an evening at the Opéra," but not by Debussy, as might be assumed. Three years earlier, at the age of seventeen, the same young man had written in his journal that he aspired to become "a somebody": either a man of letters, a musician, or an artist. And indeed, he was talented enough to choose any one of the three professions, or all three, if he so desired. Less than a decade later Pierre Louÿs became the well-known French man of letters, the author of the widely read and acclaimed *Aphrodite*, who exerted one of the most significant influences on Debussy, but who did not meet him until 1893.

Pierre-Félix Louÿs lost his mother at the age of nine and was

[1] Philippe Quinault (1635-1686), French dramatist and librettist.
[2] José Maria de Hérédia (1842-1905), poet, was born in New Orleans. With Coppée, Sully-Prudhomme and Verlaine, he belonged to a group called *les Parnassiens*.

brought up by his half-brother, Georges, Baron de Louis, twenty years his senior, a man of considerable wealth in the French diplomatic service. When their father died Pierre, then eighteen, inherited a small fortune of three hundred thousand francs. By that time Louÿs's way of spending his youth had wrecked his health—he had tuberculosis—and his doctor, Professor Potin, warned him that he had only three more years to live unless he would change his curriculum. Taking into serious consideration this verdict, Louÿs divided his fortune into three parts, one for each year, and rich and independent, carried on with even more abandon.

"In those days," said Paul Valéry, the poet, "Pierre Louÿs was the most timid, the most haughty, the most fastidious, delicate and most stubborn of young men, with a captivating charm I have seen only in him. . . . his talents, his interests, his vast culture, astonishing and well founded, his enthusiasm sometimes bursting into violence, his irresistible and overwhelming caprices, the charming surprises that he alone knew how to make—all the traits of a man unique in friendship. . . ."

In this one sentence Valéry summarized the recollections of a whole Pleiad of poets, artists, journalists, musicians and writers (Francis Viélé-Griffin, Henri de Régnier, Ferdinand Hérold, André de Tinan, Pierre Quillard, André Fontaine and others) who used to congregate at Pierre Louÿs's. In his apartment in an old house at 1 rue Grétry at the back of L'Opéra Comique, he had a most remarkable collection of books, some of them so rare as those at the Bibliothèque Nationale in Paris or the British Museum in London; paintings, drawings, sketches and Oriental tapestries which, magnifying glass in hand, he showed to his friends, describing in minute detail their origin and history. There were also many coded manuscripts on paleography to which he claimed to have discovered the keys. And sometimes, sitting on the floor with legs crossed in Turkish fashion, he would entertain them with a children's toy that was in vogue, while a barman passed exotic concoctions. He had already published his *Astarté*, written his first poems, translated (during 1891) *Les Poésies de Méléagre* and started on *Chrysis* (later to become *Aphrodite*), but he also busied himself with compiling recipes for drinks, exotic dishes, and martingales (systems of betting for gamblers), not to speak of his heavy social schedule. He was generous in helping many less fortunate comrades, and was particularly remembered, as Valéry said, for the way he liked to give his friends pleasure—by leaving anonymous presents at their homes: gloves, handkerchiefs, ties, flowers, perfume, or rare bibelots and books.

As if predestined, Debussy found in this young man, eight years younger than himself, the taste for the rare and the precious that he, Debussy, with the careless air of an English lord, had always possessed. In Louÿs Debussy saw the personification of his ideal—freedom from material worries, independence of any ties, freedom to devote his life to the service of beauty and art—the only *raison d'être*, in Debussy's estimation, worthy of a true artist. And with him, at last, he discovered the height of intellectual pleasure in the fruitful exchange of esthetic opinions that were no longer mere endless arguments, useless except as fuel for their own fire.

In contrast to Debussy, who "lived," so to speak, in the world of dreams, of the unreal and symbolic, Louÿs saw true beauty in sensuality. He admired the antiquities, the expressions of erotic mysteries, but not the cold classics; he was against Christianity, as he was against anemic puritanism with its vague ecstasies over chaste pleasures. Louÿs shared his vast knowledge of ancient literature and art with his new friend and evoked in Debussy an interest in a source that has served French art from Ronsard to Giraudoux, from Rameau to Ravel. Louÿs was a brilliant talker and he liked to spend long nights in discussion, since he slept till midday—one more reason for the empathy that Debussy so strongly felt.

When the two men met, Louÿs had started on his "third and last year," according to his doctor's diagnosis, with a considerable portion of his fortune still left to be spent methodically and royally, while Debussy was in a singularly cheerful frame of mind, stimulated by a whole sequence of recent events: the relative success of *La Damoiselle élue's* first performance, followed by a monthly income from Hartmann; he had at last not only discovered a play (*Pelléas et Mélisande*) to suit his purpose, but had already sketched two scenes and, what was not least important, at that time his courtship of Mlle. Thérèse Roger was progressing successfully— there was every reason for Debussy to plan ahead.

Louÿs's and Debussy's mutual spontaneous sympathy soon called for closer intimacy, and Debussy contrived an "ideal solution" for the problem. He suggested that the two should rent a house together. They were shown several establishments and their choice fell on one at 62 Boulevard Bourdon in Neuilly, a select residential suburb of Paris. It was beautifully situated at the end of a long allée of trees "Lemartine-like," as Louÿs observed, with a large lawn at the back of the house. The mansion had eight bedrooms and could easily have been divided into two parts, but while they were waiting for the legal arrangements to be completed they changed their minds. "Since best friendships can rarely withstand the test of an obligation to live together," as Louÿs said and Debussy agreed, they eventually renounced the whole idea. Instead, Debussy moved to 10 rue Gustave Doré, to a modest little apartment with Gaby *dans nos murs* and a few pieces of their own furniture, and Louÿs stayed on in his apartment on rue Grétry. But the two friends remained inseparable.

Pierre Louÿs followed every step in Debussy's creation of *Pelléas*, although at first he showed little enthusiasm for Debussy's choice. He was the first one to hear the early sketches for the "fountain in the park scene" (Act IV, Scene IV) with which Debussy began working on his score, and it was Louÿs's interest that prompted Henri de Régnier to write to Maeterlinck. And when Debussy said that perhaps he should see the author, Louÿs took him to Belgium.

They spent a whole day with Maeterlinck at Ghent. "At first he assumed the air of a young girl being introduced to her future husband," Debussy later reported to Chausson, "but after some time he thawed out and was charming." Debussy thought that when Maeterlinck spoke of the theater he seemed a very remarkable man—he spoke of extraordinary things with delightful simplicity; but when the conversation turned to music, Maeterlinck betrayed a complete ignorance—"when he speaks of a Beethoven symphony he is like a blind man in a museum."

Debussy found the visit well worth while, for Maeterlinck not only agreed to the cuts he suggested, but himself offered a few important and useful ones, and the whole interview passed in an atmosphere of extreme cordiality, each thanking the other for the great honor and infinite pleasure.

Upon his return from Belgium Debussy decided he had been too hasty in announcing that the "fountain scene" was completed. After spending a sleepless night—"one that brings wise counsel"—he had to admit, he said, that it was not at all what he wanted. What he had there was "a duet written by Mr. Anybody-you-please with an obvious appearance of Wagner." He tore the whole thing up and started over again, this time with "a little compound of phrases" he thought more characteristic, trying to be both Pelléas and Mélisande. "I have been searching for Music behind all these veils by which she hides herself from even her most ardent worshipers," he said.

It was then that Debussy discovered that silence might be used as a means of expression. "Don't laugh," he warned. "It is perhaps the only way of bringing the emotional value of a phrase into relief. If Wagner used silence," he argued, "it seems to me it was only in an extremely dramatic way, imitating a little certain other dubious dramas in the style of Bouchardy, d'Ennery and others." [1]

These were but the first steps in a work which would take Debussy ten years to complete and many more years to perfect. No other composer—with the possible exception of Meyerbeer, who was content to have his operas produced at intervals of ten years, and Borodin, who worked on *Prince Igor* for seventeen years—has ever worked harder and revised his score as much as Debussy did with *Pelléas et Mélisande*. The chief reason for his slow progress on the score, after the initial upsurge of enthusiasm, was his lack of assurance in the technique which he wished to employ—"Previous research in pure music has led me to hate classical development, whose beauty is merely technical and of interest only to

[1] Joseph Bouchardy (1810-1870) and Adolphe Philippe d'Ennery (1811-1899), popular dramatists known for the facile effectiveness of their technique.

the highbrows of our class." Besides, Debussy, craving friends to help him shake off the Wagnerian influence, found himself again in the company of a Wagner enthusiast—Louÿs placed him on the list of his favorite composers above Bach and Beethoven.

"After several years of passionate pilgrimage to Bayreuth I began to entertain doubts as to the Wagnerian formula, or rather it seemed to me that it could serve only the particular case of Wagner's genius," Debussy said. "He was a great collector of formulas. He assembled them all into one which appears original to those who are ill-acquainted with music. And without denying his genius, one may say that he placed a period to the music of his time in much the same way as Victor Hugo did for poetry. The thing, then, is to find what comes after *Wagner's time* but not after *Wagner's manner*."

Such a declaration was an insult to Louÿs, for his admiration for Hugo bordered on violence. And as for Wagner, Louÿs said that if he was not the greatest man that ever lived, he certainly was the man who since the origin of art understood better than anyone that an action has different gradations. "He even wrote a theater-piece *Lohengrin* which has no other subject," Louÿs explained. "Lohengrin," Louÿs quoted Mallarmé, "is a gentleman who arrives and departs—there is nothing else dramatic in the piece."

But their discussions of Wagner did not always end on a humorous note. Sometimes they became so violent that Debussy, after returning home, would write and beg Louÿs to forgive his outburst of temper. He hoped, he said, it would not affect their friendship: "If you wish, I will learn by heart one of Victor Hugo's longest pieces and recite it barefoot on my knees in the Place de la Concorde."

This Debussy did not do, but pecuniary circumstances forced on him almost as humiliating an ordeal for his views on Wagner. While trying desperately to escape from the Wagnerian sounds in his head, he could not reject an opportunity to earn some extra money by performing Wagnerian operas at society musicales.

Unwittingly Debussy had made a reputation for himself as a

"Wagnerian pianist" when on May 3, 1895, at a public lecture given by Catulle Mendès, he played the scores of *Des Rheingold* and *Die Walküre* on two pianos with Raoul Pugno, one of the most outstanding French pianists. Debussy, however, derived little joy from being connected with this event because he felt that his participation endorsed Mendès' pro-Wagnerian bias. "This work [*Die Walküre*]," Mendès said in the course of his lecture, "announces the spring of a new music and the death of the old worn-out formulas." "That's not what I think, but that doesn't seem to matter," Debussy said with resignation. But both Lerolle and Chausson were concerned with Debussy's constant material difficulties and they saw a good opportunity in his unusual ability for playing Wagner scores—they arranged a series of musicales at the homes of Paris society, where Debussy was to perform everything from *Tannhäuser* to *Parsifal*.

"Our good Debussy does this for the same reason that a man carries a trunk—to earn a few coppers," Lerolle remarked to Chausson, "I believe he is happy to think we were able to get about a thousand francs for him." Whether for "a few coppers," or a thousand francs, it was in Debussy's nature to do his work to the best of his ability, and although some listeners complained that they could not hear the words, Lerolle thought they should have considered themselves fortunate that in some parts of the score Debussy did not sing anything but *tra, ta-ra, ta-ta*, since he played and sang with such energy that at the end of the first act of *Parsifal* he was near collapse. Lerolle had to take him out and give him something warm to drink, and Debussy swore that had it not been for Lerolle, who was there to turn the pages, he would have, at one point, closed the score and gone home.

The thousand francs was one consolation, the other that, fortunately, after his Wagnerian ordeal he did not have to go to see Louÿs but could visit Chausson, who was more sympathetic on the subject. Debussy would go to Chausson's country place where he could rest, perhaps forget Wagner, and talk over the problems of his own work in the happy atmosphere of a home that was open to him as his own. "Bring with you something to do," Chausson would suggest. "I rejoice in advance about the wonderful day we are going to have. Bring with you something to work on; Lerolle will paint in the garden, and I would like to finish my own battles. We will work, each one in his corner, which will not stop us from getting together later on."

Chausson was in the midst of his *Roi Arthus*. He had already twice rewritten the first two acts and often found himself in a common predicament with Debussy. Speaking of Wagner's powerful influence, Debussy advised Chausson to give up worrying over what he called "the frame."

We both have been taken in by the same German, Richard Wagner. We too often decide upon the frame before we have acquired the picture, and sometimes the richness of the former causes us to overlook the poverty of ideas—and I am not speaking of the cases where magnificent trappings are used to decorate ideas that are not worth a twenty-cent doll. One would profit, it seems to me, by taking the opposite course—that is, to find the perfect design for an idea, and then to add what is absolutely necessary in the way of ornament; for, indeed, certain composers are like those priests who clothe wooden idols with peerless gems. Look at the poverty of the symbols that are hidden in Mallarmé's last sonnets and then take a look at the works of Bach, where everything prodigiously concords with presenting an idea in its full value, where the light frame never overpowers the principal theme....

It was at this junction in their discussions that they turned for support to the school of thought opposite to Wagner's—that of the Russians, and particularly of Moussorgsky. Just when Debussy made his first acquaintance with Moussorgsky's *Boris Godunov* has often been disputed, some musicologists even implying that he knew the score while he was in Russia. If he did, he certainly kept his secret well, but the following has been firmly established:

In 1874 Camille Saint-Saëns brought the score of *Boris Godunov* in its first edition from Russia—that is, before the opera was heavily retouched by Rimsky-Korsakoff. Discarding it as the work of a maniac, an obscure and grotesque orator, Saint-Saëns turned this single copy in France (at that time) over to Jules de Brayer, a professor of music and an organist at Chartres who was interested in contemporary work. Six years later, when, through Robert Godet, Debussy met de Brayer, he borrowed the score from him. According to Godet, Debussy did not read the whole composition through because there was no French translation of the text. Thus not till his visit at Chausson's in 1893 did Debussy have the opportunity of understanding the opera, which for the rest of his life he admired as a masterpiece in modern music literature. (A familiar photograph of Debussy in shirt-sleeves at the upright piano, playing for his hosts, was supposed to have been taken on this memorable occasion.)

Boris was not the only Moussorgsky composition that was thoroughly analyzed at Chausson's. ".... and the new Moussorgsky perhaps will arrive!" Chausson wrote Debussy, meaning the *Pictures at an Exhibition* and the two song cycles *Without the Sun* and *The Nursery*. "Borrow everything you can of Russian music," Chausson said in the same letter, no doubt suggesting that Debussy bring other scores with him. Debussy did "borrow" many scores for the studies at Chausson's, and later on in his "borrowing" went even further than might have been expected—those who know the Pimen scene in *Boris Godunov* can plainly hear the echoes of it in the first act of *Pelléas*.

Like most French musicians, Debussy did not like Tchaikovsky and preferred the Mighty Five. But even among the Five, he spoke only of Moussorgsky as "this god of music." When Moussorgsky was hardly heard of in France, Debussy knew at least this much about him: that he was born in 1859 and died in 1881—"and thus," Debussy said, "it is apparent from these dates that to become a genius he had little time to lose. He lost none, and he will leave an indelible impression on the minds of those who love him or will come to love him. No one has ever appealed to the best that is in us in deeper or more tender expression. He is unique and will remain so, for his art is free from artifice or arid formulas. Never was refined sensitivity interpreted by such simple means. It is like the art of an inquisitive savage who discovers music at every step made by his emotions. Neither is there ever a question of any definite form; or rather, this form is so manifold that it cannot possibly be likened to the recognized or orthodox forms. It is achieved by little consecutive touches linked by a mysterious bond and by his gift of luminous intuition. Sometimes, too, Moussorgsky produced the effect of shuddering, restless shadows which close around us and fill the heart with anguish."

These were Debussy's general impressions of Moussorgsky's works. (Unfortunately he did not leave any criticisms of *Boris Godunov* as he had hoped to do.) But while in complete accord with Moussorgsky's esthetic principles Debussy differed in his choice of operatic subjects. In *Boris Godunov* Moussorgsky dealt with "the people" as his hero (Rimsky-Korsakoff's version changed it to Boris' personal drama), while Debussy's *Pelléas et Mélisande* was to portray the fate of two individuals. Moussorgsky's music was realistic and hard, as his subject was historical. "But the drama of *Pelléas et Mélisande*," Debussy maintained, "in spite its fantastic atmosphere, contains the human element much more than do the so-called 'documents on life.'" On one point, however, their conception of modern opera met: the characters in their drama were to sing like real people and not in the arbitrary language of antiquated opera traditions.

Often Debussy found difficulty in realizing his theories and he felt like abandoning the whole project. "I have spent days in pursuit of this 'nothing' from which Mélisande is made and sometimes I did not have the courage to tell you about it," Debussy confessed to Chausson. "Besides, this sort of struggle is known to you, but I don't know if you have gone to bed (as I have done) with a vague desire to cry because during the day you have failed to see someone you love very much."

Every scene, every character in his slowly progressing score caused him anguish. "Now it's Arkel who worries me, the old Arkel who is disinterested and has a far-seeing affection for those who are about to pass away.... And one has to express all this with *do, re*, *mi, fa, sol, la, si, do!* Oh, what a profession!!" Debussy exclaimed in desperation.

He fretted and fussed and by the end of May (1894) he had at last finished the first act, and Louÿs invited a few friends to hear this first audition of *Pelléas*. "Bring the third scene, if it is ready, the one with the hair, even if it is not completed," Louÿs urged him.

Debussy was one of those composers who was not only able, but found it stimulating, to work on several compositions at the same time. While *Pelléas* seemed to absorb his whole being, he was working on *L'Après-midi d'un Faune* and was planning still another work, this time in collaboration with Louÿs. But the project died in embryo because Louÿs had discovered that Georges Rodenbach had already used the same subject in his one-act play *Le Voile*, presented at the Comédie Française in May 1894. "Never mind," Louÿs said, "I have something else." This "something else" did not materialize for over a year, for meanwhile Louÿs had suddenly changed his plans and Debussy had to be patient with him.

A month later, in July (1894) Louÿs started on his annual journey to Bayreuth. He had been there in 1891 and 1892. In 1895 there was no Festival, thus there was one more reason for the pleasure with which he anticipated the forthcoming performances of his favorite composer. He left Paris way ahead of the Festival's opening, to visit André Gide, who was taking a hydrotherapeutic cure at Champel near Geneva. Gide had just returned from Biskra, where he had spent the winter, and the stories about his adventure there, and one in particular, about Ouled Naïl Meriem, so excited Louÿs that he immediately contrived a plan to go there to find her. He wrote Debussy and invited him to join him in coupling with little Arab girls "strictly Sahara-like!"—"If, thanks to Hartmann, you'll pay for your ticket," Louÿs wrote, as he quoted the prices, "(430 francs *aller et retour*, first class; 218 francs, second; and 170 francs, third class), I will blow you to your expenses for two months."

But Debussy was not the type of a man who on a minute's notice would embark on an expedition to the Near East in search of the erotic, nor did Louÿs's invitation come at an appropriate time. "This

way of killing time *à la Mitylène* [1] is very charming in books,"
Debussy said later to René Peter, "but not for me. I am, you know,
for things positive and regular.... This little genre of amusement
without any result doesn't mean anything to me. I find it silly...
empty and unbecoming. I make love, beautiful love, bare and simple. It is much too noble a thing to let all the unnecessary monkey
business make it revolting and get under one's skin."

The record of Debussy's life shows that he was far from a fanatic
believer in what he said—he had too many "occasional" exceptions
to his rules to have a good argument—but Louÿs's proposal definitely came at the wrong moment. Debussy was in the midst of
a courtship of Catherine Stevens, which he took very seriously.
Beautiful, tall and proud, Catherine had a lovely singing voice, but
she was also a daughter of the well-known Belgian painter Afred
Stevens, and Debussy soon had to abandon his original strategy for
bringing "their mutual attraction to more immediate and less idylic
results." Instead, because of his "reputation"—Debussy realized
that it had reached Catherine's ears—he had to proceed cautiously.
To join Louÿs in his amorous escapades would be to repeat the
disastrous *volage* he made in Brussels at the time of his engagement to Mlle. Roger, with the same consequences in prospect.

Besides, there was his work, which he could not very well put
aside, especially *L'Après-midi d'un Faune*, already accepted by the
Société Nationale and scheduled for a performance on December
22; *Pelléas*, which seemed to take longer than he expected; and
a new idea for a composition he planned to write for Ysaÿe. This
last one he sketched out as "an experiment with the different combinations that can be obtained in one color—like a study in gray in
painting." It was going to be a piece for violin with orchestra. The
orchestration of the first part of the composition was to consist entirely of the string instruments; of the second—flutes, four horns,
three trumpets and two harps, and of the third—of both groups.
"I hope this will appeal to you," he wrote Ysaÿe, "for the pleasure
it might give you is what I am most concerned with."

Debussy was speaking of the *Nocturnes* in their original version.

---

[1] Mitylene, the island of Lesbos.

And he talked so much about it that against his own rules he revealed the origin of his inspiration: *Nuages* had its starting point, so to speak, when he was crossing a bridge near the Place de la Concorde and his attention was caught by the clouds of a gathering storm and the sound of a horn from a passing boat; and *Fêtes* was a memory evoked by the popular festivities in the Bois de Boulogne with the Garde Républicaine's orchestra playing the retreat.

Debussy did not join Louÿs, but he heartily approved the sudden change in his friend's itinerary. "After all, Bayreuth is a dull assignment, it is a narrow-minded world," he wrote him, as if to score one more point in their everlasting arguments about Wagner. "How much better is Biskra, which should teach us *de combinaisons nouvelles.*"

Louÿs made a *bon voyage*, stayed at Biskra long enough to contract a fever from the infernal seasonal heat there, and to seduce Meriem, with whom he settled down at Constantine in Algeria for the rest of his African trip. ". . . She is the most beautiful, the most graceful and the most delicate being I have ever seen," Louÿs wrote to Gide. "Unfortunately it is no more possible to drag this little animal along in a civilized city than to present a panther in a drawing room. . . . I beat her like a little dog, but rest assured I will not spoil her for you, but . . . I beat her and not with a flower." His *Chansons de Bilitis* begun in France were completed at this time and dedicated to Gide "in memory of Meriem ben Atala."

Two months later Louÿs returned to Paris with a burnouse and endless stories of his erotic discoveries, and remained in the city long enough to see his *Chansons de Bilitis* published in December of the same year and to attend the first performance of Debussy's *L'Après-midi d'un Faune.* Debussy was "enchanted" with the *Bilitis* and of course enjoyed Louÿs's almost Erik Satie-ish hoax. The "*Chansons de Bilitis,* translated for the first time from the Greek," actually never had any other author than Pierre Louÿs. But to make his characterization authentic Louÿs interpolated into the selection of his poems several titles of songs which he said "were

not translated." The fact that he had already published a translation of the *Poésies de Méléagre* only added to the credibility, but,
of course, there is no denying that the narrative is so well kept in
an antique atmosphere, and every detail so perfectly chosen, that
it achieves a complete illusion. Debussy insisted, however, that there
were erudite Germans at Leipzig University who criticized Louÿs's
French and even found faulty translations in the text. *Bilitis* is a
series of 143 poems in prose, each one written like a sonnet, yet the
whole presented as a novel. In these *chansons* the poet unrolls
the life of a woman in the world of Greek courtesans two thousand
years ago.

If Debussy did not write his *Chansons de Bilitis* until several
years later, it was only because he found himself too busy. Just as
at the Brussels' concert, he was still working on the score during
the rehearsals. In his final version he shortened the *Prélude, Interlude et Paraphrase Finale à l'Après-midi d'un Faune* to *Prélude
à l'Après-midi d'un Faune* and either incorporated the other two
parts—they were barely sketched—or omitted them entirely. A
short explanatory note, most probably written by Debussy, was
attached to the score: "It evokes the successive echoes of the Faun's
desires and dreams on a hot afternoon." It certainly was less expressive than the one he wrote a year later to Camille Chevillard, the
conductor of the *Concerts Lamoureux*, who asked him for more
precise instructions in regard to the solo flute part: *"C'est un berger
qui joue de la flute, le c ... dans l'herbe."*

L'Après-midi d'un Faune was conducted by Gustave Doret on
Saturday and Sunday, December 22 and 23, 1894, at the Salle
d'Harcourt, 40 rue Rochechouart. For the first time the Société
Nationale had opened its doors to the general public and Debussy's
friends, strong in their devotion, if not in number, arrived to acclaim the work. Unfortunately there is no reliable report of this
first audience's reaction: some recalled later that the piece was
played to an accompaniment of boos and hisses in the audience,
others said that it had such an instantaneous success that it had to
be repeated. There are even two versions of Mallarmé's own opin-

ion. Debussy said that after the performance Mallarmé sent him a copy of *L'Après-midi* with the following inscription:

> *Sylvain d'haleine première,*
> *Si ta flûte a réussi*
> *Ouïs toute la lumière*
> *Qu'y soufflera Debussy.*[1]

And yet one of Mallarmé's close friends said that when asked about Debussy's work, he remarked it was *"du même, au même."*

The critics were far from unanimous in their enthusiasm. There were some who repeated Debussy's own words: "It was only logical that it should run the risk of displeasing those who like only one brand of music and remain faithful to it, despite its wrinkles and its thick make-up." Others, as usual, dissected and minutely scrutinized the composition, trying to bring it into line with the stereotyped classics or other familiar compositions, condemning it for the predominance of Wagnerian and Russian influence and borrowed themes, which, they said, deprived the composer of his own style. There were a few critics who gravely announced that "Debussy lacked heart and vigor" and "was as vague as Mallarmé's poem;" and Charles Darcours, who up till then had been Debussy's champion, declared in *Le Figaro* that "such pieces are amusing to write, but not to listen to."

A few years later, even after *L'Après-midi d'un Faune* had gained a foothold on the programs of Edouard Colonne and André Messager, Debussy's masterpiece was still the despair of the critics and the term "indefinable" used in analyses of the piece seemed to have been especially coined for it. Somehow the critics had failed to see that it was a most individual work—indeed, without parallel even in his own art—conceived beyond the limits of reality in the world of dreams and leaving "delightfully superficial, almost phantom-like, impressions."

---

[1] Woodland spirit, at first breath,
If thy flute persuades us,
All the radiance will be heard
That streams from Debussy.

Furthermore, Debussy's own declaration echoing Heinrich Heine, that "his music is the art of the inexpressible, whose role begins where inadequate words fail. . . ." was misinterpreted so that it raised a question on moral grounds: whether such music should be approved or rejected by respectable audiences, since Debussy was portraying the sensual pleasures of a faun, a demi-god, in a not exactly intellectual pursuit on a hot afternoon. (Edouard Colonne had to omit the explanatory program notes because "too many young ladies attended his concerts.")

L'Après-midi d'un Faune brought Debussy's name into the foreground among the French contemporary composers, but it caused more criticism than praise—"*Pelléas* is my only hope," Debussy repeated over and over again. There was no question of collaborating with Louÿs on the "something" he had in mind which was to bring an immediate success, because a few weeks after the performance of *L'Après-midi* Louÿs departed for Spain, presumably to do some work, but actually with the same aim as in his previous journey to Algeria. He spent three months there adding a whole new list of names of young girls in their teens with whom he "exercised the same art as that of Don José and Carmen in Bizet's opera"—to add a realistic touch to his adventures he chose to live in Seville on the same rue du Candilejo.

In his letters to Debussy Louÿs said nothing about the work they were to collaborate on, for, as he said, "he did nothing with his ten fingers, except unmentionable things." Louÿs confided that with the exception of the rich variety of his paramours there was nothing new to tell, that he was composing a waltz, a romance and a bolero (Louÿs once said that he knew by heart more music than literature, and he probably did), and naïvely reported to Debussy his discovery of songs which did not end on the tonic. Debussy's reply expressed his sincere hope that the little girl friends had more original charms to offer than this latest musical find, which seemed to be keeping Louÿs from the work he had promised to do.

In March Louÿs returned to Paris with "five francs in his pocket," the last left from his fortune. He told his brother that everything he owned would have to be sold at public auction unless he supported him until he found a way to earn his own living. Thus Louÿs came to the end of the first part of his incredible record, while Debussy had to accept an end of one of his no longer unusual stories—his love affair with Catherine Stevens.

After many months of carefully preparing the ground for the final step, Debussy decided to ask the girl to marry him. Alfred Stevens' better days were a thing of the past. His paintings had brought him a fortune but he lived a wildly extravagant life and although at one time he had owned a whole street of houses (the street was named after him) now he was reduced to living in a modest studio and a couple of rooms, driven to painting numbers of small canvases for art dealers because of his debts. As Catherine and Debussy sat in front of the fireplace discussing their financial problems, Debussy said: "Tell me, Catherine . . . when my *Pelléas* is played—and it will be played if not in Paris, then in Brussels— I will become rich. Then I will go to see your father and ask him for the hand of his daughter. Do you think he will give it to me?" Catherine, disconcerted and moved by this sudden avowal, was silent. "Let's wait till *Pelléas* is played, and then we'll talk about it," she said. Debussy understood. Years later Catherine said that she would have married Debussy "despite his reputation with women," if it were not for the brilliant young doctor on whom she had already decided. Debussy's visits with her became less frequent until one day he asked her to return the manuscript of the song *En sourdine* which he had dedicated to her. His publisher, he said, had asked for it. Later, when the composition was published among the *Fêtes galantes*, he "affectionately" presented her with a copy. To Catherine's surprise the piece was dedicated to another woman. "This," Catherine said, "was his only revenge."

CHAPTER XI

BOHEMIAN PERIOD—THE BREAK
WITH GABY

THE FAILURE OF the doctor's prediction of Louÿs's imminent death and the last five francs in his pocket touched off an artistic collaboration between the two friends in the hope of solving one of their immediate mutual problems—the threat of financial bankruptcy. Louÿs had no desire to do any work, but since his brother had offered him an income he felt compelled to do something. Shortly after his return to Paris he announced that he had been commissioned by Léon Carvalho, the director of the Opéra Comique, to write a libretto for a children's fable to be performed on Christmas Day by the Opéra Comique, and that Debussy was going to compose the music for it.

Grimm's "Fairy Tales" suddenly appeared on Louÿs's working desk and he spent many nights carefully reading *Blanche-Neige* (The Snow-maiden) in search of inspiration, while changing his future heroine's name in his mind from Geneviève to Kundrynette and, finally, to Cendrelune. In a "once-upon-a-time" story, which eventually he spun into two acts with ten scenes, Cendrelune, a poor little girl ill-treated by her "horrid stepmother," wants to run away into the woods. Neither the wise elderly village woman nor the saints to whom Cendrelune prays succeed in dissuading her from following fairy enticements into the woods. She enters the enchanted garden convinced that there, at last, she will find the mother whom she lost as a child.

Debussy became so enthusiastic about the project that he talked

to Hartmann and the three of them were in the midst of long conferences about the production when Louÿs suddenly declared that
the whole thing was no good, that no one would be interested in
it, and that, if he wrote it in his own frank and original way, it
would only disgust most people. After all, Louÿs explained, the
story turned around a struggle of two religions for a little unhappy
peasant girl, who ends by deserting the Church for Demeter's
temple. "I believe a book can be written about it," Louÿs concluded,
"but to put this on the stage in 1895—that is impossible. It will
appear pedantic, boring and unnecessary. Such a subject needs
seventy-five paragraphs of explanations and cannot be recited by
our cast."

Therefore, he suggested, if Debussy wanted to do something besides *Pelléas,* they should take a well-known story, which he,
Louÿs, would rejuvenate as best he could, and which would not
confuse anyone. In the back of his mind he had *Faust,* but, of
course, he knew Debussy would not listen to it. *Ariane* would make
much too long an opera, but there were other subjects, he said—
Psyché for instance, "one of the most dramatic and charming stories."

But neither Debussy nor Hartmann were ready to give up
Cendrelune—all they wanted Louÿs to do was to make a few
changes in his scenario. Louÿs pondered over their suggestions another night and finally refused. This religiosity, this triumph of the
lily over the rose and of Chastity over Love was utterly strange to
him, he said. "Write your own *Cendrelune,* you are perfectly capable of it," he told Debussy, and this would have been the end of
any further discussion of the project had Debussy not held tena-
ciously to the idea that had become dear to him. "Never mind
Hartmann's insistence on change; we'll strangle him. *But we must
do 'Cendrelune'!*" Debussy pleaded and Louÿs promised to attend
to it: "Pierre Louÿs has the honor to inform his master, friend and
collaborator Claude, that he has rented an apartment right near
him, 11 rue Chateaubriand, which on an incalculable scale will fa-
cilitate the production of a superb *Cendrelune.* The house has two
entrances. Please notify the pusilanimous ladies," Louÿs signifi-

cantly concluded his message, and for weeks Debussy's collaborator disappeared out of his sight. "Silence is a lovely thing and God knows that the blank measures in my *Pelléas* score testify to my love for that sort of expression of an emotion, but yours has really over-extended all the measures," Debussy complained, but in vain.

While Louÿs gave the impression of being fickle in the way his enthusiasm would suddenly change to complete disinterest, ac-tually he was almost as tenacious as Debussy once an idea took real root in his mind. Only, unfortunately for Debussy, it was not on *Cendrelune* that Louÿs rested his hopes of getting out of his finan-cial predicament. And though he never spoke of it, another plan had been germinating for years.

In 1883, at the age of eighteen, he saw Sarah Bernhardt in Vic-torien Sardou's *La Tosca* and was "so overwhelmed" that he wrote her. But not till a few years later, when he started on the second of his "three final years of life" was he actually introduced to her in London. "And what do you do?" Sarah asked. "I am a poet, Ma-dame," Louÿs replied, as he bent to kiss her hand. "I could have guessed it from the way you blushed. Write me a play, then," Sarah suggested. These were the last words she ever said to him, for he never met her again, but for years the dream of writing a play for Sarah Bernhardt never left his mind. During the month of July 1892 Louÿs wrote his first draft of the play "commissioned by Sarah Bernhardt," a drama in three acts, sixty pages of prose and poetry. He may or he may have not known Bernhardt's back-ground, but he thought the play written for her should be based on the legend connected with her first name. He called his drama *Chrysis*.

The play remained in his desk until this crucial junction in his life when, practically penniless, with nothing already written to offer a publisher, he spoke to Alfred Vallette, the editor-in-chief of the *Mercure de France*, a literary magazine, who was not interested in discussing mere ideas. Louÿs decided to rewrite *Chrysis*, to make a novel out of it under a new title *L'Esclavage*, and departed to the country home of an old friend, A. Ferdinand Hérold, at Lapras in

Ardèche, promising Debussy, in vague terms, that he would get to work on *Cendrelune*.

A month later Debussy received from his collaborator a more specific account of his past and future plans.

January	*Repos* [rest]
February	*Repos*
March	*Repos*
April	*Repos*
May	Plan for *Cendrelune*
June	*Repos*
July	
August	*L'Esclavage*
September	
October	
November	*Cendrelune*

There was nothing that Debussy could do except to write him that Mélisande sent her love to Cendrelune.

Debussy differed from Louÿs in his attitude toward his financial situation. Whereas Louÿs was in a fever to find some way out of a position he had never known before and could not get used to, Debussy had long since resigned himself to failures. He behaved as if success were an acquaintance who promised to call, and if his guest would arrive hours late, he would still be glad to see him. He believed in *Cendrelune* as a sure financial success, but he was helpless against Louÿs's procrastinations. And meanwhile, like Louÿs, he also reviewed his accomplishments during the past months.

He told his friends how "Pelléas and Mélisande began to sulk and no longer wanted to come down from their tapestry," and how, therefore, he had been forced to "play with other ideas." He worked on, but had not yet completed, the *Nocturnes*, several piano pieces, the *Images*, and of course, thought of *Cendrelune*. "Then," Debussy said, "a little jealous, they [Pelléas and Mélisande] returned to bend over me, and Mélisande, with the soft, ailing voice, which you know she has, said to me: 'Leave these little longings, favorites of the cosmopolitan public, and keep your dreams for my hair. You know well that no tenderness is like ours.'"

Debussy complained that the scene between Mélisande and Golaud (in the second act) was the most difficult to do, for it is then,
he said, "that one suddenly has a premonition of catastrophes, it is
there that Mélisande begins to lie to Golaud and is enlightened
about herself, aided therein by this Golaud, a fine man all the
same, who shows that it is not necessary to be entirely frank, even
with little girls." Then Debussy told of completing the scene in the
tower and the one in the underground caverns—"filled with subtle
terror and mysterious enough to give vertigo to the best inured
souls! and the scene on leaving these caverns, filled with sunlight,
but with sunlight bathed by our good mother the sea. . . ." He also
disclosed that he had written a scene for "Yniold with the little
sheep." In this scene, he said, he put something "of the compassion
of a child to whom one of the sheep first gives the conception of the
game in which he cannot take part, and also of the pity which people eager to be comfortable no longer feel. . . ." And if the scene
between Yniold and Golaud frightened Debussy—"for this I had
to have profound and sure things at my command," he said—and
Golaud gave him nightmares, he was extremely happy about the
one before the grotto. "This scene," he explained, "tries to express
all the mystery of the night, where amid so much silence, a blade
of grass stirred from its sleep makes a really menacing noise. . . .
Then there is the nearby sea which speaks its sorrows to the moon,
and Pelléas and Mélisande, who are a little afraid to talk amid
so much mystery. . . ."

And finally Debussy told how he planned for the scene of Mélisande's death to have an orchestral group on the stage in order
"in some sense, to have the death in all sonority." This, he said,
was the same idea he was trying out in the combination of instruments in his *Nocturnes*. There also he wanted to use separate groups
of the orchestra to develop new nuances in an ensemble. But eventually he gave up the scheme in both cases. "In France," he said,
"every time a woman dies on the stage, it must be like *La Dame aux
camélias;* it suffices to replace the camelias with other flowers and
the woman with a princess in a bazaar! People cannot conceive that
one leaves discreetly, like one who has had enough of this planet,

the Earth, and is going away where the flowers of tranquillity blossom. . . ." "One does not dare enough in music," Debussy concluded, "because of the fear of some sort of divinity called 'common sense'—the most wretched thing I know, which after all is nothing but an established belief to excuse the existence of so many imbeciles!"

During the spring of 1895 Debussy finished the score of *Pelléas*. Then, either spurred by Louÿs's energy in pursuit of improving his financial affairs, or because of Louÿs's constant delays with the scenario for *Cendrelune*, Debussy once again went to London with the same aim as on his two previous journeys there: to find a publisher, or to arrange for performances of his work, or, perhaps, to find some kind of a permanent post in a musical institution. But the three weeks in London were fruitless, even though Camille Saint-Saëns, whom Debussy, by chance, met crossing the Channel, introduced him to Sir Robert Parry at the Royal College of Music. Fruitless, except that he was offered an opportunity to have his *Pelléas and Mélisande* used as background music for the forthcoming production of Maeterlinck's play. This Debussy refused.

"What do you care," Louÿs said, when upon his return from Lapras Debussy told him of the proposition. And Louÿs reminded him of how "the old miserable one [Wagner] had sold his 'scenario' of *The Flying Dutchman* to Paul Foucher for five hundred francs and two months later composed his own opera for the German theaters." Debussy refused to listen to Louÿs and perhaps because of Wagner's example remained adamant as far as his own score for *Pelléas* was concerned, but as he held the exclusive rights from Maeterlinck, he graciously agreed to let Gabriel Fauré compose the music for the planned performance of the play in London (1898). And after rereading *Pelléas* once again he began quietly to revise the first version, which was far from satisfactory to him. "And when *Cendrelune?*" he asked Louÿs.

Louÿs returned to Paris sooner than Debussy expected, but not because of the promised work on *Cendrelune*. Louÿs hated living in the country, he hated walking and he hated bicycling on the unpaved roads. Back in Paris he vanished again from Debussy's sight.

For weeks at a time he was carousing with his friends in the Latin Quarter, returning to his apartment only occasionally and only because he had to complete *L'Esclavage*, the first installment of which had already begun to appear in the *Mercure de France*. Then at the end of November [1] as he sat at his desk at two in the morning, he wrote: "My dear Claude, do you have the courage to compose in twelve days a ballet in three scenes, thirty minutes of music, to my scenario with this title: *Daphnis et Khloé* (with a beautiful K)?" Debussy must have been surprised by his choice of subject and for good reason.

Pierre Louÿs's interest in *Daphnis et Chloé* dated back to 1889, when, as a boy recently graduated from high school, he read Jacques Amyot's (1559) translation of an ancient myth and in his enthusiasm wrote to André Gide, then his closest friend: "... It is a delight. It is absolutely exquisite. I don't know anything more gentle, more chaste, more young. It makes one think of the busts of Donatello. Do you see? These lifted eyelids on astounded faces. It is so deliciously naïve. And what language! He is extraordinary, this Amyot! And how sixteenth-century this is. Oh! you see, I can't tell you what I felt reading it. The first part is a masterpiece, absolute and complete. The three other parts depart a bit too far from the main subject, but each time one returns to the grotto and nymphs, each time Daphnis again sees Chloé, it is enchanting. ..."

Years passed after this youthful outburst of admiration. Gide was no longer Louÿs's friend, his taste and interests had changed, and in a twenty-eight-page-long study of this work Louÿs remarked, among other things: "The stupidity of the subject! Daphnis, the fifteen-year-old shepherd, has a flock of fifty sheep *qu'il fait saillir et qu'il double à chaque portée*. He sleeps every night with Chloé, the thirteen-year old shepherdess who sees *ses béliers*. They want to unite but they don't know how. It is up to Lykainion to reveal to Daphnis the secret (!) of love. Can it be that such a subject, the most stupid in the world, has given birth to *Daphnis et Chloé?!*" Apparently Louÿs had forgotten that when he first read *Daphnis*

[1] November 27, 1895.

et Chloé he wrote to Gide that one should read it at the age of eighteen, when one is "too curious to feel and too naïve to understand. Later on one becomes too blasé to enjoy it and too sceptical to 'believe that it happened.'"

Debussy could not fathom how at a time when Louÿs was engrossed in his *L'Esclavage* he could be interested in *Daphnis et Chloé*, and he wanted to hear more about this sudden new change in Louÿs's opinion of the work. As it turned out, the idea for the ballet on this subject came from Alphonse Franck (later the director of the theater Gymnase and of the Théâtre Édouard VII.) He was asked to organize a few productions at the Théâtre La Bodinière on rue Saint-Lazare and Louÿs already saw sold-out houses and the end of Debussy's and his own material worries.

"I am working on the scenario. You will have it Saturday. Between now and then you must start looking for melodies," Louÿs urged Debussy. "Here are the essential indications: Chloé, *chantefable un peu conne, mais tendre.*[1] Daphnis, a flute player. Thus, the theme should be pastoral—ardent and naïve. You arrange this. Lykainion, a well-experienced person, *très portée sur sa figue.* Voluptuous, but without any passion.

"You remember the scheme of the plot:

    I: C. and D. don't know.

    II.   L. teaches D.

    III.   D. teaches C.

    Curtain.

"We need for the first section a theme constructed like the first phrase in *Parsifal*, i.e. it should go as far as the dominant, but I have no plan for it. For the second section I visualize an extended theme which has nothing to do with theme I, but it could be joined by it in Section III.

"Good advice, all this, eh?

"The score should begin with a theme for a flute . . . and so that we shouldn't lose time, couldn't you pinch something from the *Faun's Afternoon* [in English in the original] by a certain Debussy?

[1] Allusion to *Chantefable un peu naïve*, a poem by Albert Mockel, Belgian writer (*Mercure de France*, Paris, 1891).

They played it, three months ago, at the Colonne concerts; M. Gauthier-Villars said it was very good.

"Here you are. We must hurry up, old man. It will be played fifteen times, that is a promise, without counting the revivals. And it will be paid for in banknotes."

Nothing came of this project and not only because Debussy remained cool toward the *Daphnis et Chloé* which fifteen years later served another French composer, Maurice Ravel, as a subject for one of the masterpieces in the literature of music and ballet. There were other reasons. Since Debussy showed less enthusiasm for *Daphnis et Chloé* than he did for *Cendrelune*, Louÿs took his negative attitude as final, and as he believed he had in *Daphnis et Chloé* a sure success, in his haste to get on with it he approached Massenet with the same proposition. This did not go very well with Debussy. However, when Massenet declined the offer, Louÿs returned to Debussy who, before plunging into work with the speed Louÿs requested, still wanted to have more details about the nature of the music Louÿs was imagining.

Was it going to be for xylophone, banjo or Russian bassoon? —and where was the work going to be produced? This last question was of even greater importance to Debussy, who zealously guarded his works from being performed "anywhere." While these "negotiations" dragged on for weeks, something else had happened in Louÿs's "pursuit of big sums of money," as he called his unusual, nervous behavior, that changed his plans and affected those of Debussy, including *Daphnis et Chloé*.

The four installments of *L'Esclavage* (August, September, November, 1895, and January, 1896) in the *Mercure de France* not only did not produce the effect Louÿs anticipated, but he had to pay a part of the expenses of publication. This, however, did not shake his faith in the novel, and he was willing to gamble another five thousand francs, undoubtedly borrowed from his brother, on its publication in book form. With this sum of money he persuaded a not too enthusiastic publisher to bring out the novel under still another name: *Aphrodite*; but on one condition—Louÿs was to be paid two francs from every copy of the book sold. *Aphrodite* appeared in the bookstores and again remained unnoticed by the public, until a senator, M. Béranger, intervened in the name of morality. The unpleasant connotations of an "affair" reached Louÿs's brother's ears and threatened to embarrass him in his official position of Ambassador to Egypt. Thereupon Baron Louis wrote a letter to François Coppée, then the director of the literary department of *Le Journal,* a Paris daily, and asked him to hush up the case.

Originally Coppée had been among those shocked by *Aphrodite,* but after receiving the letter, he reread the novel and discovered it to be a masterpiece. On April 15, 1896 he published his editorial which began: "You have not read *Aphrodite?* What do you do with yourself between meals? For your information, I want you to know that since *Salammbô* there has been nothing written in so pure a French and so perfect...."

Coppée's article launched a sale of one hundred and fifty thousand copies, thus not only returning to Louÿs the fortune he had recklessly squandered, but providing him with an income for the rest of his life. At the age of twenty-six Pierre Louÿs became as famous as Pierre Loti and Gustave Flaubert and his *Aphrodite* was to be adapted for a play with Debussy's music—so far the most lucrative proposition offered to his patient "collaborator."

But again Debussy was in no hurry to start on a project before he was sure that it would be presented to the public as a work of art. Not even *Aphrodite,* obviously a gold mine, could stir him from his principles of artistic integrity, not even when time and again he had to borrow small sums of money from Louÿs to keep alive, because he had no pupils and no income to speak of from his already published works, and he and Gaby were, as he said, in a *"purée noire, verte, multicolore et jusqu'au cou!"*

Debussy preferred to work quietly on *La Saulaie,* Louÿs's translation of D. G. Rossetti's poem "Willowwood." This, at least, was going to be an important work written in the light of his "latest discoveries in musical chemistry," he said. And then he still was thinking about *Cendrelune,* occasionally talked about it to Louÿs, and when Louÿs was once again leaving for Spain and Algeria to recuperate from his success, brought him as a *bon voyage* present the old *Cendrelune* scenario, begging him to work on it. Meanwhile he continued revising the score of *Pelléas*—his only hope, as he had been repeating for the last four years.

Early in the fall Debussy had taken this second version of his opera to his old friend Ysaÿe in Brussels. Debussy had dedicated the opera to him and he was anxious to have Ysaÿe's opinion. With Théophile, Ysaÿe's brother, at the second piano and Ysaÿe and Debussy playing and singing the parts, they went through the score, which made a great impression on the Belgian musician. "I saw the opera through my ears," Ysaÿe said, but some of his severe criticism almost made Debussy tear up the score upon his return to Paris, had it not been for Louÿs who talked him out of it. Instead, he followed Ysaÿe's suggestions and began, once more, to revise it.

Ysaÿe, on the other hand, unaware of all this, tried to get a performance of *Pelléas* at the Théâtre de la Monnaie in Brussels and at the theater in Ghent, and only when these projects failed did he offer to perform some excerpts from the score at one of his symphony concerts. As a matter of fact, it had already been announced for the second regular subscription concert to be conducted by Ysaÿe when Debussy first heard about it. No arguments would prevail against Debussy's firm attitude toward the presentation of his opera. He brushed aside the comparison with the brilliant fate of Wagner's works, which were first introduced at symphonic concerts.

MY GREAT FRIEND [Debussy wrote Ysaÿe]: [1]

I am touched by your letter and your friendly concern for Pelléas and Mélisande—these poor little creatures so difficult to introduce to the world. For even with you as their godfather this world does not want to be convinced. Now I am going to tell you humbly the reasons against your opinion concerning a performance of fragments from *Pelléas et Mélisande*. First of all, if this work has any merit at all it lies particularly in the connection of the action on the stage with the music. It is, therefore, evident and indubitable that this qualiy will be lost in concert form and one could not blame anyone for not understanding the remarkable eloquence of the silent intervals with which the work is strewn. On

[1] October 13, 1896.

the other hand, the simple technique can gain its true significance only
on the stage, while in a concert performance they would throw at my
head the American wealth of Wagner and I would appear as a poor man
who cannot afford to pay for "contrabass tubas"! In my opinion Pelléas
and Mélisande must be presented *as they are*, and then it will be a matter
of taking or leaving them, and if we have to fight at least it will be
worth while...."

Instead of *Pelléas*, Debussy proposed to send *La Saulaie*, which
he hoped to have ready by December, and the three *Nocturnes*
"written *for* Eugène Ysaÿe, the man I love and admire," Debussy
wrote. "Besides, these nocturnes can be played only by him. Even
if Apollo himself would ask for them, I would have to refuse him."
But he never completed *La Saulaie* (only one page was found
among his manuscripts), and the three *Nocturnes*, at least in their
original form as a solo violin piece with orchestra, had a different
fate, along with a plan for violin sonatas also intended for Ysaÿe—
they became a victim of Debussy's relationship with Ysaÿe as a consequence of events in Debussy's personal life.

So poor that only Louÿs's help kept him from "sleeping under
a bridge," Debussy for some time found solace in a new love affair,
but an unexpected turn of this affair completely threw him out of
his groove and uprooted his more or less placid life with Gaby during the last ten years. Whether because his biographers at this
point had enough of Debussy's love affairs and did not bother to
investigate this case while the information was still fresh in the
memories of the few who knew about it, or because it turned out to
be one of many episodes in Debussy's history that were hermetically
sealed by him, it has never been ascertained who was the latest subject of his heart "still susceptible to flutter," as he said to Louÿs.

It has been stated positively but erroneously that his last paramour was none other than his future wife Lily Texier, but Debussy
did not meet her until some eighteen months after the "drama"
took place in his apartment early in 1897. Therefore, the following
is purely my conjecture, based on dates and on Debussy's circle of
acquaintances at that time. One sentence in a letter to Louÿs in
reference to the whole story: "You would probably say, 'It is all his

own fault,' but here it is—I am sometimes sentimental, like a *modiste* who could have been Chopin's mistress," may serve as a clue to a hypothetical—and I stress this word—dénouement. Among Debussy's friends at this period of his life there was only one woman whom he respected as a great artist—Camille Claudel, the sculptress, Paul Claudel's sister. She was Rodin's pupil. "I have shown her where to find gold, but the gold she found was entirely her own," he said about her.

But she was not only his pupil. The beautiful, dark, blue-eyed young woman was at one time Rodin's great passion. Debussy must have met her after Camille Claudel had accepted the tragic situation—Rodin would not leave Rose, with whom he shared his whole life. Godet told of many an evening at his home when Debussy played for Claudel. Not particularly interested in the language of sounds, Claudel nonetheless eventually became a devoted listener. "You don't need to explain," she would say as she touched Debussy's icy hands at the end of a piece.

Traces of this relationship remain only in Camille Claudel's works, "Sirènes" and "Faunesses" among them, and her "Valse," which Debussy always kept on his mantelpiece. Yet it has been stated positively that Debussy and Claudel, six years his senior, were lovers. If this is true it could have happened only at this particular time. Fearing unpleasant publicity over the "drama," Claudel withdrew from the awkward situation and left it to Debussy to handle it in his own way.

Louÿs, the friend Debussy needed most, was far away. After the success of his *Aphrodite* he had gone to the Near East, and months passed before Debussy knew where he was. First, Louÿs received a letter from Gaby (the only one of Gaby's letters which has survived, except for a few lines of greeting she sometimes added to Debussy's letters). Gaby wrote at nine in the evening on Saturday, January 23, 1897:

My dear Pierre,
    Claude is gone to the Nationale, where he is playing Lekeu's quartet. I am alone and sad, even more sad than the weather outside and this is

saying little. I envy you in a land which I imagine beautiful, gay and full of sunshine. I thank you from my heart, my dear Pierre, for the bananas you sent me. It gave me a double pleasure: the first, that you thought of me, and the second—the satisfaction of my gourmandism, because it is a fruit I love so much.

This morning we received your telegram. Claude will write you to-morrow; he would have written you sooner, if you had not forgotten to give us your address. Write us soon and tell us about your health, and then tell me if it is really warm in Algeria. It is so cold here that your letters will warm us (at least our hearts). Claude doesn't know I am writing you, but I will tell him when he comes home and he will give me authorization to send you his sincere regards and a good handshake.

As for me, I kiss you on your left cheek and I am as always your little friend.

GABY

Claude did not write on the morrow. Two weeks passed before he felt calm enough to write a long letter and to explain that his silence had been caused by an "unpleasant story," a story on which, he said, Paul Bourget may have collaborated with Xavier de Montépin (known for his popular melodramatic love stories in the news-papers).

"Gaby, with her eyes of steel," Debussy finally came to the point, "found a letter in my pocket, which left no doubt about the development, well advanced, of a love affair with everything romantic in it that is necessary to move the most hardened heart. Where-upon! . . . drama . . . tears . . . and a real revolver. . . . All this is barbarous, unnecessary and does not change anything at all. Kisses and caresses of the body cannot be effaced with an India-rubber eraser. It would be quite an invention! India rubber to erase adul-tery. Besides, this poor little Gaby had just lost her father and this intervention of death calmed down for the moment these little pe-culiar stories."

Debussy's rather cold account of the "drama" showed that his relationship with Gaby had reached a point from which there was no return, and his cruel attitude toward Gaby's unhappiness was a fair warning to his future lovers. For when he mentioned "a real

revolver" he did not say that Gaby shot herself and that she had to
be taken to a hospital. After leaving the hospital Gaby "found a
refuge" with Madame Chausson, and later on, at Madame Chausson's suggestion of "a little change of surroundings," Gaby went
for a visit with the Ysaÿes in Brussels. Debussy said nothing at the
time. But because of what he considered "taking Gaby's side," he
cut off his relationship with his two dearest friends and their families. When two years later Ernest Chausson was killed while riding
a bicycle, Debussy did not rush to the side of the grief-stricken family, whose home, only a few years previously, was as his own. It
was up to Pierre Louÿs, two days after the accident, to remind Debussy and to offer to join him in paying last respects. "Would you
send me your visiting card?" Louÿs wrote Debussy. "I will attach
it to mine on a wreath I am going to send."

Debussy's attitude toward the Ysaÿes was similar. Evidently he
felt so strongly about it that, after five years of silence, he made an
allusion to his hurt feelings in a letter to Ysaÿe on December 30,
1903.

My dear friend,

I understand that in the near future you are going to play the three
Nocturnes. I don't need to tell you of my joy. I only regret that, for the
most wretched reasons, I shall not be able to be present at this performance, which, I am sure, will be the one I have dreamt of. It has been
a long time, my dear friend, since I had the pleasure of seeing you. But
whatever may have been said to you about me (friends sometimes have
a funny way of arranging things), believe me, I have never forgotten
all that I owe you in artistic emotion and beauty, and you will never lack
my most fervent admiration.

This was the last letter Debussy wrote Ysaÿe. It was no longer
written in the old-time "younger brother" vein. He used the more
formal *you*, instead of *thou*, no longer "dear great friend," but
simply "my dear friend," and instead of "fraternal embraces" there
was nothing left but "fervent admiration." Debussy said "the performance I dreamt of," but he did not say that the nocturnes Ysaÿe
was going to play were no longer the same he had been working on
years before, "written *for* Eugène Ysaÿe, the man I love and ad-

mire...." Nor did Ysaÿe know that *Pelléas et Mélisande* was no longer dedicated to him. Debussy blamed the rupture in their friendship on "friends who have sometimes a funny way of arranging things," clearly pointing to the Ysaÿe and Chausson families.

Louÿs was the only one among his close friends in whose friendship he could trust, Debussy said at the time of Gaby's "drama." Probably not realizing how seriously Debussy was shaken, if not by Gaby's "tears," then by the frustrated latest love affair, Louÿs sent him *L'Adieu*,[1] *a song*—he himself wrote the words and music—in a "very Montmartre" style with a *nota bene:* "do not be reminded of Chopin's third étude." Debussy preferred this sort of expression of "condolence" to what he regarded as "mixing in other people's business." At the age of thirty-five Debussy had definitely established in his mind principles and answers to questions regarding life and human relationships; his habits were never to be disturbed, his opinions were no longer flexible.

After several weeks of "exile" Gaby returned and found no visible change in Debussy's behavior or in their home. It was as if she had been out to do her shopping in the neighborhood. Line, the Angora cat—Debussy's cats were always Angora and always were called by the same name, which they inherited from each other—tiptoed, as usual, through a mass of papers on Debussy's desk, while he was working. Debussy's habits did not change in Gaby's absence. He got up late in the morning and he went to bed late at night. He took his time in "starting the day": he devoted special attention to his coiffure, every hair meticulously arranged in its place, as he did to the careful examination of his shirts and suits before he would put them on. The large cravat had to have an almost scientifically studied effect of casual disorder, and he considered that rolling one's own cigarettes was one of the elementary rules of a citizen worthy of the name, like using a straight, instead of a safety razor—with his beard it was an easy argument. Before going to bed he would sonorously blow his nose *à fond,* for snoring was to him the height of bad manners. An atheist, he was as superstitious as an old peasant

[1] See Appendix.

woman. Before retiring he placed his shoes so that the toes pointed outwards, otherwise it would bring bad luck. "Not to tempt the Devil," no matter how curious or how excited he may have been about the contents of a letter or a package, he would first arm himself with a large, ornate paper knife and then carefully cut the envelope in the right place and the right direction, as he would work endlessly to undo the string knots on a package instead of simply tearing them open. He would not sit at a table with twelve others, nor walk under a ladder.

There was, however, one change that could not escape Gaby. He was restless and he could not concentrate on anything. He tried working on *La Saulaie,* he even started on *Daphnis et Chloé,* but put it aside—he did not know what to do with it. "Music," he said, "escapes me." He said he was broken, and Gaby could no longer put the pieces together.

"You don't work because you have a hard life, and you have a hard life because you don't work," Louÿs told him, when upon his return he found Debussy in a state of deterioration. And to get him out of this vicious circle, to distract him, and to bring him back into "circulation" with friends who had not seen or heard of him for some time, Louÿs proposed giving a musical evening at his home. To bolster Debussy's ebbing morale he selected a program where Debussy's works would appear on equal terms with those of Bach and Beethoven. As Louÿs owned a Mustel organ he asked Debussy to choose an organist for the performance, and himself engaged the Belgian Crickboom Quartet, with Ysaÿe's name conspicuously absent in his plan. "I suggest this program," Louÿs wrote Debussy:

1. Prelude and Fugue   Bach
   (*Mustel*)

2. Quartet Op. 10   Debussy
   (*the Belgians*)

3. Toccata and Fugue in B flat major   Bach
   (*piano—you*)

4. Quartet XV and Fugue   Beethoven
   (*the Belgians*)

5. Scene (of your choice) from *Pelléas* Debussy
   (*piano—you*)

6. Entr'acte and buffet Pierre Louÿs

7. "The *Archduke* Trio" Beethoven
   (*you and the Belgians*)

8. Toccata in F Bach
   (*Mustel*)

"We'll invite ten friends, no more. I like the program, don't you?" Louÿs wrote at the end of his note, and as he never missed an opportunity to tease Debussy he added, "You don't think Wagner has been given too much of a place?"

The little musicale was a success and had an immediate beneficial result. At Louÿs's suggestion, his old friend M. Floury, the owner of *L'Image*, a literary and artistic magazine (originally founded by a group of wood carvers in 1896), asked Debussy for a composition. It had been a long time since Debussy was approached with an offer for a publication of his work and he was very pleased with it. He thought of doing one of Louÿs's *Chansons de Bilitis—La Chevelure* ("The Hair"). Since Debussy never met Meriem herself, with whom Louÿs in 1894 was engaged in the art of love, it is a matter of conjecture whether his choice of *Chansons de Bilitis* was prompted by his meeting her sister Zohra, a young and voluptuous Algerian whom Louÿs had imported on his recent arrival in Paris. In those days of depression Debussy spent more time in their company than at home.

During the following months he wrote two more songs: *La Flûte de Pan* and *Le Tombeau des Naïdes*. The collection of these exquisite musical poems is the only work combining the names of the two friends that is left of all their endeavors in collaboration. For as well as Louÿs knew Debussy, his projects—it was always up to him to choose—seemed to have been doomed by one and the same obstacle: Debussy's refusal to have his art "degraded" to the level of a popular work.

Shortly after Debussy had composed the *Chansons de Bilitis*, once again an opportunity to pull Debussy out of his financial pre-

dicament presented itself. M. de Lagoanère, a composer and conductor, but at that time the director of the Olympia, the music hall,
offered to do a ballet based on Louÿs's *Aphrodite* and once again
Louÿs tried to persuade Debussy to write a score for it. "Don't say
no too quickly," Louÿs argued. "Naturally, the theaters' reputation
depends on what they offer, their qualities and respectability are
based on good or bad plays.... Now, I know that many whores
are to be seen at the Olympia, but not as many as at the Opéra.
Those who speak of the public speak of a collection of idiots;
whores nowhere add a remarkable intellectual element, but they, at
least, bring with them some perfume which is not entirely false,
and, here and there, a beautiful head. And then, they have a superior merit over the honest women—they live frankly, etc., etc.,
etc. (see my *Aphrodite*)."

But not even three to four thousand francs with more income to
come from the performances outside of Paris would tempt Debussy.
He would not have his music performed in a music hall. He preferred quietly to revise *Pelléas* and occasionally reminded Louÿs
that he was still waiting for the promised scenario of *Cendrelune*.
"I need something to love," he pleaded with Louÿs. "Without it I
will become an idiot and there will be nothing left for me but to
commit suicide, which is even more stupid." And Debussy was not
jesting.

Working on the *Chansons de Bilitis* was like the last spark of a
once prodigious energy. While Debussy frankly admitted that he
did not like all the *Chansons de Bilitis*, it was one of Louÿs's works
that inspired him most, ever since he read it when it first appeared
in print. And Louÿs's presence in Paris and his constant concern at
the time when Debussy thought he had reached the end of his road
were like a cure to an invalid. But when Louÿs's idyll with the
"daughter of the African desert" came to an end and Louÿs went
to Marseille to start Zohra on her homeward voyage, Debussy felt
completely abandoned. Now, he said, he knew he was facing a dead
end.

During the following three months he brooded and did nothing.
Occasionally he would pick up the three *Nocturnes*. This score, he

mused, had once held the promise of great hope, which suddenly turned to despair, and then to mere emptiness. Besides, he confessed, he could do nothing whatsoever while something was happening in his personal life. Debussy was still suffering from his last unfortunate love affair. He believed that only from a *souvenir*, from a memory, from something that had passed could one extract emotions of real value. "Those who cry while they write masterpieces are implacable humbugs," he said. Another month passed and Debussy's depression reached its lowest ebb. "Nothing has changed in the black skies that are the background of my life," he wrote Louÿs, in April, 1896, "and I don't know where it all is leading if not to suicide, a stupid dénouement to something that merited perhaps something better. And all this because I am too weary to fight against idiotic impossibilities, utterly distasteful. You know me better than anyone, and you can afford to say that I am not just an old fool," he concluded, as if explaining the logic of his final decision and the reason for the "sonorous words" with which he had "no intention to bother" his friend.

Louÿs became alarmed. "... I cannot tell you how absurd the letter which I received today is. Four years ago I also had similar thoughts but at that time no one had made an eulogy to me, and the day I was financially ruined, without a penny left from my fortune, without a publisher ... I also had my hand on a revolver. I certainly would have used it, if it were not for my brother. And I would have made the most stupid mistake. . . ."

Debussy had no wealthy brother. He was thirty-six, not twenty-four. Still, Louÿs's compassion and sudden return to Paris kept Debussy's spirit alive for another few weeks, long enough for him to hear good news. *Pelléas et Mélisande* was accepted by the Opéra Comique.

CHAPTER XII

FIRST MARRIAGE—DEBUSSY A PLAYWRIGHT

DEBUSSY's *Pelléas et Mélisande* was accepted by the Opéra Comique, but accepted *en principe*—that is, without specifying either a date or even a season for the production. And if *Pelléas* was not given its first performance until several years later, it was not entirely the theater director's fault. Debussy's score was far from completed when André Messager, a composer and conductor responsible for introducing many contemporary works, finally decided to show *Pelléas* to Albert Carré, the newly appointed director of the Opéra Comique. It was still only a vocal score with Debussy's indications for orchestration. During the following years Debussy kept taking back his *Pelléas*, working on it up to the last days of the rehearsals and even the first performance. "To complete a work is just like assisting at the death of someone you love," Debussy once remarked in reference to his work on *Pelléas*.

Besides—and this in part would explain his constant changes in the orchestration—Debussy was not as happy about having it performed at the Opéra Comique as might have been expected. The theater was much too large, he thought, the intimacy of his piece was going to be lost, and he hated the large crowds of spectators. He always had hoped that Comte Robert de Montesquiou, an eccentric rich dilettante, would give, perhaps, two private performances at his Pavillon des Muses, and, preferably, for a select audience. This would have suited Debussy much better.

But if there was one man who was happy about it, it was Pierre

Louÿs. "Now you must not monopolize this hall with *Cendrelune* on the day after your *Pelléas*," he told Debussy, mentioning *Cendrelune* with an obvious sigh of relief, and he was ready with new projects to follow *Pelléas*. "In my opinion, despite the inconveniences of opera, you must do something else for this sort of *colisée*. I know, you are afraid your music will fade away in it and the architecture of the place would influence the piece I am going to suggest to you, as it did all the others that were given there for the last twenty years. But I know what you need too well to be mistaken. What you need—listen to this vocabulary—it is a text, which, on the whole, is *discreet* and *energetic*, of an *intense* emotion and never declamatory. If you and I had a little guts, we would do *Hamlet*, because this is exactly what you would do best, and to hell with M. Thomas.[1] Now, of course," Louÿs added as an afterthought, "this sort of 'adaptation' would interest me less than to write an original work, but we can talk about it next Monday when we dine on rue Boissy-d'Anglase, if you are free. Hereafter, and at last, I am sure you are going to start working again. One can even work for you," Louÿs cheerfully ended his note of congratulation on the acceptance of *Pelléas*.

They dined together and they talked about it, but nothing came of Louÿs's new project. The mere acceptance of Debussy's score by the Opéra Comique was not a sufficient stimulus either to shake him out of his inertia or to alter his preconceived ideas of an artistic production. *Hamlet* would have been a tremendous undertaking. They never spoke of it again. And as if to illustrate once again how strongly he felt about the performances of any of his works, Debussy even refused Louÿs the favor of accompanying a singer in the *Chansons de Bilitis* at a lecture on the poems to be given by Achille Ségard, an author well known in literary circles.

"The *Chansons de Bilitis*," Debussy explained his point of view, "in marvelous language contains everything there is of gentleness and cruelty in passion so that the most subtly voluptuous people are forced to recognize the childishness of their games vis-à-vis the ter-

---

[1] Ambroise Thomas's *Hamlet* had been given at the Opéra on March 9, 1868.

rible and seductive Bilitis. Would you tell me now, what can my little music add to a rendition of the pure and simple language of your text? Nothing at all. I would even say, it would inadroitly disturb the emotions of the listeners. Why then tune Bilitis' voice to major or minor scales, when her own voice is the most persuasive in the world? You are going to say: 'And why did you write the music?' This, old man, is another story . . . it's for another décor, but believe me, when Bilitis is present we should let her speak alone." And to soften his latest rebuff to his friend, Debussy spoke of "other difficulties, entirely material, as, for instance, in finding a young woman who would wear herself out in studying these three songs for the sake of our esthetics, merely contenting herself with the assurance of our consideration." Speaking of himself, as a performer, he confided to Louÿs that the emotional perturbations in his life during the past months had played such havoc with his nerves that he had developed "an unpleasant habit, almost a mania, of scattering a handful of false notes whenever I play for more than two people . . . ," and he did not welcome the idea of appearing in public.

Besides, he did not need to tell Louÿs that the nominal acceptance of *Pelléas* had not changed his situation. He was just as broke, just as lonely and unhappy. Gaby was still living with him, but the day when Debussy heard the news about *Pelléas* was not the one she was dreaming about. It came too late. For ten years Gaby had accepted and, as those who knew her life with Debussy well said, "sublimely" managed *la misère à deux,* staving off the creditors, keeping up his spirits, time and again carrying the whole load of financial responsibility, tiptoeing while he was working, and hoping that some day she too would reap the fruits of her suffering and sacrifice. But the day of *Pelléas* arrived after they had said farewell to their life together and their relationship, or what was left of it, hung on a thread Debussy was not particularly careful about.

Debussy led an aimless life. During the last two years he had written one piece and that only because of his new friendship with René Peter, a young writer. He first met Peter when, as an ardent Wagnerian in his student days, Debussy played and sang excerpts from the German's operas at the home of Maurice Vaucaire, the poet, and the twelve-year-old René happened to be there with his parents. Debussy was eight years older than René and had the aura of the Prix de Rome. René listened with awe to Debussy's every word. Later, when he grew up, he had attended the Bayreuth performances and exchanged a few letters with Debussy, only by that time his enthusiasm for Wagner was not shared by the advocate of the old days. Then years passed and a mere chance brought René Peter to Debussy's doorstep.

Monsieur V. (Peter would not disclose his name), a "financier-poet," blond, bald and with a long mustache, had written a tragedy called *La Fille de Pasiphaé* which he felt needed some music, and he asked René to serve as an intermediary with Debussy. Shortly afterwards Monsieur V. was seen leaving Debussy's apartment in a rage, brandishing his manuscript like a whip in the hand of a circus director and shouting at his host: "Monsieur, I am offering you half of my glory!"—"Keep it all," Debussy said and closed the door. But René stayed; he was just what Debussy needed, and during those years when Debussy felt lonely and abandoned, became one of his closest friends.

From their discussions of literature, Peter was surprised to learn that Debussy must have read all of Balzac, but did not like Dumas *père*, and felt that Victor Hugo's works had "a bit of parade" in them. Debussy loved Dickens and was annoyed by the disdain in which a certain class of English society held their national writer. He admired him more than Thackeray. *Bleak House*, in his opinion, was one of Dickens' greatest novels and he never tired of re-reading *The Pickwick Papers*, *Dombey and Son* and *The Old Curiosity Shop*.

Debussy insisted that there was something of Sophocles in *The Old Curiosity Shop*, particularly in the idea that the old bric-a-brac merchant, ruined by gambling, and Nelly, his granddaughter, decide to abandon their shop and their dishonest clients, to go begging on the street, "free at last," and that at the end of their journey little Nell feels she is going to die and is very happy. This, he thought, was an admirable dénouement and made him think of

Oedipus, only with the roles inverted—it is not the mistaken old man, but Antigone who is happy in the serenity of death.

Debussy sometimes recited the description of little Nell's last hours almost by heart, just as at other times he would rage about the room quoting from *Dombey and Son*. "Let him remember it in that room, years to come! The rain that falls upon the roof, the wind that mourns outside the door, may have foreknowledge in their melancholy sound. Let him remember it in that room, years to come!" For while reading about inflicted pain, Debussy suffered physically, Peter observed, "as if it were done to him, and he rebelled against injustice imposed by brute force on those weaker in combat"—a curious revelation, in view of Debussy's personal relationships, as we shall see.

Debussy loved children's books with illustrations. Nothing, he found, was as restful. His active mind could never be at a standstill and to do nothing was irritating, but "to let a tired soul reincarnate, so to speak, in a child's world—it is refreshing," he said. "Afterwards, my brain is again in order, like a room that is well swept." He would read Andersen's fairy tales before starting on a work by Tolstoy or Schopenhauer.

René Peter showed him the manuscript of his novel *La Tragédie de la mort*, and Debussy took such an interest in it that he did all he could to help with its publication. He enlisted Louÿs's influence with the committee of the *Mercure de France* and plagued Louÿs so long for a preface to Peter's novel that it almost caused a quarrel between the two old friends. Later, when the book was to be adapted for the stage, René asked Debussy for a short piece of music to accompany the scene between the mother and her dying child. Without the usual argument Debussy agreed to compose a berceuse, and if a long time passed before René received the piece, it was only because Debussy took his contribution most seriously.

This was the first Peter–Debussy collaboration. It was based on a different relationship than that of Debussy and Louÿs. Although René Peter and Louÿs were of the same age, in their relations with Debussy Louÿs was the dominating figure, often as unreliable as he was despotic, while Peter's adolescent admiration persisted from the first days of their acquaintance and placed Debussy in the position of mentor to an apprentice. Indeed, Debussy not only advised René in the revision of his novel, but actually, during the following four years, twice a week gave Peter "lessons" in drama writing, not of the accepted style and form, which Debussy held in utter contempt, but of his own.

Their friendship, not as intimate as that of Debussy with Louÿs, was spurred by the particular situation in Debussy's domestic affairs, rather than based on common intellectual ground. Debussy was lonely and restless and, except for an occasional game of bezique with Gaby, looked for diversion in his nocturnal visits to cafés, and René was his constant companion.

The Chez Weber dominated the third café period in Debussy's history. The topographical location of Chez Weber on rue Royale, near the Madeleine, amply spoke of its clientele's superior social position to those of the Chat Noir and Chez Pousset—everybody who was anybody in the arts or literature sooner or later passed through the door of Chez Weber. Like different factions at a world congress, they gathered in groups at tables specially reserved for them: the literati, the painters, musicians, and even politicians. On one night or another one was sure to see Léon Daudet, Charles Maurras, the painter Paul Robert, the famous caricaturist J. L. Forain, the poets P. J. Toulet and Jean de Tinan, Reynaldo Hahn and Marcel Proust, André Tardieu, Charles de Chambrun and Léon Blum. Occasionally Whistler would be looking for Pierre Louÿs, or Oscar Wilde would come in to order a glass and a bottle of Vichy water to refresh the sunflower (*la fleur alchimique et solaire*) which he carried in his hand like a little sacrament of nature. Marcel Proust usually arrived around seven thirty in the evening to "partake of a few grapes and a glass of water," gravely announcing that he had just got up, that he had a cold and a headache, that the noise made him sick and he was going back to bed, and, after throwing a few glances of utter contempt at his fellow citizens, remained till the early hours of the morning.

Debussy strolled in "after dinner." He did not join any of the groups, not even when such a subject as the Dreyfus case would unite them in furious discussions. Debussy was not interested and did not take at that time a definite stand in the "affair" that troubled the mind of every other French citizen. He sympathized with Lieutenant-Colonel Picquard, because "among all these ugly people here is one who likes arts and music," he said, but after hearing Jean Jaurès, the famous socialist, he asked René Peter to drink a toast with him to the prisoner on Devil's Island.

On opening the evening paper he always bought at the same newsstand near the Madeleine, Debussy skipped the political news section, skimmed through the theatrical and music page, carefully folded the paper and, after putting it into his coat pocket with "I'll read it later," ordered Welsh rarebit with a glass of English pale ale. Debussy never took part in gossip. He was indifferent to "other people's business," and if he was forced to listen to a long adventure he might, with a distant look in his eyes, say "Just imagine! ..." and with this dismiss the matter.

Marcel Proust was his admirer and once managed to drive Debussy home in his carriage, which always stood waiting for him at the door. Of this tête-à-tête both men retained different souvenirs. Proust complained that Debussy did not listen to him and missed the subtle and profound ideas he was delivering, while Debussy thought Proust was long-winded, condescending, and a bit of a concierge. Proust invited him to his house, to a party he would give in his honor with a few interesting friends, artists and people of "the best company," but Debussy refused to be honored. "You know, I am a bear. I much prefer we see each other again in a café. Don't hold it against me, I was born this way."

But "in a café" he would not be drawn into the discussions of the latest theatrical production, or music, or literary work. He would much rather play a game of his own invention. It consisted of guessing a person's character, occupation, and social position from the way he looked and behaved at the table, without hearing a single spoken word. Debussy called this sort of amusement "lifting the mask of false humanity" and René Peter was his faithful partner.

Sometimes, when an evening at Chez Weber seemed dull, Debussy and Peter would move next door to a little bar, Reynolds. There they were sure to find plenty of "human material who have taken off their masks." These were the clowns from the Nouveau Cirque, jockeys and the dancers who used to come there after their shows. It was noisy and gay and Debussy enjoyed conversing with them because they did not know who he was.

"Well, well, monsieur is an artist, perhaps?" Footit, the famous clown, asked, as he joined Debussy and Peter at their table.

"But you are also ... I think—" Debussy started.

"Oh no, I am a clown."

"That is also an art."

"An art of receiving kicks and doing pirouettes."

"We the musicians, we also do pirouettes and we also receive kicks, but with us it is either our reputation or our public who gives them. ... And you at least know how to fall back on your feet without hurting yourself, while we ..."

"But you have the glory."

"Yes, when it comes ... and even then it is open to question. ..."

"Oh, well. Everyone knows *Carmen* and *Mignon*."

"Do you know who wrote them?"

"Why ... Gounod."

"That's it! That's exactly what I meant. The glory, yes, it consists of being ignored by thirty million Frenchmen ... as well as Englishmen ... and detested by some forty fellow artists. ... What will you have to drink?"

They would remain there until the closing hour. The lights were put out, the first vegetable carts on their way to the market passed them as they started for home. The distant song of a bird would stop Debussy. "Listen to the lovely sound of the dawn. It is fresh, it sings. ... What a joyous festival ... while awaiting the great definitive rest. ..."

Debussy knew he led an aimless life and it seemed there was nothing he could do about it. Occasionally he gave a piano lesson or coached a singer. Twice a week he went to his friends, the Lucien Fontaines, where he conducted an amateur chorus. He even composed the first two of the three *Chansons de Charles d'Orléans* for the group, but it bored him. Madame Fontaine asked him to write some music for a pantomime for her. For a while he toyed with the idea—he felt he should do it because of their friendship, then he gave it up.

Days and weeks went by, monotonous in their similarity, without any apparent hope for change. At about this time, with René Peter and his friends, Debussy met a young woman who was working in one of the *maisons de couture*. Rosalie Texier had been in Paris for two years. She came from Bichain (near Villeneuve-la-Guyard, Yonne), a little village in Burgundy, two hours away, where her father was the railroad stationmaster. She was frail and beautiful but provincial, and Debussy thought she was *gnangnan* and he liked to imitate her little mannerisms. She took his teasing good-naturedly. They were not particularly attracted to each other. She preferred Gaby and Gaby liked her. The two became close friends. Occasionally Debussy was seen with Gaby and Mlle. Texier, or later on with Mlle. Texier alone, but no one thought much about it. Mlle. Texier was a friend of Debussy's friend Gaby.

When, in March 1899, Pierre Louÿs returned from his last trip to Algeria he found that Debussy had moved from rue Gustave Doré. His new apartment was at 58 rue Cardinet on the fifth floor with a small balcony facing the street, and Gaby was no longer with him. Gaby had left, this time for good, but where she went and how she lived became a mystery like her first meeting with Debussy. Over twenty years later Alfred Cortot, the pianist, recognized Gaby at the Grand Théâtre in Rouen dressed in the pinafore of a humble working woman. Gaby had been offered large sums for the letters, manuscripts and her souvenirs of the great musicians of her time, but nothing would make her part with them. There is one manuscript, however, now in a private collection, that bears Gaby's name —either it never reached her or she was willing to make it an exception. But in my story I have not yet come to this last facet of her relationship with Debussy.

Debussy did not see much of Louÿs, for although he was in Paris the windows of his apartment did not show any lights for many weeks. Louÿs was going through what he called a "volcanic" period, and he promised to explain everything in a short while. And indeed, ten days later, he announced to Debussy that "because of her love for a rich rhyme, inherited, no doubt, from her father, Mlle. Louise de Hérédia is changing her name to Louise Louÿs, which is more symmetrical and has more equilibrium."

In 1894, when Louÿs reached the last of his fatal "three years," Debussy had agreed to compose a funeral march worthy of his stature. Now, in the spring of 1889, Louÿs asked Debussy to write two hundred bars of music for organ, a piece "pompous, lustful and ejaculatory in character" to be played at his wedding at the Saint-Philippe church.

"You wouldn't refuse your old comrade this, would you?" Pierre Louÿs wrote, as if he were afraid of Debussy's usual arguments about the respectability of the performance of his work. Debussy did not refuse, and in his letter of congratulation there was a touch of envy. "If the piece will not be beautiful, it will at least be fraternal and accompanied by the inevitable emotion of a debut, expressing feelings so far unexplored by me. I am afraid it is my old bond with *Music* that prevents me from marrying!"

Did Debussy fear that with Louÿs's marriage he was going to lose his last friend? The man who said that he abhorred sentimentality begged Louÿs to give him his inkstand as a souvenir.

"Here is the inkstand out of which all my books were written. I am very touched by your asking me. I am delighted to give it to you. Your friendship filled my bachelor days. It still reserves for us many long hours, isn't this true? I love you," Louÿs wrote in a note accompanying the gift.

But Louÿs's happiness left him little time for Debussy, and Debussy felt it. Was the year of 1899 predestined to be the year of decision for both of them? Debussy had not found "the dream of his dreams," but the more he mused about his lonely existence the more the idea of marrying Mlle. Texier took on a vivid reality. He was even ready to forgive her "not quite bourgeois past," as he magnanimously referred to her love affair with a young businessman when Debussy first met her. Lily-Lilo, as he had been calling her for some time, was afraid it would not work out. She certainly had good reason to think so, but when Debussy wrote her that he would commit suicide unless ... she agreed. They were married on October 19, 1899. Louÿs, Satie and Fontaine witnessed the ceremony and left the two to have their nuptial luncheon by themselves, as Lily asked.

But if Debussy's love for unresolved chords extended beyond his musical scores, he made at least one exception. Whether before his wedding or after, during the same months of October he wrote this inscription on the first sketch of *L'Après-midi d'un Faune*: "*À ma chere et très bonne petite Gaby, la sûre affection de son dévoué Claude Debussy.*" Perhaps Gaby, undoubtedly feeling that "enough is enough," came to fetch her things and Debussy then presented her with the score as an "adieu" gift. Or perhaps Debussy, ("clearing the decks" for a new life) had a fleeting, remorseful feeling toward his behavior with Gaby and meant to leave this for future reference—this cannot be ascertained, for nothing further to illuminate his gesture has been recorded.

Otherwise Debussy was hardly well prepared for the momentous event. His parents were against his marrying Lily. To them it was a "misalliance," ridiculous as this may sound, and Debussy did not tell them of his marriage until a year later.

According to an accepted story, on the morning of their wedding Debussy gave a piano lesson so that he could pay for their first meal. They returned to rue Cardinet without a cent to start "a new life." It was not new and it was *du même au même* in more than one respect, as Lily learned only too soon, but there was *Pelléas* and "I will be rich when my *Pelléas* will be played."

"Please remain seated," Debussy warned as he was about to break the latest news to his old friend Robert Godet. "Mlle. Lily Texier has changed her disharmonious name to Lily Debussy, much more euphonious, as everyone will agree,"—imitating Louÿs's announcement of his own wedding; he went on: "She is incredibly blond, beautiful as in a legend, and she adds to her virtues that she is not in the least 'modern style' [in English in the original]. She does not like the kind of music 'Willy' H.G.V.[1] approves, but has a taste of her own: her favorite song is a roundelay about a 'little grenadier' with a red face who wears his cap over one ear like an old trouper.... It is inoffensive and not very provoking esthetically."

Debussy did not need to make excuses for Lily. Anyone could see that he had married neither a princess nor an intellectual giant. He married a simple, provincial, beautiful girl who apparently cared enough for him to take his threat of suicide seriously and whose devotion to him from the first days of their life together gained her the respect of all his friends. She was a real woman, a better wife than many a man can boast. Debussy seemed to be happy. He spoke of working again, of completing the new version of the three *Nocturnes* and *La Saulaie*. He saw a great beauty in Rossetti's poem, great possibilities for a musical composition, but he had lost the habit of working. His financial situation without any prospect of improvement weighed heavily on his mind—in "the little Debussys' existence there was more love than beefsteak," he confessed. Debussy did not know how to get started on his work. Everything served as an excuse for further delay. The production of *Pelléas* was going to change everything, he hoped, but meanwhile the premiere of Charpentier's *Louise* at the Opéra Comique and its general acclaim plunged him into an even deeper depression.

Both Louÿs and Debussy, although not sitting together, were at the dress rehearsal and both came away indignant. Louÿs reported to Debussy that he would have booed the opera had he not been a guest of Charpentier's friend, that Mendès came up to tell him that "the opera was admirable, a historical event, etc., etc., etc.," adding that "Debussy should do something similar," but that d'Indy, in a pathological state of fury, walked out slamming the doors, and that he heard that Massenet after reading the score refused to listen to such garbage.

"It seems to me necessary that this work should have been written, produced and acclaimed. It supplies only too well the need for that cheap beauty and idiotic art that has such appeal," Debussy

[1] Henri Gauthier-Villars.

raged. "You see what Charpentier has done. He has taken the *Cris de Paris* which are so delightfully picturesque and human, and like a filthy Prix de Rome he has turned them into sickly cantilenas with harmonies—to be polite I will call them parasitic. But by God, it's a thousand times more conventional than *Les Huguenots,* using, although it does not appear so, the same technique. And they call this Life! Good God! I'd sooner die right now. What you have here is something of the feeling after the twentieth half-pint, and the sloppiness of a *Monsieur* who returns home at four in the morning, falling all over the cleaning woman and garbage man. And this man imagines that he can express the soul of the poor!!!! It's so silly that it's pitiful. Of course M. Mendès discovers his Wagner in it and M. Bruneau his Zola. And they call it a true French work! There is something wrong if you add all this up. It's more silly than harmful. But then, people don't very much like things that are beautiful—they are so far from their nasty little minds. With many more works like *Louise,* any attempt to drag them out of the mud will completely fail.

"I assure you that I'd rather have *Pelléas* played in Japan, for our fashionable eclectics might approve of it—and I can tell you that I would be ashamed."

To aggravate Debussy's gloom further, two months later Georges Hartmann, his publisher, died. During the past seven years Debussy had received a monthly allowance of five hundred francs as an advance on royalties from his work. But Debussy's published works did not cover the advanced sum at any time, nor had Debussy supplied Hartmann with any new compositions during the last three years. Hartmann was going to publish *Palléas,* but the score was still on Debussy's desk, still far from being completed. Hartmann left his business affairs in disorder, with a certain General Bourjat as the executor of his will. The General demanded an immediate settlement of his business—that is, the reimbursement of the money Debussy owed Hartmann, threatening him with court proceedings. There was nothing Debussy could do about it.

Was it because he had become disillusioned during the last two years about the fate of his compositions, with Hartmann's death dimming the hope for further publications, that Debussy decided to try his hand in a purely dramatic field? Or was it because of his friendship with René Peter, to whom he gave lessons in drama writing? In either case, at this time when he could not bring himself to compose, Debussy actually worked on a play in collaboration with his "pupil," entitled *Brothers in Art*.

In the plot of this dramatic satire, mostly conceived by Debussy, the sinister character of a famous but lecherous painter finds the way through his important position in the league of "Brothers in Art" not only to prevent other talented painters from achieving success, but to compromise the honor of his favorite pupil's young wife. Debussy used Lily and himself as models. Since Debussy himself wrote the entire second scene of the play it is an interesting document, perhaps as valuable as his letters, where he lets a stranger see at least some part of his intimate life and hear him speak his ideas and convictions aloud.

The scene is laid in the Maltravers's garret studio. As the curtain rises, Maltravers draws Marie, who works near a window. Raland, the sculptor, paces up and down the room: he is rolling a piece of clay in his hand and whistles a song by Rollinat.

MALTRAVERS *(to Raland)*: What are you thinking about?

RALAND: Nothing. *(Silence.)* What a musician, this Rollinat!

MALTRAVERS: No ... what a poet!

RALAND: Oh? *(Silence. He goes to a bench. He looks into a tobacco box.)* Look, there is no more tobacco. . . .

MALTRAVERS: My dear man, Marie has no shoes!

RALAND: Damn it! It's about time for this league of "Brothers in Art" to do something. . . .

MALTRAVERS: Why?

RALAND: Why? Because I am too fat. I suffocate here.

MALTRAVERS: You have a wonderful reason. If all your reasoning is as strong, I suggest you make a piece of art out of it. . . .

RALAND: It is all very well for the two of you to be like little coffee buns. But it's different with me. I should whistle and walk about like an elephant in the springtime! You, Maltravers, you can do and re-do the architecture of nothingness. Marie there can sew one dream after another with silk thread without any rest; this silent existence satisfies you. . . . But I, I need action, noise, I need people!

MALTRAVERS: You are not exactly a man of the garrets.

RALAND: What do you expect? I need space. Listen, I want to work in a marble quarry. From it I would bring out a crowd of torsos and rumps intermingled and unfolding themselves like the curves of the sea when she pretends to be wicked, and above all I want to do a statue of Fate. You will see what a menacing thing this will be.

MALTRAVERS: *(After a while)* Well . . . I see Fate smiling, but as a wound would smile at a knife! And isn't it logical, this smile? Doesn't she know that honest people build dreams to forget, some of them, their misery, others—their disappointments, and that she is there to do it over at her whim? Have you observed with what care she scatters the little white pebbles on the road that leads to misfortune so that people will not lose their way?

RALAND: The little white pebbles, these are the amateurs . . . because of baldness. . . .

MALTRAVERS: If you like. And isn't she there to serve the rogues? Because it seems as if she were invented especially for the rogues, this Fate; and this shows how much right she has to smile. Nevertheless, here is ten *sous* and I recommend the tobacco merchant downstairs. And while waiting for better times, rest assured that we love you here.

RALAND: Oh you, you are really an artist of the good old time! *(He leaves.)*

MALTRAVERS: Old fool, go! And to think that this man looks like an imbecile when he wants to and is a genius when he doesn't want to. . . . We are the poor little Buddhas who utter screams which we consider sublime and capable of changing whatever to whatever! We are nothing but the more or less delicate instruments which are directed by hands that came out of I-don't-know-what shadow, and we don't do anything but execute orders dictated by a mysterious power. *(He takes the drawing on which he was working and carefully studies it.)*

MARIE *(Comes quietly to her husband, stands back of him and looks over his shoulder. Then she gently takes his head into her hands and makes him look at her.)* Oh, how I love you!

MALTRAVERS: My darling! *(They kiss)* You see, you have something extraordinary. You are a delicious woman and nothing else.

MARIE: I am trying to make myself so small that I will not disturb the dreams of my big fool.

MALTRAVERS: Yes, you don't play the role of a Muse, that horrible scarecrow; you don't arrange your hair to imitate women on frescoes; you smell good and you are sweet like a peach, without bothering yourself with the latest success of Monsieur Houbigant; you don't dress yourself up, which saves time and which is, of course, my fault. . . .

MARIE: In short, I am perfect. . . .

MALTRAVERS: Oh no, thank God! You have faults in your qualities, but fortunately not the faults that make women so tired at the end of the day. A woman must remain a little girl, even when she has children of her own—first, to teach them to be children, and then to prevent them from becoming little bits of the calculating and administrative bourgeoisie. Just imagine Madame Durtel's children [according to René Peter Mme Durtel was the beautiful and coquettish wife of the artist powerful at the league of "Brothers in Art"]—that woman resembles an advertising billboard and speaks a mixture of salon *argot* and English.

MARIE: You must not say such bad things. After all, don't we owe him this league which is going to help us?

MALTRAVERS: Well, then, God help her not to resemble him! Her manners, her way of talking! . . .*(Imitating her)* 'This exhibition completely annihilated me . . . I am like a wheat field after a storm . . . like a wine merchant's bed . . . *broken down, my dear!*' [English in the original.] She should be whipped!

MARIE: You are going too far. . . .

MALTRAVERS: Well, after all she is only a painted doll who is useful to this old rascal Durtel.

MARIE: Oh, how you speak of him! He has good qualities. First of all he is very amiable ...

MALTRAVERS: Don't fall for it.

MARIE: And then, one can always get away from him. He and his league don't stand in the way of a beautiful dream.

MALTRAVERS: Durtel does not dream, except when he has an audience. You can be sure that if he has founded this league and taken up the *cause célèbre* "make place for the young," it is merely so that the old ones can ride them....

MARIE: Durtel is not old.

MALTRAVERS: Those who have succeeded are always old and the young ones always swallow the dream of Utopia. Poor things! ... they will come like fatalistic sheep to the slaughterhouse.

MARIE: I have confidence....

MALTRAVERS: That is fine! Confidence is a moral scarf which keeps your heart warm while awaiting the inevitable draft of air.

(Raland returns; he is smoking two cigarettes at the same time and makes enormous clouds of smoke.)

MALTRAVERS: *(To Raland)* So this is what you mean by domestic economy?

RALAND: *(With a sigh of satisfaction)* Ah ... now I feel better. Say, I have been thinking ... since you go every Sunday to the Lamoureux concerts, you certainly should know more about music than I do. From today on whenever I'll speak of Rollinat I am going to say: "What a poet!" But as a musician he has talent, doesn't he?

MALTRAVERS: You should lose this habit of speaking of talent with such vehemence. Really, when they use this word it seems to me as if I hear them speak of Mr. X's fortune. Talent! Actually it is only change from a coin ... and very often false! Talent ... it only serves to identify mediocrity. Would you ever think of saying that Michelangelo or Rodin had talent? Leave this word to the so-called amateurs of art; it is so simple for them to put everyone into the same salad basket, and particularly all those little ones—nobody is as wicked as the mediocre! And, of course, as they are the majority they are always right. We are dying and we will die because of Mediocrity! She has the force of inertia and adapts herself faithfully to so many people.... Don't laugh, it is very serious. If you think about it, one can make a social problem out of it. For instance, how do you expect a worker to make a beautiful piece of furniture since the invasion of "modern art"?—this style which imposes aggressive-looking chairs and pieces of furniture that frighten children, wallpaper which gives you nightmares? Even the door locks demand a special study to explain their enigma.

RALAND: Perhaps this may explain why so many people sleep under the bridges....

MALTRAVERS: It is not as far-fetched as you may think. Look, instead of the false "modern style" one might invent a "modern soup," where the poor people would find a real soup....

(Someone knocks on the door. Heldebrand enters.)

A director of one of the Paris theaters heard that René Peter was working on a play with Debussy—a musician whose opera had been accepted by the Opéra Comique—and he thought this so interesting that he, on the spot, commissioned the play for his theater. At first Debussy was pleased—"it certainly does not seem to resemble anything already known," he said.

But on second thought Debussy saw a certain amount of danger in this audacious enterprise, unless it was a masterpiece. And then there was still another aspect to consider—the play definitely had "social significance, perhaps [is] even a bit anarchistic," he remarked. And of course the obvious resemblance of the hero to one of the authors might cause an adverse public reaction. "We have to be careful, very careful..." Debussy said, after looking silently for a long time at his collaborator.

A few days later Debussy rejected the whole project. After the first excitement, he said, he was able to examine coolly the wisdom of such a step, as well as carefully to reappraise the merits of the play itself. It seemed to him that he had not made a sufficient study of the characters. "One does not invent, alas," he said.

He was sorry about disappointing René Peter. As for himself, he said with a shrug: "I am an old romantic who has thrown the worries of success out the window."

After Debussy's death the manuscript of the play was found in a secondhand bookstore. The entire play was in Debussy's handwriting, completed without his collaborator. René Peter saw the manuscript and said that "without artist's vanity he had to admit that this work did not belong to the list of Debussy's best."

Thus another Debussy project went overboard and at a time when he had no idea what was going to happen to *Pelléas,* when he had lost not merely his only assured income and his publisher, but every hope of finding another who would offer the same terms. "Destiny really is cruelly ironic to me! ... I found the only publisher who would adjust himself to my delicious little soul and he had to die!!! I am not wicked, but I could kick the whole Universe...."

Debussy's destiny was cruel enough to strike him once again and in a more vulnerable spot. During the month of August 1890 his "little Lily" had to be taken to a clinic, La Maison Dubois. Lily was operated on.

"But that was not all," Debussy wrote Louÿs. The doctors discovered that her organism was generally run down and "just between us," Debussy confided, "she has the beginning of tuberculosis in the tip of both lungs." This, Debussy was advised, should be treated without delay. Lily should be taken to the Pyrenees for at least three or four months. "You can imagine our sufferings, and if you would add to these the miserable financial situation that has been plaguing me for some time, you will understand that I am at a loss to know which way to turn."

CHAPTER XIII

DEBUSSY A MUSIC CRITIC—
LA REVUE BLANCHE

DEBUSSY HAD no means of taking Lily to the Pyrenees and Louÿs, the only friend who might have helped him, was not only sick himself far away in Spain, but had suffered from similar bad luck in his own matrimonial life. Madame Louÿs had to be hospitalized in Barcelona. "What poor little creatures are these women," Louÿs pondered. "If they don't marry, they become ill, so they say, because of their chastity. And when they try to have a child, it's even worse. . . ."

There was nothing Debussy could do but to take care of Lily as best as he could. Gradually, during the autumn, Lily's health began slowly to improve, although Debussy remained anxious—"her life hangs on something so frail and her whole system is completely shattered," he said. He practically never left her side and it was during these months that he forced himself to complete the first two of the three *Nocturnes*. The scheduled public performance of the *Nocturnes* was not an event, in Debussy's opinion, of any consequence in his artistic or financial affairs, and as his relationship with Hartmann's heirs was hopelessly entangled, for once Debussy was ready to accept Louÿs's latest proposition.

In debt, with a sick wife on his hands and no money to pay the rent, Debussy had no time to thrash out the old argument about "popular presentation" of his work and he agreed "to compose eight pages for violins, silences, and chords for brass instruments which would give what one calls 'the impression of art' " according to

Louÿs's prescription. These were for a selection out of Louÿs's *Chansons de Bilitis* to be "recited and mimed" at the Théâtre des Variétés after an initial performance at the Salle de Fêtes of the *Journal*, a Paris daily.

On December 9, 1900, the first two parts of Debussy's *Nocturnes* were played at a Concert Lamoureux and the performance scored a sensational success. No one could have been more surprised than Debussy himself. Practically all the reviewers joined in praising the work and at last spoke of the long overdue recognition of "an extraordinary musician in their midst." Even the most antagonistic among them who only recently had labeled Debussy's music as "the despair of the critics," and the kind that "defied analysis," suddenly changed their opinions and with boundless enthusiasm declared it to be "pure music, conceived beyond the limits of reality, in the world of dreams, amidst the ever-moving architecture that God builds with the mists, the marvelous creations of the impalpable realms. . . ." As though quoting Debussy, they stated that "M. Debussy does not demand of Music all that she can give, but rather, that which she *alone* is capable of suggesting. He looks upon music as the art of the inexpressible, whose role begins where inadequate words fail. . . ."

The composers, led by Paul Dukas, Debussy's old friend, and Alfred Bruneau, also wrote eulogies to the suddenly discovered great personality in the musical world. "The *Nocturnes*," Bruneau wrote, "recall the strange, delicate, vibrating 'Nocturnes' of Whistler, and like the canvases of the great American painter, they are full of deep and poignant poetry. . . ." And placing him in the very front rank of artists, Bruneau spoke at length about Debussy the man, who should at last be well known by the public.

This musician, whose works are rarely performed, is one of the most original and remarkable artistic personalities of the day. He is little known by the crowd, goes nowhere, composes, I fancy, only when he feels inclined, and lives like a recluse, scorning all noisy publicity. What an admirable and rare example! And what a lot of valuable time some men waste nowadays in preparing their publicity, writing and distributing notices that proclaim their own glory. Having shut himself up in this haughty seclusion, M. Debussy seems intent on expressing the transient impressions of the dream he is in quest of, rather than the eternal passions of the world which he shuns.

This testimony, although true in some respects, nevertheless showed how little even his close friends knew about his personal life. The irony of it may have amused Debussy, but this was the way he wanted to be. He waited for success to come to him; he would not seek it. Even during these months of dire necessity he was loath to reveal how badly he was in need of work that would pay him more than artistic praise.

"I hear that your friend Antoine is going to give *King Lear* at his theater," Debussy casually remarked to René Peter. "I imagine it will need some music. It would amuse me to do it, but, of course, much less than to go to see him and ask him about it.... Well, I thought, if you had an occasion ... But you must not, above all, tell him that I have asked you.... Tell him that this is your idea ... and only yours, you understand, so that he will not think that I am trying to approach him ... otherwise, I would just as soon give up the whole idea...."

André Antoine, the director of the Théâtre Libre, knew nothing about Debussy, though he remembered him as "the dark fellow who used to come to Chez Pousset with a woman with green eyes." —"Well, what? Is he also a genius?" Antoine asked Peter who was trying to arrange a meeting between the two. Debussy became very reluctant when Peter told him they could see Antoine in his dressing room during a performance. "I don't want to appear to beg. It is neither my genre nor my taste." But finally he let himself be persuaded.

There is no doubt that Debussy was not an ideal collaborator and perhaps his attitude, or lack of the right attitude, thwarted more than one project, but his negotiations with Antoine to write incidental music for Shakespeare's *King Lear*, as recorded by René Peter, seem to be characteristic.

Debussy went out of his way to make clear to Antoine that it was he, Antoine, who wanted him to write the music.

"This is of no importance," Antoine said. "I have to be on the stage in ten minutes. . . . You'll excuse me if I speak frankly? Well, I don't understand a thing in music; it bores me. I consider musicians utter bores . . . not all of them, but most are bores both as musicians and as men. You understand? Excuse me—this is to explain to you why when I thought of doing *King Lear,* it did not occur to me to occupy myself with this detail. But, *en principe,* only of course on one condition, that it will not take much space, that it will not disturb the text and that it will not distract attention. . . . It's something to think about. There are even some people who might be amused by it. . . . Not me, not me! It's just like your Wagner. . . ."

"Oh! *my* Wagner!" Debussy protested, ready to leave.

But Antoine said he liked the idea—"I like your name, it will look very artistic on the program. For the rest I depend on you. But don't cram it too full. You have a good six months to do it in. Good-bye!" And Antoine excused himself, going to get dressed for his entrance.

King Lear was one of many projects never to materialize. How much work Debussy did on the score will never be known, except for a rough draft in pencil of the *Fanfare* (for three trumpets, four horns, two harps, three kettle-drums and one drum), and *Le Sommeil de Lear,* a *berceuse* (for flute, horn, harp and strings).[1]

From his further relationship with Antoine a letter has survived in which Debussy told him that it was impossible to have the score ready for the agreed date, and that he would need at least a thirty-piece orchestra—"otherwise we shall have a miserable little noise, a sound like flies rubbing their legs together. . . ." Most probably Debussy waited for Antoine's next move, and Antoine, on the other hand, expected Debussy to bring him the score. By the time they reached this stage in their "negotiations," Peter could not serve as intermediary—the "stormy events" in Debussy's personal life during the following years had blown their friendship out of existence.

The music to accompany Louÿs's *Chansons de Bilitis* had a dif-

---

[1] Completed at a later date and posthumously published in October, 1926.

ferent fate. Debussy wrote the score (for two flutes, two harps and celesta), and attended many unsatisfactory rehearsals with the models engaged to represent the ten songs, "some of them draped in veils, others without anything on except their two hands and a posture—three quarters in reverse," as Louÿs described it. The scheduled spectacle again aroused the wrath of Senator Béranger. The performance, nevertheless, took place on February 7 before a selected audience of three hundred, but it neither created the sensation of a scandal, as Louÿs anticipated, nor gave any valuable publicity to Debussy. "Graceful music, ingeniously archaic, composed by M. de Bussy, Prix de Rome...." was the way Debussy was referred to in the *Journal*'s notice [1] of the event, as if it was still 1891 and not 1901 after the sensational success of his *Nocturnes*. The promised performances at the Théâtre des Variétés never did follow this one and only public audition (at the *Journal* they even claimed that there was no record of this performance), and later Debussy used some of the written score for the six *Épigraphes antiques* (piano four-hand, since orchestrated by Ernest Ansermet).

Except for the time wasted on rehearsals, Debussy, needless to say, did not regret the sudden collapse of Louÿs's latest project. "Life is too short for joy and too long for trouble," he said as he thought again of the success of his *Nocturnes*, hoping that it might still prove to be the turning point of his career.

Even though at first there were no signs of any radical change of his situation, judging by the inscription on the score of the *Nocturnes*, Debussy seemed to have greeted the New Year of 1901 in a happy frame of mind. "This manuscript belongs to my little Lily-Lilo. All rights are reserved. It is a proof of the deep and passionate joy I have in being her husband. Claude Debussy—at the peep of January, 1901." Two months later, most probably through Louÿs's intervention in his behalf (Louÿs was an old friend of the publisher and the editors), Debussy was asked to write musical criticism for the *Revue Blanche*, a magazine of a limited circulation but with a certain prestige in literary and artistic circles.

---

[1] *Le Journal*, February 8, 1901.

This provided him with a forum far more appropriate for the expression of his views in the field of his knowledge than the one he attempted to challenge with his dramatic play. He managed, however, to include almost verbatim some of its ideas. Debussy made his debut as a music critic in April, 1901:

Having been invited to speak of music in this magazine, may I explain in a few words the way in which I intend to do it? In this space you will find sincere impressions actually experienced, rather than criticisms. These resemble much too often brilliant variations on a theme: 'You are wrong, because you don't do as I do,' or else 'You have talent, I have none; this cannot continue any longer....' I am going to try to discover in works the various impulses that gave them birth, and what they contain of inner life—far more interesting than the game which consists in taking them to pieces, as though they were watches of curious construction.

People seldom remember that as children they were forbidden to open the inside of dolls (surely in itself already a crime against mystery), they still insist on sticking their esthetic noses where they have no business. If they no longer demolish the dolls, they explain, they take them to pieces, and thus kill the mystery in cold blood. It is more convenient; moreover, it gives them something to talk about. My Lord, utter ignorance may excuse some, to be sure; but others, more vicious, do harm with premeditated malice. These dear little mediocrities should be defended at all costs ... they have the support of a faithful little clique.

I will speak little of works well established either by success or by tradition. Once for all—Meyerbeer, Thalberg, Reyer...are men of genius; otherwise it is of no importance.

On Sundays, when the good Lord is kind, I am not going to listen to any music. I am making my excuses in advance.... And finally I should like to insist on the use of this term *Impressions*, which I value because it enables me to shield my emotions from any parasitic esthetics.

During the following eight months Debussy contributed eight articles, either covering musical events or on music in general. They were written in a sort of loosely connected bantering style, marked with bitter sarcasm. Debussy language may have been considered picturesque—still it was baroque and old-fashioned. Debussy loved to write: he enjoyed writing letters and he enjoyed writing reviews and articles. But he was not a music critic in our sense of the word. If it were ever discovered that he was well acquainted with Bernard Shaw's music criticism one might then have the key to their kinship, except that Debussy knew more about music than Shaw.

His column often dealt with extraneous aspects of the performance—the looks or behavior of the interpreters on the stage, cleverly depicted to be sure, but out of place in a serious review. The articles reflected not so much his *Impressions* as his theories, and having been given a pulpit, he preached (and not without venom) against not only masterpieces and their creators but "the Holy of Holies." At last he had an opportunity to harangue against established reputations, accepted rules and traditions, and while cloaked in mockery and exaggeration, often unfair and contradictory, his remarks were sincere and not entirely lacking in wisdom.

"I love music too much to be able to speak of it otherwise than with passion," he asserted with defiance. "Shall I even succeed in avoiding that faint suggestion of bias which colors the best of motives and causes the most convinced advocate to lose his head? I dare not hope it."

Wagner was his *bête noire* and he went out of his way rather than miss an opportunity to berate the composer's works. He would say that Wagner's music was irresistible as the sea and in the next breath say that Isolde sounds like a cat in heat. He said that *Parsifal* was a masterpiece—that is, the music only—and when he had to review a Wagner program he was annoyed by the audience's enthusiasm: he hated Wagnerism more than Wagner. "This persistent delirium . . . God forgive me, but it was enough to make you believe that all those people were the more-or-less natural offspring of Ludwig of Bavaria." He considered it a form of snobbery: "Two and a half hours of music [*Rheingold* in concert form] during which you are torn between a natural inclination to go away and a desire to sleep after having politely begged your neighbor to wake you at the last bar, to join in the applause. Irony apart, this is the attitude of many well-bred people. They submit with more or less elegance to being bored, and if they do not go away it is because they must appear eloquent and well-informed. Otherwise, what object would they have in coming?"

And when he suggested that *The Ring* should be performed at the Opéra he made it clear that its purpose would be "thus to be rid of it—the pilgrims of Bayreuth would no more worry us with their German *gasonades*."

As if the event were especially contrived to irritate him, the Berlin Philharmonic Orchestra under the direction of Arthur Nikisch came that spring to Paris to commemorate Wagner's anniversary. Before he gave the German musicians their due for impeccable execution, Debussy said that it was sufficient to have elegant poses and a lock of hair, romantically tousled, to assure success with the Parisian audience and Nikisch had both.

He was no less critical of "domestic" affairs in French musical life. He spoke at length about the "curious institution situated in the Place de l'Opéra. The Paris Opera house," he said, "for a man who was not properly warned, resembles a railway station and the inside—a Turkish bath establishment, a place where they keep on making a strange noise which the people who have paid for it call music. . . . You must not altogether believe them. Thanks to special privileges and State subsidiaries anything may be produced at this theater. It matters little that the boxes are installed with carefully thought-out luxury—'loges à salons,' called this way because there one may sit in comfort and hear nothing of music; they are the last salons where conversation is still indulged in. In all this I do not blame the genius of the directors, since I am convinced that the best will would encounter a solid wall of stubborn officialdom through which no searchlight could penetrate. Nothing short of fire or revolution would bring a change, but even the revolutionists never bother about these monuments. Yet, what beautiful things could be done there. . . ."

Debussy repeated, now in print, everything he had said already so many times about the Conservatory, the Institut des Beaux Arts and the Prix de Rome, and he gave his opinion about "concerts in the open air." "These," he said, "should be in keeping with the natural scenery." Why, he asked, should military bands monopolize the squares? "I can imagine music specially designed for the open air, all on big lines, with daring instrumental and vocal effects which would have full play in the open and soar joyfully to the treetops. Certain harmonic progressions which sound abnormal within the four walls of a concert hall would surely find their value in the open air. Perhaps this might be a means of doing away with these little affectations of overprecision in form and tonality which so encumber music. Thus art might find regeneration and learn the beautiful lesson of freedom from the efflorescence of the trees. Would it not gain in grandeur anything that it might lose in charm of detail? It should be understood that vastness of effect should be aimed at and not bulk. Neither should one weary the echoes with the repetition of excessive sounds. One should rather make use of them in order to prolong the harmonious dream.

"So, the very air, the movement of the leaves and the perfume of flowers would work together in mysterious union with the music, which would thus bring all the elements into such natural harmony that it would seem to form a part of each.... In this way it could be proved without a doubt that music and poetry, alone of the arts, dwell in space.... I may be mistaken, but it is my belief that this idea will be the dream of future generations. In our day music will, I fear, continue to be rather stuffy."

And Debussy repeated again that in his opinion art cannot be reduced to the level of a mere intellectual trick—"Art is the most beautiful deception; and no matter how much a man may wish to make it the setting for his daily life, he must still desire that it remain an illusion lest it become utilitarian, and as dreary as a workshop. Do not the masses as well as the select few seek therein oblivion, in itself a form of deception? The smile of Mona Lisa probably never really existed—still its charm is eternal. Let us then avoid disillusioning anyone by clothing the dream with too much reality."

These interesting remarks were interspersed into his reviews, which invariably began with a complaint, almost a yawn, that it was a lovely day outside, the sun was shining and it was a crime to sit and listen to what ... to music, played by whom?

Fortunately before he wrote his third article he was reminded once again that his true calling was that of a composer. "As you are after all ... my old Pierre," Debussy wrote Louÿs, "I don't want you to learn through a stranger that: *I have a written promise from M. A. Carré that he will present 'Pelléas et Mélisande'* during the next season of the Opéra Comique."

This meant a great deal of work—he had not completed the orchestration. Yet the short time left before the rehearsals were to begin would not accelerate his pace. He worked slowly and in the first days of August (1901) took the score along to Bichain where, near his parents-in-law, Lily and he had been renting a small house for their summers. But the end of the month brought the end to his concentration on *Pelléas*. He had had enough of it and after reading Pierre Louÿs's recently published *Le Roi Pausole* decided he should compose a symphonic suite based on this work.

"For a long time I have been walking in the company of this little neurotic Mélisande, who cannot stand violins unless they are divided in eighteen parts (she is so frail)," Debussy wrote Louÿs, "and suddenly she said to me: 'Last night I dreamed of Roi Pausole. He is a remarkable man and you should compose a symphony for his royal personage where you would bring to life his travels to recover things that were never lost....'"

This last attempt at a Pierre Louÿs–Claude Debussy collaboration, the first of Debussy's own choice, was forgotten soon after Debussy's return to Paris. He had neither the time nor peace of mind because of all the annoyance, he said to Louÿs, "which represents to me that place called the Opéra Comique."

CHAPTER XIV

PELLÉAS ET MÉLISANDE

"How will the world get along with these two poor creatures?"
Debussy had written to Lerolle in 1894. "...They are so difficult
to introduce into the world..." he had complained to Ysaÿe in
1896. For ten years these were Debussy's thoughts about *Pelléas
et Mélisande* and there is no doubt, now that the opportunity had
finally arrived, that his sole concern was with the best possible way
of presenting his work. He certainly had not the slightest premonition of the "drama" his opera would cause even before the curtain
rose for the dress rehearsal, a "drama" which involved two beautiful, ambitious and jealous prima donnas, their lovers, and Debussy,
implicated only because of this concern with the forthcoming production.

The two prima donnas, Georgette Leblanc and Mary Garden,
have both written their memoirs and have stated the case, each
according, I presume, "to her best knowledge and belief," as contra-
dictorily as one would expect. Of these two accounts of the story,
Georgette Leblanc's, written some twenty years after the events
took place, is shorter and calmer, as befits the loser in a contest,
while Mary Garden's, as told from a memory of fifty years, is so
emotional—perhaps understandably—and so vague about dates,
that it can serve only as an illustration of the characters entangled
in an intrigue that gave Debussy an unnecessary headache.

Both women were singers well known to the audiences of the
Opéra Comique, and both were closely connected with Albert Carré,
the director, and André Messager, the conductor, who had the de-

cisive voices in choosing the cast. Mary Garden had had a two-year-long love affair with Messager and says in her memoirs that Carré had asked her to marry him. Georgette Leblanc had recently married Maeterlinck and in her story insinuates that Carré was not entirely indifferent to her. Such were the cast and the aphrodisiac atmosphere into which Debussy stepped with his score of *Pelléas et Mélisande*.

According to Leblanc—and it does not sound improbable—during or at the end of the summer of 1901, Debussy went to see Maeterlinck, who was then living in Paris on rue Raynouard in Passy. While Debussy played his score, Maeterlinck smoked his pipe and, having neither understanding nor interest in music, fell half asleep from boredom. Behind Debussy's back Georgette Leblanc made a desperate effort to keep her husband awake. Before Debussy left, they spoke of possible choices for the roles and Leblanc expressed her ardent desire to sing Mélisande. Maeterlinck agreed and Debussy was "enchanted." They arranged immediately to study together, and they did—two or three times at the Maeterlincks' and twice at Debussy's apartment on rue Cardinet. Debussy seems to have been perfectly satisfied with Leblanc.

Meanwhile, an important conference was held at the Café Weber between Carré, Messager and Debussy. Many names were suggested and discarded in connection with the casting, and whether because they were reminded of a similar situation when Carré and Messager had spent months searching for the right person to play *Louise* before they discovered Mlle. Marthe Rioton, or for more personal reasons, Carré brought up the name of Garden and her sensational debut while substituting for Rioton, who fell ill during a performance of *Louise*. Debussy knew nothing about Mary Garden, but Carré insisted: "I think even her charming inexperience is an asset in this case."

Thereupon it was arranged for the cast to meet Debussy at Messager's apartment and to hear his work. "Debussy played his score and sang all the parts in that deep, sepulchral voice of his, but with an expression that grew more and more irresistible," Messager said. "The impression produced by his music that day was, I think, a unique experience. At first, there was an atmosphere of mistrust and antagonism; then gradually the attention of the hearers was caught and held; little by little emotion overcame them; and the last notes of Mélisande's death scene fell amidst silence and tears." Mary Garden says that she burst into "the most awful sobbing," and Madame Messager began to sob along with her, and both of them fled into the next room.

On January 13 the rehearsals began and a few days later Maeterlinck read in the newspapers the name of Mary Garden as Mélisande and not that of his wife, Georgette Leblanc. Enraged—he was going to stop the production—Maeterlinck appealed to the *Société des Auteurs,* basing his complaint on the fact that the registration of *Pelléas* at the Society on December 30, 1901, was illegal, since it did not have his signature, and reserving all rights regarding the performance until he should be given the list of the cast for his approval. Called on for an explanation, Debussy quoted Maeterlinck's written authorization dated October 19, 1895, giving him the right to produce the opera "when, how and wherever" he liked. And as for Maeterlinck's assertion that only a few months previously Debussy had agreed to give Lablanc the role of Mélisande, Debussy denied it, saying that he had not committed himself any further than the casual "we will see."

On February 7, following Maeterlinck's formal complaint, Victorien Sardou, then presiding over *La Commission des Auteurs,* summoned both parties for the committee's next session, and on the 14th of the same month Debussy declared his firm stand in regard to Garden. The *Commission* proposed that both sides submit to arbitration. Debussy accepted. Maeterlinck promised to give his answer, and a week later announced that he had decided to appeal to the courts, bringing the case also against Carré, whom he considered equally responsible. On February 27 the court decided in Debussy's favor on a purely legalistic basis.

Brandishing his cane, Maeterlinck told Leblanc that he would use it on Debussy "to teach him how to live," and as their apartment was on the street level, walked out of the window with the air of a crusader on his way to revenge. Debussy took refuge in an armchair when the unexpected guest entered his apartment and Lily rushed to him with the smelling salts. She begged the poet to leave. What else could he do, Maeterlinck said later, "All crazy, all sick, these musicians!"

But Maeterlinck was not through. Leblanc was worried that Debussy would send his seconds to Maeterlinck, and Maeterlinck threatened to challenge Carré to a duel. Debussy had betrayed him, Maeterlinck raved. But the true villain was Carré who, he said, was taking vengeance on Leblanc because a few years previously, when Leblanc sang *Carmen* at the Opéra Comique, she had refused to become his mistress.

Debussy had no intention of fighting a duel, he had far more serious things on his mind. The rehearsals began in the middle of January and for three and a half months continued till the day of the performance—forty-one rehearsals with the cast, not counting those with the orchestra alone. Soon the initial enthusiasm began to sag. Debussy had left the copying of the orchestra parts to an inexperienced musician, a piano student, who though conscientiously counting all the "rests" would forget to mark the changes in meter and tonality and often simply mistook sharps for flats. This caused frequent interruptions during the rehearsals and the orchestra men rebelled. "A despicable pack of hounds," Debussy growled, and himself tried to help, explain and correct wherever he could.

Some members of the orchestra, particularly from the brass section, were so moved by Mélisande's death scene that they would come up to Messager and say: "We have very little to do in this part, and we don't know how it sounds to you here at your desk, but when Arkel says 'If I were God I would have pity on men' . . . that is truly beautiful." But there was a large section of the cast and musicians who were tired out from the unusually long rehearsing and were getting bored.

To Debussy all this was mere detail. For Carré had asked him to write some more music for the entr'actes in order to give him time to change the scenery. It had to fit what was already written and not disturb the composition as a whole. When not at the theater, Debussy worked at his desk, while Messager kept sending letters and

Debussy at the age of thirteen.

Two wall plaques mark the apartment in Saint-Germain-en-Laye where Debussy was born.

Mme. Nadejda von Meck and two of
her daughters (Sonia is on the right).

Sonia von Meck at the age of sixteen.
*Two hitherto unpublished photo-
graphs from originals in the Tchaikowsky Museum at Klin, Russia.*

Mme. von Meck's trio—Vladislav Pakhulsky, Peter Danilchenko, and Claude Debussy. *An unpublished photograph from the Tchaikowsky Museum at Klin, Russia, taken in Italy in 1880.*

M. Vasnier.

Mme. Vasnier.

Debussy playing for the first time the score of Moussorgsky's *Boris Godounov* at the home of Ernest Chausson in 1893. Left to right: Mme. Henri Lerolle (seated in black dress), Raymond Bonheur (chin in hand), Henri Lerolle, Chausson (turning pages), Mme. Chausson (seated on couch in white dress).

Lily Debussy in 1899.

Lily and Debussy in 1902.

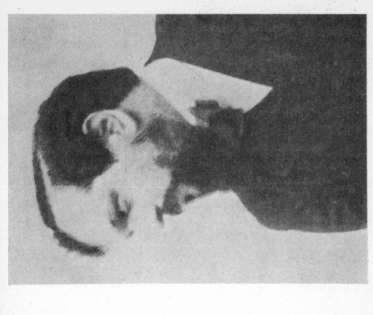

Debussy at Pourville, 1904. *Collection of Mme. Gaston de Tinan.*

The second Mme. Debussy at Pourville, 1904.

With Mme. Debussy in the garden of their Bois-de-Boulogne home, 1905.

Debussy with his daughter Chouchou in the forest at Mouleau, 1916.

"La Belle Gaby."

telegrams asking for the music for the next scene and threatening
to cancel rehearsals. These were piled together with notes from
bailiffs and summonses to court for nonpayment of debts. Debussy
spent the nights composing, rearranging and adding to his score to
fit the needs of Carré's production and certainly did not think of
Maeterlinck, who on March 19 came to the Opéra Comique, sat
through two rehearsals, first of the orchestra and later of the whole
company, and then without a word to anyone walked out. No one
expected to hear from him again. But no one knew that Maeterlinck had changed his tactics.

He was not going to leave this "affair" in the hands of justice
alone. He went to a fortuneteller, in good faith, as he said; that is,
if he did not entirely believe in clairvoyant force, he was open-
minded about it and was ready to put it to a test. The whole business with *Pelléas* seemed to him an excellent occasion for such an
experiment, since, he said, in this intrigue several powerful and
hostile wills were engaged in a struggle against him. "The forces
were well balanced and according to human logic it was impossible
to predict the outcome and who was going to be the victor," Maeterlinck wrote later on, describing in detail his visit to the fortuneteller.[1]

Maeterlinck chose the most famous clairvoyant in Paris. During
her trance the middle-aged woman claimed to have incarnated herself into the spirit of a little girl named Julia. Sitting across the
table from Maeterlinck, she asked him to concentrate on the subject
of his trouble and to speak to her as he would to a girl of seven or
eight. Then her hands, her eyes and her whole body went through
convulsions Maeterlinck found disagreeable to witness. With her
hair disarranged, the expression of her face completely changed to
a naïve and childish one, her voice a high descant, she began her
discourse.

Maeterlinck was inclined to believe her as she slowly described
not only the places, but the faces and the characters of everyone
involved in his "trouble."

[1] In Maurice Maeterlinck's collection of six essays, *The Future* (not translated into
English).

"But how will it all end?" said Maeterlinck. "Will I be the one who will win, or the enemy who resists me and wishes me ill?"

"Ah, this [that is, the future] is much harder to tell," the voice said—and particularly because the enemy was not against Maeterlinck but "because of another person."—"I cannot see why he detests her!" the voice continued. "Oh, how he hates her, how he hates her! And it is because you love her that he does not want you to do what you want to do for her."

"But," Maeterlinck anxiously asked, "will he go to the extreme, isn't he going to compromise at all?"

"Oh, don't worry about him. I see he is sick and will not live long."

"Nonsense!" said Maeterlinck, "I saw him the day before yesterday. He is perfectly well."

"No, no ... this does not mean anything," the voice reassured, "he is sick, it does not show, but he is very ill. He is going to die soon."

"But when and how?"

"He is covered with blood. I see blood around him, everywhere."

"Blood? Does it mean a duel?" [Here Maeterlinck wrote in parenthesis: "I was thinking for a while of finding a pretext to fight my adversary."] "Or an accident, murder, vengeance?" ["He was an unjust man without scruples who had hurt many people," Maeterlinck commented.]

"Oh, don't question me. I am very tired ... let me go.... Be good, I will help you...."

The same crisis of convulsions was repeated as at the beginning of the séance and the woman regained her own expression and her own voice as though she woke from a long sleep.

Apparently Maeterlinck followed her advice "to be good," for he did not challenge Carré. A short while later Carré actually fell ill, had to be operated on and almost fulfilled the prophecy.

Maeterlinck was not, however, at the end of his resources. When the rehearsals of *Pelléas* reached a peak of excitement and confusion because only two more weeks were left before the opening night, he sent a letter to *Le Figaro* which was published on April 14:

DEAR SIR:

The management of the Opéra Comique has announced a forthcoming production of *Pelléas et Mélisande*. This performance will take place against my wishes because MM. Carré and Debussy have disregarded my most legitimate rights. Actually M. Debussy, after having agreed with me on the choice of an artist, the only one in my opinion capable, following my intentions and my wishes, of creating the role of Mélisande, decided, supported by M. Carré's unjust opposition to my choice, to deny me the right to intervene by abusing a letter which I wrote him in all confidence some six years ago. This inelegant gesture was joined by strange practices, as is proved by the bill of acceptance of the piece, obviously antedated in order to establish that my protest came too late. Thus they succeeded in excluding me from my work and from then on it was treated like a conquered land. Arbitrary and absurd cuts have made the piece incomprehensible; they have preserved passages that I wished to suppress or improve as I did in the libretto which has just appeared and from which it will be seen how far the text adapted by the Opéra Comique differs from the authentic version. In short, the *Pelléas* in question has become strange and hostile to me, almost an enemy, and, stripped of all control over my work, I am reduced to wishing its immediate and decided failure.

This latest missive added fuel to the growing gossip, intrigue and criticism in connection with a work that had not yet been presented. "If Maeterlinck, the author himself, is against it, why argue about it?" was the common attitude. Debussy wrote and telegraphed Godet for his advice on what to do about Maeterlinck's letter. It was decided that Debussy should ignore it. But Carré wrote Octave Mirbeau, Maeterlinck's old friend, hoping through him to calm the furious poet. It was in vain. Mirbeau regretted the ridiculous attitude taken by Maeterlinck—"I have never seen a man so possessed by an evil spirit of a woman"—but he said there was nothing he could do against his blindness. "I cannot ask him to reason, for he does not reason any more."

Six months after the first performance of *Pelléas et Mélisande* Maeterlinck conceded his defeat. At the end of 1902 he wrote: "Julia's prophecy came to pass in part—that is, without my triumph in the major point, the 'affair' turned out, nevertheless, satisfactory in other aspects." [Carré had engaged Leblanc for a title role in Dukas' *Ariane et Barbe-Bleue*, an opera written after Maeterlinck's play.] "As for the death of my adversary, it has not happened yet and willingly I release the future from keeping the promise given me by an innocent child of the unknown world." But Maeterlinck never forgave Debussy. In 1909 he attended a performance of *Pelléas et Mélisande* at the Manhattan Opera House in New York. He walked out after the first act.

But to return to 1902 and Paris, the dates of the dress rehearsal and the first performance were set. "I don't need to say how necessary it is for me that you should be there..." Debussy wrote in a hurry to Pierre Louÿs.—"You can count on me, Claude, I have invited five friends to fill the box with applause. Thank you and good luck!" These were the notes exchanged by the two friends just before they went into the Opéra Comique to see the fate of Debussy's "dream," for they were well aware of the antagonism which they were certain the performance would evoke.

April 26, 1902 happened to be a sunny spring day and a crowd of invited spectators mixed with curious passers-by filled the Place Beaulieu, waiting for the doors to open for a dress rehearsal. But one more blow was to strike Debussy's work even before the curtain rose on the first act. It has never been discovered who instigated this calumnious deed—a printed "select program," ridiculing the opera, was sold for ten cents a copy.

This is a story of the Middle Ages. Or better still, a legend [read the pamphlet]. A castle and a dark forest serve as décor. Twelve scenes, twelve tableaux. The story is told like the captions in a comic book.

Scene I: Golaud, an old widower, little Yniold's father, while losing his way in the forest meets a girl, also lost there. He takes her with him and marries her.

Scene II: Arkel, his old father, who hears of this sudden union, does not object; he is a fatalist. Nothing useless ever happens, he says.

Scene III: Pelléas, Golaud's brother, takes a walk with his little sister-in-law in the shadowy dark gardens. Ha, ha!

Scene IV: Mélisande, always accompanied by Pelléas, is going to wash herself in the fountain; she loses her wedding ring, which glides down to the bottom of the pool.

Scene V: Pelléas and Mélisande are looking for the ring ... in a dark grotto.

Scene VI: Mélisande is working at a spinning wheel [meaning Mélisande is combing her hair] and the perfect love with Pelléas. The little Yniold, a terrible child, sees it ... and he intends to talk.

Scene VII: Mélisande sings as she combs her hair ... Pelléas helps her. He puts his hand into her hair. He is covered with it. He wraps it like a scarf around his neck. They hear some one coming ... Heavens! It's the husband.—"What are you doing here?"—"I ... I ..." stammers Pelléas.—"You're only children," says the good fellow, but a bit nervous, nevertheless.

Scene VIII: Golaud and Pelléas take a walk in the subterranean passage. There must be something to it.

Scene IX: Golaud tire les vers du nez du petit Yniold, who innocently lets the cat out of the bag.

Scene X: The old father Arkel gossips. Suddenly Golaud arrives with blood in his eye. He orders Mélisande to bring him his spear. He discourses incoherently. He threatens the young woman. Father Arkel thinks he's been drinking.

Scene XI: Near the fountain. Love duet between Pelléas and Mélisande. Naturally the husband, spear in hand, surprises them. He strikes his brother, who falls dead. The horrified mistress—Mélisande—runs away.

Scene XII: Mélisande lies in her bed, dying. The murderer husband is in despair; he begs his wife's forgiveness. Nevertheless, he wants to know the truth ... if the lovers have betrayed him completely. The good fellow Arkel ingeniously discloses that Mélisande is the mother of a little girl. The guilty one was not even conscious of it, she must see it to believe it. Thereupon she dies. Golaud cries.

And here you are! This little drama is a masterpiece and Maeterlinck is a genius. At least, this is what they say.

Rumors, but unfounded, had it that Maeterlinck was the author of this pamphlet. But it is doubtful that the poet could have chosen this sort of hara-kiri. However, it certainly had a devastating effect on the audience, which, lacking the regular programs not supplied at the dress rehearsals, had to consult this "select program" during the performance. It set the tenor of the general reception of Debussy's work.

At first the audience exchanged astonished glances, then they smiled and spoke of wasting a good day of sunshine, and finally their tempers rose until the comments on the play were heard through the hall. "Give us some real music...when will they stop tuning their instruments? What, no overture, no ballets, no little women, no chorus, no duets...?" Every sentence was accompanied by repartee from the crowd and many a time Messager turned around at his conducting desk and faced the audience, trying to silence them. And when Mary Garden's heavy Scottish accent was heard in "*Je ne suis pas heureuse*" the whole house roared. "Look at that...the little woman...she is not happy, that's funny! Ha, ha! Never mind, her young brother-in-law will take care of that as soon as she stops combing her hair. He'll distract her!"

During the intermissions laughter and mockery filled the corridors. The little Yniold was referred to as *le petit Guignol* and the opera was rechristened *Pédéraste et Médisante*. Some arguments led to fist fights, and the police had to be called in. Throughout the rest of the evening the audience behaved as if in a market place and when Golaud lifted Yniold up to see if Mélisande and Pelléas were near the bed, screams of "Enough, that will do!" almost stopped the performance.

Lily sat in her box as pale as if she were about to faint. Debussy locked himself up in Carré's office, where short bulletins were sent to him. "Why did the author want Mélisande to be pregnant?" questioned some as they were leaving the theater. "Did she have to have a baby before she died? She could just as well have waited another fifteen days. Then she would have had the audience's sympathy all for herself and not divided with the orphan and his future."—"Debussy, Debussy..." screamed the young partisans of the composer. "Shut up, you idiots!" were the last words heard in the hall.

Debussy remained outwardly impassive. On leaving the theater, he thanked Carré and Messager. He joined Lily and René Peter and they took a ride in the Bois de Boulogne. Debussy said nothing about *Pelléas*. He spoke of the beautiful sky of the "dying day." Peter said later that he had never seen Debussy so proud, so "above human poverty." What Debussy's true thoughts were puzzled even his closest friends. Six years later he revealed them, but this time for publication:

The scenic realization of a work of art, no matter how beautiful, is always contrary to the inner vision which drew it in turns from its alternatives of doubt and enthusiasm. Think of the charming life in which your characters and you yourself dwelt for so long, when it sometimes seemed that they were about to rise, tangible, from the silent pages of the manuscript. Is it any wonder if you are bewildered on seeing them come to life before your eyes through the intervention of such and such an artist? It is almost fear that is experienced; and one hardly dares to speak to them. In truth, they are like phantoms.

From this moment, nothing remains of the old dream. The mind of another interposes between you and it. The setting materializes under the deft movements of sceneshifters, and the birds of the forest find their nests in the orchestral woodwind. The moon is lit up, the curtain curtails or prolongs emotion. Applause—aggressive noises resembling the sounds of a distant fête where you are but the parasite of a glory which does not always prove to be what you desired. For to succeed in the theatre most often implies a response to anonymous desires and assimilable emotion....

In 1902, when the Opéra Comique staged *Pelléas et Mélisande*, I experienced some of those impressions, although the production was carried out with the most scrupulous care. Perhaps my anxiety was futile, but at any rate it will bear out what I wish to say later. I had always realized that the personality of Mélisande would be difficult to interpret. I have done my best to express in terms of music her fragility and her elusive charm; there was also her attitude to be considered, her long silences, which a single wrong gesture might frustrate or render meaningless. The most difficult point of all was Mélisande's voice, which sounded so gentle to my inner ear—for the most beautiful voice in the world may be unconsciously fatal to the individual expression of a given character. It is neither my business nor my intention to describe here the various phases through which one passes during the period of the rehearsals. As a matter of fact, these were the pleasantest hours I spent in the theater. I saw examples of admirable unselfishness and came in contact with great artists. Among them one young woman of very marked individuality stood out. I hardly ever had to make any remarks to her; little by little the character of Mélisande took shape in her; and I waited with a strange confidence mingled with curiosity.

At last we came to the fifth act—the death of Mélisande—and I cannot describe the amazement I experienced. That was indeed the gentle voice I had heard in my inmost soul, with its faltering tenderness, the captivating charm which I had hardly dare to hope for, and which has since forced the public to acclaim the name of Miss Mary Garden with ever-increasing fervor.

The audience's reaction during the dress rehearsal had, however, further repercussions. It reached the ears of the Under Secretary of State for Fine Arts, and Debussy was told to make two cuts in the score if he wanted to see his opera performed at all. Thus, the little boy's scene with the sheep in the Fourth Act was suppressed and another scene, between Golaud and Yniold at the end of the Third Act, was censored. There was nothing Debussy could do about the first cut, but he managed to save the second "offensive" scene by compromising with the government representative. It was agreed to omit fifteen bars in the original score from the dialogue between Yniold and his father: "No, father dear."—"And the bed? Are they near the bed?"—"The bed, father dear? I don't see the bed. ..."—"Hush, they might hear you."

Three days later, on April 30, *Pelléas et Mélisande* had its official première. The performance faced a much quieter audience, but the reception was far from enthusiastic acclaim. And Debussy still had to endure one more trial—the critics' opinion. In Europe, contrary to the practice in the United States, the reviews usually appear weeks later, but Catulle Mendès' piece was published in the *Journal* on the following day, May 1st. Debussy and his friends had good reason to be worried about Mendès. Neither they nor Mendès had forgotten Debussy's sudden loss of interest in the opera *Rodrigue et Chimène*. They saw him at the dress rehearsal and he came again to the première. Was this a good or bad omen? Was Mendès going to repay Debussy for what had happened ten years previously, or was Mendès too much of an artist himself to be influenced by personal feelings where a work of art was concerned? Mendès' article answered these questions, if not entirely satisfactorily.

He had many flattering things to say about Debussy as a musician, but he had a great many "buts" once he started analyzing the opera. "Every artist had noted the collaboration of Debussy and Maeterlinck with great pleasure. By their delicate and subtle sensibility, the similarity of their emotions and dreams, their fraternity, one may say, the young geniuses of the poet and the musician seemed perfectly matched. One expected—what is so rare in an opera—a really homogenous work, as though inspired by one man and in which the spoken drama would of itself develop into a musical drama. If our hope was not always deceived, it was too seldom realized," Mendès said, thus making it clear right from the start where his further detailed analysis would lead.

"There was often disagreement, sometimes divorcement, just when we expected that perfect concord more indispensable in this work than in any other." Mentioning, as if in passing, the continuous monotony of expression, which he said could not be made "musical," Mendès spoke of the "distance" and the "differences" between the poet and the musician which, despite some enchanting places in the drama, caused the uncertainty of the opera's success— "We must have been mistaken in our equal sympathy with Maeterlinck and Debussy." After giving his due to everyone connected with the production, Mendès concluded his review with a statement that after witnessing two performances he was left with one desire: "... to hear without elocutionists Debussy's score performed by one of the symphonic orchestras, and to see the charming lyrical tale of Maurice Maeterlinck, lyrical in itself without singers or musical instruments, on the stage of one of the Paris theaters."

Mendès' reaction not only had an immediate effect on the attendance at the following performances, but it encouraged other critics to open a whole barrage of abuse which threatened to doom the opera.

"Rhythm, melody, and tonality are three things unknown to M. Debussy and he deliberately scorns them," Arthur Pougin, a former violinist who became Fétis's successor on the *Biographie Universelle des Musiciens,* wrote in *Ménestrel.* "His music is vague, irresolute, colorless, and shapeless; it lacks movement and life...."

Louis de Fourcaud, an experienced art critic, professor of esthetics and history of art at the École Nationale des Beaux-Arts in Paris, wrote in *Le Gaulois:* "This score is the outcome of special theories of which I could never, under any circumstances, approve. By dint of indulging in cerebral subtleties and an unwholesome craving for originality and novelty, the composer has attained to a doctrine of complete negation. He renounces melody and its development, he renounces the symphony and its deductive resources.... The only really interesting elements in the work are the harmonic combinations.... This nihilistic art, which curtails everything, which throws off the bonds of tonality and liberates itself from rhythm, may amuse those who are *blasé,* but it cannot arouse any deep emotion in our hearts.... What we aspire to is a really deep, human art, not continual effects of titillation which are fundamentally morbid. One cannot serve ideals without ideas. One cannot quench the thirst of souls with questionable pharmaceutical beverages."

One could quote pages of similar criticism which kept appearing in the Paris dailies and the weekly and monthly reviews. The voices of musicians and critics such as d'Indy, Paul Dukas, Gaston Garraud, Calvocoressi and Marnold, who took up the cudgels in Debussy's defense, were lost in the avalanche of these diatribes. They affected not only the attitude of the general public, but that of the Paris musical institutions as well. Debussy was ridiculed at the Schola Cantorum, and Théodore Dubois, the director of the Paris Conservatory, issued a formal decree forbidding students of composition to attend the performances of *Pelléas* under penalty of immediate expulsion. (Maurice Emmanuel and Émile Vuillermoz, later eminent critics and musicologists, were the victims of this order.)

It was entirely due to Carré's adamant stand that the opera survived these attacks. In the most ingenious way he kept the performances alive by filling the vacant stalls with the enthusiastic youth who usually sat in the galleries. But the press was against him, against Debussy, until finally the critics began to indulge in long criticisms of each other. At this point *Le Figaro* proposed that Debussy answer the critics and on May 16th Robert de Flers interviewed him for this purpose.

It was not easy to find out what Debussy thought of the reviews of *Pelléas et Mélisande*. He smiled, spoke quietly in his soft voice, but his answers were brief. "For the last ten years, monsieur," Debussy told de Flers, "*Pelléas et Mélisande* has been my daily companion. I do not complain of this long labor. It has given me joy, an intimate satisfaction, which no mere words, no criticism can diminish. Besides, some of the critics have understood me perfectly and divined my intentions. I owe my thanks to MM. Gaston Garraud [*La Liberté*], Camille de Saint-Croix [*La Petite République*], Gustave Bret [*La Presse*], André Corneau [*Le Matin*], and to Henry Bauer for his fine article in the *Figaro*.

"After an almost embarrassing amount of praise, M. Catulle Mendès states that I have not adequately rendered the 'poetic essence of the drama' and that my music is 'independent of it.' And yet, in all sincerity, I made every effort to identify the two. I wanted them to express themselves individually, independently of me. I let them sing within me, and I tried to hear them and to interpret them faithfully. That was all. M. Gauthier-Villars finds fault with my score because the melodic pattern is never to be found in the voice, but always in the orchestra. I wished that the action should never be arrested, that it should be continuous and uninterrupted.... I know that I have very much 'alarmed' M. d'Harcourt. I greatly regret it. In speaking of me, he mentions 'noisy *arrivistes*.' He need not be uneasy. He evokes the Holy Trinity of music: melody, harmony, and rhythm, whose laws may not be violated. That is very well put. But is there any law in existence that forbids a musician to blend these three elements? I think not. In any case, although I have read through his critique carefully twice, I have not been able to fathom the meaning of all M. d'Harcourt's remarks. No doubt they are exceedingly profound. The same critic alludes to the 'awakening of Mélisande.' Perhaps he is confusing it with the awakening of Brünnhilde....

"I have tried to obey a law of beauty which appears singularly ignored in dealing with dramatic music. The characters of this drama endeavor to sing like real persons, and not in arbitrary language built on antiquated traditions. Hence the reproach leveled at my alleged partiality for monotonous declamation, in which there is no trace of melody.... To begin with, this is not true. Besides, the feelings of a character cannot be continually expressed in melody. Also, dramatic melody should be totally different from melody in general.... The people who go to listen to music at the theater are, when all is said and done, very like those one sees gathered around a street singer! There, for a penny, one may indulge in melodic emotions.... One even notices greater patience than is practiced by many subscribers to our state-endowed theaters and even a wish to understand which, one might even go so far as to say, is totally lacking in the latter public.

"By a singular irony, this public, which cries out for *something new*, is the very one that shows alarm and scoffs whenever one tries to wean it from old habits and customary humdrum noises.... This may seem incomprehensible; but one must not forget that a work of art or an effort to produce beauty are always regarded by some people as a personal affront."

And in concluding the long interview, Debussy said that he did not claim to have discovered everything in *Pelléas*, but that he had tried to trace a path that others might follow, broadening it with individual discoveries which would, perhaps, free dramatic music from the heavy yoke under which it had existed for so long.

But to make matters worse, as far as the illustration of his principles was concerned, the original quality of the production declined rapidly. Messager, to whom Debussy was bound by close friendship after many months of working together, had left the Opéra Comique after the première of *Pelléas* and gone to Covent Garden. For personal reasons, he broke with Carré on account of Mary Garden. Henri Büsser, an inexperienced conductor, took his place. Without having had a rehearsal of the work in its entirety, he "simply did not know what to do with the score," Debussy complained. "He looked as if he were about to take a cold bath. The orchestra admirably supports him, blowing the finest nuances, while he lunges with his stick into the singers' feet without knowing what they are singing." The cast was not doing any better either. "Périer (Pelléas) sings with a voice that sounds as though it came from his umbrella," Debussy cried in desperation, and since Messager had gone, Garden did not even look at the conductor's desk. Debussy did not blame her.

Debussy came to every rehearsal, every performance, but he was at a loss how to help or to prevent an obvious disaster. Then, on April 20, the seventh performance was sold out and for the first time Debussy witnessed a cheering house. He could not understand what had happened. "You can explain this any way you like," he wrote Messager.

It was Sunday and Pierre Lalo of *Le Temps*, the chief music critic of the Paris press, probably in the longest article to appear in a daily newspaper, covering almost as much space as a whole page of The New York Times, hailed *Pelléas et Mélisande* as a masterpiece in musical literature. "It is a glory for the director to have presented this work, and it is a glory to have presented it in the perfect way he did," Lalo ended the review that turned the tide and decided the fate of Debussy's opera.

Lalo's article was not a mere review, it was a thesis on *Pelléas et Mélisande*. After describing the plot in detail in three and a half columns, Lalo said that the opera had a few grave faults, but far greater qualities, and he spoke first of the faults—of the characters who talk and move as though in a dream, surprised by what they say and do, passive, irresponsible, dominated by the strange force of destiny, often talking and moving without any reason that is clear to either the spectators or the characters themselves.

The details seemed to him "only to add to the indecisiveness, and the superfluous symbols to augment the obscurity. The action in the play was dragging; after two acts it hardly gets started—these two acts which contain scenes with endings so abrupt that one could not understand what they are supposed to serve." And yet, in these scenes he found great beauty, delicacy and a force of emotion that suited music and particularly Debussy's music.

Perhaps Lalo had been waiting these three weeks before writing his own piece in order to study the critiques of *Pelléas*, for he referred to them in almost chronological order and disposed of every one.

"This music has singular beauty, and originality that is singular. Originality is everywhere; the originality is spontaneous, harmonious, without system and without effort. To quote Madame de Sévigné, 'it is the most astonishing, the most surprising, the most remarkable, the most incredible, the most unexpected, the most rare, the most worthy of envy! ...

"There is nothing, or almost nothing of Wagner in *Pelléas et Mélisande*," Lalo categorically stated to all who spoke of Wagnerian influence on Debussy's work. "Not the dramatic form, nor the musical form, nor the rapport between the music and the text, nor the voices with its instruments, nor the composition and its development, nor the harmony nor the orchestration comes from Bayreuth."

And after criticizing those French composers who imitated Wagner, Lalo continued: "The declamation is in high relief, it is rapid, fluent, singing and natural in its inflection, full of nuances, expressive and always musical.... The song is supported by sumptuous and profound harmonies and a most poetic and colorful orchestra. It does not need a complicated apparatus of leading themes nor a Wagnerian symphony to reveal the souls of Mélisande, Golaud and the old Arkel. The expressiveness of their words is sufficient, and that of the harmony and the orchestra. The instrumentation is eloquent, yet the most discreet in the world: it is afraid of noise, it does not suffocate the voice, and one does not miss either a word or a note. Here again is its singular virtue, far from mediocre."

Here Lalo compared Debussy to Moussorgsky, but only in exterior details, and summarizing the question of influence said: "Where then should one place Debussy and his music? A disciple of Wagner? In no way. A disciple of César Franck? Not at all. Massenet? No more than the others. Who then? What is it then that does not resemble anyone so that one does not know what to think or what to say...? Should we pretend that people have actually made an effort to have their own opinion, and to evaluate someone unknown? Has anyone tried to understand him? It is much easier to negate and to laugh. For they have laughed in the hall and in the newspapers, they have denied this work the most elementary qualities. They have proclaimed that it has no melody, no rhythm, no harmony, not even, to speak frankly, any music at all.

"This sort of temporary judgment is eternal," and Lalo said that since "Debussy's art cannot be likened to the classics, or Wagner, or the Italians, they say there is no music in it. It will need time to discover it." Lalo pointed to early criticisms of Wagner and gave another example: " 'He has abandoned harmony in the pure meaning of the word....' You would think I am quoting a reference to Debussy. Not at all. This was written about Bizet in a review of *Carmen* which appeared in *Le Figaro*."

Lalo divided the "enemies of *Pelléas*" into several groups. First. the man in the street. He was amused and laughed at it. Then the theorists—"they are mostly Wagnerians. These successful revolutionaries are the most conservative. They do not admit nor comprehend that one could dream of another art, except the one of which they are the apostles. The house of music belongs to them . . . they admit only music written according to their prescription.

"Then there are musicians, and excellent musicians, who cannot sincerely enjoy music different from their own. This is their right. But I would like to remind them that they were the ones who were the most vehement assailants of Wagner. And finally there are those people of good faith, the true friends of music, and those I ask, if they have not heard *Pelléas* yet, to hear it, or if they have, to hear it again. And since in time they will have to join those who enjoy and love this work, wouldn't it be better to do it now?"

If Debussy still did not know why on that night at the Opéra Comique they were turning people away, Pierre Louÿs's short note must have explained to him on the following morning. "You must be satisfied with Lalo's article," Louÿs wrote. "For the last fifteen years that I have been reading newspapers, never has a musician had anything of the kind written about him. I have never seen a journalist attack everyone to make the place so neat at someone's feet. Critics, public, musicians—he did not leave out anybody."

The remaining seven performances out of the fourteen played during the months of May and June were given to sold-out houses, but the proceeds did not cover the deficit. And Debussy's immediate reaction to Lalo's article was to start on a new project, another lyrical work. He chose Edgar Allan Poe's "The Devil in the Belfry." It was not a passing whim, for the more he delved into the subject, the more firmly the idea of setting the story to music got hold of him.

Debussy's choice of the story does not need psychiatric analysis. It is self-evident. In Poe's tale of the borough of Vondervotteimittiss, "the finest place in the world," where "the good burghers were fond of their sauerkraut and proud of their clocks," and were convinced that their happy existence would never experience a reverse, Debussy saw an allegory of the French musical world. And the press and his colleagues who plagued his works with criticism were obviously in his opinion well depicted in the "good burghers" in this fantastic story, who "at special meetings" adopted three important resolutions: "That it is wrong to alter the good old course of things, that there is nothing tolerable out of Vondervotteimittiss, and that we will stick by our clocks and our cabbages." Debussy saw himself in the "foreign-looking man" who came over the hills to Vondervotteimittiss to upset the old order of things.

He wrote Messager for his opinion. "From this tale one could draw something in which reality can be mixed with fantasy. One would find also that the ironic and cruel devil is much more of a devil than the sort of red clown who is illogically preserved for us by tradition. I want to destroy the idea of the devil as the spirit of evil. He is simply the spirit of contradiction, and perhaps it is he who inspires those who do not think like everybody else. It would be difficult to argue that those people are not necessary."

But Debussy was tired. He wished the performances of *Pelléas* would come to an end because, he said, they were treating it like an old piece in the regular opera repertory; the singers were improvising, and the orchestra became heavy—"a feat that seems almost fantastic and incredible, and soon one will be forced to prefer *La Dame Blanche*.[1] You know I am no good at pretending and humbugging people in order to revive their courage."

Also, there was one more decision to be made. Périer was not going to sing during the following winter season and it was not easy to find someone to replace him—Debussy must have written the role of *Pelléas* for his own voice: too high for a baritone, too low for a tenor. Carré offered a solution to the problem. He told Debussy they should engage Madame Jeanne Raunay, a singer then at the peak of her popularity, for Pelléas. "Carré got this idea," Debussy reported to Messager, with whom he was in constant correspondence, "when Madame Raunay confessed to him 'slightly irregular' love for Pelléas, which in relation to our problem, curiously resembles a lyrical onanism, or, speaking in less medical terms, narcissism. Well, as a matter of fact, after all, Pelléas has nothing of a hussar's amorous behavior and his belated virile resolutions are suddenly frustrated by Golaud's spear—thus there should be no inconvenience in such a substitution."

Debussy wanted to have Messager's advice. It was not switching the sex that he was anxious about, but the sonority of her voice. He said he was guided more by curiosity than taste in this experiment. A few days later, however, Debussy heard Madame Raunay sing some fragments from *Pelléas* with "the voice of a passionate old gentleman a little out of breath," and the project was abandoned. M. Rigaux, a young baritone, was engaged for the season of 1902-1903.

"Neurasthenia," Debussy said, "is a sickness which belongs to luxury, and I don't believe in it." But he was worn out and needed rest. He went to London for a short visit with Messager. Mary Garden, "our Garden," as Debussy called her, was having a great success at Covent Garden. It did not surprise him—"you would have to have your ears stopped up in order to resist the charm of her voice. As for me, I cannot conceive a *timbre* more gently insinuating. It almost resembles an obsession, it is so hard to forget."

---

[1] *La Dame Blanche*, composed by François-Adrien Boïeldieu.

After a few happy days with his friends Debussy had to return home. Lily had been taken very ill and they decided to leave immediately for the country. "Truly, the ironical and cruel god who directs our destinies makes us pay dearly for the purest of joys," Debussy said.

CHAPTER XV

PAUL-JEAN TOULET—DEBUSSY'S REVIEWS IN *GIL BLAS*

THE DEBUSSYS were an ailing couple when they arrived in Bichain. Lily was suffering from an acute kidney attack, and Debussy "looked like a squeezed lemon." They both needed to get away from Paris, from work and worries. During the whole month of August Debussy did not write a single note. Bichain, if not always inspiring, had a particular charm for him. "Here in Bichain the minutes pass, one knows not exactly how. I have a feeling of being at the other end of the world.... One cannot deny that the movement of the trees against the river banks forms a counterpoint less poor than our own ... but the people here are less lovely than the setting. I need not tell you that when *L'Angélus* gently orders the fields to go to sleep, you never see anyone striking that solemn pose of the lithographs," [1] Debussy wrote to his friends in Paris.

In this little village he could forget *Pelléas*, the Opéra Comique, the public, and "all those so-called artists. Ah! those sinister black-guards!" Debussy scoffed. "One should really hear with what a constipated air they discuss Art! By God, all of life is Art! It is voluptuous emotion (or sometimes religions ... it all depends). Only 'intelligent people' don't know voluptuousness, except on spe-cial occasions." But to start a new work suddenly seemed a danger-ous enterprise where he "might fracture his spine." Debussy preferred to do nothing and to enjoy the country as did Lily, who

---

[1] Allusion to the well-known Jean François Millet's pictures, "L'Angélus" and "Les Glaneuses."

soon began to feel better and with her suntan looked like a farmer.

"Nature," Debussy said, "the mother of all of us, treats me well and returns to me the iron health and muscles of steel of a 'young locomotive.' " Unlike Lily, he never was seen working in the fields. And though he had a small garden of his own, he would rather watch his father-in-law digging the ground—it satisfied perfectly his ambition for farming. "Nor is everyone made to be a sportsman," Debussy said and he insisted that he was very happy doing nothing. But this was not entirely true. Debussy was incapable of remaining idle for long. While he may have not composed anything, he was planning a new work in collaboration, this time, with Paul-Jean Toulet.

Toulet was a poet five years younger than Debussy. The two had met at Chez Weber during Debussy's café days. Through his mother Marie-Emma Loustan-Lalanne, Toulet was related to Charlotte Corday. He was proud of Charlotte as he was proud of another distant relative—Pierre Corneille. Leaning over a whisky and soda, so thin that he looked almost emaciated, this tall man with arched shoulders and a mouth twisted by irony would speak quietly, rubbing his nervous hands together, to an ever-present audience of friends carried away with delight and admiration by his subtle intelligence, his caustic remarks, his aphorisms, his wit and banter, his wistfulness and his bitterness.

Toulet belonged to a wealthy family of landowners and his independent means allowed him to indulge all his whims. He spent many years in Algeria and Morocco "experimenting," *à la* Pierre Louÿs, in erotic "extravaganza," only he went one step further. He became a drug addict, smoked opium and hashish, and wrecked his health. In Paris for fourteen years he tried unsuccessfully to interest publishers in his works, generally of an exotic nature. But as most of them were not published until after his death,[1] Toulet was known only to a small circle of literary men and artists. Léon Daudet, one of the familiar visitors at Chez Weber, could not understand "how Toulet and Debussy, these two sophisticated natures, when put together did not throw off sparks. They were not exactly

[1] Paul-Jean Toulet died in 1920.

cool to each other, but there certainly were no signs of any attraction between them," he said.

"Why, what utter nonsense!" Toulet exclaimed. "Debussy and I, from the first day of our meeting, we were friends like two pigs." But Daudet was right. Their friendship was not apparent in public, for soon after their meeting Debussy married and ceased to be a companion in Toulet's nocturnal life. "I love Toulet because he never needs to sleep," said Santiago Rusiñol, the famous Spanish painter, as Toulet after Chez Weber's closing hour would lead his friends to a bar at the Café de la Paix and, later on, to finish up the evening, to some small *bistro* near the Gare Saint-Lazare that stayed open all night.

"Respectable people," Debussy said, "speak of Toulet as a Bohemian. I do not understand them. In Paris Toulet leads the best regulated life in the world. He gets up every afternoon between three and four, and every morning from seven o'clock on you can find him in bed." On one occasion, historical for Toulet, he got up at noon. Debussy invited him to a rehearsal of *Pelléas*. Soon afterwards the two began discussing using Shakespeare's *As You Like It* as an opera, with Toulet preparing the libretto for Debussy's music.

This idea of adapting Shakespeare's play was not new to Debussy. Long ago, during his Prix de Rome days, Maurice Vaucaire asked him to collaborate with him, and, according to René Peter, they started to work on it. But nothing came of it. Later, Debussy spoke about it to Louÿs, but it did not arouse the latter's interest. Now, from Bichain, Debussy wrote Toulet: "I would like to have some news of *Comme il vous plaira*. I am constantly thinking about it and I would like to think of it 'through' you (you won't hold this against me)." It sounds like his former pleadings with Louÿs for the *Cendrelune* libretto. By the time Toulet sent him his first draft Debussy had returned to Paris because of the *Pelléas* rehearsals.

This collaboration was like that with Louÿs in another respect. Toulet suddenly decided to go to Tonkin to visit the Hanoi Exposition. "Surely one does not go every day to Tonkin," Debussy tried to excuse this procrastination, but he wanted to have all the material

Toulet could supply before his departure, "because I am so sure we have something really admirable," he told Toulet.

"The second plan you sent me suits me perfectly," Debussy wrote him. "Don't you think one should heighten the interest of the first scene by the introduction of a chorus offstage which would emphasize the various incidents of Orlando's fight? These could be the exclamations: 'He's down! No, he's not! Ah! He's no coward!' But, all joking aside, I think that musically it will be quite original. Also, I would like to have some songs sung by a group of people. The Duke is rich enough to have the Chanteurs de Saint Gervais [a well-known choral society] and their conductor come to the Forest of Arden—we must find a beautiful ceremonial for the betrothed and have it all end in perfect joy. I agree with you, in the last scene we should leave all these people in the Forest of Arden. Whenever you can replace the exact word by its lyrical counterpart don't hesitate. This does not mean that the tone in which the two scenes are written does not please me—quite the contrary. I suggest it because of your fear of being too rhythmical. . . .

"I have an idea which I offer you for what it is worth: couldn't we use the scene between Charles the Wrestler and Oliver (Shakespeare's Scene 1) as an introduction?"

A few days later Toulet sent Debussy the first scene, which he said he had already started before he received Debussy's letter.

As the curtain rises [Toulet wrote him], the opening scene would have an agreeable effect (on the right, Celia bending over the balustrade and Rosalind, coming from the garden, slowly walking toward her) which wouldn't be possible if there were another scene before it. But it seems to me that the important exposition should be in the dialogue between Celia and Rosalind, while Oliver's conversation with the wrestler would show Oliver's hatred of Orlando, which it would be better to soften and make less melodramatic. Don't forget that Orlando's departure, an important event, should not be clear in this scene, since it is decided later, because of the Duke's whim. Therefore we can introduce Oliver and the wrestler in the second and third scenes.

At the end of the first scene between Celia and Rosalind, Oliver appears and speaks of the wrestler. Then the wrestler comes to warn Oliver that his brother Orlando has challenged him. This should be followed as it is in Shakespeare, only shorter, and above all much softer. The presence of the young girls will not spoil the scene, for Oliver's intentions are not to kill his brother but to give him 'a good lesson.'

Except for this, I am very enthusiastic about your suggestion to have the exclamations from the chorus during the fight. The young girls will remain silent—a sign of emotion—and Oliver will comment sarcastically.

Debussy and Toulet had just enough time to exchange two more short notes and then Toulet departed, leaving Debussy anxious to have more details of this "little human fairy tale" and begging Toulet not to forget him "in yellow Tonkin."

A year later a Paris newspaper facetiously spoke of Toulet working on the libretto for a Shakespeare play in Indo-China and sending bits of it from the Far East to Debussy, but if there was a correspondence nothing has survived. While Debussy did not give up the project and during the following years occasionally reminded Toulet, as he used to do Louÿs in regard to *Cendrelune*, he did not return to it himself until fourteen years later.

The time which Debussy could spare from rehearsals of *Pelléas* he devoted to work on "The Devil in the Belfry," to preparing the score of *Pelléas* for eventual publication, and to three pieces for piano whose titles he particularly liked: *Pagodes, La Soirée dans Grenade,*[1] and *Jardins sous la pluie.* "When one cannot pay for travel, one should substitute for it with one's imagination." However, he added, he had to admit that there are other ways than composing music for piano.

Lily's health worried him, but he could not leave Paris. He was in debt. The General was pursuing him with his demands, and Debussy still had not found another publisher. Besides, he felt he had to attend certain official functions, even if they afforded him no pleasure. He was made a member of the Prix de Rome jury and, to the astonishment of many musicians, on January 3, 1903, he was decorated with the Legion of Honor. But it was no surprise to Debussy; in fact he asked: "What am I supposed to say to a man who

[1] Inspired by a postcard from Manuel de Falla.

announces something I have already known?" Debussy meant all the preliminary steps customary to such awards that had been taken by the Ministry of Education. Only six months previously Debussy had sworn to René Peter that he would reject the decoration and when Louis Laloy, a music critic instrumental in arranging it, asked him for the name of someone connected with politics in France, Debussy answered: "I have known only one such man in my life. He was Monsieur Wilson, a charming man who cordially hated music. But this was twenty years ago; since then I have remained where I am. This first relationship seems to have been decisive." Twenty years ago, at the Château de Chenonceau, where Madame von Meck was visiting, Debussy had in fact played piano for Madame Pelouze, Wilson's daughter, President Jules Grévy's granddaughter—Debussy's only contact with officialdom in France.

Perhaps Debussy was joking, for Daniel Wilson had later been involved in a notorious scandal caused by the exposure of traffic in the decorations of the Légion d'Honneur. Because of it, his father-in-law Jules Grévy was forced to resign in his second term as President.

"Nevertheless, despite an attitude which would have discouraged the most well-meaning friends," Debussy said, he was decorated with the ribbon. He accepted it only to please his parents, he added. "And there is no reason to think that I have become a better man because of it."

The official sign of recognition did not relieve him from financial problems, and to help the situation, which did not seem to improve from year to year, Debussy took a post as music critic on *Gil Blas,* the Paris daily. He wrote twenty-four articles during that season. Some musicians, perhaps to excuse the occasional flippancy as well as the animosity and barbed tongue of his criticism, have said that "he took little interest in these notes, which he wrote from the sheer necessity of earning some money." I doubt this.

On the contrary, Debussy was extremely conscious of everything he wrote—be it an article or a letter. He used his sense of form and composition as he did his sense of the sound of every word. When he wrote, he heard it as if it were a piece of music played back to him. That later on, when he planned to compile his articles into a book,[1] he thought it wise to edit and to tone down many of his opinions, does not prove that at the time he was writing them he did not sincerely believe in what he was saying.

Actually this "digest," published posthumously, does not do justice to the original reviews. The selection of twenty-five articles includes two essays which had already appeared in *La Revue Blanche*, . written in the form of a discourse between Debussy himself and an imaginary personage called *Monsieur Croche, Antidilettante* (Dilettante-Hater). Debussy may have borrowed this idea from Toulet who, while he was in Indo-China, wrote *Letters to Myself*, or from Paul Valéry's *Soirées avec M. Teste.* It has also been stated, I think erroneously, that Debussy invented this ghost "to provide himself with a peg on which to hang his own more surprising theories—theories which at that time ran the risk of being considered scandalously blasphemous.' Debussy had freely voiced his opinion and had made much stronger statements than those ascribed to M. Croche, and was not afraid to sign his name. I think it was his flair for the theatrical that dictated his choice of this particular form.

Nor does the fact that Debussy, sometimes verbatim, sometimes slightly changing the wording, would repeat in *Gil Blas* what he had already published in *La Revue Blanche,* just as in letters to different friends he would express the same idea in identical terms, prove how little he cared for "these notes," but rather show how firm he was in his conviction and in the way he said it.

Thus, in his first article in *Gil Blas* [2] Debussy restated his credo as a music critic and added for the benefit of "those fierce reviewers who love to destroy all mystery" that murder is one of the fine arts.

Debussy never was impartial in his reviews and he was honest enough to doubt such a possibility. He praised the works of Dukas and d'Indy, whom he considered his friends. But he was careful not to betray his old grudge against Chausson, as he was cautious when speaking of Fauré.

"Chausson's freedom of form never mars his harmony of pro-

---

[1] *Monsieur Croche, Antidilettante,* Paris, 1921.

[2] January 12, 1903.

portions. . . . His music, abandoning everything in the nature of narrative description, becomes the very sentiment that inspired the emotion. Such moments are precious in the work of an artist," Debussy said. ". . . Alas, that on hearing it my feelings should be turned to pain by the thought that he is no longer with us, that we shall never see again the sincere kindness of his smile."

Debussy wrote only once about Fauré, after he heard the *Ballade* for piano and orchestra at the Société Nationale: "The *Ballade* is almost as lovely as Madame Hasselmans, the pianist. With a charming gesture she readjusted a shoulder strap which slipped down at every lively passage. Somehow an association of ideas was established in my mind between the charm of the aforementioned gesture and the music of Fauré. It is a fact, however, that the play of the graceful, fleeting lines described by Fauré's music may be compared to the gesture of a beautiful woman without either suffering by the comparison."

Among the performers, the conductors were his favorite target. Debussy always poked fun at their behavior on the stage—the toreador-like pantomime which he said certain conductors with an international reputation affect. "This fashion of sticking banderillas in the head of an English horn, or striking terror into unfortunate trombones with the gesture of a matador," was very disconcerting. As he noted later, "The orchestra men usually remain cool as Greenlanders—they've seen worse before." He mocked the fascinating effect of the lock of hair à la Nikisch affected by the young conductors, noting 'its sad and weary droop in soft passages, intercepting all communications between the music and the audience, and its proud rise in warlike passages."

Among the conductors he preferred Richard Strauss, who had no "crazy lock of hair, nor gestures of an epileptic" and he thought that Strauss was about the only original musician of young Germany. "He resembles Liszt in the remarkable skill of his orchestral work, and our Berlioz in his anxiety to prop up his music with literature. . . . There is no doubt as to the anecdotes the music endeavors to tell and the likeness of the orchestra to the crazy illustration of a text. . . . The art of Strauss is certainly not always so definitely fantastic, but he undoubtedly thinks in colored pictures and he seems to outline his thoughts by means of the orchestra. The method is unusual and not hackneyed. In addition, Strauss employs it to carry out the development in a manner peculiarly his own. It is not the severe architectural manner of Bach or Beethoven, but a development in rhythmic colors. With amazing *sang-froid* he super-imposes on one another tonalities that are utterly unrelated. He does not care in the least whether or not they are nerve-racking, he only aims at making them alive."

Debussy's enthusiasm for Strauss' orchestration was surpassed only by his admiration for that of Rimsky-Korsakoff, after he heard the latter's *Antar:* "It would be impossible to describe the charm of the themes, the dazzling orchestral and rhythmic effects. I defy anyone to remain insensitive to the spell of this music; it makes one forget life, one's neighbor in the stalls, and even the desirability of maintaining a correct attitude. You just want to shout for joy. With difficulty you limit yourself to making an absurd noise with your hands, but that is certainly poor thanks to a man who has given you moments of happiness."

But Debussy seldom left the concert hall in a happy frame of mind. And when to a program he found distasteful he would add an unfortunate personal prejudice, the result was as malicious as it was unjust. The attitude he took toward Edvard Grieg, because of what had happened when the latter was invited by Colonne several years previously, was one of the most characteristic.

"M. E. Grieg is that Scandinavian composer who was anything but friendly toward France at the time of *l'Affaire*..... [the Drey-fus case]," Debussy wrote in an article entirely devoted to Grieg. "In his answer to Colonne's invitation to conduct his orchestra, M. Grieg nervously declared that he never again wished to set his foot in a country where liberty was so misunderstood.... France certainly could do well without M. Grieg, but it seems that M. Grieg cannot do without France, since today he is quite willing to ignore his quarrel and is ready to cross the frontier in order to conduct the French orchestra which was formerly the object of his Scandinavian contempt. . . . Besides, *l'Affaire* is nearly dead and Grieg is almost sixty!

"For a while I thought that I would give only color impressions of Grieg's music! To begin with, the number of Norwegians who usually frequent the Colonne Concerts was tripled; we have never before been privileged to see so much red hair, or such extravagant hats (the fashion in Christiania seems to me rather behind the times). At last I saw Grieg. His front view suggests a genial photographer. Seen from the back, the way in which he wears his hair makes him look like those plants called sunflowers, dear to parrots and to the flower beds at small provincial railway stations. In spite of his age, he is vivacious and wiry, and he conducts with a nervous attention to detail which emphasizes every nuance and distributes the emotion with unwearying care."

When Debussy finally got around to reviewing Grieg's music, he said that the songs "are Grieg *à la* Schumann" and that *Le Cygne*, a drawing-room favorite, was among the more sophisticated. "In this orchestral cuisine the savor of the harps mingles with the lemon flavor of the oboes, the whole being steeped in the juice of the stringed instruments. There are pauses, too, which thrill the audience, and so we have the unfailing formula of the encore. It is very gentle kind of song, very colorless—music suitable for sending wealthy convalescents to sleep. There is always a note that clings to a chord, like a water lily on a lake, tired of the moon's gaze, or . . . a little balloon blocked by the clouds. This music is so ineffably charming that it is irresistible."

Of the Grieg concerto he said: "His treatment of the piano is quite in tradition, and I have never understood why he breaks in here and there with blasts of warlike trumpets which usually announce the beginning of a little cantabile passage that sends the audience into transports (Trumpets! . . . your candor is abused)."

And while he was at it, Debussy disposed of another foreign visitor, this time from the United States: "At last the King of American music is within our walls! That is to say that during a whole week, Mr. J. P. Sousa 'and his band' will reveal to us the beauties of American music and how to use it in the best society. One must really be singularly gifted to conduct this music. Thus, Mr. Sousa beats time in circles, or he shakes an imaginary salad, or sweeps up imaginary dust, and catches a butterfly out of a contrabass tuba. American music may be the only kind which can find a rhythm for unspeakable cakewalks. If so, I confess that at present this appears to be its sole claim to superiority over other music ... and Mr. Sousa is indisputably its king."

With a few exceptions, Debussy was kinder to the musicians who were no longer alive. César Franck—whom in his student days he called a modulating machine—now "was a man devoid of malice, and the discovery of one beautiful harmony sufficed to make him happy for a whole day."

He was not, however, charitable toward Wagner, and must have been sharpening his pencils when at the end of April, 1903, he was sent by *Gil Blas* to cover Wagner's tetralogy at Covent Garden in London. To the great surprise of his readers he wrote an enthusiastic account of Hans Richter (1893-1916), the German conductor who was in charge. But upon his return from London he wrote more of his impressions of Wagner's Tetralogy and on Wagner in general.

"It is hard to imagine the state to which the strongest brain is reduced by listening for four nights to *The Ring*. A *leitmotiv* quadrille is danced, in which Siegfried's horn executes a strange vis-à-vis figure with the theme of Wotan's spear, while the curse motif performs the most maddening 'gentlemen's chain.' It is worse than obsession. It is possession. You no longer belong to yourself. You are but a *leitmotiv* moving in an atmosphere of tetralogy. No ingrained habit of courtesy will in future prevent us from hailing our fellow-beings by the cries of the Walküre: Hoyotoho! ... Heiah! ... Hoyohei! ... Isn't it gay? Hoyohei! What will the newsboys say? Heiaho! Ah, my lord! How unbearable these people in skins and helmets become by the fourth night! ... Remember they never appear without the accompaniment of their accursed *leitmotiv*. Some of them even sing it! Which suggests a harmless lunatic who, on presenting his visiting card, declaims his name in song...."

After repeating several times how tiresome is all this "pompous palaver in high helmets and without definite warrant," Debussy proceeded to analyze the libretto of the *Ring of the Niebelung*.

Having pointed more than once to Debussy's free hand in "borrowing," I feel reluctant to mention that his analysis is so similar to Tolstoy's [1] that it puts to question the originality of his treatment of the subject.

But Debussy was sensible enough to admit that "... in moments of tedium, when one really does not know whether to blame the music or the drama, passages of unforgettable beauty suddenly appear and silence all criticism. ... It is irresistible as the sea. Sometimes it lasts but a moment, often longer...."

At various times Debussy wrote enough about Wagner to have published it as a book. But his final judgment remained the same: "Wagner was—if one must express oneself with some of the grandiloquence that becomes him—a beautiful sunset that was mistaken for a dawn." And he has been quoted to have said: "Wagner can never quite die. He will eventually feel the cruel hand with which time destroys the most beautiful things. Some splendid ruins will, however, remain, in whose shade our grandchildren will dream of the past greatness of the man who, had he but been a little more human, would have been great for all time."

Debussy breathed a sigh of relief when he finished his account of Wagner's performances in London, and was ready to forget it, except that he was haunted by the last impression of his journey. On the way home he found himself in the same compartment with a fat young man who constantly whistled Siegfried's *leitmotiv*. To survive the ordeal, Debussy heroically countered with *La Marche Lorraine*.[2] "I would much rather be taken by this young man for a traveling salesman than a musician," Debussy said.

[1] Tolstoy: "Wagner's *Niebelungen Ring*, a type of counterfeit art. Its success and the reasons thereof," included in the collection of essays *What Is Art?* but originally published separately.

[2] By Louis Ganne, French composer (1862-1923).

CHAPTER XVI

A THUNDERBOLT

Upon his return from London Debussy received an unexpected call. Eliza (Mrs. Richard Jr.) Hall, the president of the Orchestral Club in Boston, "debarked" at 58 rue Cardinet and asked Debussy for the composition she had commissioned. As Debussy told his friends, the piece had been "commissioned, paid for and eaten almost a year ago," and he could have added that he had forgotten all about it. Mrs. Hall, Debussy said, not content just to be an American, had a strange and extravagant hobby: "for reasons of her health," she said, she played saxophone. She studied under G. Longy, the French oboist of the Boston Symphony Orchestra, and through him commissioned several composers, including d'Indy, Fauré, and Debussy, to write for her.

"The tenacity of these Americans is proverbial," Debussy told Messager, and he assured Mrs. Hall that "with the exception of Rameses II" nothing occupied his thoughts as much as this composition he was working on. He even had a title for it: *Fantaisie*, or *Rapsodie orientale*. For a while Debussy searched for "new combinations calculated to show off this aquatic instrument"; he wondered whether "the saxophone indulges in romantic tenderness like a clarinet," but after making a few sketches laid it aside in favor of something better.

In the first part of July, 1903, the Debussys went for the summer to Bichain and it was there that he started a new composition: *La Mer*.

"You perhaps did not know," Debussy wrote Messager, "that I

was destined for the fine life of a sailor and that it was only by chance that I was led away from it. But still I have a great passion for the sea. You will say that the ocean doesn't wash the hills of Burgundy and that what I am doing might be like painting a landscape in a studio. However, I have endless memories and, in my opinion, they are worth more than reality, which generally weighs down one's thoughts too heavily."

But Debussy was fated to be continually interrupted in the writing of this, one of his major works. By the time he had sketched out the three movements they had to return to Paris, where the rehearsals of *Pelléas et Mélisande* left him so little free time that he did not even continue as music critic for *Gil Blas*. And before he knew it, Debussy said, it was spring again, summer was approaching, and another year had passed without bringing the slightest change in his financial situation.

At the end of June, 1904, the Debussys were getting ready to go to Bichain for the summer as usual. Debussy chose the scores he intended to take with him and Lily attended to all the other matters connected with the journey. They visited a few friends, as they always did before they left for the summer, and they had some of them for lunch or dinner at their apartment. And if on occasion one of the friends would see tears in Lily's eyes, Debussy would explain —it was because they did not have any children. "Don't be discouraged," he was told, and they spoke of other things. They made engagements to make the rounds during the forthcoming celebration of the 14th of July, one of Debussy's favorite entertainments, and there was no apparent reason to anticipate any change in his domestic affairs. But on July 14th Debussy left 58 rue Cardinet and did not return.

For some years, most probably since 1901 (for that is when a young man by the name of Raoul Bardac began to study composition with him), Debussy had known Madame Bardac, his mother, a couple of years older than Debussy or about his age. Emma, born Moyse, was the wife of Sigismond Bardac, a wealthy banker, and was well known in Paris society for her charm, her interest in the arts, and particularly in music. She sang at society musicales and

Gabriel Fauré dedicated his *Bonne Chanson* to her. It has been rumored that Fauré wanted to marry her. I might mention here parenthetically that Debussy did not like Fauré, perhaps because their taste met on this one point.

The Bardacs lived in beautiful private homes ("never in an apartment!") first at 30 rue de Berry and later at 52 rue de Bassano, and at the beginning of their acquaintance with Debussy, Lily came several times with Claude to dine with them. But the Bardacs did not think much of Lily. At least, this is the impression I gained when talking about her with Emma's daughter Madame Dolly de Tinan. Lily, they thought, was beautiful to look at, but . . . she was from a different world, hoi polloi; also her conversation was not interesting—she was intellectually their inferior. Lily must have sensed this, but nevertheless, she encouraged Debussy to go without her to their home, to "attend their musicales"—it was necessary for his career.

And this was the beginning of the end of Lily's happiness with Debussy. *"Elle l'a pris par la gueule,"* Lily said later. It was more, however, than just the good cooking and excellent wines that drew Debussy to Madame Bardac's home. After spending ten years with Gaby and five years with Lily in what seem to have been harmonious relations, it must have occurred to him suddenly that he was neither another Mozart to be contented with Constanze, nor Goethe with Christiane. The five-foot-tall Emma with green eyes and golden, almost red hair was the woman he had longed for—a woman of the world, beautiful, a brilliant talker, "his intellectual equal," and whose singing was enchanting. Perhaps she reminded him of Madame Vasnier, the first great passion of his youth. "In love," Paul Dukas remarked, "Debussy was particularly sensitive to the 'decorative' side." Madame Bardac had everything.

After an evening with her, to come home to find Lily silent, or pouting, suspicious, or perhaps even jealous, was an ordeal that, in Debussy's eyes, "plainly showed the abyss which separated them." The little Lily-Lilo whom he loved for her ravishing beauty, her vivacious spirit and courage, this *midinette* who had the most perfect poise and sense of discretion, who in their dark moments of despair, never complaining of her own troubles, would distract him with a single "funny word"—this woman's voice now "froze the blood in his veins," he lamented. Debussy had ceased to love her, but Lily loved him more than her own life.

When she learned that his "morning walk" on that fateful July 14 took him all the way to Pourville near Dieppe, where he remained with Emma, Lily shot herself, almost fatally. According to Mary Garden, who said she saw a great deal of them just before this happened, Lily told her later that she had written a letter to Debussy and expected to be dead by the time it reached him. But Debussy returned in time to get her to a hospital. There, without taking off his hat, he sat in the waiting room until a doctor told him that Madame Debussy would live. "Thanks," Debussy said, and left.

A man leaving one woman for another is an everyday occurrence and would hardly have offered sufficient material for a "scandal," but in Debussy's case it was not only his behavior, but rather the circumstances of both women and their relationship to the career of a great artist that raised almost a social problem. It involved a wealthy society woman, a wife and mother of two grown-up children, a much younger poor woman "of the people," and an artist whose name was constantly in the public's eye. It was of interest to everyone.

Paris was aroused with indignation and buzzed with rumors. How could a young woman who had sacrificed "her best years" be discarded, without any further ado, for another because of obvious material advantages? Had the two lovers paused to think of the unfortunate woman's future? A story was spread that when Debussy saw Lily in the hospital while she was recovering and she said she could not live without him, he told her not to be discouraged— "After all you are still young and pretty." This remark was interpreted as an "exhortation to prostitution."

Money played a cardinal role in the "authentic reports" as well as in the mean gossip widely circulating in Paris, for it was generally believed to have been the prime cause of the drama. Debussy and his father, who happened to be with him when they took Lily to the hospital, were accused of pocketing two hundred francs Lily had left in an envelope addressed to a friend who had lent her the sum, and, according to another version, a one-hundred-franc bill left by Mary Garden on Lily's night table at the hospital was missing. "What of it ... she has but a few hours to live," Debussy's father was quoted as having said.

There was no question of where general sympathy lay. Their old friends rallied around Lily and a subscription to pay Lily's hospital bills was started by Nico Coronio, one of Debussy's pupils. To donate to this fund was considered a public expression of disapproval of Debussy's behavior.

As had happened in Gaby's case with the Chaussons and the Ysaÿes, Debussy severed his connections with every one whose name was signed on the list. Although Pierre Louÿs generously contributed to the fund—he was sincerely fond of Lily—on the condition that his name should not be used, Debussy heard about it. It brought the end to the longest and closest friendship in his life. On learning what had happened, René Peter rushed to Lily's bedside and offered her his services. That was enough for Debussy. He would not see him any more. Seven years later his feelings were unaltered—he refused to come to Peter's wedding, making it clear why, and in another short note he said: "... believe me—it is no paradox—that distant friendships are the ones that remain the dearest, because they are protected from a life that has mean teeth." And there were many others, including Mary Garden, Messager, Carré, and even Maurice Ravel, who innocently lent his name to Misia Edwards, a wealthy patroness of the arts, for her contribution to Lily's fund.

As if nothing had happened, Debussy spent the month of July with Emma at Saint-Hélier on the island of Jersey. He was correcting the proofs of *Fêtes galantes* to have them ready for publication by Durand. "Speaking of *Fêtes galantes*," he wrote Jacques Durand, "I beg you not to forget the dedication, which should read: 'Pour remercier le mois de juin, 1904' [to say thank you for the month of June, 1904], followed by these letters: À.l.p.m. This may be a little mysterious," Debussy commented, "but one must do something for the sake of a legend!" He meant "*À la petite mienne*"—to my little one. This time it was Emma.

Debussy was shrewd enough to know that this dedication would outlive what he called "malicious gossip." But if he thought he was contributing anything worth while to the legend about his behavior with Lily he was mistaken. He would have done better to follow his own advice to others "not to be too smart." As once before with Catherine Stevens, he took his revenge. But it was a gesture of an impotent rage, and the whole idea of this sort of legend only showed that while Debussy may have been a suave gentleman he was far from a chivalrous one.

"... It is a lovely country," Debussy informed his publisher. (Whether Jacques Durand took any sides in the "drama" has never been established—at any rate Debussy could not afford to cut him off.) "I am quiet, and what is even better, I work with perfect freedom, something that has not happened to me for a long time.... The sea has been very good to me, she is showing me all her robes." He was working on *La Mer*. Debussy pretended to be happy and untouched by the "affair." His reference to "perfect freedom, something that has not happened to me for a long time" was another untrue remark and, if also intended for the legend, unworthy of Debussy.

A month later, for the rest of the summer, Emma and Claude went back to Pourville. There he worked on *L'Isle joyeuse* and a transcription for piano duet of his quartet. But in September Debussy admitted that "these are really the last good days, for they already inject into the hearts of poor city folks the mean melancholy connected with the approaching days when one has to return to the accursed Paris."

Debussy was frightened of the accursed Paris, he spoke of wanting to complete *La Mer*, but there was still a great deal of work to be done on the orchestration—"just as stormy and changeable as .... the sea!" But he spoke in a different spirit when he wrote not to a businessman but someone he hoped was his friend. Here is his letter to Messager, dated September 19, from Dieppe:

My very dear friend:

You have a perfect right to be annoyed with me, but you must admit that for a while I have imagined that you had abandoned me, particularly since only through Madame Messager did I learn of your friendly desire to see me when you were in Paris.

As for my life during these last months, it has been exceptionally strange, much more than one could wish. It is not easy to give you the details. I will find it somewhat embarrassing. It will be better to do it when we will be alone with a glass of whiskey like old times.

I have been working...not as I have wished.... Whether because of the worries, or because I wanted to surge too high? It doesn't really matter! I have fallen too often and hurt myself.

There are many reasons for it. I am going to tell you some day...if I find the courage, because they are particularly sad.

As one has to live one's life, after a certain time, in regretting the old days, I miss Claude Debussy who worked so happily on *Pelléas*, because, just between us, I cannot find him again—and here you have one of my misfortunes among many others.

I hope to see you in Paris in October, if you will return....I need your dear and true friendship very much.

This was the last affectionate letter between the two friends. Like so many others, Messager disapproved of Debussy's behavior.

In October Debussy returned to Paris and took an apartment at 10 Avenue Alphaud, which was near the Avenue de la Grande Armée. It had been presumed that his life with Lily was ended, except for a formal divorce. To those with whom Debussy was still on speaking terms he complained how he suffered and how sorry he was, but it was stronger than he—he could not love Lily any more.

But in Mary Garden's recently published memoirs,[1] the one-time close friend of the Debussys reveals an epilogue to the drama, which Miss Garden says she alone knew and was making public for the first time.

In this story, Lily, radiant with joy, told Garden that Debussy upon his return to Paris had written her and asked her to come to

[1] *Mary Garden's Story*, published by Simon and Schuster, Inc., New York, 1951.

see him. "I have been visiting Claude every night," Lily said. Then, after a few weeks, Lily came again to see Garden. "I had hoped I would regain his love and bring him back," Lily cried. But one night Debussy had said: "Lily, I won't be seeing you again." Lily told Garden that she was too stunned to say anything. She just stood there in a stupor and waited for Debussy to speak again. He paused a few moments and said: "I am going to be a father." Then without saying another word, Debussy showed her out of the apartment.

CHAPTER XVII

DEBUSSY LOSES HIS FRIENDS

EXCEPT FOR ERIK SATIE, who always remained indifferent to his personal affairs, Debussy lost all his former friends. Even Pierre Louÿs, "the only friend in whom I can have full confidence," as Debussy had said at the time of a similar crisis with Gaby, now took a stand "against" him. It is true, however, that during the past two years their relationship had deteriorated to a point where they hardly saw each other and only occasionally exchanged short notes. There could have been several reasons for it: Louÿs's purely professional jealousy of Debussy's interest in working with Toulet, or René Peter; his own disappointment whenever there was a question of collaboration with Debussy, or, perhaps, because of his own life after his marriage, his own matrimonial difficulties. Whatever may have been the cause, it was Louÿs who took leave, so to speak, and Debussy deeply felt his loss and tried over and over again to rescue what was left of the old friendship. Debussy wrote him, on June 17, 1903:

The exorbitant fact of not seeing you for over one year could not be explained by death. . . . You are the friend whom I have certainly loved most and I console myself for the lack of your presence by imagining that you are in a *décor* so distant that all hope of communicating with you is impossible.

If sometimes someone insists on having seen you, then I, for my part, insist that he is mad. Your sending me your book disturbs the pattern of this dream a little. Imagine! I had tears in my eyes—so strong was my emotion on seeing your handwriting.... I am going to send you something soon that will remind you of "other things." It is sad, after all. You send me a book, and I reply with music. And this is all that is left of a life that is dead.... How much more I would have loved a handshake of the old times, alas! Now I can only imagine it.... But I am always your true friend. Aggravated by age,

CLAUDE DEBUSSY

Some time after Debussy left Lily he wrote Louÿs:

I have not replied immediately to your two letters, because the first one hurt me, and the second made me laugh. Besides, you cannot imagine how I agree with you about our relationship. It is absurd, chimerical and incomprehensible. We are not even dead, which could have served as an excuse. And yet I have a chronic desire to see you, aggravated by the little effort we make to satisfy it....

CLAUDE

They never saw each other again, nor exchanged any letters. They left no further trace of their former friendship. Many years after Debussy's death, Louÿs would occasionally reminisce about the days on the rue Grétry. But there was no warm note connected with Debussy's name.

Debussy began a new life, where, to quote from his reproach to Louÿs, the *décor* was going to be "so distant that all hope of communicating with him was impossible." Toulet was another friend with whom Debussy was not ready to part. A few years passed before, by chance, at an exhibition at Durand-Ruel, Debussy saw him. "I was surprised that you did not shake hands with me, according to our old habit. If you had been alone I would have asked you to explain—it seemed so impossible to me that your usual point of view would approve the attitude of certain of my so-called friends!" Debussy wrote as soon as he returned home, and asked Toulet for an answer. The misunderstanding was patched up— Toulet's remark that the only news he had of Debussy came to him through "others," and he did not always share their opinion, reassured Debussy. But this, as I said, happened several years later, and meanwhile, left without friends, without money to meet not only the old obligations but also the new problem of settling his affairs with Lily, Debussy was incapable of concentrating on his work.

Pelléas, once his "only hope," now became his only salvation. For years Debussy had been scheming to get most of the profit for himself from the publication of the score. He thought of bringing it out at his own expense, guaranteed by a list of subscribers. But the project fell through. Then he asked Fromont, the music publisher, for twenty-five thousand francs for the score and Fromont, after deliberating for a long time, refused. Fortunately, Durand came to Debussy's rescue. The Durand firm took over from Fromont the offer for *Pelléas* and signed a contract with Debussy on terms similar to those of Hartmann, only this time Debussy's monthly allowance was doubled from five hundred to one thousand francs.

But even with this major burden off his mind, Debussy was too restless to do more than make a few plans for future compositions —two groups, for one piano: 1. *Reflets dans l'eau,* 2. *Hommage à Rameau,* 3. *Mouvement;* and one for two pianos: 1 *Gigues tristes,* 2. *Ibéria,* and 3. *Valse,* which he marked with a question mark.

Debussy refused to accept the humiliating fact of being boycotted, and for a long time made every effort to mend the old ties. It was in vain. No one would answer his letters or come to see him. Ten months went by before Debussy received a friendly word. It came from Louis Laloy, a close acquaintance. He had not seen him since the lunch Laloy had with Lily and Debussy early in July, a few days before he walked out of 58, rue Cardinet. Laloy was in the Jura and only upon his return to Paris in October had learned from Romain Rolland what had happened during his absence. Laloy waited a few months and then, in April, wrote Debussy, apparently making it clear that he took "no sides" in the case. Debussy was touched, and answered [1] shortly before or after he closed the door on Lily:

[1] April 14, 1905.

My dear friend:

First, I want to tell you that you have never ceased being my friend. And your friendship has become even dearer by the simple test—but yet so rare!—that you have just passed by writing me with clairvoyant sympathy. If you only knew how people have deserted me! It is enough to make one forever disgusted with everyone who calls himself a man.... I shan't tell you all that I have gone through. It's ugly, tragic and sometimes it ironically resembles a novel worthy of a concierge. Well, I certainly have suffered a great deal, morally. Was it because I had to pay some forgotten debt to life? I don't know, but often I have had to smile so that no one would see that I was going to cry. I will try to find the Claude Debussy of old. If he seems a little worse off for worry, don't hold it against him, but think of his friendship for you, which remains unshakable.

According to the old rules of the Paris Boulevards a man who suffers must show it, otherwise his friends who wish to comfort him feel deceived; he does them wrong, he is ungrateful, selfish, secretive and even plain cruel. Debussy felt sorry for himself and all his letters to his friends carried like a *basso obstinato* the same lament. Two months later, in June, he could no longer bear his situation and he fled to Eastbourne (England)—"fled from all these sad and peculiar stories, from myself who was allowed to think only by permission of a bailiff."

Debussy stayed at the Grand Hotel. At first he was pleased with his choice of self-imposed exile. "It is a pleasant and even charming spot," he said. "The sea displays itself here with a correctness strictly British. In the foreground there is a lawn, combed and well kept, where little English tots, important and imperialistic, fight. But what a wonderful place for work! ... No noise, no pianos, except for the charming pianolas, no musicians discussing paintings, and no painters discussing music.... At last, a lovely place to cultivate one's egoism. Besides..." and here Debussy probably unconsciously expressed one of his innermost feelings, that hatred for poverty which in those days must have been stronger than ever, "until now I have seen but one poor man, and he too looked rather comfortable.... During the vacation season they must be hiding the poor."

He completed *La Mer*, worked on *Images*, and suddenly decided to rewrite *Reflets dans l'eau*, already started in Paris. But three weeks passed before he could see clearly "in his imagination," and before his "thinking functions" returned to him. In his letters he talked again and again about nature, afraid to mention the real cause of his unhappiness. "Well, I am trying to forget the man I am to become the man I should be, if this will please the gods. All these metaphysics, mixed with mechanics, can neither be useful, nor clear, but metaphysics is the art of saying the most stupid things in obscure language."

Debussy blamed everything and everybody except his guilty conscience. He was humiliated but thought he could laugh it off and not show his true feelings. But he would not admit it—he was trying to run away from himself and now he blamed Eastbourne. What had nothing to do with metaphysics and became only too clear to him was that by the end of August he had had enough of Eastbourne. The drafts were killing him, he was suffering from neuralgia, and the once "charming" pianolas and local festivities were getting on his nerves. He said they were chasing him from this country that he had thought was so quiet, and he did not know where to go. For a few days he went to London, then back to Paris. There he felt he was walking the streets like a stranger. He did not meet or call on anybody and finally went to Bellevue (Seine-et-Oise) for the rest of the summer. This, he said, was a much better place for him. "It was not patronized by tourists, except for a few neurotic Americans who couldn't find their special brand of whisky, and two or three Russians forgotten by the Japanese." [Russia was at war with Japan.]

As if Debussy had nothing else to worry about, Eliza Hall, "the saxophone woman," as Debussy called her, "was claiming her *Fantaisie*" and he sincerely believed that her patience deserved to be rewarded. But he just could not force himself to the task, particularly after he had heard her perform (d'Indy's *Choral varié*) at one of the Société Nationale concerts. In his memory still lingered the sight of her in a pink frock playing saxophone, and the picture was so incongruous that he shuddered at the idea of contributing anything to it.[1] Instead he completed *Images*, corrected the proofs and made a two-piano arrangement of the score.

At the end of September Debussy left Bellevue with a heavy heart and returned to Paris—Camille Chevillard needed him at rehearsals of *La Mer*, scheduled for its first performance on October 15. Of the two principal conductors in Paris, Debussy felt more sure with Chevillard. Édouard Colonne made him nervous. The last time Colonne had conducted his work, in December, 1902, speaking of *La Damoiselle élue*, which he had decided to revive, Colonne had said: "I see clearly what one must do—it must be very naïve, very white." Debussy could not conceal his uneasiness, but the worst had happened at the first rehearsal. Colonne suddenly suggested that Debussy should conduct himself. Debussy knew his limitations in this field and refused, but he did not want anyone to know about it and he certainly did not want to run the risk of being asked again. "After all, one shouldn't disgust people," he said, strictly confidentially.

Although Chevillard was not always easy to get along with, Debussy was used to working with him. "I want this to be a little more delicate, a sort of flowing. . . ." Debussy would suggest to Chevillard during a rehearsal.—"Slower?"—"No . . . more flowing . . ." —"Faster?"—"No, no . . . more flowing . . ."—"Gentlemen," Chevillard would turn to the orchestra, "let's start again," and he would play it all over again without the slightest change. But at least there was no danger that Chevillard would suddenly turn the baton over to Debussy. "When I have to conduct I am sick before, during, and after," Debussy said.

Whether he sincerely believed in his role of the "injured party," or was ignorant of the emotional strength of public opinion, Debussy certainly had courage to present at that time a new work that was sure to create a controversy. The most ardent admirers of his

[1] In 1911 Debussy sent Mrs. Hall the incomplete rough draft entitled *Rapsodie Mauresque*. Later Roger Ducasse orchestrated it and it was performed by M. Mayeur after Debussy's death at the Société Nationale on May 11, 1919.

music felt they had been deceived. From the title of the composition they expected another sea piece like the grotto scene in *Pelléas,* or like *Sirènes* in the *Nocturnes.* Chevillard's vigorous interpretation accentuated Debussy's clear-cut and unambiguous composition, for despite the titles for every movement, *La Mer* is not a programmatic piece.

The original title of the first movement, *La Mer belle aux îles sanguinaires,* was chosen for the sake of the verbal contrast between the words *belle* and *sanguinaires.* This and the original title of the last movement, *Le vent fait danser la mer,* were eventually changed at Jacques Durand's suggestion to *De l'aube à midi sur la mer* and *Dialogue du vent et de la mer.* In giving these titles Debussy was observing an old French custom, carrying on the tradition of the XII and XIII century clavecinists, who invariably gave fanciful and ornate titles to their keyboard pieces. Actually it is composed like a symphony in three movements: Allegro, Scherzo and Finale; and it was Debussy's first major orchestral work since the *Nocturnes.*

The reception was rather cool and opinions differed. Pierre Lalo, whose article had saved *Pelléas* from an early death, spoke frankly of his disappointment: "If the three pieces included in *La Mer* were the work of anyone but M. Debussy, they would have delighted me. It is only when I compare him to himself that I am disillusioned...." And Lalo "compared" *La Mer* to the grotto scene in *Pelléas,* "where a few chords and a single orchestral rhythm gave the atmosphere of night and of the sea...."

"It seems to me," Lalo went on, "that in *La Mer* the sensitivity is neither so intense nor so spontaneous; I think that Debussy desired to feel, rather than actually felt, a deep and natural emotion. Listening for the first time to a descriptive work of Debussy, I have the impression of beholding not nature, but a reproduction of nature, marvelously subtle, ingenious and skillful, no doubt, but a reproduction for all that.... I neither hear, nor see, nor feel the sea."

Gaston Garraud in *La Liberté* went further in his analysis of the three symphonic pieces, which he said did not give a complete idea of the sea, but depicted only a few of its aspects as seen at close quarters. "Nor do they express the essential characteristics of the sea, but rather those ever-delightful frolics in which the sea exhausts its divine energy, and the lively interplay of water and light that bewitches us; the magic spell of foam and wave and spray, whirling mists and splashes of sunlight." Nor had Gaston Garraud found the term "sketches" well adapted to the pieces, for, he said, their structure, though slight, illogical, but strong as in all Debussy's compositions, was clearer and more definite than in his previous works.

"There is also less originality and inventiveness in the ideas," Garraud pointed out, "which suggest now the Russians, now César Franck. The atmosphere is less subtle, less exact; the vision is rendered with a sensitivity that is as delicate as ever, but seems to lack freshness. And the rich wealth of sounds that interprets this vision with such accuracy and intensity flows on without any unexpected jolts, its brilliance is less restrained, its scintillations are less mysterious. It is certainly genuine Debussy—that is to say, the most individual, the most precious and the most subtle expression of our art—but it almost suggests the possibility that someday we may have an Americanized Debussy."

The closing remark was certainly unfounded and uncalled for in a musical review and betrays only that the author was not free from the general attitude of musicians toward Debussy's personal life, perhaps influenced by such platitudes as "now that Debussy is rich he will not write any good music," attributed to Léon Daudet.

But not all the critics were ready to discard the piece by merely comparing it to Debussy's previous works. There were some among them who already had achieved a calm and objective point of view, and who saw a new phase in Debussy's evolution, accepting Debussy's almost "possessed" endeavor not to repeat himself. ". . . The inspiration is more robust, the colors are stronger, the lines more definite. . . . One has the impression that M. Debussy, after diligently exploring the domain of sonorous possibilities, has here considerably condensed and clarified the sum total of his discoveries, and his music tends to acquire the absolute eurhythmic quality that characterizes all masterpieces. . . ." It is significant that this recognition should have been voiced by M. D. Calvocoressi, a music critic, not one of Debussy's devoted friends and admirers, but, on the contrary, the spokesman for a whole clan of musicians who had been championing another French composer, Maurice Ravel, in a controversy then at its beginning.

Meanwhile, not only *La Mer*, but all of Debussy's works as well as his esthetics came in for a most thorough examination in a dispute that is now a matter of history. But before I give an account of this often confusing quarrel, I would like to relate some of the pertinent details of Debussy's personal life.

Two weeks after the first performance of *La Mer*, on October 30, Debussy became the father of a little girl, Claude-Emma, or "Chouchou," as he nicknamed her. The joy of the "fulfillment of one of his most cherished hopes" overwhelmed and frightened him. Both he and Madame Bardac were in the midst of what was referred to as "double divorce," and whereas Madame Bardac's freedom was granted with generous alimony from her husband, Debussy was involved in the most disagreeable court sessions in which his life with Lily was disclosed by the plaintiff in all its details. Judgment was pronounced against Debussy.

The Bardac fortune has been estimated in so many different figures that it is impossible to be accurate about it. Some report that Madame Bardac was to receive an income equal to sixty thousand dollars a year, others say ten thousand. Madame Gaston de Tinan, Madame Bardac's daughter, told me "it was comfortable," whatever figure this may imply. There was also talk of Madame Bardac's expecting to inherit a large fortune from her uncle Daniel Iffla, known as M. Osiris, the philanthropist. Thus, even if the twenty-five thousand francs paid by Durand for his *Pelléas* were swallowed by divorce expenses and the initial financial settlement with Lily, Debussy started his life with Emma "fairly comfortably off," to use the same expression.

They bought a house near the Avenue de la Grande Armée and furnished it luxuriously, the house where Debussy spent the rest of his life, living in the eyes of musicians and Paris society, in luxury and a "distant *décor*."

What was not known at that time was that several years later

Madame Bardac's income was to be drastically cut down, that after his death her uncle would leave his fortune to charity and the Pasteur Institute and not to his niece, and that Debussy would find himself in financial straits even greater than before, since he lived with his family on a higher scale. He was forced to accept engagements as a conductor or a pianist—both odious to him—and for the rest of his life he had more financial lawsuits than "finances."

But "public opinion" never forgave Debussy for his desertion of Lily. Two years later, in 1908, came a revengeful blow in a form which left Debussy utterly helpless.

CHAPTER XVIII

DAY OF JUDGMENT

FOR YEARS Debussy had been dismissing his "domestic dramas" as banal and "worthy of a concierge." He said this at the time of his break with Gaby and he complained in identical terms about the "scandal" that was "created" about his leaving Lily. It may have been true in reference to some newspaper stories and gossip. But when a banal story is taken by a dramatist, who, rejecting all conventions, prejudices and fiction, presents a play constructed with the most scrupulous respect for logic and sentiment, captivating in the beginning and developed to the end in its noble spirit, when its true, simple words and literal portrayal of the situation evoke tears from the most insensitive and blasé spectators and at times is so moving that it makes the whole audience rise from their seats—then the banal story becomes a work of art.

Bataille's [1] *La Femme Nue* ("The Woman in the Nude") was a drama written as though from shorthand notes of Debussy's most intimate life.

The favorite theme of Bataille's plays was the *vetue* (clothed) and the *nue* (naked)—the haves and have-nots—and since, as a painter more interested in portraits than landscapes, he had a good eye, and, as a musician accomplished enough to write his own music to his plays,[2] he had good ears, it was not surprising that the authenticity of his characters could not be disguised. If Lily, Debussy and Madame Bardac were mere names in the newspaper stories, Bataille

---

[1] Henry Bataille (1872-1920).
[2] *Le Songe d'un Soir d'Amour.*

recreated them life-size for the general public. Of course, Lily, in his play, was a composite of both Lily *and* Gaby.

Twenty years later, in his essay on Henry Bataille, J. B. Besançon wrote: "Perhaps Bataille let himself be too much inspired by a recent adventure of a great Parisian composer and did not sufficiently free himself from the actualities." Indeed, no mere amateur in hard realism, Bataille showed that he was no stranger to "nuances" and "suggestion." Effectively using Debussy's own favorite device in composition, Bataille, through fleeting sentences here and there, innocent and coincidental remarks, made clear, down to the smallest details of his play, his one purpose: to offer Debussy's case to public judgment as a social problem.

It has been reported that the whisper of Debussy's name pervaded the corridors of the Théâtre de la Renaissance, where *La Femme Nue* opened on February 27, 1908. It created a sensation. The play was acclaimed as a masterpiece. Newspapers carried detailed accounts of the plot and columns were devoted to praise by the critics, some of them written by Debussy's personal acquaintances, journalists who had interviewed him recently, or with whom he had worked on *Gil Blas*. Never has there been, at least to my knowledge, such a Hamlet-like situation. Debussy may well have remembered his remark in reference to his own play, that "one does not invent, alas." And there was nothing that Debussy could do about it. To protest, to try to stop the play or to sue Bataille would have been to admit the authenticity of the plot. Besides, Bataille "explained" his play in an interview (republished on May 2nd in the theater program) in such a way that no successful action for libel could have been taken.

"The title of the play," Bataille said in reference to its provocative nature, "should be understood in the exact sense of the word as well as in the most liberal metaphoric conception of it, since it concerns a type of being who serves naked as a model for painters, as she is 'naked' in life. This nakedness is not obscene, but rather grave and sacred. The title is even three-fold metaphoric, because one must add to the innocent heroine of my play the primitive and original 'nakedness' of a rich soul in all its instincts, without any other attire except this mysterious and precarious beauty.

"Next to her, you will see the *vetues*, those 'clothed,' if one may say so, beings enriched not only by their social position but by all the secular crystallization of the spirit, by all the resources of their flexible conscience and all their weapons, among which marriage should be considered as the strongest. . . .

"I have placed the discussion in the only social milieu where it could happen, the only one where the triple metaphor could take place—that is, in the artists' circle. They, the artists, are the only ones, in reality, who should ascend without any trouble (that is if they wish) to the great natural morality. They are, after all, the free individualists by definition. . . .

"My play, therefore, can be dedicated to the glory of the 'instinctives,' to those beings who keep in the depth of their innocent souls the most beautiful morality in the world. It is they who are the most beautiful force and theirs is the most persuasive example."

It is a matter of conjecture whether Bataille knew about the play Debussy had been writing at one time in collaboration with René Peter, for Bataille also presents his musician as a painter. But it has never been denied that Bataille knew Lily (he was Pierre Louÿs's friend, knew René Peter, Toulet, and many other friends of Debussy) and perhaps he attended the court proceedings in Debussy's divorce at which, it was reported, Lily spared no words in describing her intimate life with the composer. Perhaps he gained access to the court transcripts. None of Debussy's letters were published at that time, and certainly not one of Lily's words was recorded except in court. Thus it is improbable that Bataille could have written dialogue so closely resembling in substance the original, unless he had some "documentary" help. In any event, in his play Bataille for the first time offered Lily's side of the story, without which Debussy's drama cannot be told completely, and up to now, never has been. It has never been published in English and as it would be impossible to incorporate Bataille's entire play in this volume, I feel compelled to give a synopsis and to quote directly a few scenes most pertinent to Debussy's relationship with Lily.

As the curtain rises Pierre Bernier, the painter, and Louise Cassagne, his mistress (the chief characters in the play) are anxiously awaiting the results of the contest at the Société Artistes Français.[1] From the snatches of conversation of various artists who keep coming out on the terrace of the restaurant for refreshments, the audience learns that Pierre is a poor Bohemian artist who had submitted his painting, "The Woman in the Nude." He had been unknown until an art critic devoted a long article in *Le Figaro* to it and acclaimed it as a masterpiece.[2] There are three rounds of votes and Pierre has steadily been gaining, but he keeps to himself at his corner table and does not want to show his excitement to his friends.[3]

His mistress, Lolette (or Loulou, as Pierre calls her [4]) is well known to the artists and models who gossip about her at their tables.[5] Lolette was a model before she came to live with Pierre and it was she who posed for the "Woman in the Nude." Simple and honest—"an instinctive type"—she has no worldly manners but would do anything for Pierre, whom she loves and admires for his talent, his capacity for work, his courage and endurance. The audience also learns from the conversation of Lolette with her sister, who comes to join them, that Pierre does not think Lolette has any maternal instinct.[6]

Pierre has struck a hard bargain for the price of the painting and an option for two more canvases with a prominent art dealer, provided he wins the prize. A few minutes later he wins, and at once begins negotiating for the sale of the same picture with a Government representative, shocking Lolette's sense of honesty.[7]

---

[1] Bataille sets the first act in the atmosphere of an unusually warm day, as was April 27, the day of *Pelléas'* dress rehearsal.

[2] Pierre Lalo's review of *Pelléas et Mélisande*.

[3] During the decisive hours of *Pelléas* at the dress rehearsal open to the press, Debussy remained in Carré's office and saw no one.

[4] Debussy called Lily "Lily-Lilo."

[5] Madame Berthe Bady, the famous actress, was costumed in the same old-fashioned style and hair-do as Lily Debussy.

[6] Debussy often explained Lily's tears by the fact that they did not have any children, and some have attributed Debussy's final break with Lily to this lack.

[7] Debussy was known to have sold the same composition to two publishers.

Crowned with success, Pierre (alone with Lolette) tells her that now he is going to keep his word ("when my Pelléas is played and I become rich," as Debussy told Catherine Stevens and, no doubt, Gaby) and marry her. Lolette bursts into tears. What has she done to deserve such happiness?—"the happiness of growing old together," as she says. "What have you done?" Pierre exclaims. "You were courageous in those wretched days, you were sincere and kind and a good sport! I owe you a good part of this prize." And what about her past? Lolette asks—he deserves a much better woman. "Bah!" says Pierre, "that was not your fault . . . life is life." This is a happy moment for them. "It takes a day like this one," Pierre says, to bring to the surface all "the painful memories" of their life together, and for them to dare to speak frankly of their past. And they tell each other about the first night they spent together, how jealous Pierre was and how sorry Lolette was she has never made him jealous since, how she belongs entirely to him. But the life of misery is over, they say, Lolette won't need to cut francs into centimes any more, she too can realize a few dreams she had—"to eat a lot of *marrons glacés*, and in winter wear a Chinese pink carnation, and buy a bicycling outfit in green velvet and a small hat with a touch of sealskin." "Tonight," Pierre says, "everything belongs to love. We'll walk down to the boulevards . . . we'll just walk about, we'll look at my name in the evening papers, and then we'll take a train to go and dine far away . . . like lovers . . . far, far away. To Saint-Germain [1] . . . would you like to?"

In the next act, Pierre has become rich. He has invited a few old friends to his first little party and both he and Lolette are showing their guests the sumptuous duplex, explaining some unfinished installations. The old comrades are cordial to him, but when alone speak of him as a *parvenu*. Lolette's natural delight in showing off her new possessions and her lack of "lady-like" manners annoys Pierre. It leads to conversation with Garzin, an old painter. Here Bataille speaks himself: [2]

---

[1] As previously mentioned, Debussy was born in Saint-Germain-en-Laye.

[2] Pierre Louÿs's two letters—they have not been found—at the time of the crisis with Lily, which made Debussy "cry and laugh," may have been written on the same theme.

"Don't you listen to them... let them talk, my boy," Garzin tells Pierre. "I too have married my mistress... she was a girl from a farm in Argeles. Don't think I did not suffer on account of her —men are dastardly cowards! Sometimes, in a drawing room, or on the street, when we run into friends, her coarseness embarrasses me. I'm still ashamed of it, although I try not to show it. What does it matter that she is so simple, so common that she makes us blush before our friends? She is the finer of us two, the one who has the right to say those words, the only truly noble ones: 'I love you!' And she loves you, this little one, terribly.... You only have to see how hard she is trying tonight, to follow the movement of her naïve eyes, turned toward you as if toward the sun..."

"Yes, I don't deny it," Pierre says. "But it's annoying, just the same, when a man develops and the quality of the one he loves remains inferior. It's not too much to ask that she should follow you upwards."

"Inferior? Pooh! What is that?" says Garzin. "Look at Chardin [1] ... a kitchen table, an apple—nothing but an apple. But the soul is there... everything is there."

"Still, you can't hold it against me for not being contented with an apple all my life," Pierre says.

"My boy... nature, nothing but what is natural—that is for us, the artists!" Garzin replies. "This is the only thing that is beautiful. You must go to a natural woman, to the natural morality, as we look for a motive—to the skies, a tree. The rest—prejudices, the conventions, everything that is false in life—this is not for us. On the contrary, you must respect in your little woman everything that is awkward, naïve, and bare.... She is charming, because there is nothing in the world so beautiful as the instinctives."

"I am not sure..." says Pierre. He is interrupted by the sudden entrance of Princess Paule de Chabran, whom he did not expect. From the first words spoken between them the audience is aware of their intimacy. Pierre has been painting her portrait, but this is her first visit to see how he lives and to meet some of his friends.

[1] Jean-Baptiste Chardin, 1699-1779.

In the ensuing scene with Pierre, the Princess speaks freely of her relationship with him, amused by his awkward ways with a woman of society, which under her guidance will improve, she assures him. She has a slight German accent, acquired in her childhood.[1]

PRINCESS: I was born a Blochental, my darling—extremely rich, it's true, but after all only a Blochental; you certainly know the hostility attached to the race. . . . I wanted to have all the Parisian aristocracy at my feet; I have had them—I bought them. I am satisfied.[2] Now they bore me. . . . How insignificant my dreams are! As soon as I realize them, I am bored. I'm not sure I have not ruined my life . . . you are laughing? You are wrong, you don't understand. . . . After all, I was destined for art . . . with my millions I should have done what Ludwig of Bavaria did, only with more taste. But you, you are a little bourgeois. Why did you marry this woman? She is not worthy of you. It's surprising for a sophisticated man like you, it's shocking. . . . She's nice, of course, but so common—you'll excuse the word, so "Montmartre." You are not annoyed with me? She doesn't even take proper care of herself.

PIERRE: You're crazy. What do you want . . ? It was a lovely day and I was happy. . . .

PRINCESS: But you still love her—yes, a lot. . . . one can see it in your eyes when you look at her; you're worried about her, about how she behaves. You are a little bourgeois, that is all. . . .

Lolette walks in and is surprised to see the Princess in her home. The Princess explains her visit. Their house was on her way and she thought she might drop in for a few minutes. She has brought them a painting she has done. She also is an artist.[3]

[1] The Princess's hair-do resembled that of Madame Bardac.

[2] Madame Bardac was a Jewess. This was supposed to have been an additional reason for some of Debussy's former friends to turn against him. On the other hand, it was reported that Madame Bardac's uncle, M. Iffla, did not leave his fortune to his niece because she had married a gentile. Debussy was the loser in both cases.—Bataille's portrayal of Madame Bardac may have been exaggerated because of his prejudice.

[3] Madame Bardac was known in Paris society as a musician.

Alone with Princess de Chabran Lolette, nervous and intimi-
dated, bluntly tells the Princess that she and Pierre adore each
other. Of course, she says, sometimes she annoys him and they quarrel, but these things happen in every marriage and she loves Pierre
"as no one in the world could love him...."—"He is my whole
life," she says. "The woman who would take his love away from
me would commit a crime—a horrible crime...." The Princess interrupts her, laughing, and reassures her: "Don't worry! I like you
both very much, but... how should I say it?" She examines Lolette
with her monocle. "You are neither of you from my *milieu*.... I
consider you both my friends, but I have no other ambition in my
personal relationship." Lolette believes her and promises to prove
what a good friend she will be.

But the party ends badly. Lolette overhears Pierre's and the
Princess's avowal of love. She makes a scene, while Pierre tries to
get his guests out of the house. Left alone with Lolette, he reassures
her and then carries her in his arms to her room.

Thus in the first two acts Bataille establishes his characters and
the situation as it was before Debussy made his final decision to
leave Lily. It has been reported that he wanted to make the break
several times before, but somehow the jealous scenes with Lily were
patched up. In the Third Act, Bataille brings the drama to a climax
at Prince Paule de Chabran's home.

Lolette comes to see the Prince, hoping to find an ally in him.
"They are trying to get rid of us," she tells him. "We have the
same interest—to defend ourselves." But the old Prince does not
see it that way. He is too preoccupied with the financial settlement
he is expecting and he has no use for emotional outbursts that may
interfere with it. Above all, he does not want a scandal.[1] The Prince
lectures Lolette on the strength of organized society, where the
power is in the hands of the rich and she is helpless. He advises her
to be practical and make the best of it. Lolette leaves him, but not
his house.

She hides in the garden. After the Prince discusses some details

---

[1] It was said that M. Bardac had a mistress of his own and had no objection to divorcing
his wife.

of his settlement with the Princess he leaves her with Pierre, who has just arrived. Lolette's return interrupts their love scene.[1]

LOLETTE: (*To the Princess, who starts for the door*) Wait ... don't go away! If you move, I'll scream, I'll call—I'm ready to summon the whole street!

PIERRE: (*Running toward her*) Not here, not here! Don't make any scenes. . . . Come on, let's go.

LOLETTE: Be still, you! I'm not talking to you. It's to that woman there! Honestly! They steal your husband and then don't even let you talk about it for two minutes! I'd like to have a talk with you—and we're going to have it.

PRINCESS: (*Sitting down again*) But madame, I'm not running away. You could have come directly to me, I would have received you. . . .

LOLETTE: I was hiding in the garden. (*Pointing at Pierre*) I saw him walk in . . . I knew you were here, and that I was going to find you all sprawled out. . . . Hey, are you afraid, you, woman? You're not quite sure . . . you keep looking at my hands. Perhaps I have a revolver in my bag—you can see it, can't you?

PIERRE: Now, I beg you, please, please, Lolette . . . be reasonable. Come, come . . .

LOLETTE: Be quiet, you! I have disturbed you—it was so charming, just the two of you! (*Looks the Princess up and down with utter contempt*) Now, would you please look at her get-up? You've chosen well, my dear, my congratulations! And your eyes, your horrible eyes, both of you! (*Turning to Pierre*) Tie your tie again properly, you idiot!

PIERRE: This grotesque scene has lasted long enough . . . get out now, I order you, or I'll use force. . . .

LOLETTE: I've told you, I'm going to talk. I want to talk to both of you—nothing is going to stop me, not even your threats. . . .

PIERRE: You're crazy. Come away.

LOLETTE: No, no!

---

[1] Whether or not the following scene took place in just this way, there is no doubt in my mind that the problem was discussed by all three: Lily with Claude, Claude with Mme. Bardac, and perhaps even Mme. Bardac with Lily.

PRINCESS: Don't interfere, please . . . madame has the right, we do owe it to her. We must have a talk. Nothing is simpler. . . .

PIERRE: Oh well, perhaps a good discussion, frank and final. . . . It shall be as you wish. Go ahead!

LOLETTE: (*Looking at him*) A coward, a coward! (*Suddenly she puts her hands over her eyes*) It's horrible. You cannot understand how horrible it is to see you both like this. (*She is crying and trembling.*)

PIERRE: (*With regret*) Why did you come, my child?

PRINCESS: Please sit down, madame, I beg you. My most sincere desire is to make good, as far as possible, the wrong I have done you, to assure you a comfortable life worthy of you, and of a kind your husband could not afford. And I admit this would be only a small compensation.

LOLETTE: Now it's charity! And *your* charity, of course! I'd be ashamed to accept it . . . but if I don't I can go and die on the bare floor! That's the alternative.

PRINCESS: My offer, as I see it, cannot be called charity. Believe me it will be much more generous than anything that is usually called by that name.

LOLETTE: I should hope so! You're taking everything away from me and you think you are not going to do anything to make up for it. Money? I should say I'll need money, and lots of it! You're rich, you . . . when one pays for the luxury of getting a man, one should learn what it costs.

PIERRE: Lolette!

PRINCESS: Congratulations, madame. On this ground we'll understand each other much better. Let's talk about the practical side. Let me explain how I see it and you can tell me if I'm wrong, if it will not be satisfactory to you. . . . First of all, your means will be assured, you'll have a regular allowance. And this income—

LOLETTE: (*Interrupting her with sudden fury*) But I don't want your dirty money—keep it! Do you really think I am going to soil my hands with it? Can you give me back the man I love, without whom I feel I wouldn't be able to breathe another day? Yes, yes, it's horrible to admit such cowardice! You take everything away from me with your money.... You've bought him, but you are not going to get me in the bargain! I've listened to your proposition, both of you ... I refuse, I refuse everything! There will be no divorce. I will remain ... and it will be you who is going to leave! (*She shakes her fist at the Princess.*)

PRINCESS: (*Pulling herself together*) This certainly cannot go on much longer. You have to choose between us, M. Bernier ... and right now. One of us has to say good-bye to you, and forever.

LOLETTE: Yes, and it's not going to be me. (*To Pierre*) You have no right to leave me. What is going to become of me? Just think of it ... should I get myself a lover? You have made me faithful to you, and I cannot love anyone else. How can I look for a new life, run from one man to another to find one who would take care of me? Must I return to prostitution? If you'd left me where I was, yes ... but now, I couldn't do it. It's your fault, you've given me a conscience. What for, good Lord? Each time I failed, you dragged me back to the "heights." Well, I am there! At last I've become the woman you wanted me to be, now I can no longer change back. That's finished, and you have a duty to perform. It's me whom you have to keep and you are going to keep me....

PIERRE: I've made you what you are, I've helped you to attain a certain social standing. I'm leaving you on a higher plane which can serve you as a springboard. Life is far richer in its resources than you think. You can remake your circle of friends, like everybody else in the world you can find a better love than mine, and far, far happier....

LOLETTE: Ah! so it's me you're condemning? I can feel it! You've made your choice—go and be happy with her, you brute! It will never be like Loulou's love ... your little Loulou, your poor barefoot Loulou! What we have been to each other cannot happen twice. I've taken it as she never would have: I had your youth, but also your misery and we pulled our yoke together. Those were the days, when your pants were worn and you didn't have four shirts in your drawer. (*To the Princess*) Oh, by God, this was not the elegant gentleman *you* know! It was *la purée*, *la purée noire*... Pierre, Pierre, what have you done? (*She cries*).

PIERRE: My poor girl, if you knew how I am torn, torn to pieces...

LOLETTE: (*Taking him by the arm*) Oh, this is impossible! (*To the Princess*) You see, he has pity on me! You're not going to take him away, you are going to leave him to me! You have no idea what you're doing! Don't do this, don't do this... have pity! Look, I am on my knees to you, madame, I don't scream, I don't threaten, I beg... have pity on me! Come away, Pierre, let's go, my dear, my love—you do love me a little, don't you? Come, I beg you—let's go home, shall we?

PRINCESS: I don't want to be the cause of such unhappiness. Monsieur Bernier, you are free!

LOLETTE: You see, Pierre, she says it herself! It was a bad dream. It's finished now, let's go home. (*She pulls him by the arm. The Princess takes his hat from the table and is going to give it to him. Pierre makes a negative sign to her which does not escape Lolette. Lolette straightens herself and gives a horrible scream.*) Ah! I saw you—you made a sign to her to keep quiet! I was there, on my knees—I have humiliated myself, but you have decided to go to the limit. Oh, how I hate you both, how I hate you! But you're not going to get away with it. You'll see... you —*la gueuse*, and you—*maquereau! maquereau!!*

PIERRE: Come, come, Loulou!

LOLETTE: Yes, yes—and I'll scream as much as I like! You're not frightening me, I'll resist, I'll resist... (*Suddenly she stops. She remains this way for a few seconds, then she makes a gesture of utter despair.*) Ah! no... look, I understand—it's all over.... You're going to have what you want. Do you have pen and ink here?

PIERRE: What are you going to do now?

LOLETTE: Leave me alone. (*She writes, dictating to herself*) Monsieur, I am asking for a divorce... from my husband, Monsieur Bernier.... Please consider this request as final. (*Pierre and the Princess look at each other while Lolette writes. Pierre starts toward Lolette, who pushes him away without lifting her head*)

Shoo, shoo ... the address ... All you have to do is to mail it. ... (*She gets up without looking at anyone*) It's finished between us, Pierre. It's what you both want—here you are!

PIERRE: Well now, come ... (*Takes his hat to accompany her.*)

LOLETTE: Ah, no—now I order you not to follow me. It's all finished. You have what you wanted, now leave me alone. No more, no more, it's all over. . . .

PIERRE: But where are you going?

LOLETTE: (*Without turning around*) What difference does it make now?

The last act takes place in a private hospital in Neuilly in Paris. Lolette is there recovering after attempted suicide. The bullet has remained in her lungs, but she is going to live, she has been told. At one time Lolette had had trouble with her lungs.[1] The Princess comes to visit her; she brings her flowers and still hopes to "arrange" everything. She promises to give Pierre back to Lolette.

"Ah," Lolette says, "if it were up to you! It's *he* who does not love *me*. . . ." Lolette knows that Pierre has been lying to her. Her sister has been spying on him and has reported to her that Pierre spends every night with the Princess.

When Pierre comes in the Princess leaves them alone. Lolette tells Pierre she knows all about it, but she repeats that he had made her one of the happiest women in the world and she asks him for the last time if she could take the place of the Princess—"perhaps gradually push her away. . . ."[2]

It is then, after explaining to her how he plans to take care of her—to take her to the South of France, to visit her there—that Pierre tells her that he does not love her any more. ". . . I would like to love you, Loulou, as I used to, as you still love me, but what can I do if I don't—if I cannot? One has to resign oneself. If the will were enough to bring the past to life, I swear that you would be the happiest woman, for you don't know how true it was when

---

[1] Lily began to develop tuberculosis during the first years of her marriage to Debussy.

[2] After Debussy "left" Lily, upon his return to Paris, he asked her to come to see him. Lily spent many nights with him hoping to win him back.

you said a minute ago, 'I know that you suffer because you cannot love me any more, Pierrot.' Oh, you will never know how I suffer! It's a terrible thing to see your former love die within you ... it's as if one wanted to come to the rescue of a child and would say, 'my little one' and he disappeared the more you hugged him. It is not my fault...." [1]

The play ends with Lolette returning to the poor painter, where Pierre originally had found her.

This is the weakest point of the play. Actually Lily's situation was worse than Lolette's—she had no one to return to and nowhere to go. There are only two reports available on Lily after her "Debussy days." In her memoirs Mary Garden says that Lily came to see her backstage after a revival performance of *Pelléas* at the Opéra Comique in 1925.

"Oh Mary, you are back with *Pelléas!*" Lily cried. "It's so marvelous, and you know—Claude is with me! I bought myself two tickets, one for me and one for him. Claude is with me tonight, right there in the seat next to mine ... his spirit is there in the house. I feel him everywhere. Don't you?"

"Then suddenly the door of my dressing room opened and in came a man with an old lady on his arm," Garden continues her story. "She was dressed in black, walking with a cane, and as she came toward me her lips trembled and she couldn't say anything. Then she broke into a fit of sobbing. And this was the second Madame Debussy..."

Madame Bardac did not see Lily, who walked out without saying a word. When Madame Bardac left, Garden turned to Aristide Briand, the Prime Minister, who had happened to witness the scene, and asked: "Which of them do you suppose really loved Debussy for himself?"

"I suspect they both did—each in her own way," Briand said.

A few years later, in 1929, Léon Vallas gave a series of lectures on Debussy at the Sorbonne. Lily attended them like a student and after Vallas made allusions to the "picturesque circumstances of his

---

[1] Indeed, Debussy said just that to his friends.

marriage," Lily, says Vallas, told him, "not without malice," that what he said was "almost true," and thereafter "confided many a touching intimacy," which Vallas refused to reveal. What more could Lily have added to what Bataille had made public already?

La Femme Nue was considered the best play Henry Bataille had written. It was given again in 1911, 1916, 1923, 1928, I understand a moving picture was based on it, and an opera by Henri Février, composer of *Monna Vanna*. Bataille's play must have had a devastating psychological effect on the composer. The drama was on display for everyone to see, not for one night but for years, and in Paris, where Debussy lived and could not escape being reminded of it whenever he looked at the theatrical page or passed the billboards on the street. Public opinion had branded him and he knew it.

Up to this day musicologists have been puzzled by the question of what happened to Debussy during the second part of life that caused his creative ability to wane. If it is no longer an enigma to me, it is because I believe that even a man of lesser sensitivity than Debussy would have broken down under the circumstances.

There is no trace of Debussy's reaction to the play. In an undated letter to Jacques Durand in Cannes, written during the following month of March, Debussy said: "There is a letter for you at the Hôtel Gonnet which contains the most circumstantial news. . . . Do claim it imperiously, because I declare myself incapable of remembering the details which may amuse you. As for the Parisian *tourbillon,* you will permit me to pay little attention to it. We laugh, by mistake, at American 'bluff' because we cultivate a sort of artistic 'bluff' ourselves, which one of these days will hit us in the face—very disagreeably for French vanity."

Debussy ends his letter by saying: "Don't think of me as a pessimist because of the tone of this letter. I hate this sort of attitude, only from time to time people disgust me and I have to cry out to someone who won't take it for a sickness."

The letter Debussy mentioned was not published. His remarks may have been in reference to the play or they may have had bearing on a musical "affair" then brewing in Paris.

CHAPTER XIX

DEBUSSYSM

DEBUSSY'S ALREADY unhappy life was to be still further troubled. In my biography of Maurice Ravel I have given a detailed account of *L'Affaire Ravel*, as it was called; *Le cas Debussy* ("The Debussy Case") was the other side of the story.

In the spring of 1902 the success of *Pelléas et Mélisande* was questionable. In fact there is no doubt that had it not been for Lalo's article hailing it as a masterpiece and Carré's clever management of a claque recruited from Debussy's ardent admirers, the opera might have gone into oblivion. At about that time Jean Lorrain, a reporter on the *Journal*, began to throw darts against the production in his "Pall Mall" column, and on January 4, 1904, he published a long article that opened the campaign against Debussysm. As humorous as it was malicious, it could not escape public attention:

Just as they were convulsed with admiration over the sunny *pizzicati* of that little masterpiece *L'Après-midi d'un Faune*, they have now declared that we must go into raptures over the deliberate dissonances of the lengthy recitatives in *Pelléas*. Those long-drawn chords and those perpetual beginnings of repeatedly announced phrases have an enervating effect. A kind of titillation that is at first pleasurable, then exasperating, and in the end, cruelly painful, is inflicted on the ears of the audience by the continual repetition of a theme that is constantly interrupted and which never terminates. This work with its limbo-like atmosphere and its occasional little shocks so very artistic (oh, my dear!) and so upsetting (you can imagine!) received the united votes of a public consisting of snobs and poseurs.

Obviously Lorrain was no match for Lalo in arguing the musical merits of the opera and, having offered these generalities, he centered his attack on a certain group of people in the audience, a subject far more congenial to his style.

"Thanks to these ladies and gentlemen, M. Claude Debussy has become the head of a new religion," Lorrain announced, and he went on to say that the Opéra Comique took on the atmosphere of a sanctuary, that the audiences wore an air of compunction, exchanging meaningful glances and *mous* full of complicity, that after the preludes, which were listened to in a religious silence, the initiated greeted one another in the corridors, fingers on lips, and that peculiar handshakes were hastily given in the semidarkness of the boxes by men with crucified expressions on their faces and eyes with a faraway look.

"Music is the last religion left in this century without faith," Lorrain continued, comparing *Pelléas* to performances of Wagnerian operas at the Châlet theater, "which in ardor and hypnotic faith remind one of early Christian meetings in the catacombs. But at least," he said, "the Wagner followers are sincere. They come from all classes of society and the humility of their clothes, the ugliness, sometimes sublime, of their suffering faces, testify to the strength and even violence of their belief. M. Debussy's religion has more elegance; the neophytes fill the orchestra seats and the first tier of boxes..." and to illustrate his point Lorrain described them as ever-present in the audience during the past two years.

... That fair-haired girl, too frail, too pale, and too fair, who has evidently got herself up to look like Mary Garden... her fingers listlessly turning the pages of the score placed on the edge of the box, or that whole group of good-looking young men (nearly all Debussysts are young, very young), ephebi with long hair skillfully brushed in bangs across their foreheads, those youths with plump, pallid faces, deep-set eyes, velvet-collared frock coats, with slightly puffed sleeves, the redingotes a little too tight at the waist, with satin cravats that thicken their necks, or floating Windsor ties, nonchalantly tied over an open collar when the Debussyst is in a business suit, and all wearing on their little fingers (because they all have beautiful hands) some kind of precious ring from Egypt or Byzantium and all appearing in couples. Orestes and Pylades *communiant* under the guise of Pelléas and Mélisande, or the personification of perfection of a son with lowered eyes accompanying his mother (they all love their mothers) and all, all 'drinking in' Miss Garden's gestures, Jusseaume's scenery, Carré's lighting effects, all of them archangels with the eyes of visionaries, who at impressive moments whisper in one another's ears words that reach the very depths of the soul...the *Pelléastres!*

And to make sure that his readers would not misunderstand his pun, Lorrain devoted the second part of his article to a detailed description of the character and occupation of a prototype with "the most beautiful hand in Paris."

The article annoyed Debussy, for despite being an obvious exaggeration, there was a bit of truth in it. Indignant, he wrote Louÿs about it, but Louÿs advised him to ignore it. This was one of the last suggestions Louÿs gave him before the end of their friendship. Debussy, nonetheless, wrote a protest. It was not published. It would have been forgotten if at the time of *La Mer*'s first performance, Debussy's new friend Laloy had not written an extravagant eulogy. Thereupon Camille Mauclair, the writer and art critic, who later (after Debussy's death) claimed to have been entrusted by Maeterlinck with judging the score of *Pelléas* before he gave his authorization, wrote an article reviving the idea of Debussysm as an unhealthy cult. Mauclair called it "Debussyitis, a peculiar form of intoxication, a disease that should be studied and treated by pathologists."

"I should never have imagined that *Pelléas* could produce such an effect," Mauclair said. "One would think those people had been listening to a revolutionary hymn. They smell blood and gunpowder and they fall under a kind of hypnotic spell. It is very curious. A mixture of saltpeter, Cretan bhang, hashish, and curry works them up to a state of rabid mysticism. They run about like those Malays who become prey to a murderous frenzy known as *amok*."

The history of French music is marked by definite stages of its evolution when protagonists and their adversaries formed groups—ready, like fanatics, to defend their faith. In the eighteenth century they fought for French music against Italian, then came the Romantics and later the Wagnerites, the Parnassians, the Symbolists, the Impressionists; they were divided into those who were for or against the Academy, Prix de Rome, Conservatory and Scola Cantorum, Franckists and d'Indysts, and after the performance of *Pelléas,* as Édmond Bailly predicted—Debussysts.

As happens in the French Chamber of Deputies during periods of crisis (and each new major musical event invariably caused one), the warring parties regrouped, coalesced, or formed new ranks among the various partisans. But none of their discussions stirred so much furor and confusion as the appearance of Maurice Ravel and his adherents. Even such critics as Garraud, Marnold and Lalo found themselves now fighting against, and then defending again, the same new tendencies.

Ravel was thirteen years younger than Debussy, but he became known as a composer earlier in his life, so that the development of his art right from its beginning ran parallel to that of the already mature Debussy. His first recognition came even before he had supplied a sufficient basis for it; he had a whole cadre of admirers before there was anything to admire, if one may say so, for, in contrast to Debussy, Ravel lived in close friendship with his fellow musicians. He belonged to a group of talented young artists. They called themselves *Les Apaches*, because each such coterie felt it had to have some kind of name. Florent Schmitt, the composer, Tristan Klingsor, a poet and musician, Dmitri Calvocoressi, the music critic, Maurice Delage, another composer, and Ricardo Viñes, one of the most prominent pianists at that time, were the "early Ravelites," whose headquarters were at Delage's studio on the rue de Civry, where they met and held their discourses. Viñes, Ravel's closest comrade from his childhood, who as a pianist was usually called upon for the first performances of new works, and Erik Satie, another friend of Ravel's, were the only links between this group and Debussy. For although Debussy knew *Les Apaches* personally, his relationship with them, while cordial, remained always distant.

Ravel's and Debussy's names were first linked when at a concert in January 1902 Viñes played Debussy's piano pieces called *Es-*

tampes: Pagodes, La Soirée dans Grenade and *Jardin sous la pluie,* and the Ravelites were surprised by the close resemblance of *La Soirée dans Grenade* to Ravel's *Habañera,* composed in 1895. Ravel remembered well that on March 5, 1898, at a concert organized by the Société Nationale, after the first performance of *Habañera,* which passed without particular notice by the audience, Debussy had borrowed the manuscript of the piece. Debussy later explained that he had mislaid the piece before he had a chance to examine it carefully, but the Ravelites accused him of what they called the "well-known Debussy trait of borrowing" from other musicians.

Later, in March, 1904, another Debussy composition, *L'Esquisse,* was published, first by *Paris Illustré* and later in the same year by the Édition Schott of Brussels under the title *D'un Cahier d'Esquisses,* a composition which also bore a definite resemblance to *Habañera.* The *Habañera* incident has always been considered as the prime reason for the cooling off of the relationship between the two composers. Actually, Debussy paid no attention to the allegations of plagiarism and, as if to show his unchanged feelings for Ravel, he wrote him concerning Ravel's quartet shortly before its first performance in March 1904: "In the name of the gods of music and in mine, do not touch a single note of what you have written in your quartet." But when a few months later Ravel joined those who subscribed to help Lily, the Ravel-Debussy relationship met the same end as the rest of those on the list. Thus, when in 1907 the Ravelites and the Debussysts came to a real battle, the two composers were no longer "on speaking terms."

The sparks began to fly because Pierre Lalo in his not unusual criticism of Ravel had touched a sensitive spot. He questioned the originality of Ravel's piano works, something Ravel was particularly proud of and with good reason.

"I would like to call your impartial attention to the following point," Ravel wrote Lalo. "You expatiate at some length upon a certain type of writing for the piano, whose invention you ascribe to Debussy. But the *Jeux d'eau* appeared at the beginning of 1902, at a time when there were only "Three Pieces for Piano" composed by Debussy, for which, I do not need to tell you, I have a passionate admiration, but works which from a purely pianistic point of view did not contribute anything new. I hope you will excuse this legitimate claim."

Ravel had the satisfaction of putting Lalo in his place, and Lalo swallowed the pill but he did not forget it. A year later the performance of Ravel's *Histoires naturelles* created one of those scandals the French relish as a real proof of success. The concert hall was a battlefield of bravos and screams of "throw them out."

"There has been no other such frenzied success in the annals of the old Société Nationale," Louis Laloy reported, but in the eyes of most of those in the audience and those who heard about it, it was a regular scandal, a *lèse-majesté* crime.

The discussion was picked up by the newspapers and blown up into what was called *L'Affaire Ravel*. All sorts of arguments, theoretical as well as historical, were brought into a dispute which no longer centered on Ravel's latest work alone. All the "warring sects" joined the conflict with Debussysts and Ravelites as the main forces.

Debussy was the only one who kept aloof. After the first performance of *La Mer* and the birth of his child he was engrossed in his personal affairs, which were far from settled. If during all his former emotional perturbations he was incapable of working, one can easily imagine that the latest thunderbolt in his drama with Lily destroyed his capacity to concentrate. Withdrawn into the privacy of his home, Debussy nevertheless was well aware of the brewing storm, in which his name never left the foreground. If he could, he would probably have left Paris so that he would no longer have to "breathe this enervating Paris air; not be obliged to have talent; to pluck ideas as one would pick a flower, that's not bad! Is this possible in Paris, where the spitefulness of one hundred mouths lies in wait for you, and everybody is a genius?—at least for one evening," he wrote Jacques Durand, probably the only man with whom he was then in constant contact, primarily because of business.

Durand urged Debussy to work (after all, Debussy had signed a contract to supply a certain number of compositions), and Durand was also concerned with having Debussy's works played during the season. He suggested a Colonne program of Debussy's works arranged in chronological order, but Debussy declined—he was afraid of being accused of scraping the bottom of his drawer just to keep his name on concert billboards. He realized only too well that he had not completed, nor had ready for performance, anything new, and he admitted: "I continue to stagnate *dans les usines du néant*, if I may say so.... You cannot imagine the anguish this state of mind can cause you ... even without mentioning all painful and unpleasant things, I have to endure the fact that I can no longer think with the same freedom. It is idiotic—imagine a blind brain."

Debussy said he was doing all he could to overcome this "bad period," but he was not always satisfied with his progress. Yet he must, he will succeed, he said. "I give you my word," he promised Durand. He worked on *Ibéria* and talked again about Edgar Allan Poe's "The Devil in the Belfry"—"but if Music does not reserve a single smile for me, then she must have a really brutal heart," he said with resignation.

During the summer Debussy went with his family to Puys, near Dieppe. But if Durand hoped that the "change of scene" would bring the long-expected fruitful results, he must have been disappointed when he finally heard from him. "Here I am again with my old friend, the sea; it is always endless and beautiful," Debussy wrote in almost his old bantering vein. "It is really the one thing in Nature which restores you best to your place. But people do not respect the sea sufficiently ... they should not be permitted to dunk their bodies, deformed by everyday life; why honestly, all these arms and legs gesticulating in ridiculous rhythms—it's enough to make the fish weep. In the sea, there should be only *sirènes*, and do you suppose those estimable persons would consent to return to waters frequented by this rather low company?

"The hotel where we live is managed by a certain Monsieur X and he is a dangerous man.... He does his own marketing and brings the most horrible provisions, he brings bad luck to fish, to meat ... in short, he is a patent murderer. But as his hotel is the only one in this place, he smiles at all remarks and continues his sinister mission.

"Please excuse these details of the domestic economy, but Carlyle, being a dyspeptic, knew what he was talking about when he said that an artist should eat better than anybody else. Well, what can we do? As for music...I have a feeling that there are three ways to end *Ibéria;* should one play it *à pile ou face* or look for the fourth way?"

One would almost believe that the sea restored Debussy to himself. But except for reading the proofs of the German translation of *Pelléas,* then in the process of publication, he did not do anything during that summer or the following winter, or, indeed, in the following year.

"Sincere admirers of the creator of *Pelléas*—who daily increase in number—have long been deploring the silence of their favorite composer," Émile Vuillermoz, at one time an ardent Debussyst, wrote in *La Nouvelle Presse.*[1]

From the depths of his no doubt laborious retreat, M. Debussy does not condescend to send them anything but old compositions that have been lying by, and revivals or republications of early works. These old productions, under new titles and in new shapes, are being systematically passed in review to the great sorrow of musical epicures, who are partial to first editions and unpublished works.

This *Jet d'eau* [Vuillermoz referred to a recent performance at the Concerts Colonne of an orchestral version of a vocal composition written in 1887]—a mere extract from the *Cinq poèmes de Baudelaire* which all Debussysts know by heart—will not satisfy their thirst for novelty. Besides, there is something contemptible about the facile manner in which the composer of the *Nocturnes* has orchestrated this old song, in order to ensure that his name should not be banished from the Colonne concert posters during the entire winter season. The instrumentation of the piece lacks fluidity, freshness, and brilliance. The dear, familiar technique that characterizes *Pelléas* is used haphazardly, without any descriptive justification. The piano version is preferable to an orchestral score that has neither coherence nor color.

[1] February 26, 1907.

One wonders whether, during his long period of idleness, M. Debussy is not losing that marvelous skill, that instinct which has made him one of the most remarkable poets of the modern orchestra. If that is the case, I see only one remedy for his disastrous situation. Let the composer of *Pelléas* read the works of the young composers who are regarded as his pupils; let him listen to his 'junior class,' which contemporary critics are ridiculing—a little too readily, perhaps. There, very skillfully treated, he will find all the new sonorous effects which he seems to have forgotten. The master can draw a useful lesson from the works of his impudent disciples, and he will realize with amazement the dangers that lie in wait for him. If he does not resolutely take his place once more at the head of the contemporary musical movement, the composer of *Pelléas* will find that the young generation of parasites which has grown up around his work is writing *Debussyst* music—better than he.

Debussy did not pick up the gauntlet. Pierre Lalo did instead.

A month later [1] he wrote a blistering article in his Sunday column in *Le Temps* taking up the question of Debussysm.[2]

It is an incontestable fact that the great majority of young French composers write "Debussyst" music.... At the present time it is fashionable to hold a certain opinion about "Debussysm." This opinion can be summarized as follows: "M. Debussy was the most eloquent speaker for a whole generation of musicians, who, nourishing the same intentions as he, have been writing for a long time in silence and obscurity his most successful discoveries." ... He only was fortunate to be the first to publish the discoveries which belong to all. The young French musicians do not owe a thing to him. Between them and him there is no question of influence, or imitation, but that of coincidence and of natural similarity. It is an error and pure injustice to maintain that they resemble M. Debussy; one could just as well say that Debussy resembles them....

It would be not entirely wasteful to pause and consider this new theory. No doubt most musicians who belong to this group are at the beginning of their careers and their reputation does not transcend the narrow limits of their own little coterie. But they represent the future, and it is they who will make the music of tomorrow in France.

One must tell them at once: their theory does not seem to me to be

---

[1] March 19.
[2] Lalo's article is given in full in my book *Maurice Ravel*.

anything but an impudent mockery; it cannot be justified either by the dates of the works or by the character of the compositions: neither by history nor by esthetic values.

Let us take history first. Debussy's first works are already twenty years old. *La Damoiselle élue* and *Printemps* are of 1888, *Les Ariettes* of 1889, *Cinq poèmes de Baudelaire* of 1890, *L'Après-midi d'un Faune* of 1892, *Les Proses lyriques* of 1893, and at this time *Pelléas et Mélisande* was already begun. From that period on—that is, more than fifteen years ago—Debussy's personality was completely formed. Where was the generation of the young musicians then, who today pretend that they owe nothing to him, and that they invented at the same time as he did the art which is in error attributed to him? ... What have his rivals and their successors produced that could give them even a shadow of some kind of reason to claim a part in the foundation of the art which they now practice and to dispute the right of Debussy to his glory as its creator?

... As for the character of the music, the presumption of these young people is no better founded than when the question was put to the test of history. All that is precious and admirable in Debussy's art—all that makes his a profound originality—is a new sensitivity, a sensitivity marvelously intense and delicate, a sensitivity toward nature, which lets him evoke the soul of things without any descriptive anxiety.

What is there in common between this art, which flowed from the very source of poetic sentiment, and the art of the diligent little composers who claim this art as their own? In none of their works have they succeeded in evoking nature. They have never expressed an emotion or passion of a human soul. They do nothing but write notes, combinations of chords, and the tone coloring of different instruments; they have in common with Debussy only the technique of composing. And this technique they have borrowed directly from him.

... It is possible that they might have been endowed with the same sensitivity as Debussy, and that in fact there was one way of feeling for a whole epoch; but it is impossible, it is absurd, to suppose that a whole generation of composers should have rediscovered in themselves, should have spontaneously re-created a technique invented exactly fifteen years ago by a musician they all know exceedingly well. One must remind them once again: the dates are there.

These young people, by the way, do more than just claim a part in M. Debussy's art. They have recently begun to push M. Debussy out of 'Debussysm,' even to discard him altogether, to point out to him that he has, hereafter, nothing to do with this business, since he never did have much to do with it of any importance. They let him know that his own 'Debussysm' is today a bit primitive, that he has been by-passed, that now everybody is 'doing Debussy' better than Debussy himself.

This is terribly funny, one cannot go much further in the grotesque than these conceited, pompous simpletons do.

...It seems to me that only a few years ago, when speaking of the first works of the counterfeit "Debussysts," I pointed to the dangers to M. Debussy himself. The results already have proven that I was right. I hope that I will not be even more right in the future. I hope that the vulgarization and exploitation of "Debussysm" by clever and mediocre composers will not make too ephemeral the future of a delightful art and will not turn us away from loving the exquisite musician as his work merits.

Far from resolving the question of Debussysm, Lalo's article gave new impetus to a continuing polemic. In the spring of 1907, Vallas, then the managing editor of *La Revue musicale de Lyon*, asked Jean Marnold to give his opinion on *L'Affaire Ravel*. At that time Marnold, besides being the founder and editor of *Mercure musical*, held the post of music critic on *Le Mercure de France* and was considered by both Ravelites and Debussysts as an authority on the science of musical theories. A close friend of Ravel and a champion of his music, Marnold spoke more of Debussy than of Ravel in his answer to Vallas, published as an open letter on May 1, 1907: [1]

...The question of "Debussysm" is a complex one and interesting to elucidate from the purely musical point of view, the only one appropriate to the subject, in my humble opinion.

Nothing could be more childish than the way it recently has been presented in many instances in the musical press. It is just as absurd to maintain that Debussy *invented* nothing, as to imagine that he *invented* all the harmonic material which he uses and in which lie the most important and most marvelous characteristics of his art.

...Actually, the so-called present "Debussysm" is only a phase of the eternal process between the consonance and dissonance. Therefore, one

[1] Marnold's article is given in full in my book *Maurice Ravel*.

who would consider intervals of a fourth or sixth as consonant intervals, or who would introduce the interval of a third in a final chord, is already in his own way "doing Debussysm." Does this mean that one is imitating Debussy or is doing as he does? Can one be accused of having plagiarized his "technique"?

There is a similar naïveté in reproaching our young musicians for making use of "Debussyite" harmony. At all times artists have legitimately exploited the harmonic resources which they owed to a predecessor's genius, whether far or near. But, on the other hand, our musicians have the best reason to practice "Debussyite" harmony—that is, without simply copying it. They could not make use of any other kind and they should make use of this particular one.

Harmonic evolution, as a matter of fact, is strictly *determined* by the nature of the phenomenon of sound. From the time of the origin of our music this evolution has followed a progressive march from the most simple to the more and more complex, while the gradual familiarization of our senses with the correspondence of different intervals—at first known as dissonance, and later accepted as consonance—has rigorously followed the order of the series of the constitutive harmonies of the musical sound.

Then the hour of "Debussyite" harmony struck. It would have been impossible to put this in practice some hundred years ago. Today Debussy's claim is inevitable. Certainly, the glory belongs to Debussy for having penetrated the surrounding vibrations of the sound. Without his genius we might have come much more slowly and imperfectly, for Debussy's gesture is without comparison, without precedent, no matter how far back we go in the history of sound. But was the author of *Pelléas* not born at a time when we were somehow "doing Debussy" without knowing it?

And it has always been that way. Masterpieces are factors, unconscious as well as conscious, in the evolution of music. Exploring this evolution one will find that in each epoch the material of the art work is always different, but is determined by the harmonic development of the preceding one and is common to all contemporaries; and, what is interesting to note, the more one withdraws from the present, the more the originality of the creator pales.

...It is very likely that a lack of familiarity may currently lead some to a confusion of Debussy and Ravel, and none can boast of having escaped this initial impression. Thus it would be appropriate to be on one's guard against hasty and bold judgments.

One cannot prevent the future generation from using its own language, different from that of yesterday. It was of this that I wrote in July of 1904 in the *Mercure de France*. One need not fear to appear as an imitator of Debussy. Without copying him, one should follow him. Claude Debussy's art does not consist solely in his harmony; it also lies in his particular way of using it, which belongs only to him—it is made of something that only he could "create" and the radiant beauty of which disdains time and imitators.

Marnold closed his article with a sudden, but final, statement that in his opinion Ravel was a genius. This brought to an end, at least in the press, the long controversy over Ravel's individual gifts and independence of Debussy, but it did not restrain musicians from further probing into Debussy's art and Debussysm.

Nine months later, in February 1908, *L'Éclair*, a Paris daily, asked Maurice Leclerq to interview Debussy in connection with the planned commemoration of the twenty-fifth anniversary of Wagner's death.

"The influence of Wagner?" Debussy repeated Leclerq's question. "Do you really believe that there are any influences, masters and disciples of a school? There are masters, of course ... that is, the musicians on whom this title is bestowed. But there are no disciples ... no more. And if there are no disciples, then there are no leaders, no heads of a school." Debussy got up from his chair as he continued. "And this, sir, is not only in music, but also in literature, painting, sculpture—in all the arts. Today all musicians and artists are highly individual ... personal. They take the greatest care not to show any influence in their works. . . ." Debussy began to pace up and down the room. "Admiration of great works remains. We have never had as many admirers as we have today, but admirers are not disciples. No, there are no heads of a school which can have an influence. The head of a school should have an original ... special technique, a doctrine of his own, *his own* grammar. Today a musician or an artist who is famous has only one occupation—to create his own individual works. He has not time for disciples. This is the case of all contemporary musicians ... Wagner and others. But you are not going to publish this?" Debussy suddenly asked. "I was only talking. If you want to please me, leave me out of this. Or if you insist, then write just one line, something neutral." Debussy returned to the table and wrote on a piece of paper: "I consider Wagner's curve to have been accomplished. Wagner was and will remain a great artist. Claude Debussy."

This interview was not published at that time. But eighteen months later *La Revue du Temps présent*, in its zeal to settle the Debussy question once and for all, sent out questionnaires to a number of noted musicians, men of letters and artists in France and abroad.

1: What is the actual significance of M. Claude Debussy, and what should be his role in the evolution of contemporary music?

2: Is he a really original personality or merely an accidental phenomenon?

3: Is he the representative of a fruitful innovation, of a formula, or a tendency capable of creating a new school—should he, in fact, create such a school?

Out of twenty-eight answers only a few were in Debussy's favor, among them those signed by Ernest Ansermet, Camille Chevillard, Carré and Garraud. Romain Rolland asked to be excused: "I have too much work to do to answer questionnaires. My friend Jean Christophe [1] would answer for me: 'I don't particularly like all your modern French music very much and I am not mad about your M. Debussy. But what I can't understand is that, being so poor in artists, you have to quarrel about the greatest one you have. As for the question of whether he is the leader of a school, and what this school will be worth, one can simply say that every great artist has a school and that all schools are evil. Would it be better, perhaps, not to have great artists? Jean Christophe.' "

Among the negative answers the prize should go to Monsieur A. Chéramy, who said that he did not have the honor of knowing

---

[1] Hero of Rolland's ten-volume novel of that name, portraying the life of a musician of genius in the contemporary world.

Debussy personally but considered him a remarkable musician, admirably gifted and "very clever"—"I am tempted to say: very sly. I think that at the beginning of his career he reasoned in the following way: 'I am not a genius. Nature did not give me the power to create great works, but I know my craft as well as anybody. Therefore, I will use my knowledge to do something that was not done before me. Mozart had said: Melody is the essence of music. After him, Wagner wrote: No music can be created without melody; music and melody are inseparable. Well,' Debussy said to himself, 'I will write music without melody.... No more melody or singing—only curious and unexpected harmonies, nothing precise, everything just in halves, half suggested, half attempted —and in all this I will put the refinement, sensuality, declamations and harmonies which will enchant certain ultra-impressionable and neurotic natures.'

"With this subtle and morbid esthetics he wrote *Pelléas*, a curious work and nothing more. It is something like Verlaine or Mallarmé, a work without grandeur and lacking in emotion, a work which does not offer a trace of human feeling. Nothing is more monotonous and tiring than all these incoherent murmurings, this musical dust that is ready to fly away at the first blow, these whisperings and caresses of these fragile lovers who take their spasm of a second for great triumphs of love and passion. M. Debussy's lovers appear to be tired from birth and are afraid of action. And Pelléas' love impresses me as a treatise on neurasthenia and impotence.

"Debussy will remain a pure accident without a future in the history of art, and to compare him to Wagner is sheer madness. I think that in ten years no one will speak of *Pelléas* and I am waiting with curiosity mixed with anxiety for Debussy's next opera. Debussy's school would perish immediately. Pelléas and Mélisande were not made to reproduce."

This long diatribe on three simple questions, along with other answers, an article by Raphaël Cor, "Claude Debussy and the contemporary snobbism," as well as excerpts from newspapers and magazine articles, were collected by two enterprising journalists, C. Francis Caillard and José de Bérys, and published in book form under the title *Le Cas Debussy* in 1910. It was then that Leclerq's interview was added to the volume, an interview which Debussy had expressly asked not to have made public. Leclerq, besides being untrustworthy, was also a mind reader. To explain Debussy's reluctance to have the interview published, Leclerq said he knew Debussy's thoughts: "Who knows what may happen in the future? No leaders of a school, no disciples, nothing but admirers! But I must be careful. If tomorrow it should occur to them to bestow on me the first title and connect my name with a new school of thought—why be in their way?"

Five years later, in 1913, for the first time in the ten years of wrangling Debussy told Calvocoressi what he really thought about the whole business. "I consider it almost a crime. The former policy of allowing artists to mature in peace was far sounder. It is wicked to unsettle them by making them the subjects of debates that are, generally, as shallow as they are prejudiced. Hardly does a composer appear than people start devoting essays to him and weighing his music down with ambitious definitions. They do far greater harm than even the fiercest detractors could."

Debussy knew that these remarks were going to be published and he spoke with the dignity of a master.

But while the bickering over Debussysm was at its height, Debussy met by chance his old friend René Peter. "Those Debussysts annoy me," Peter said to him. "They annoy you?" Debussy replied. "They are killing me."

CHAPTER XX

ILLNESS

WITH HIS second marriage Debussy was to begin "a new life." Whether this optimistic dictum was realized to his satisfaction is a question not easily to be answered by an outsider. To be sure, he had at last achieved what he had been striving for all his life—the décor, the surroundings he had always envied, and a luxury not to be compared with his past. From the modest little apartment where he lived with Lily he had moved to the most select residential section of Paris, near the Avenue de la Grande Armée and the Bois de Boulogne—a long way from the Montmartre garret he once had shared with Gaby. Debussy's beautiful private home was decorated and furnished on a less theatrical scale than Richard Wagner's "Wahnfried" in Bayreuth, although the comparison may not be farfetched (only Debussy's was in good taste). There he lived, in the harmony of his family: his little daughter Chouchou whom he adored, and his wife, who anticipated his whims and shielded him from the "outside world." The "Claude" or "Monsieur Debussy" of Gaby's and Lily's days was referred to as "*Le Maître.*"

He had achieved fame. His *Pelléas* had been translated into German, Italian and English. In 1907 it had a triumphant success in Brussels, where eight performances were given during four weeks. Two months later it was presented in Frankfurt and a year later in Munich and Berlin. In April, 1908, Toscanini conducted the first performance at La Scala in Milan and in 1909 it was played in Rome. Invariably *Pelléas* caused controversies and in Italy there were riots between those for and against the work. While Giulio

Gatti-Casazza, the director of the Metropolitan Opera Company of New York, was searching for a "perfect" Mélisande for his planned production and Debussy, declaring he did not know one (Mary Garden's name was among those who had helped Lily), suggested Lina Cavalieri, Oscar Hammerstein engaged four major artists (including Mary Garden) from the original Opéra Comique cast and imported them to the United States for performances at the Manhattan Opera House during February 1908.

His other works, *L'Après-midi d'un Faune* and *La Mer*, had been played abroad, but nothing pleased Debussy as much as the growing interest in his music in England, promoted by two new admirers, G. Jean Aubry, a writer and a music critic, and André Caplet, the composer and conductor.

This was not the first time that Debussy turned to England for recognition, but now, with things as they were in Paris, it was particularly gratifying that at last *he* was sought and it was not *he* who was seeking. Although he still believed that the English had only officially established sympathies for music, with Handel and Sullivan amply satisfying their needs, he was unusually cooperative in supplying the data of all his compositions to Jean-Aubry, who had organized a series of performances for a lecture-concert tour. And as a final accolade, the first book on Debussy was to be written by an Englishwoman, Mrs. Franz Liebich. It appeared in 1908 and it bears the following appropriate and revealing motto: *"L'âme d'autrui est une forêt obscure où il faut marcher avec précaution, Claude Debussy."* (The soul of a stranger is an obscure forest where one should walk with caution.) [1]

But Debussy's happiness was far from complete. The dream of financial independence was short-lived. Soon after their marriage Madame Debussy's private income was seriously cut down as I have mentioned before, and the increasing financial demands of the scale on which they chose to live forced him to find new ways to earn more money. He had to accept occasional engagements to conduct his works—the aspect of musical activity he enjoyed the least.

---

[1] *Gil Blas,* March 2, 1903, re. Siegfried Wagner at Concert Lamoureux.

For Debussy was well aware of the lack of improvement in his conducting technique, and since the engagements were of an "occasional" nature they did not offer him the possibility of acquiring sufficient experience. The mere fact that he would conduct only occasionally and for relatively small fees is further evidence of how often and how badly he was in need of funds, for what he earned was a mere drop in a bucket, as he said himself. Or was he doing it more or less out of pride?

"Since I saw you last," Debussy told Toulet, "I have made my debut as the conductor of an orchestra. . . . It is amusing while you seek out the colors with the end of the little baton, but after a time it resembles a man exhibiting some kind of freak, or a performance where your success is not much different, it seems to me, from that of an acrobat after a dangerous stunt. I am going to play this game in England, later in Italy. . . ." Here Debussy paused, and then, perhaps indulging in a bit of indiscretion, added as an afterthought —"Life is full of surprises."

Nor was he as free to compose whenever he had an inspiration. Durand et fils perhaps were generous in providing him with a monthly allowance, but they were not Maecenases, they were in the publishing business and Debussy was constantly urged to supply them with the works he owed under the terms of their bargain. If Debussy's "supply" to Durand during those first years after his second marriage consisted in rewriting, orchestrating and reorchestrating his old works, it was partly because of his constant occupation with a plan for another major lyrical work. Ever since the first performance of *Pelléas* in 1902, Debussy had been interested in the works of Poe, who, he thought, "had the most original imagination in the world."—"He struck an entirely new note, and I shall have to find its equivalent in music," Debussy said as he returned to this search from whatever else he had been working on in the meantime.

At first he chose Poe's "The Devil in the Belfry." While he often announced that the preliminary planning of the work was about to be completed, it took him years to formulate the structure of the piece in his own mind and to focus his main ideas in proper perspective. How much he actually finished, how much was only in the form of sketches or general plans will never be known, for as Debussy said to his friend Dr. Valléry-Radot: "After my death there will not be a note left of my plans." Debussy destroyed them all.

But from what he said at the time he was working on it, it is clear that both in the choice of subject and the plan of its treatment his chief preoccupation was to create something so entirely different that "the people who are so kind as to hope that I shall never be able to escape from *Pelléas* will see that they were very much mistaken."

"Surely," he said, "they must realize that if such a thing were to happen I would immediately devote myself to the cultivation of pineapples, for I think it is quite disastrous to repeat *oneself.*"

This partly explains why *As You Like It*, one of the projects Debussy seriously considered with Toulet, was laid aside; its legendary setting was too reminiscent of Maeterlinck's play (including the forest). And returning again and again to Poe's poem, Debussy anticipated with glee how "the same people will think it shocking of me to have deserted the shadowy Mélisande for a cynical, pirouetting devil, and they will once more make it a pretext for accusing me of eccentricity."

For besides having discovered in Poe's work the material "for a play which would be a happy blending of the real and the fantastic," Debussy was fascinated by the very idea of "the devil represented as cynical and cruel—much more devilish than the red, brimstone-breathing clown that has, so illogically, become a tradition with us," as he once wrote to Messager.

Debussy contrived an original way of portraying his hero: he was not to sing, but to whistle, and the major singing parts of the piece were to be given to a crowd, but here again Debussy had set himself a new problem. In his opinion crowds had never been successfully represented on the stage. He pointed to two examples: Moussorgsky's *Boris Godunov* and Wagner's *Die Meistersinger*. "The populace, the people in *Boris* do not give the illusion of a real crowd," Debussy said. "First one group sings, and then another, there is no third group. They sing alternately and usually in unison. And in

Meistersinger," he scoffed, "that isn't a crowd, but an army, highly organized in the German fashion and marching in ranks."

What Debussy hoped to achieve was "a scattered effect, something more divided, more detached, something that would appear unorganized and yet be regulated, a real human crowd in which each voice would be independent but where all the voices, when united, would produce an impression of concerted movement."

He must have made a great many experiments. Four years after he first chose the subject he wrote Durand: ". . . . Apropos the Devil . . . I think I have discovered a rather novel method of handling the voices; it has the additional merit of being simple. But I hardly dare to have faith in it, and it must remain a secret between us. . . . I am still afraid that one of these mornings I shall realize that the idea is idiotic."

Debussy did not disclose his secret, and apparently he did not succeed with this "novel method," for another five years passed and in February, 1911, he was still describing his problem, this time to Godet, in the same terms as he previously did to Durand.

"I should like to achieve a choral style that would be at once perfectly simple and perfectly mobile. I do not consider the *placage* in *Boris* any more satisfactory than the persistent counterpoint in the *Meistersinger* finale, which is nothing else than cold-blooded disorder. There must be some other solution, some clever device to 'cheat the ear.' It is the very devil! Not to mention the stupid way they have of arranging the chorus as if they were in a bathing establishment: one side for men, the other for women—another difficulty that I shall have to overcome. And then you will see what long, outlandish words people will use to describe a very simple thing. . . ."

By this time, however, the general character of the work had definitely taken shape in his mind; it was to be a burlesque—a biting sarcasm—and to serve as an antithesis to another work, also based on a Poe story: "The Fall of the House of Usher," which was to be tragic in its portrayal of "the progression of anguish." Debussy visualized the presentation of both works at the same performance. He began working on the libretto for "The Fall of the House of

Usher" during the spring of 1908, but only after he more or less discarded another idea for an opera.

Mary Garden tells that he had planned (that is before his second marriage) to compose a *Romeo and Juliet,* and Carré remembered him speaking of "another *Don Juan*"—nothing further is known about these plans. A new *Tristan* was also seriously considered for a while by Debussy. In August, 1907, the Paris newspapers announced that *L'Histoire de Tristan* by Claude Debussy was going to be performed during the following year at the Opéra Comique. This came as a surprise to Debussy, particularly since *Le Temps,* usually considered a reliable newspaper, also carried the same news item. Actually Debussy had only talked about it with Gabriel Mourey, who was going to use for his libretto a new adaptation of *Tristan et Yseult* by Joseph Bédier.

Debussy admitted that the project was "so attractive and tempting" that it made him quite nervous to think of the moment when he would receive the libretto and have to start working on it. Upon his return to Paris from Pourville in September, 1907, he spent hours with Mourey arguing and planning, and they no doubt had many more similar sessions, but nothing came of it. The twelve bars of "one of the 363 themes in *Roman de Tristan,*" written in a letter to Durand, is all that is left of Debussy's *Tristan,* which was to be (and this information is based entirely on rumor) "a descriptive, anecdotal epic drama, tragic and comic by turns."

Two years later [1] Debussy wrote Mourey: "I prefer your idea of *Le Marchand de Rêves.* This one, being indefinite, permits us anything and is exactly what we need, because there is more fairyland in our time than M. Clemenceau imagines. One simply has to find it. . . ." This was the last time Debussy referred to *Tristan.* At that time he had already dedicated a whole year to the work on "The Fall of the House of Usher."

"It is an excellent way to steady one's nerves against all sorts of horrors," Debussy said as he plunged deeper into the atmosphere of Poe's story. "There are moments when I lose the feeling of

[1] March 29, 1909.

things around me, and if Roderick Usher's sister were suddenly to walk into my home I wouldn't be a bit surprised."

For twelve months, from June, 1908, to June, 1909, "the world outside" ceased to exist for him. "The heirs of the Usher family did not leave me in peace," Debussy said, until, at last he could announce that he had almost completed the long monologue of "this poor Roderick. It is sad enough to make the stones weep . . . because, actually, there is the problem of the influence which the stones have on the state of mind of neurasthenics." But much as Debussy wished the world to cease to exist and leave him to his work, he was constantly interrupted just because the world did not cease to exist—"I am guilty of about ten acts of incivility an hour."

In February, 1908—"life has so many surprises"—Debussy went to London to conduct *L'Après-midi d'un Faune*. This was not the first time the English had heard *L'Après-midi* and *La Mer* at Queen's Hall; in 1904 Sir Henry Wood had already introduced this work, but apparently Debussy's music was still above their heads.

. . . As in all his maturer works, it is obvious that he renounces melody as definitely as Alberich renounces love; whether the ultimate object of that renunciation is the same we do not know as yet. . . . [wrote *The Times*.]

For perfect enjoyment of this music there is no attitude of mind more to be recommended than the passive, unintelligent rumination of the typical amateur of the mid-Victorian era. As long as actual sleep can be avoided, the hearer can derive great pleasure from the strange sounds that enter his ears, if he will only put away all idea of definite construction or logical development. . . . Mr. Debussy is a master of coloring, and there may be some good reason for his abandonment of that element of music which has been considered as the most essential of all from the earlier ages until now. . . . At all events the practical result of this music is to make the musician hungry for music that is merely logical and beautiful, and many regrets were expressed by those who were obliged to leave the long concert before the Unfinished Symphony.

But the reviews were much too familiar to Debussy to discourage him and he came to Queen's Hall to conduct a concert on February

27 with *L'Après-midi d'un Faune* and the *Nocturnes* on his program. This time it was a success. "*Fêtes* was encored," Debussy reported to Durand, "and it only depended on my strength to get an encore for *L'Après-midi d'un Faune*.... But I was ready to drop—a very bad posture for conducting anything."

Debussy was seriously ill. The first symptoms of the disease appeared during the summer of 1907, when it was still considered to be merely intestinal trouble. Debussy followed a strict diet, and at times felt so tired that he walked as if in a daze—like a man who has forgotten the number of his hotel room, as he described it. Shortly before he came to London he had to be given morphine, cocaine and other drugs for the constant pain. Debussy had cancer of the rectum. He had to forego his engagements in Manchester and Edinburgh and return to Paris. But in May he went again to London, this time to assist at the rehearsals of *Pelléas*. He got along very well with Cleofante Campanini, then the conductor at Covent Garden, although he could not refrain from remarking that "Campanini beats time as if he were working a water pump—a disturbing spectacle, particularly when accompanied by trombones."

To prepare the opera Campanini was given only four rehearsals, including the dress rehearsal, and Debussy sympathized with him, but he was driven to utter despair by another "circumstance"—"a stage director by profession, and surely born in Marseille [1]—all this put together (called Mr. Almans) sees ceilings where there is nothing at all and imagines all sorts of things ... I have rarely had a stronger desire to kill anyone!" Debussy complained to his friends. The result was that, sick as Debussy felt, he had to be "an electrician, mechanic and God knows what else ..."

The dress rehearsal, in his opinion, was deplorable; it lacked everything, and Debussy was sure that with the stage director's good care nothing would be left of the opera at its first performance. "What do you expect?" Debussy shrugged, "it is the same old story: the theater directors want to do in eight days work that takes a month. Naturally it is mediocre and there is no joy in it."

---

[1] In France, one "born in Marseille" is a braggart and an exaggerator.

When the final curtain came down on the *Pelléas et Mélisande* debut at Covent Garden and for fifteen minutes the audience called the composer, Debussy was resting in his bed at the Palace Royal Hotel. He learned of the sensational success, such as had not been known for years in England, from Campanini, who on the following morning came to tell him about it "in his *Polichinelle* manner" and embraced Debussy as if he were "some medal blessed by the Pope."

The triumph of *Pelléas* at Covent Garden might have had a far-reaching importance in the evolution of theater music had not, practically during the same week of May, another event taken place in Paris that radically turned the trend of artistic activities to a new groove—the ballet.

During the past three years Sergei Diaghilev's importations of Russian art had monopolized the Paris spring season. Having made his debut in Paris during the month of May, 1907, at the Salon d'Automne, where he exhibited an immense collection of Russian paintings and sculpture lent him from Imperial palaces, museums and private collections, Diaghilev had followed up his success with the presentation, in 1908, of a series of five concerts at the Opéra. He introduced to Parisian audiences the masterpieces of "Russian Music Through the Ages," with the élite of Russian artists taking part. Rimsky-Korsakov, Glazunov, Chaliapin, Scriabin, Joseph Hoffman and Rachmaninoff were heard in programs of works by Glinka, Borodin, Cui, Balakirev, Moussorgsky and Tchaikovsky, as well as the composer-performers' own compositions. In the following year Diaghilev caused a sensation with Chaliapin in *Boris Godunov,* and now, in 1909, he played his highest trump—the Russian Ballet.

To attribute Diaghilev's success merely to the perfection of his performances, dazzling colors and virtuosity would be to minimize the importance of the new trend he introduced in Western Europe, then vacillating between symbolism (England), cubism (Italy), and expressionism (Germany). He provided a new form of expression for composers, since music in his ballets did not serve as an accompaniment but was an integral part. Two objectives distinguished Diaghilev's enterprise: to restore the grace and elegance of the old ballet through the perfection of new techniques, and to completely regenerate the ballet by enlisting for its service every available talent from all the arts.

Originally Diaghilev's *Saison Russe* was under the patronage of the Russian Government—it served as propaganda for Russia, moving closer to an *entente cordiale* with France. But after Grand Duke Vladimir, Diaghilev's chief sponsor, died in 1908, and intrigues against Diaghilev at the Russian court cut off its subsidies, the Russian Ballet ceased to be the Russian Government's instrument and Diaghilev became his own master. He was free not merely to seek advice among the French artists, but to give them a share in the Ballet's creative work.

Diaghilev devotees are still debating his talent and merits, but they are unanimous on at least one point—he had a genius for choosing the right men for his projects. Some ascribe it to chance, others to his intuition. Be that as it may, as I have said in my biography of Ravel when describing in detail Diaghilev's relationship with the French artists, to be associated with the Russian Ballet was a distinction, to have one's work performed by this glamorous group of élite artists was a unique opportunity and an honor, and to be able to take part in it was an unforgettable experience. Among all the eminent musicians who came in contact with this organization and delighted in following closely the various stages of the productions, Debussy never departed from a certain detachment of attitude. This curious stand can easily be explained.

Having fought Wagnerian domination, Debussy could hardly have been expected to greet a new foreign influence with enthusiasm, even though his feelings toward their merits were not the same. He recognized the wide possibilities which ballet offered to composers. But something more personal was an even stronger barrier to his association with the organization. "Diaghilev is a great man and Nijinsky is his prophet, unless it is Calvocoressi," Debussy said, and thus divulged the main reason for his aloofness. For Calvocoressi was the spokesman for the Ravelites, a member of the Apaches, a group so closely knit together that "what was known to

one was immediately communicated to all." A musicologist, Calvocoressi made the Russian contemporary's works his chief subject,
and through his correspondence with Mily Balakirev served as a
channel for their importation into France.

At the beginning of his ambitious plan for the historical concerts
of Russian music, Diaghilev called on Calvocoressi to help him with
translations of some of the works scheduled for performance and
to prepare the program notes. Gradually Calvocoressi became his
close associate and the Apaches joined in advising Diaghilev whenever the question of Parisian taste arose. It was the Apaches who
talked Diaghilev out of productions of Tchaikovsky's *Queen of
Spades* and *Eugene Onegin,* and insisted on Moussorgsky's *Boris
Godunov,* and later on, when "the barbarian hordes" of the Russian
Ballet arrived, helped them in their frenzied rehearsals wherever
they could, so that they celebrated the triumphant success of the
Ballet as if it were their own.

Besides Calvocoressi there was Misia Edwards, a close friend of
Ravel and the Apaches, who became Diaghilev's confidante, ad-
viser and financial sponsor of his projects, in fact "the only woman
he would have married, if he could," as Diaghilev himself confessed. Long before, during Debussy's meagre Bohemian days,
Pierre Louÿs introduced Debussy to this handsome young Polish
woman (she was born Godebsky), then married to her first husband, Thadée Natanson, the founder of *La Revue Blanche.* She was
the Muse of the literati and painters: Renoir, Bonnard, Vuillard
painted her portraits; Mallarmé spent nights listening to her play
Beethoven; Paul Valéry, Jules Renard, Henri de Régnier, Colette
and Willy used her apartment on the rue Saint Florentine as their
"second home," where Toulouse-Lautrec left his "small masterpieces" sketched on tablecloth and napkins. But Debussy snubbed
her—"just another Polish woman to take your hat off to when you
see her on the street," he remarked to Louÿs. After Misia divorced
Natanson and married Edwards, a millionaire and the owner of
Le Matin, she joined that high Parisian society which Debussy,
some said, hoped to enter through Madame Bardac's door, but

never did. And Misia brought his wrath on her head when she generously contributed to the fund for Lily.

When Diaghilev found himself without the Grand Duke's support, he turned to the "rich and powerful" in Paris, and Misia was his prime minister and ambassadress-at-large. Naturally once Diaghilev decided to engage French composers, Calvocoressi and Misia suggested Ravel first, and Ravel was commissioned (1909) to write a ballet, of all things—*Daphnis et Chloé*.

Upon his return from London Debussy no doubt read the reports of the Ballet's success, the eulogies to Nijinsky, Karsavina, Rubinstein and Pavlova and the future plans of the company, but he was not going to offer his services to Diaghilev. During the following June and July Debussy worked exclusively on "The Fall of the House of Usher" and "The Devil in the Belfry"—". . . I fall asleep with them, and when I awake I find the dark melancholy of one or the *ricanement* of the other." And he certainly did not breathe "the intoxicating air of the Russian Ballet" which Diaghilev claimed pervaded the Paris spring. It was up to Diaghilev to come to him.

This Diaghilev did a year later, in August 1909. Meanwhile in May, 1908, Debussy received a visit from Gatti-Casazza. After having lost to Hammerstein the first performance of *Pelléas* in New York, Gatti-Casazza hurried to Paris to buy for the Metropolitan Opera the rights for Debussy's future works—the three operas: *La Légende de Tristan*, "The Fall of the House of Usher" and "The Devil in the Belfry"—"or whatever you can do," Gatti-Casazza added, begging Debussy to sign an agreement with him.

Debussy was reluctant. "I must tell you honestly that of the three works, there barely exists the sketch of the librettos; and as to the music, I have written only some vague ideas. How can I honestly sell you such embryonic compositions?" he asked. But Gatti-Casazza succeeded in making him sign the contract and accept "an advance of money which Debussy himself wanted to be very modest"—two thousand francs. "Do not forget that I am a lazy composer and that I sometimes require weeks to decide upon one chord in preference to another," Debussy said, bidding him good-bye. "Remember also that you are the one who insisted on making this agreement and that probably you will not receive anything."

A year and a half later when Gatti-Casazza came to see him again, Debussy said: "You know, the operas that I am to write for you will be further delayed on account of a new fact. I will not write an opera, but a ballet, because, after all, it is better to have to do with mimes than with singers."—"Well," Gatti-Casazza said, "let us make an agreement also for a ballet."—"Oh, no," interrupted Debussy, "never! I have already abused enough of your courtesy, faith and patience. No contract; and when the ballet is finished I shall offer it to the Metropolitan before anyone else."

But the Metropolitan never "received anything" from Debussy. He was by then negotiating with Diaghilev.

"... Of course I don't have a ready subject for a ballet," Debussy said after a session with Diaghilev and one of his associates. "And here they talk to me about the eighteenth century in Italy ... for Russian dancers, which seems to me a little contradictory." According to Debussy, Diaghilev's companion spoke French too well for Diaghilev, causing a little confusion in the conversation. This, however, in no way prevented him from understanding the main points of the proposition and the material advantages to be derived from Diaghilev's plans to perform his work "in Rome, Moscow, etc. ..." In reporting to Jacques Durand, he asked him to take care of the business side of the agreement to be sure not to let Diaghilev get away with anything—Debussy himself claimed not to understand "business." As Diaghilev would not need the piano score until January 10 and the orchestral until the first part of May, "with these dates" Debussy agreed to try.

Eventually he wrote a small booklet for the proposed ballet and called it *Masques et bergamasques,* but beyond discussing the title, whether it should be changed to *L'Éternelle aventure,* or *L'Amour masqué,* nothing was accomplished. Durand published the little brochure, but he doubted that Debussy ever wrote any music for it. This time Debussy could not have claimed that the conventional plot of a Venetian masquerade in the *commedia dell' arte* vein would not have been presented in the proper decor, worthy of his art, for if there was anything that won his enthusiasm for the Russian productions it was Diaghilev's care and taste.

Instead, Debussy continued to work on Poe's stories. "I do as much as I can," he told Durand, who had been impatient with him for some time. "It's in those moments that I find the best way to satisfy my taste for the inexpressible. If I succeed—that is, as I hope —to express this 'progression of anguish' that is supposed to be 'The Fall of the House of Usher,' I think that then I will well have served music, my publisher, and my friend Jacques Durand." Debussy said he dwelt in "The House of Usher"—"it has nothing of *La maison de santé* and sometimes I come out with nerves tight as the strings of a violin."

But because of financial expediency Debussy had become less fastidious about the "artistic" presentation of his work. At this time he had agreed to write a ballet for Miss Maud Allan, an English dancer, to a scenario written by W. L. Courtney. It was to be an "Egyptian ballet," entitled *Khamma,* "dealing with some sort of legend about a high priest and a crowd of worshipers of the god Aman-Ra," he said. Intended as a music hall number, "that queer ballet with its trumpet call, which suggests a riot or an outbreak of fire and gives one the shivers," in Debussy's words, could not hold his interest for long. He sketched out the work, composed a few pages, but never himself completed this commission for Maud Allan, whom he called too English for words. He frankly admitted that "other arguments of a different sonority," and reasons of what he called "domestic economy" had forced him to accept the contract, and he turned over whatever he had already written of the ballet to Charles Koechlin for orchestration at the first opportunity.

Debussy was ill and depressed and there were weeks when he could not work at all. Nevertheless, he did write the first book of his *Préludes,* a group of piano pieces including the well-known *Ce qu'a vu le vent d'ouest, La Fille aux cheveux de lin, La Cathédrale engloutie, Danse de Puck* and *Minstrels,* and orchestrated the waltz *La Plus que lente* in a way that would be more appropriate for a "five o'clock tea" than for "genre brasserie." Debussy wrote two books of *Préludes,* each containing twelve. The second book was not complete till three years later, but, as he said himself, not all of them were good and they were not meant to be played as a whole, for he called them *Préludes* advisedly—that is, short pieces to be played before more important ones, and some of them, like *Danseuses de Delphes* and *Des pas sur la neige,* to be played only "*entre quatre-z-yeux,*" he said.

Sick and downhearted, Debussy was further irritated by the "international atmosphere" which was then cultivated in intellectual circles. Debussy was a chauvinist, though, of course, he thought of himself as a nationalist. It was plain in his writings, as it was in his casual references to foreigners. With the exception of the English, where his attitude showed a touch of inferiority complex, his feelings for "other Europeans" were colored by hostility or sarcastic contempt. "It is a mistake to believe that qualities peculiar to the genius of one race can be transmitted without injury to another—a mistake that has often harmed our music, for we are apt to adopt guilelessly formulas into which nothing French can enter," Debussy said, and he believed that "since every race is endowed with musical instinct, customs, forms and spiritual needs peculiar to itself, frontiers are not purely geographical fictions—to abolish them would be as futile as it is idealistic."

When, during the summer of 1910, he was asked to participate in the Festival of French Music to be held in Munich, Debussy answered: "What business have we there? Have we been invited to come? No! Well, what is the meaning of this? It is quite evident that we have been more than hospitable to German musicians. What will remain of our present infatuation fifty years hence? We delight in everything that comes from outside. We clap our hands like children over a work that comes from afar—from Scandinavia, from the Germanic or the Latin countries—without gauging the true value and solidity of the work, without asking ourselves if our souls can really vibrate in sympathy with souls that are foreign to ours. We have reason to be thankful when we do not imitate, stammeringly, what these people say in their language, when we do not rhapsodize over false Italianism in music or false Ibsenism in literature, and when some of our people do not make fools of themselves in their attempts to become exotic. There is no reason why the Germans should understand us. Neither should we try to absorb their ideas. Besides, though Munich may be well chosen from the political point of view, as the *Figaro* says, it cares nothing for our art. Concerts of modern music are only attended by a few music lovers. People will go out of politeness to hear French music. They will applaud, perhaps, with that Germanic courtesy that is so difficult to put up with. I am convinced that our art would not make a single conquest in Germany. This may even, perhaps, be regarded as a means for bringing about a rapprochement by the propaganda of our works! Music is not made for that . . . and the hour is ill chosen!"

Debussy may have made this speech in answering the inquiry, but actually his refusal had a different reason. The financial part of the proposition did not appeal to him. For two months later, because of a better offer, he accepted an invitation to Austria-Hungary to conduct several concerts and in November he went to Vienna. There an unpleasant surprise was awaiting Debussy, the conductor. *La Mer*, the *Nocturnes*, the *Petite Suite*, *L'Après-midi d'un Faune*, and his recently completed *Ibéria* were scheduled for the program, for which there was insufficient time to prepare—at least, that is, for a man with as limited experience in conducting as Debussy.

He was told that since Richard Strauss had conducted *La Mer* in 1907 the orchestra knew the score. "Ah! my friend, if you could only have heard this!" Debussy reported to Durand. "The *Nocturnes* was a similar adventure." He decided to leave them off the program. "And I assure you it was quite a feat to put *Ibéria* into shape in two rehearsals," Debussy wrote later to Durand. "Without wishing to claim that this accomplishment should be engraved on the tablets of eternity, I assure you it was not so simple, and my nerves are shattered. Don't forget that these people could understand me only through an interpreter—in the form of a doctor of law, who might have completely distorted my ideas, who knows! . . . On the other hand, I cannot think of any means of expression that I did not use: I sang, I gesticulated like a character in an Italian pantomime, etc. . . . it was enough to move the heart of a buffalo.

Well, they managed to understand in the end and it was I, after all, who had the last word. I was recalled as often as a dancer, and if the idolizing crowd did not unyoke the horses from my carriage it was only because I was in a simple taxicab."

Debussy said that from this experience he could draw only one conclusion: he was not made to be a composer capable of practicing his profession in foreign lands. "It takes the heroism of a traveling salesman, and to consent to a sort of compromise is definitely repulsive to me."

Nonetheless he went on to Budapest, where to his surprise his chamber works were going to be performed in the large Redoute Hall, which to Debussy resembled Hammam, a well-known Turkish bath establishment in Paris. "Fifteen hundred people to hear the *Children's Corner* seems startlingly out of proportion," Debussy remarked. The Waldbauer Quartet played his Quartet and Debussy was applauded by an enthusiastic audience of musicians, painters and literati who came to hear the works of an "impressionist."

He preferred Budapest to Vienna—"a city with a heavy make-up, where they abuse Brahms' and Puccini's music, and where the officers have chests like women, and women have breasts like officers." His irritation with the Viennese musicians reached its climax when at a banquet given in his honor a toast was proposed congratulating him on the "abolishment of melody." "Dear Sir! My music aims at being nothing else but melody!" Debussy replied indignantly.

His short stay in Budapest spared him similar official receptions and left him in peace to enjoy the few hours he had before returning to Paris, long enough to observe that "The Danube is beautiful, but it refuses to be blue, as the famous waltz claims it."—"The Hungarians are liars, but charming people. There is something French about their enthusiasm that brings us more quickly into sympathy with them than with our so-called Latin brothers..." He bought as gifts some exquisite embroidery and "the most marvelous chocolates made by Monsieur Gerbaud, a Swiss and a real genius." And he took with him an unforgettable "souvenir" of a gypsy violinist. "Radich," Debussy said, "was the violin itself! In an ordinary, dirty café he gives you the impression of sitting in the shadows of a forest, and he extracts from the bottom of the soul that special melancholy which we seldom have occasion to use. . . . He is capable of getting the secrets from a safe."

But there was one thing that intrigued Debussy and made him look forward to his return to Paris with even more pleasure. It had no relation to his trip, except that it was in Vienna that he received a letter from Gabriele d'Annunzio.[1]

MY DEAR MASTER:

One day, long past, on the hill of Settignano, the native country of the most melodious Tuscan sculptors, Gabriel Mourey spoke to me of you and the "Tristan" with profound expressiveness. I already knew and loved you. I used to frequent a small Florentine circle, where a few serious artists were passionately interested in your works and your "reforms."

Then, as today, I suffered from the lack of ability to write music for my own plays. And I have wished for an occasion to meet you.

Last summer, while I was imagining a long-contemplated mystery play, a young woman, a friend of mine, used to sing one of your most beautiful songs with that inner voice that you need.

Do you like my poetry?

Two weeks ago in Paris I wanted to go and knock on your door. Someone told me you were away.

Now I "cannot keep quiet." I am asking you if you will see me and let me tell you about this work and this dream.

Just send me a word. I will come.

At least I would have the joy of telling you of my gratitude for the beautiful thoughts that you have cradled and nourished ceaselessly in my mind.

GABRIELE D'ANNUNZIO

[1] November 25, 1910, from Arcachon, France.

CHAPTER XXI

LE MARTYRE DE SAINT SÉBASTIEN

FOR SOME TWENTY YEARS d'Annunzio had been nursing the idea of writing a mystery play, *Le Martyre de Saint Sébastien,* but not until he reached the age of forty-five and was told by an "oracle" that he was to meet a violent death during July of the following year did he feel it as a compulsion. Two other events, far more realistic than an oracle's prediction, were also partly responsible for this new departure in his rich literary career. Long before the first days of that "fatal" July, d'Annunzio was chased by his creditors from his Tuscan villa. "France, France, without you the world would be all alone," d'Annunzio said as he chose the land of his "exile." And there, in the spring of 1910, when he came to Paris he saw for the first time Ida Rubinstein in *Cleopatra,* one of Diaghilev's productions.

The exotic beauty of this young dancer had conquered Paris. Musicians, sculptors, painters and reviewers became poets when speaking of her, and d'Annunzio sent a message, like a last S.O.S., to his friend Comte Robert de Montesquiou-Fezensac: "I have just seen *Cleopatra.* I cannot control my excitement, what is there to do?" Montesquiou had the answer—"to write a work that would in an exceptional way bring to light the unique qualities of this artist and would raise her to the skies."

"Have the characters in mystery plays ever been presented in the nude?" d'Annunzio asked. He was told that men play the women's parts. "Then I will take revenge for the feminine sex— Ida Rubinstein will play Saint Sebastian. Tall, slender, and flat-chested, she is absolute perfection for this role. Where could I find an actor whose body was so ethereal?"

A few months later d'Annunzio installed himself in the Villa Saint-Dominique at Moulleau, near Arcachon, and began to collect material for his play. A whole iconography of Saint Sebastian filled his rooms, on a harmonium he had the score of Bach's Saint Matthew's Passion and books, pamphlets, letters and telegrams containing valuable information on his subject arrived daily at his door.

He made frequent trips to Paris to do research on the origin of Christianity and to study old texts at the Bibliothèque Nationale, both religious and secular, of fables, miracles, poems, and the lives of the saints. In the *Acta Sanctorum* he discovered a discourse by a saint on the joys of Paradise, and he had someone read to him "The Death of Saint Sebastian" from a fifteenth century manuscript. Many a night Louis Vierne, the blind organist at Notre Dame, would play the works of the great masters for him in the cathedral, and upon his return to Moulleau d'Annunzio would try to improvise on his harmonium.

"There is music between every syllable, between every verse," he said. "There is music in every isolated gesture and in every movement of a crowd." But he could not write his own music. He infused Rubinstein with such fantastic descriptions of the play already ripe in his imagination that the dancer became as inspired as he and was impatient to see it produced. "We must do it next spring, if we have to move heaven and earth," she said.

At first Rubinstein suggested Roger Ducasse (not Paul Dukas, as has been erroneously stated), but much as the composer was attracted by the opportunity to collaborate with d'Annunzio, he declined because he had no free time. Ida Rubinstein held Florent Schmitt's acceptance *en principe* in reserve, but Montesquiou insisted on first trying to interest Debussy, and both of them told d'Annunzio that it would be best if he himself would ask the composer.

"... How could I not love your poetry?" Debussy wrote d'Annunzio from Vienna. "The mere thought of working with you gives me a sort of fever."

Ten days later at a *petit dîner tout intime* given by the producer Gabriel Astruc at the Café de Paris for the Debussys and Rubinstein, the date of performance was agreed on: May, 1911, at the Théâtre du Châtelet.

For the first time Debussy had every intention of having his score ready for the deadline. It was less than five months away, but since d'Annunzio's script was not completed until the first days in February, it left Debussy even less time. "Not without a bit of terror I look forward to the moment when I will have to start composing," Debussy wrote d'Annunzio. "Shall I be able to do it? Shall I be able to find the right music? This anxiety perhaps is laudable, for one should not penetrate a mystery armed with arrogant vanity."

Debussy was intrigued by "the mixture of intense vitality and Christian feeling that characterizes the subject, in which the worship of Adonis is united with that of Christ." The mystical theme appealed to his inner esthetic sense, and, according to Jacques Durand, once Debussy started on his score he wrote it in a state of exaltation.

"Debussy withdrew into his mortal shell, into the domain of pure feeling where he entertains all the emotions and gives himself up to the intoxicating delights of ecstatic raptures," wrote a journalist who interviewed Debussy on behalf of *Excelsior*. There was more poetry than truth in these words, for two more months passed before Debussy wrote the first notes of the score. The journalist did not miss the opportunity to mention "the secluded little corner, not far from the Bois de Boulogne, the narrow study most artistically decorated in fabrics of bronze and tawny hues where a deliberate simplicity reigns," but apparently he was ignorant of the fact that the upkeep of this particular decor forced Debussy to accept engagements both as pianist and conductor, and thus interfered with his own work.

He had concerts scheduled for the month of March: he had to conduct at the *Cercle Musical* his own orchestration of Erik Satie's *Gymnopédies*, the orchestral version of *Children's Corner* and the *Chansons de Charles d'Orléans*, and to accompany Jean Périer and

Maggie Teyte in a few songs. (Maggie Teyte was the new Mélisande in the revival of *Pelléas*—some critics said that she was engaged to succeed Mary Garden because the "high-brows considered it essential that Mélisande should have an English accent.") And at another concert, which was to take place four days later, Debussy was on the program, this time as a pianist, in a group of his piano *Préludes*.

All these performances required rehearsals, practice, time and nerves, and if one remembers that Debussy was a sick man it is to his credit that he was willing calmly to discuss the question "whether his new project means the renaissance of religious music?"

"It would take me months of concentration to write adequate music to d'Annunzio's subtle and mysterious drama," Debussy said. "I feel obliged to limit myself to such music as will be worthy of the subject—probably a few choruses and some incidental music. I labor under the distressing obligation of having to be ready by May.

"In my opinion the writing of sacred music ceased with the sixteenth century. The beautiful, childlike souls of those days were alone capable of expressing their passionate, disinterested fervor in music free of all admixture of worldliness...."

Debussy always thought of himself as an atheist and, unaware of the possible consequences of such a declaration, he took this inopportune occasion to offer it in print to the public. "I do not practice religion in accordance with the sacred rites. I have made mysterious Nature my religion. I do not believe that a man is any nearer to God for being clad in priestly garments, nor that one place in a town is better adapted to meditation than another. When I look at a sunset sky and spend hours contemplating its marvelous, ever-changing beauty, an extraordinary emotion overwhelms me.

"Nature in all its vastness is truthfully reflected in my sincere though feeble soul. Around me are the trees stretching up their branches to the skies, the flowers perfuming the meadows, the gentle grass-carpeted earth . . . and my hands unconsciously assume an attitude of adoration. . . . To feel the supreme and moving beauty of the spectacle to which Nature invites her ephemeral guests!— that is what I call prayer...."

Since 1903, when Debussy left *Gil Blas,* he had not written many articles and granted interviews only occasionally. This may have been the reason why he welcomed this chance to speak at length of his work in general and to forewarn the critics of his new project in particular.

"Who will discover the secret of musical composition? The sound of the sea, the curve of the horizon, the wind in the leaves, the cry of a bird, register complex impressions within us. Then suddenly, without any deliberate consent on our part, one of these memories issues forth to express itself in the language of music. It bears its own harmony within it. By no effort of ours can we achieve anything more truthful or accurate. In this way only does a soul destined for music discover its most beautiful ideas. If I speak thus, it is not in order to prove that I have none. I detest doctrines and their impertinent implications. And for that reason I wish to write down my musical dreams in a spirit of utter self-detachment. I wish to sing of my interior visions with the naïve candor of a child.

"No doubt, this simple musical grammar will jar on some people. It is bound to offend the partisans of deceit and artifice. I foresee that and I rejoice at it. I shall do nothing to create adversaries, but neither shall I do anything to turn enmities into friendships. I must endeavor to be a great artist, so that I may dare to be myself and suffer for my faith. Those who feel as I do will only appreciate me the more. The others will shun and hate me. I shall make no effort to appease them. On that distant day—I trust it is still very far off—when I shall no longer be a cause of strife, I shall feel bitter self-reproach. For that odious hypocrisy which enables one to please all mankind will inevitably have prevailed in those last works."

Bitter as he may have sounded, Debussy's main concern was the shortage of time to complete his score. He was used to being his own master—to thinking, planning, to correcting and rewriting at his leisure. "It takes me weeks to decide to substitute one chord for another," he repeated over and over again. February passed, then the first weeks of March, and Debussy still had not begun to write his score. The days were flying by—"it's always tomorrow," he complained. "It is annoying, it is unbearable."

D'Annunzio commuted between Arcachon and Paris, but the collaboration by correspondence was only another source of irritation to Debussy. He needed him at his side. "Please forgive me for saying this," he finally wrote d'Annunzio. "When you are near me, I hear music suggested by your words, and yet I still need some practical points of direction. Your letters, to a painter and musician, resemble an enchanting forest of images, a forest where I feel like Tom Thumb."

Furthermore, Debussy thought it would be impossible to comply with Ida Rubinstein's request to detach the dances from the rest of the score so that she could "plan her gestures."—"They are organically bound up with the words, either already said or those to be said later. Protect me!" he begged d'Annunzio. Finally, two months before the scheduled date of the performance, referring to his play, he wrote d'Annunzio, "It is so high, so far off, that it is terribly difficult to find the right kind of music," and began to write his score.

D'Annunzio was very busy. Ida Rubinstein was a dancer and a beautiful woman, but that was not sufficient for the role of Saint Sebastian. It was up to d'Annunzio to create an interpreter. "I can say that he gave me my voice...," Rubinstein said later. "He brought me a complete revelation of myself, of everything I did not know about myself." Having inspired her enthusiasm for her role, d'Annunzio fed the "sacred flame," as only this poet knew how—in his letters, written like poems, he informed her of his work's every detail, told her of the literature she should read that would put her into its atmosphere, and even taught her to shoot with a six foot bow and arrows, which he ordered from an old archer in Paris. "Tell me if I can stay as long as necessary," Rubinstein asked him, whenever she was free from her concert tours, "until every word, every gesture will be the way you hear it and the way you see it." And when the rehearsals started both of them moved to Versailles so that they could see each other constantly and be near Paris.

D'Annunzio also took charge of the production, held long conferences with Léon Bakst, who did the decors, Armand Bour, the stage director, and Astruc. "Generally speaking, I ask from my interpreters an excellent diction and a corporeal sense of rhythm, for my octosyllables often have the weight of bronze or ebony," d'Annunzio said, but he would never forget to see if the chosen actor had straight legs and well-arched feet.

"Monsieur Bour must find me four or five leaders for the crowds scenes," he wrote Astruc in haste. "He also must find me seven or eight young women with harmonious voices and expressive faces.... The Emperor's role is grandiose, played on all the strings of a cithara. Monsieur Romuald Joube no doubt has straight legs and is not flat-footed. I beg you to see Madame *la Comtesse* Venturini (4, rue de Messine) for the role of the 'feverish girl.' She plays Night in *The Blue Bird*.... Please engage Mademoiselle Paz Ferrer (22, rue d'Antin)! She has eyes of somber flame and a warm voice in a mournful mouth.... One must not forget that the atmosphere of this liturgic drama is 'miracle.' The second and third acts are truly the summit of the supernatural. I need extraordinary masks, eloquent bodies.... *La Voûte des Planètes* is a problem; the *Paradis* is another problem. I have some ideas. But right now, try to find slaves, archers and magicians and feed them with everything that is terrifying...."

At the same time he was thrown into a fever of excitement when he heard that Henry Russell, the director of the Opera in Boston, had asked for the privilege of giving the first performance of *Saint Sébastien*. D'Annunzio did not know what to do. "Monsieur Astruc is going to the United States," he wrote Debussy. "He can arrange a lot of things for us there, particularly since my Mystery—as you know—is strictly orthodox and cannot shock anyone."

Meanwhile Debussy worked like a slave—"without having time to look over his own shoulder," he said. But the time left before the opening night was too short. To help him with the orchestration André Caplet was at his side, but even with his and a copyist's assistance the last pages were written after the rehearsals began, and were brought to the theater one by one with Debussy's last changes and corrections in pencil. "Here is Saint Sebastian's last cry... and I am not at all angry that it is his last. I can do no more..." Debussy, exhausted, wrote in a note attached to the last pages of the manuscript.

At the Théâtre du Châtelet the large dancing hall served as rehearsal studio. Caplet was going to conduct, and three men, D. E. Inghelbrecht, Émile Vuillermoz and Marcel Chadaigne, were in charge of choruses. Debussy did not attend any rehearsals until the choruses and the orchestra were ready for ensemble work. "They performed with such magnificence that no one who had the privilege of hearing the first contact of the voices and orchestra would ever forget," Vuillermoz said later. "The work was so strongly imbued with a magic of its own that it could hardly be approached on a level of familiarity. It was unfolded and laid out before the composer with amazing veneration and respect." Debussy, who usually controlled his emotions, wept. "It must have been a unique moment in his artistic life and experience," Vuillermoz remarked.

Indeed it was, for destiny, Debussy's "old enemy," was against him. Two weeks before the performance the Vatican put d'Annunzio's works on the Index, and ten days later Cardinal Amette, the Archbishop of Paris, threatened with excommunication any Roman Catholics who might attend *Le Martyre de Saint Sébastien*. Debussy and d'Annunzio were dumbfounded, particularly since as far back as January d'Annunzio had thought he had obtained approval from "an erudite and intelligent Abbé," who, after listening to a few scenes from the "Mystery," told d'Annunzio that "he had never before heard such lyrical expressiveness in glorifying the love of Jesus."

In the eyes of the Church d'Annunzio had confused pagan rites with a Christian cult (a confusion which historically existed at the time of the first martyrs). To save the situation, Debussy said in an interview with René Bizet: [1]

Do you imagine that my works do not contain religious precedents, if I may say so? Do you propose to fetter the soul of the artist? Is it not obvious that a man who sees mystery in everything will evidently be drawn to a religious subject? I do not wish to make a profession of

[1] *Comoedia*, May 18, 1911.

faith to you. But even if I am not a practicing Catholic nor a believer, I did not need to make a great effort to rise to the mystical heights which the poet's drama attains. Let us be clear about the word *mysticism*. You see that this very day the Archbishop has forbidden the faithful to attend d'Annunzio's play, although he does not know the work....

But let us not dwell on these annoying details. From the artistic point of view such a decree cannot be discussed. I assure you that I wrote my music as though I had been asked to do it for the Church. The result is decorative music, if you like, a noble text illustrated in sounds and rhythm; and in the last act when the saint ascends into Heaven I believe I have succeeded in expressing all the feeling aroused in me by the thought of the Ascension. Have I succeeded? This does not concern me. We have not the simple faith of other days. Is the faith expressed by my music orthodox or not? I cannot say. It is my faith, my own, singing in all sincerity.

In case it interests you, I may as well tell you that I wrote a score which ordinarily would have taken me a year, and that I put into practice what I might call my theories on incidental music. It should be something more than the vague buzzing that too often accompanies verse or prose, and should be closely incorporated with the text.

After consulting d'Annunzio, jointly with him Debussy signed a protest delivered to the press:

"The Archbishop of Paris, in a manner that was ill advised, has attacked in his recent decree a work, still unknown to him, created by two artists, who, in the course of several years of labor, have at least given evidence of their unremitting aspiration toward the severest forms of art. Without failing in the respect which the Archbishop's note itself fails to accord us, we desire to express our regret at the singular treatment which we have not deserved; and we affirm—upon our honor and upon the honor of all those who are acquainted with *Le Martyre de Saint-Sébastien*—that this work, deeply religious, is the lyrical glorification not only of the admirable athlete of Christ, but of all Christian heroism."

But the Archbishop remained adamant. Besides the Church's general opposition to the play itself, one aspect of the performance was regarded as "extremely objectionable: the representation of the saint by a Jewish woman dancer." Some journalists and critics, including Vallas, maintained that "to further her theatrical ambitions, she had commissioned two of the most celebrated artists of the day to write this work for her."

The dress rehearsal was scheduled for Sunday, May 21st. It was planned as a gala performance for a large invitation audience. But Debussy's luck was again against him. On the morning of the 21st there was an aeroplane race at Issy-les-Moulineaux and the French Minister of War, caught by the propeller, was killed. Because of the official mourning the gala performance had to be cancelled. Instead, the dress rehearsal was closed to the public, except for journalists. But as the cancellation notices failed to reach many of those who had been invited, a large protesting crowd battled with police in front of the theater.

The public performance took place on the following day and had a mild success, or, as some critics reported, "barely escaped being a complete failure." The ecclesiastical interdiction kept a large number of notables from the theater and Astruc received many cancellations from "bourgeois family subscribers." The attitude of the audience was critical right from the start and mishaps during the performance caused further disparagement.

Directed more by visual effect than oral requirements, the chorus was dispersed across the stage so that sopranos were mixed with basses, tenors with contraltos, some of them lost in a crowd of extras where they could not see the conductor. Panic-stricken, they sang when they should have kept silent, or missed the cues when their support was necessary. Ida Rubinstein's first entrance on the stage evoked the genuine admiration of the spectators—her graceful silhouette resembling a Florentine painting seemed to be a perfect personification of Saint Sebastian; but the moment she began to recite, her voice, her foreign accent, destroyed the illusion.

Debussy's music was misunderstood. Those who expected it to have the major role were surprised by its "incidental" character, and others who came to see the play missed the beauty of the chorus, which appeared to them irrelevant. The audience "poured out of the theater gradually, like water from a broken vase." And the press varied in its appraisal. Most of the reviews were written not by drama but by music critics and composers. D'Annunzio's poetry was given its due recognition, but he was scorned for his use of the French language. Actually the Italian poet knew French very well. Even if he made grammatical mistakes he never failed to communicate his thought. His friends Robert de Montesquiou and Léon Blum, and, of course Debussy, had gone over the script, and if they left it unaltered it must have been because they preferred his poetic expressions to a strict pedantry.

Several critics pointed to the lack of "intimate unity" between Debussy's music and d'Annunzio's text, and claimed that the music was drowned by the avalanche of words. D'Annunzio, in his usual chivalrous manner, said, "No matter what is the critics' and the public opinion of my poem, I am convinced that everyone should recognize in Claude Debussy's score the most divine source of inspiration. For having stimulated this musical work, whatever may happen to it, I will be forgiven." But, on the whole, and leaving aside the question of "something inherently sacrilegious about it which necessarily offends Christian feeling" debated in some newspapers, Debussy's score impressed musicians with "a melodic precision, a breadth of inspiration, a boldness of coloring and expression, such as he has never before shown."

Lalo in *Le Temps* agreed with this comment, but he added: "As excellent music as it is, it is foreign to M. Debussy's real nature; it is an incident, a parenthesis, in his work and in his artistic development." On another hand, Alfred Bruneau in *Le Matin* praised Debussy's skill in writing vocal ensembles, their power, their striking and curious effects, and "the hieratic, fantastic preludes, at once religious and voluptuous, the brilliant fanfares and the lively dances." And in *La Liberté*, Gaston Garraud said: "It impressed me as being one of the finest things M. Debussy has ever written. In spite of the sumptuous coloring and the fanciful originality and marvelous diversity of the instrumental combinations, the emotion in the essential parts of the work remains intensely spiritual and of a rare purity. There are moments of ecstasy and of pain when the emotional atmosphere of *Le Martyre de Saint Sébastien* recalls that of *Parsifal*, although the works are dissimilar in feeling and style."

Garraud was not alone in saying that Debussy had written his *Parsifal*. After ten performances of the "Mystery" in its original form and several of the orchestral score alone, conducted by D. E. Inghelbrecht, Vuillermoz predicted that this work would be discovered as a masterpiece, and that Debussy's *Parsifal* was awaiting its Bayreuth.

The "Mystery" was given at the Boston Opera House on March 30, 1912, with Theresa Cerutti as Saint Sebastian, and despite its original veto by the Church it enjoyed a great success in Florence, Venice, Turin, and in Rome, only a few paces away from the Vatican. In 1913 Astruc planned to revive it at the Théâtre des Champs Elysées, but nothing came of the project except that d'Annunzio agreed to make cuts in the text, Debussy to enlarge his score, and Louis Laloy to be in charge in putting the work together. In 1914 Jacques Rouché, the director of Paris Opéra, talked of producing it there, but because of the Church's attitude was not willing to dare to risk the venture until two years later, when d'Annunzio's patriotism during the First World War won him forgiveness. In 1917, when the script was ready, Debussy, bedridden, was too ill to work—"What do you think?" he asked Godet. "I no longer know."

Since then it has been "discovered" and "revived" in concert form and in August, 1948, I had the pleasure of seeing it at the Théâtre Antique in Orange (18 miles north of Avignon) in its original version with the decors and costumes designed by Bakst.

This first-century Roman theater seating eleven thousand stands in a large dusty square, sheltered on one side by the hills. It is famous for its wall—the only one remaining of the structure—three hundred and forty feet long and one hundred and twenty-one feet high, that forms the back of the stage. The wall is virtually intact, although only two of the seventy magnificent white marble columns remain. "It is the most beautiful wall in my Kingdom," Louix XIV once said.

Here, during the prosperous Pax Romana, were given plays of Euripides, Aristophanes and Sophocles. Later, at the time of the barbarian invasion, the costly white marble and granite from the structure were used to build emergency homes to shelter refugees right on the premises of the theater. Not until the last years of the nineteenth century was the theater restored to its present state, and in the last forty years great artists—Mounet-Sully, his brother Paul Mounet, Madeleine Roch, Sarah Bernhardt, and the Russian basso Feodor Chaliapin have been starred in dramatic and operatic productions.

Where would there be a more perfect setting for *Le Martyre de Saint Sébastien?* What I saw was a breathtaking spectacle—especially the lighting effects, sometimes in color, at other times projecting scarcely visible pictures that crossed the wall like a vision. It was given by the members of the Paris Comédie Française and the Colonne orchestra conducted by Paul Paray. The problem of the choruses, which Debussy never settled, was solved by placing the singers in the pit.

I felt and wrote then as I do now, that *Le Martyre de Saint Sébastien* should become an annual event at Orange, just as *Everyman* is at Salzburg. It is the natural place for Debussy's Bayreuth.

CHAPTER XXII

BALLETS

"To tell the truth, *Le Martyre de Saint Sébastien* tired me far more than I thought possible, and the trip to Turin finished me completely," Debussy said upon his return from Italy. He had a long program of French music to conduct, including Emmanuel Chabrier's *Gwendoline* overture, Roger Ducasse's *Sarabande,* the Prelude to the Third Act of *Ariane et Barbe-Bleue* by Paul Dukas, and his own *Children's Corner* (orchestrated by Caplet), *L'Après-midi d'un Faune,* and *Ibéria.* He collapsed during the performance (June 25), and an assistant conductor had to be called in to complete the concert. Debussy blamed it on the heat, his health and fatigue. "This is how you pay for everything in this world! The old saying goes: 'Do not force your talent' and a more modern version of it is: 'Let us not be carried away.' " His doctor ordered him to rest for at least a month, but not until the end of July were the Debussys able to leave Paris and go to Houlgate, in Normandy, for the summer.

To have "something to work on," Debussy took the manuscript of the *Rapsodie pour clarinette* with him. He was going to orchestrate it, for he was sure that the pleasures of Houlgate would not be sufficient to distract him from his work on Poe's two stories. But to his surprise he found the little place pleasanter than he anticipated—the country air, the sea, and even the few people he met. He complained, however, about the "hotel life"—it was not for a man of his age, he said. There was a woman who sang one Massenet opera a day; Debussy declared it must have been prescribed for her health, and he was annoyed by the "ridiculous obligation to dress at least four times a day, which comes from the Americans and which the good Frenchmen are eager to imitate with such touching candor."—"But what one cannot prevent, one has to bear," Debussy said with resignation, waiting until he could move with his family to a little house they had rented in the country.

But the little house, "calm and noisy at the same time" (he meant that Chouchou and her friends were always either going to or coming from the beach), was as bad a place to work as it was to do nothing. Debussy was ill and restless. And he enjoyed only the last days of the summer, when, "leaving the too-crowded panorama already seen so many times," they discovered, on their trips through the country, "the beauty of Normandy—the well-kept roads, the little houses with gardens full of flowers and trees descending all the way to the sea, with no one around, and no casino on the horizon. . . ."—"And to think that people who have the good fortune to have a house in this sort of Paradise would be eager to leave it for the international noise at Trouville! Misery! Misery!" The Debussys obviously had chosen the wrong place for their vacation and he returned to Paris tired and depressed.

Meanwhile, a new development in Diaghilev's plans for the following season was taking shape. It included Debussy's *L'Après-midi d'un Faune*. Ravel was still working on *Daphnis et Chloé*, constantly delaying the final version because of long and controversial conferences with the choreographer Mikhael Fokine, Bakst, and Nijinsky, and a back-stage intrigue in Diaghilev's entourage which threatened a major crisis in the company.

Nijinsky had become Diaghilev's latest "favorite." He took him for the summer to Venice, and there, as they sat one day in a café on Piazza San Marco, Diaghilev was blessed with a divine idea—Nijinsky was to create a ballet to Debussy's *L'Après-midi d'un Faune!* If Diaghilev realized Nijinsky's complete unsuitability for the role of choreographer, he certainly had sublime faith in his own Svengalian powers, for there and then he outlined his conception of the production and thereafter spent days in museums explaining the plastic forms of the past to Nijinsky and studying ancient dances depicted on Attic vases, bas-reliefs and sculpture. When they returned to Paris Diaghilev talked to Debussy about his plan, but Debussy was against it and only through his well-known persistence did Diaghilev manage to get the authorization, given, as Debussy said, against his better judgment.

Early in 1912 Ravel at last delivered his score. Diaghilev liked the music but hesitated to produce it as a ballet. Then, during one of the conferences with Jacques Durand (also Ravel's publisher) Diaghilev suddenly reversed his own decision and announced that he would put on *Daphnis et Chloé*. What he had in the back of his mind was not clear until after the performances of the two ballets written by the two most eminent French composers. Ravel's *Daphnis et Chloé* was a fiasco. It was eclipsed by *L'Après-midi d'un Faune*, presented only a week earlier.

Fokine blamed the badly prepared production on the insufficient time left from Nijinsky's one hundred and twenty rehearsals of *L'Apres-midi d'un Faune* and on the obvious similarity of the general conception, sets and even certain details, such as the frequency of movement in profile. *L'Après-midi d'un Faune* was hailed as the last word in choreography, while *Daphnis et Chloé* remained in its shadow. It was Diaghilev's peculiar way of pitting his "favorite" against Fokine, for whom he no longer had any use. Public attention which should have been focused on Ravel's new work was obstructed by the continuing controversy over Nijinsky's *L'Après-midi d'un Faune*.

Diaghilev reveled in the "scandal"—the newspaper headlines screaming across the front pages, and men and women insulting each other whenever the subject was mentioned. It divided intellectual Paris into two camps. Editorials attacking or defending the production carried on the fight, which involved the most prominent figures in the French artistic, musical and even political worlds, including the Russian Embassy, until it was talked about everywhere —as far as Berlin, Constantinople, St. Petersburg, London and New York.

The scandal was not caused by Mallarmé's poem or Debussy's

music, as was made clear by Gaston Calmette, the editor of *Le Figaro*, in his editorial *Un Faux Pas* that set off the hostilities:

Our readers will not find, in its usual place under *Théâtre*, the review by my worthy collaborator, Robert Brussel, of the first performance of *L'Après-midi d'un Faune*, a choreographic scene by Nijinsky directed and danced by that remarkable artist. I have suppressed the review.

There is no necessity for me to judge Debussy's music, which, besides, does not in itself constitute a novelty, as it is nearly ten years old. And my incompetence is too complete for me to be able to discuss the transcription of these subtleties with the eminent critics or with the younger amateurs who tax Mallarmé's masterpiece with the interpretation arbitrarily imposed on it by a dancer.

But I am convinced that none of the readers of *Le Figaro* who were at the Châtelet yesterday will object to my protest against a most extraordinary exhibition arrogantly presented as a serious production, perfumed with a precious art and a harmonious lyricism.

Those who speak of art and poetry apropos this spectacle mock us. It is neither a graceful eclogue, nor a serious production. We saw a faun, incontinent, vile—his gestures those of erotic bestiality and shamelessness. That is all. And well-deserved boos greeted this too-expressive pantomime of the body of an ill-made beast, hideous from the front, even more hideous in profile. These animal realisms will never be accepted.

In his zeal for interpreting Debussy's own description—"The successive scenes in which longing and the desires of the faun pass in the heat of the afternoon"—Nijinsky went a bit too far. Calmette, in his article, referred to Nijinsky's final scene in which the dancer substituted for a parting kiss what appeared to be an act of onanism. Nijinsky "espoused the veil" he took from the nymph, as Misia Edwards discreetly put it.

"You are ugly! Go! . . ." Debussy said at the dress rehearsal and walked out.

But Debussy was not so disgusted as to sever his association with the organization. On the contrary, he grew closer to Diaghilev's group than before. This may have been prompted by Diaghilev's cooling off toward Ravel after the unfortunate performance of *Daphnis et Chloé*, at a time when every point gained was counted by the still warring Debussysts and Ravelites. Ravel was not asked to write any more for Diaghilev's ballet, but Debussy's *Nocturnes* were seriously considered for the following season of the company. And despite his lack of confidence in Nijinsky as a choreographer, Debussy also agreed to write a ballet for him, *Jeux*, on the theme of "a plastic vindication of the man of 1913."

Debussy was given this synopsis: "The scene is a garden at dusk; a tennis ball has been lost: a young man and two girls are searching for it. The artificial light of the large electric lamps shedding fantastic rays about them suggests an idea of childish games; they play hide and seek; they try to catch one another; they quarrel, they sulk without cause. The night is warm, the sky is bathed in a pale light; they embrace. But the spell is broken by another tennis ball thrown in mischievously by an unknown hand. Surprised and alarmed, the young man and the girls disappear in the nocturnal depths of the garden."

This innocent enough plot gained a "new look" by the time it was touched with Nijinsky's "ideology." The tennis balls, the artificial lights, etc., were left intact, but the "childish games" had a rather explicit interpretation. "The search for the ball is forgotten and they flirt, first the young man with one girl, and then with another. But as the first girl sulks and as the young man still hesitates, the two girls make love to each other just to console themselves. Finally, the young man decides, rather than to lose either of them, to take them both." Nijinsky's wife Romola added this comment: "In emotional feeling Nijinsky made a step forward. In *Faune* it was the awakening of love in a youthful being. Here in *Jeux* the feeling is modern too. Love becomes, not the fundamental driving force of life, but merely a game, as it is in the twentieth century. . . . Here he sees love as nothing more than an emotion, a pastime, which can be found among three as well as among the same sex."

No one would accuse Debussy of being a prude, but even he had some difficulty in fitting his music to Nijinsky's choreography. Diaghilev kept insisting on changes in his score. "There is something very difficult to achieve," Debussy said, as he was working up to the last moment before the opening night, "because the music has to make you accept a situation somewhat risqué! It is true, of course," Debussy mused, "that in a ballet, immorality passes through the legs of the girls and ends in a pirouette." And as he looked over Diaghilev's suggestions and notes on Nijinsky's choreography, he shook his head: "Sensuality is overflowing its banks. These Russians are like Syrian cats."

After Debussy saw the rehearsals of *Jeux* he told Godet that he seemed to be doomed to have unnecessary things happen to him, as "is happening in *Jeux,* where Nijinsky's perverted genius is devoted to peculiar mathematics. This man adds demi-semiquavers with his feet and proves the result with his arms. Then, as if suddenly stricken with partial paralysis, with a most baleful eye he watches the music go by. I understand that this is called 'stylization of the gesture'—it is ugly! In fact it is Dalcrozian, and I consider Monsieur Dalcroze music's worst enemy! And you can imagine what havoc this method can play with the soul of this young savage, Nijinsky!

"Music as you know, does not defend herself. She contents herself in opposing light arabesques to so many ill-mannered feet—they don't even excuse themselves."

Jeux was given on May 13, 1913, at the Théâtre des Champs Elysées, and was received with mild applause mixed with hisses. Debussy was in the audience, but while *Jeux* was performed he sat, smoking a cigarette, in the janitor's room.

Madame Nijinska says the public did not understand Nijinsky's ideas. The piece did not fare any better when a year later it was danced in London. "The critics complained the tennis ball was too big... and there were lengthy comments in the papers about Nijinsky's tennis trousers because they were not made according to the classical pattern," she said. The English, according to Madame Nijinska, expected to see a tennis match; "somehow the extreme *finesse* of the underlying subject escaped their understanding," she complained.

The ballet was revived by the Swedish Ballet in the early twenties and then forgotten. But Debussy's music was appreciated by some reviewers, if not by the audience which booed again when it was played in concert form on March 1, 1914, at the Concerts Colonne. In *La Liberté* Gaston Garraud said that he preferred *Jeux* to *La Mer* and to some parts of the *Images* because of "its rich, expressive tone-coloring, its breadth, and the clarity and graceful spaciousness of the lines which sustain its extremely subtle and astonishingly profuse details."

In the *Revue du Temps présent* Paul le Flem, the composer, took to task those musicians who accused Debussy of lacking a novel way of treating the details of the score: "The musicians who level this reproach at Debussy are the very people who constantly wave the banner of tradition. Why should not Debussy be faithful to *his own* tradition, to his intensely individual manner? Why should he utilize a technique that is not his? Is he to be forced to use an idiom that is repugnant to his very nature? In short, what is all this critical hair-splitting but an attempt to trump up a meaningless charge against the composer of *Pelléas?*"

"The verve and sweep of this score certainly merited a better reception," said Stravinsky, who remembered well Debussy's music, but forgot Nijinsky's choreography.

Jeux was Debussy's last collaboration with the Diaghilev Ballet, although he continued to attend their performances, was often seen in Misia Edwards' box, lunched and dined with Nijinsky and Diaghilev in restaurants in Bois de Boulogne and enjoyed a new friendship—with Igor Stravinsky. The historical date of the meeting of these two protagonists of modern music has been differently recorded. Stravinsky says in his *Chronicle of My Life* that Debussy came to see him backstage after the first performance of *The Firebird*,[1] and Laloy tells of introducing the two at his home in 1913. Debussy himself speaks for the first time of Stravinsky in his letter to Durand[2] when, referring to *Firebird*, he said, "It is not perfect, but from a certain point of view it is, nonetheless, very good, because this music is not a docile servant of the dance and at times one hears an absolutely unusual concord of rhythms." If at that time

[1] 1910.
[2] July 8, 1910.

Debussy had not met Stravinsky, he certainly made his acquaintance shortly afterwards, for a year later he wrote (. . . in Switzerland:

"Do you know that right near you, in Cla . . . e is a young Russian musician, Igor Stravinsky, who has . . . inctive genius for color and rhythm? I am sure that you would like him and his music very much. . . . He is not trying to play 'a c. . . one.' His music is all made right in an orchestral mold, with . . . any intermediary, on a design which is concerned only . . . e expression of his emotion. There are no precautions, no p. . . ons. It is childish and savage. And yet it is extremely delic . . . If you have an opportunity to meet him, don't hesitate."

Laloy may have been mistaken in thinking that Stravinsky and Debussy met for the first time at his home in the spring of 1913. But apart from this there is no reason to doubt his recollections of that afternoon. Igor embraced Claude, who gave Laloy an amused look over the Russian's shoulder. Then they sat down at a piano to play through a four-hand arrangement of *Le Sacre du Printemps* Stravinsky had brought with him. Laloy describes how Stravinsky asked for permission to remove his collar, how he struggled through the pages of his own piece while Debussy played the bass. When they finished there were no embraces, not even any compliments. Both Debussy and Laloy were speechless.

According to Stravinsky it was not the *Rite of Spring* but the *King of Stars* he had dedicated to Debussy, a composition that was never performed because of difficulties of intonation that choruses are not prepared to meet. It is not important which composition the two were reading that particular afternoon, but that they saw each other often and discussed their works. Debussy played his *Jeux*, and Stravinsky was pleased that Debussy was one of the few who realized the importance of the pages of *tour de passe-passe*, the juggling tricks in *Petrouchka* preceding the final dance of the marionettes in the First Act. Later Stravinsky always spoke of Debussy with gratitude for his sympathetic attitude toward him and his music. And how much Debussy enjoyed Stravinsky can best be evaluated from the fact that Debussy must have made an exception in his case—Stravinsky, as soon as he arrived in Paris, was taken into the circle of Rave~~lites~~ so that he was considered the "Last Apache" to join their co   n the rue de Civry.

The bette   knew Stravinsky, the more his faith in him grew, althoug   un "first impressions" remained unaltered, as can be seen from a   r he wrote Godet two and a half years later: [1]

I have rece   en Stravinsky. . . . He says: "My *Firebird,* my *Sacre,*" as a child w   my spinning top, my hoop. And it is exactly that —a spoiled ci.   ometimes puts his fingers into the nose of music. He is also a you.   ge, who wears loud ties and kisses women's hands while stepping on   feet. When he grows older he'll be unbearable —that is, he won't b ole to bear any music; but at present he is terrific.

He is friendly with me, because I have helped him climb the ladder from which he launches grenades, only not all of them explode. But, once again, he is terrific. You have seen him and have, even better than I, analyzed his hard mechanism.

Debussy's condescending manner should not be interpreted as disparagement. On the contrary, Debussy knew Stravinsky's value. It was different when he was asked for an opinion of the neo-primitives, then still in their cradle, but already noisy enough to give warning of the new æsthetics which were to replace seriousness by mere amu.   ic-hall genre and the portrayal or burlesquing of mechanization.

In Diaghilev's entourage Debussy met Jean Cocteau, then a "debutant" poet and a great Satie enthusiast, and later the driving force of "The Six," who screamed anathema against Debussy. There was more than condescending manner and bitter sarcasm in Debussy's pun when he said, referring to Cocteau, "*Qui trop veut faire le coq tôt, trop tôt finit par 'Viens Poupoule.'*" Stravinsky was the only one of the newcomers with whom Debussy found a common language. "Our era has a peculiar trait; we run after people who have hardly learned to walk," Debussy said.

Never happy with his fellow musicians, at this time Debussy missed even more acutely his former "intellectual" friends. He was bored and irritated by the middle-class society he came into through

[1] January 4, 1916.

his marriage. He made one more attempt at reconciliation with
Pierre Louÿs. But Louÿs was ill, he was going blind, and he would
not hear of Debussy.

Toulet also was ill. A fever was gnawing at what was left of his
emaciated body and he had to leave Paris. This brought to a close
the "Thursday afternoons" at Debussy's home which had been
their *jour fixe* during the past several years. "No, my dear Toulet, I do not forget you, and your friendship is too precious to stop
thinking of it. You must believe me when I swear that I am not
used to your departure," Debussy wrote.

D'Annunzio lived in the South of France and his visits, cere-
monious and stimulating, unfortunately were rare. Godet was in
Switzerland. "Sometimes I feel miserably alone..." Debussy confessed to him, "although, it could not be otherwise and this is not
the first time. Chouchou's smile helps me through many dark hours,
but I cannot worry her with stories which would be for her nothing
but wicked variations on an ogre. Thus I remain alone with my
unhappiness."

Debussy's illness was progressing and he was aware of it. He
suffered from repeated crises. "I fall into a stupid inactivity and lose
all my best force in fighting it—a game as stupid as it is dangerous,
which reminds me of a hangover," Debussy wrote Godet. "One
comes out of it a bit diminished and confused, and above all, having
lost time in fighting something that does not exist. One can no
longer answer 'Why?' Besides, one does not show off that one is
an idiot any more than one does that he is a genius—it is hard to
admit that one is growing weak."

He wished he could leave Paris. "If for family reasons my wife
did not obstinately insist on living in Paris, I would ask you to find
me a small place in Savoy where I could bathe myself in a true light
and shake off this atmosphere of false grandeur, which no matter
what one does to escape it, always ends by slipping under our door.
I am haunted by mediocrity and I am frightened... God knows it
is not a pose!

"To live and work at art in Paris is something more and more
incompatible with the spirit that reigns here. We are becoming as

silly fantasts as the Viennese ... and you have no idea what our so called 'spectacles of art' are like!"

"Why occupy the eyes with so much, when the ears have to take in everything?" Debussy remarked to d'Annunzio, discussing the latest productions in Paris. "For the past few years we have been obedient to the influences of the North joined with Byzantium, which is choking our clear and graceful Latin genius. You know this better than I do, my dear friend. And I don't know if, after having borne so much, this is not the time to act."

To act, "to put things in their proper perspective, to rediscover the true values that arbitrary and capricious interpretations have brought to a point where one can no longer distinguish a Bach fugue from *La Marche Lorraine*," Debussy agreed to write articles and reviews of the Concerts Colonne for the Société Musicale Indépendante. But in 1913 Debussy was not the crusader of *La Revue Blanche* and *Gil Blas* he had been at the beginning of the century. The revolutionary had turned conservative. His prose had mellowed.

With the authority of *Le Maître* he urged his fellow composers to follow the old tradition and the simplicity of French art. One theme runs through his writings and his "appeals"—*du goût*—taste:

"In our era where little by little we are losing the feeling for mystery, occupied as we are in seeking all sorts of systems in human endeavor, it seems to me that it was not necessary that we should also lose the true sense of the word taste. In the past century, to have taste was nothing other than a gracious way of defending one's own opinion. Today, the word has become a sort of weapon in an argument—'the blow of an American fist,' most affirmative, but lacking elegance. It has become *mauvais goût* [bad taste], where various forms and colors are engaged in an extraordinary struggle."

Debussy was not against innovations or "modern" music, he was not so much against foreign influence as he was against the indiscriminate acceptance of certain styles. "A genius naturally can do without taste; for example, Beethoven," he said. "But Mozart, who was a genius, also had in his work the most delicate taste. If we examine the works of J. S. Bach, this benevolent god to whom musicians should pray before starting on their own work to guard them from mediocrity, we would discover on every page—from the capricious arabesques of yesterday to that religious effusion for which so far we have no substitute—that it is in vain to look in his music for any lack of taste."

Debussy insisted that musicians should abstain from artificiality, and what he called mathematical formulas. He referred to Portia in *The Merchant of Venice*, speaking of the music that every being carries within himself. " 'Woe!' she says, 'to the one who does not hear it ... !' Admirable words to remember for those who, before listening to what is singing in their own souls, are anxious to find 'formulas' to serve them."

Debussy ridiculed the usual excuse for not performing certain scores—their "difficulty." "Actually," he said, "music becomes difficult each time it ceases to exist as music; the word 'difficult' serves as a screen to hide its poverty. There is only one kind of true music—the one that has the right to exist whether it uses the rhythm of a waltz you hear in a café, or the imposing frame of a symphony. And why not admit that in these two cases, at least, good taste may take sides with the waltz, while the symphony hides, and with difficulty, its pompous mediocre soul?

"Let us not be obstinate in proclaiming that we should not discuss colors or taste. On the contrary, let us discuss them, and find again *our taste*—not that it was lost, but we have suffocated under eiderdown quilts. It would serve us as the best support in our struggle against the barbarians, who have become even more dangerous since they have started parting their hair in the middle."

And Debussy repeated what he had been saying all his life: "Let us insist that the beauty of a work of art should always remain mysterious, that is to say that one can never exactly prove 'how it is made.' Let us, at all costs, keep this magic peculiar to music, for by its essence music is more likely to contain it than any other art. In the name of the old gods, let us not explain it or try to free music from this mystery. Instead, we should adorn music with this delicate observance of 'taste' and let it be the guardian of her secret."

Almost simultaneously with the publication of his views on music and advice to composers, it was announced that Debussy had chosen a subject for a new work. If *Jeux* was the last score he wrote for Diaghilev, it was not the last time that Debussy wrote "for legs instead of voices." In February, 1913, André Hellé, a painter well known for his illustrations of children's books, showed him a scenario he had written—*La Boîte à joujoux*.

"Toy boxes are really towns in which the toys live like real people. Or, perhaps, towns are nothing else than boxes in which people live like toys," Hellé said to Debussy, and he described the love story in his ballet to the composer, who was captivated by the idea. "The dolls are dancing; a toy soldier falls in love with one of them, but the doll has already given her heart to a lazy, frivolous, quarrelsome *polichinelle*. The soldiers and the *polichinelles* fight a great battle in which the poor little soldier is seriously wounded. The doll, who was deserted by the wicked *polichinelle*, takes in the soldier, nurses him, and grows to love him. They marry, have many children and live happily ever after. The *polichinelle* becomes a park attendant and life goes on as before inside the toy box."

Debussy had been contemplating two other works: with d'Annunzio a play on an Indian subject, and with Toulet a "Persian ballet." Toulet was too ill to work, and d'Annunzio's project was still only in the form of a general idea. It is easy to see how Hellé's subject appealed to Debussy, particularly because of his love for Chouchou.

"I am extracting confidences from some of Chouchou's old dolls," Debussy wrote to Durand on September 27, after completing the first two parts he had been working on during the summer. "The third part is dragging. The soul of a doll is more mysterious even than Maeterlinck himself imagines; it does not readily tolerate the kind of claptrap so many human souls put up with. There will be a money safe, but this I refuse to interpret—my lack of being used to it, perhaps? But I hope to get through with it all the same. ..." And at the end of October he announced that "all that is left is to find a theater in which to produce *La Boîte à joujoux*," adding: "In my opinion only marionettes would be capable of understanding the text and the music."

"*La Boîte à joujoux*," Debussy further explained, "is a pantomime to the kind of music I have written for children in Christmas and New Year albums—something to amuse children, nothing more. . . ." The score—that is, the piano score, for Debussy only indicated the orchestration later arranged by Caplet—had no dances, but simple movements; and it contained quotations from well-known songs, parodies of operas, bugle calls, and music-box effects—yet all "conceived in a true French spirit, clear and amusing, without posing or indulging in any unnecessary acrobatic stunts."

Debussy did not live to see the production. It was postponed on account of World War I till December 10th, 1919, when, under the direction of P. B. Gheusi, it was given at the Théâtre Lyrique du Vaudeville. Performed by regular dancers (just as when presented by the Swedish Ballet in the early twenties at the Opéra Comique) it had an instantaneous success. The charm of the score is in its sense of measure and proportion, the discreetness and harmonious quality that blend laughter and tears. It was justly acclaimed as a masterpiece.

Debussy most probably would have orchestrated the score himself had he not accepted Serge Koussevitzky's invitation to come to Moscow to conduct two concerts there, and to St. Petersburg for a program of his own works. In the Debussy family only Chouchou was well, but as ill as he was and as much as he hated to leave Madame Debussy, who had also been ailing, Debussy could not afford to refuse Koussevitzky's extremely lucrative proposition. He arrived in Moscow early in December, long before the scheduled concerts, to have enough time for rehearsals. The programs included *La Mer*, the *Nocturnes*, *L'Après-midi d'un Faune*, *Ibéria*, *Gigues*, and the *Rapsodie* for clarinet and orchestra. Debussy was pleasantly surprised. Koussevitzky's orchestra was well drilled in all the pieces. The Russian press treated him with respect, the audiences with enthusiasm, and the musicians fêted him at parties and banquets. He said he had never heard so many of his works at one time. He himself, however, except for the public appearances as conductor, confined his playing to a small circle of friends.

Debussy praised highly the artistic merits of Koussevitzky's orchestra—"obviously distinguished by an exact discipline and a devotion to music rare enough in enlightened cities of our old Europe," and he was impressed by Koussevitzky's wide scope of musical activities: his heavy schedule of concerts in Moscow, each one repeated in St. Petersburg, followed during the summer months by nomadic wanderings while living with his organization on his boat on the Volga and giving concerts in the cities along the river. "Everything beautiful, I declare," Debussy wrote to Paris, "calls up multiple qualities. These find themselves reunited in the person of S. Koussevitzky, whose burning will to serve music, it seems to me, is unlikely to be aware of obstacles henceforth."

Indeed, Koussevitzky had already solved the most vital problem, even before he became a conductor. He had married the daughter of the millionaire Konstantin Ushkov, chairman of the largest tea company in Russia. During his three weeks in Russia Debussy was the Koussevitzkys' guest and as Debussy often said he liked to "relive the past," this visit certainly offered him a perfect setting. Here was a young musician living in the "decor" of Debussy's dreams: a mansion filled with one million roubles' worth of *objets d'art*, his own orchestra, his own music publishing firm, and a boat on the Volga filled with caviar, vodka and champagne provided for his cultural excursions by his happy father-in-law.

Debussy made no effort to see any of Madame von Meck's children except Sonia. In Russia she had become known for her interest in equal rights for women and for her financial support of one of the first institutions of higher education for women in the last century, when the doors of the universities were still closed to them. The von Mecks had lost most of their fortune, but Debussy was curious to see the old fifty-room home of Madame Nadejda von Meck, of which he had "so many dear memories." It was not difficult to arrange. The irony of it was—it belonged now to Ushkov, Koussevitzky's father-in-law.

As I have said before in speaking of his visits with Sonia, nothing has been recorded. At the Tchaikovsky Museum in Klin there is a manuscript of Debussy's former pupil Nicholas von Meck's memoirs. I have a certified copy of the pages concerning Debussy's relationship with the family. Nicholas von Meck states positively that Debussy did not see anyone except Sonia, yet Edward Lockspeiser, the English biographer of Debussy, says: "There is something disconcertingly patronizing about his remarks (especially in view of the fact that they were written in 1926), and indeed when Debussy went to Moscow in 1913 his boyhood friend was only able to say that he was 'a funny, fat, and empty little man.'" This remark is not in the manuscript. Was von Meck quoting his sister's reaction to Debussy's calls, during which Debussy, in reviewing his life, might have spoken of "a life full of surprises?" I do not know.

Upon his return to Paris, Debussy had to face harsh reality. As much as it "saddened" him, he had to accept engagements to conduct in Rome, Amsterdam, and the Hague, to "earn inconsiderable sums," which made him lose "precious time."—"Oh Lord, how life is complicated and . . . mean!" He had a great success in Rome. He found the city the same, except he missed his own "twenty years." In Holland, where he conducted the Concertgebouw Orchestra, he was saluted as "a recognized authority not only in France but in the entire musical world."

Debussy had indeed become "a very important and representative personage," even in his own country. His name was suggested as a candidate for the Institut de France. The "immortals" were ready to vote for him, but Saint-Saëns, an old enemy of Debussy's independent artistic tendencies, managed to delay the nomination. This worried Debussy less than his financial affairs. No number of concert engagements with the small fees he was receiving could possibly solve his problem. He did not earn enough to support himself and his family and he was in debt. He needed large sums and his only hope was a successful theatrical production.

He was ready to do all the necessary additional work on the score of *Le Martyre de Saint Sébastien* when Astruc planned to give it at the Théâtre des Champs Elysées. But the final decision depended on Ida Rubinstein's financial backing and Debussy begged d'Annunzio to use his influence. "Astruc has not yet been received by Madame Rubinstein," Debussy anxiously wrote d'Annunzio.[1] "She is going off at any moment, supposedly 'to hunt lions in Africa!' It is a noble idea, we should not doubt it, but what is going to happen to all the beautiful projects? Can't we have some sort of guarantee before her departure? If you think I should take steps personally, I am ready! If necessary I would go to Versailles [Ida Rubinstein's home] barefooted with arms in chains! I beg you to help me in this anguish...."

The plans for *Le Martyre de Saint Sébastien* fell through, but Debussy hoped that at least one of the "beautiful projects" would materialize. There was some discussion of a film with Debussy and d'Annunzio collaborating, and of the play on an Indian theme which d'Annunzio was going to write for him. A certain Monsieur Péquin, the business manager, came to Debussy to discuss terms with him. "This man, although a businessman, is pleasant," Debussy reported to d'Annunzio, "only he pretends to have *la Diva's* instructions not to exceed twenty thousand francs as a fee! I did not feel like bargaining, especially since it would have involved endless correspondence. Monsieur Péquin is supposed to come back next Tuesday at six in the evening, armed with a contract. There is someone in this case who is in a hurry and he is Claude Debussy. It is only natural that M. Péquin wants to profit by it, since the art of doing business consists of abusing the miserable needs that sometimes artists have. Well, I am going to work with you, and this is the most important. My joy is to know you better, my hope—to see you soon. All yours, Claude Debussy."

M. Péquin came on Tuesday, but without a contract. "It seems it is not going to work, and yet it is not my fault. What is going on?" Debussy asked d'Annunzio.

MY DEAR FRIEND [d'Annunzio answered]:

Perhaps you know that my work on Saint Sebastian brought me four or five thousand francs in royalties, that is all! I have received no fee.

[1] July 30, 1913.

La Pisanelle[1] did not even pay for my life in Paris during the rehearsals. I paid my own expenses.

For the third play, after sad experience, I have dared to ask a guarantee of fifty thousand francs and insisted that your fee should be twenty-five thousand; I have based my demand on Richard Strauss' apothegm apropos the connection between hats, feathers, furs and works of art....

I cannot again work for nothing. My schedule is very heavy.

The decision, naturally, makes one wait.

This delay annoys me because of you, who needs absolutely to go somewhere to find peace and quiet. How I would like to give them to you, dear friend!

But I think this will somehow be arranged.

I press your hand with the greatest affection,

All yours

GABRIELE D'ANNUNZIO

(July, 1914)

D'Annunzio was not Pierre Louÿs. He lived like a prince and talked like a knight, but his noble spirit was spent in poetry, not in deeds. Besides, there was d'Annunzio to think about first, and he never had any money left.

"Times are hard and life for me is even harder!" Debussy wrote his publisher, his only source of financial aid, as he reluctantly accepted an engagement to participate in a private concert at Lady Speyer's home in London. "Caruso would ask as much for his accompanist as the sum I am getting! Well, it is a drop of water in the desert that these awful summer months are. Let us be grateful to Providence, even if it has an English accent!"

When ten days later he returned from London he found that his situation had not changed, that the nebulous projects had to wait while his creditors were at his door, that he did not have a single idea for a new composition and no peace of mind to work. "Paris is becoming more and more odious to me and I wish I could leave; literally, I cannot endure it any longer," Debussy said.

A week later World War I broke out.

---

[1] D'Annunzio's play written for Ida Rubinstein.

CHAPTER XXIII

WORLD WAR I

THE CALL TO ARMS did not include Debussy. He was nearing his fifty-second birthday. "At my age, my military fitness makes me just about good enough to guard a fence. . . ." But neither his profession nor his secluded way of living shielded him from the general tension and anguish.

". . . I have no *sang-froid* and even less of military spirit—never having had occasion to handle a gun. Add to this my recollections of 1870 [the Franco-Prussian War] and the anxiety of my wife, whose son and son-in-law are in the army, and you will understand my lack of enthusiasm. All this creates for me a life both intensive and disturbing, where I am nothing but a poor little atom crushed by this terrible cataclysm," Debussy said and it seemed to him that what he was doing or could do was "so wretchedly small."

Theaters were closing, orchestras were disbanded, Diaghilev and the members of his Ballet departed. Debussy's world was collapsing before his eyes and every day brought news of another old friend or acquaintance joining the army. He frankly admitted that he envied Satie, who, with the rank of corporal, "was seriously preparing himself to defend Paris," and after Paul Dukas told him that he was ready "to offer his face to be bashed in like anyone else," Debussy also declared, "If, to assure victory they are absolutely in need of another face to be bashed in, I'll offer mine without hesitation."

The initial success of the German armies, exaggerated by wild rumors, threw Paris into a panic. *Taubes*[1] as the German aeroplanes were nicknamed, were expected any day to bomb the city. The French Government was preparing to evacuate the city, and families with children urged each other to flee to the country just at the time when Debussy thought Paris had become "a perfectly charming place, since it has been rid of all these *métèques* [goons] by either shooting or deporting them." He even thought he could do some work and he asked Durand to give him something to do. "Please think of me and excuse my reliance on your friendship, but truly I have none but you," he wrote him, for he had no new ideas of his own. He was restless. To pass the time, which he said was harder than ever, Debussy joined a committee organized by the Institut des Beaux Arts to take care of the families of musicians who had gone to the front. But he soon felt that the asides of the war were more distressing than one could imagine. He found it was impossible to work. "To tell the truth, one simply does not dare," he said. "For a long time—I might as well admit—I have not been the same. I feel terribly small," he wrote Godet in Switzerland. "Ah! Where is the 'magician' you have loved in me? He has been doing nothing but morose turns and is going to break his spine in a final ugly pirouette."

Debussy had just recovered from the grippe and an attack of shingles. His financial situation was alarming—there were moments when only suicide, he thought, would bring a solution.

But this Debussy could hardly have meant seriously. He was no longer the bachelor who in a moment of despair had frightened Pierre Louÿs by communicating similar thoughts. Debussy was not only a married man with responsibilities, but there was Chouchou, the "fulfillment of one of his most cherished hopes."

All his life he strove to detach himself from his family background and he was giving Chouchou everything that his own childhood lacked. In his play, written during the first months of his marriage to Lily, Debussy had mocked Madame Durtel for her "way of talking"—mixing English phrases with what he called her

---

[1] *Die Tauben*—pigeons.

own Parisian salon *argot*. "She should be whipped," he had said. But he beamed with delight when his own child, brought up by an English governess, spoke a patois of English-French which both her grandmothers could not understand.

At the age of seven Chouchou was given her first piano lessons. "A lady in black, resembling a drawing by Odilon Redon," as Debussy said, was engaged to take charge of her early musical education. Chouchou soon discovered the advantage of her position and used it as a shield against discipline as yet unknown to her. She was pretty and frail, looked like her father, and was a spoiled child, pampered by her parents and flattered by the attention of relatives and friends. D'Annunzio, for one, treated her like the princess of his dreams and wrote her letters that would have charmed any woman who received them, and Debussy himself would often miss a concert which he should have attended because on their way to the hall Chouchou changed her mind and wanted to see a moving picture instead.

Rumors of the German Army reaching Paris played havoc with Debussy's nerves. He repeated over and over again that he had no *sang-froid*. To expose Chouchou to danger was more than he could bear and in the second half of August they left for Angers.

The expensive and tiring journey annoyed him. And after a few days there he said that a refugee's status, in that marginal life of hoping to return and meantime assisting at the kitchen of the war, can interest only specialists, those armchair strategists with whom he had no sympathy. "If the Parisians had had a little more self-confidence they would have spared themselves the ridiculous, patronizing hospitality of the little provincials," Debussy said with disgust. He was impatient to return to Paris, although he knew that nothing was awaiting him. Still, it was better than the utterly wasted time at Angers. He found, however, one solace there—the war news reached the little town much faster and was less contradictory. A few more days had passed and Debussy thought that the war situation was improving even though it had many "obscure" sides. The amateur "warriors" talked of fresh troops that were going to be thrown into the battle and the one hundred thousand

Cossacks who would fall on the enemy like an avalanche—"all a pure fantasy, so far," Debussy said.

And turning to his own field, he said: "We must save our energy for the time following the war, because if we are going to be victorious, and this we should passionately hope, the artistic activities will have a little opportunity. Never, in any era, have art and war made good bedfellows. Therefore one has to play one's part without having the right to deplore or complain. We have struck back many a blow and have suffered from revolting horrors that break our hearts. I am not speaking of the two months during which I have not written a single note, nor touched the piano. It is unimportant in comparison with the events, I know this well, but I cannot stop myself from thinking of it with sadness and regret . . . at my age, lost time is lost forever."

Debussy spent most of the time reading the papers and anxiously awaiting special bulletins. At last good news reached Angers—the battle of the Marne was won. The Debussys returned to Paris. "The lessons of patience given us constantly seem to me necessary!" he reasoned. "It is evident that armies are not transported with the same ease as chairs—a simple fact which does not occur to city folk playing with little flags on their maps."

At home he found an offer from André Charlot, the director of the Alhambra theater in London, to produce his ballet *No-yati (Le Palais de silence)*, a ballet Debussy had been talking about but Durand doubted he had ever written. "This is premature," Debussy thought. "I wouldn't like this music to be played before the fate of France was decided, because she can neither weep nor laugh while so many of our men heroically let their faces be bashed in. If I would dare, and if, above all, I was not afraid of the inevitable blatancy that this sort of composition always evokes, I would gladly write a Heroic March. . . . But again, to indulge in heroism, in all tranquility, well out of the reach of bullets—I consider it ridiculous. . . ."

Debussy said he could not work while the soldiers were practicing, some on a bugle, others on a drum. These sounds, these rhythms reminded him of the best themes of the "two Richards"—

Wagner and Strauss. "If you have a taste for moralities you may find some in this relationship," he sarcastically suggested. Another month dragged by without Debussy going near his desk. "The familiar piano sounds have become odious to me," he said. "Was it Pythagoras who continued on his mathematical problems up to the moment when a soldier put an end to them? Did not Goethe write *Les Affinités Électives* while the French occupied Weimar? These are admirable minds. I can only admit my inferiority."

In November Debussy received another message from England. This time the *Daily Telegraph* asked him to write a short composition for "Albert the King of Belgians' Book." Here was the opportunity for his Heroic March, but Debussy was slow in his progress with the score. "This is very difficult," he said, "because the *Brabançonne* [the Belgian national anthem]does not evoke heroism in souls that were not born with it." Instead of an Heroic March, he wrote *Berceuse Héroique*. "This is all I could do because the proximity of the hostilities disturb me physically, and because of lack of military spirit," he explained. The orchestral version of the composition was played during the following year at the Lamoureux-Colonne Concerts, combined on account of the war. As Debussy foresaw, its programmatic character presumably portraying "the dismal trenches in Flanders full of harassed, homesick soldiers, soothed by the strains of the patriotic melody" was more mournful and nostalgic than heroic.

"The beauty of the cannon's roar, the picturesque drama of the battlefield next to which, by comparison, all existence should appear dull, the brutal power of killing at least one *Boche,* as the only logical appeasement" to his state of mind—for these war themes Debussy had no colors in his palette. Even if he had "seen and heard" the battle, he doubted that it could be "transposed." It would always lack the atmosphere, the color of the sky, the men's faces, and above all the heroism of their souls in those moments. "Take a look at the war paintings," Debussy said. "With a few exceptions, how theatrical they are—how false, to be more precise, at least to me."

And yet he felt it was his duty as a patriot to contribute his ability to the war effort. He suffered from inactivity, and although he had neither experience nor patience for research work he agreed to take part in editing Durand's new French National publications of classical works which were to replace the German editions. The "humble domestic reasons" did not play a minor role in his decision, for he was in debt to Durand and he had no ideas, as he repeated over and over again, for original works of his own.

Discussing the project, Debussy pointed out to Durand that the four-hand arrangements of practically all the symphonies in the Peters Edition were deplorable—they sounded badly, particularly those of Schumann, which, besides, were notoriously difficult to play. It was a tremendous task and Debussy finally chose Chopin's works as his main assignment. After examining several German and foreign publications, he thought that if one had to have a written preface it should concern itself with "fantastic interpretations" in the other editions, omitting the anecdotal material already too much exploited: Chopin–George Sand, tubercular Chopin, Chopin–Balzac, or Chopin's influence on Wagner in Friedmann's edition.[1] "For a German this is not bad," he said.[2]

Consulting these publications, Debussy often found himself in a predicament trying to decide which was closest to the authentic. "The Chopin 'manuscripts' simply terrify me," he said to Durand. "How can *three* manuscripts, which are obviously not all in Chopin's hand, all be correct? You may be quite sure that only one is ... and that is where the tragedy begins. Chopin, impressionable and nervous, must have *corrected* the proofs—that is, if he had time, the poor man! That is why I have a certain amount of confidence in the Friedmann edition. It is made with a knowledge of all the other publications and shows a real taste for the Master."

Debussy regretted that his first piano teacher, Madame de Fleurville, was no longer alive—she knew so much about Chopin, he used to say. She had told him that Chopin advised practicing without using the pedal, and very little of it during a performance. And Debussy remembered in connection with "this special art" of using

[1] Breitkopf edition.
[2] Ignaz Friedmann was a Pole.

the pedal as a sort of "respiration" the occasion when in Rome he heard Liszt play and at close range watched him.

"The simple truth is, perhaps, that the abuse of the pedal is a way of concealing a lack of technique and a necessity of making a lot of noise to prevent one from hearing the music which is butchered," Debussy said. "Theoretically speaking, we should find a way to indicate this 'respiration' graphically.... Besides, it has been done. I think there is a work by Madame Marie-Jaell [1] which treats this subject."

Debussy never mentioned it, perhaps because it was obvious that he was led out of the impasse of inactivity by his constant occupation with Chopin's works. The recently "odious" tones of his *boche* Bechstein piano, thanks to his tuner, were going to sound *"à la française!"* and before two months of his editorial work had passed, he felt his creative force returning to him. Durand wanted him also to edit Bach's sonatas, but Debussy begged him to wait—he had "a few ideas" and he wanted to work on them. These were to be "cultivated" into three *Caprices en blanc et noir* for two pianos. But he had the time only to sketch them. On March 23 his ailing mother died and a month later he lost his mother-in-law. "For a long time this house has been weighing heavily on my shoulders," Debussy said. He wanted to get away and get to work. "I have suffered enough from the drought in my brain imposed by the war," Debussy complained. An old friend offered them *Mon Coin,* a house in Pourville, and early in July the Debussys moved there for the summer.

At first Debussy busied himself with "all the professions that are connected with refurbishing a house to suit one's own habitual decor"—moving furniture, hanging wallpaper, and arranging the few personal things he had brought with him. When he finally sat down at his worktable, he contemplated his new abode with satisfaction. He liked best the garden, old and neglected, with its "childish savagery," but soft and sweet—not made for those who want to play Robinson Crusoe. There was a splendid view of the sea, and

---

[1] Marie-Jaell, born Trautman.

at noon one could hear the sound of bells—like those in *Pelléas:* "if the children did not go down to the beach to bathe (*Pelléas et Mélisande*) it was because they did not feel like it.... And later in the day *l'Angélus* timidly rings the bells, as if convinced that he would bring no peace into the hearts of men," he reflected.

"Destroyed like a small village after a visit by the *Boches*," Debussy nonetheless felt an urge to work such as he had not experienced in years. Indeed, the three months at Pourville was a remarkable period in Debussy's creativity. He not only kept up with the delivery schedule of Chopin's works, but with a speed unusual for him wrote many compositions of his own. First he completed the *Caprices* sketched out in Paris before his departure. The three compositions are different in style and musical content and are not supposed to form one whole. In the first of these Debussy had taken four lines from Gounod's *Romeo et Juliet:*

> *Qui reste à sa place*
> *Et ne danse pas*
> *De quelque disgrâce*
> *Fait l'aveu tout bas*

for a sarcastic illustration of the malingerers who tried to get themselves released from military duty while their country was ravaged by war.

The second, dedicated to Durand's cousin Lieutenant Jacques Charlot, killed on March 5, 1915, is the closest to a "war piece" Debussy ever wrote. It has bugle calls, rumblings of drums suggesting the distant sound of guns, and a Luther chorale as a symbol of the German war spirit. Of the three compositions, dissatisfied with the first version, he worked longest on this one. "The *Ballade de Villon* against the enemies of France" seemed to him too somber in color, too black, almost as tragic as a "Caprice" of Goya. He kept it for days "to make sure" before sending it on to Durand. After a sleepless night "that brings good counsel," he made a final change. "This alteration," he said, "was absolutely necessary for the sake of the balance of the piece; besides, it makes things clearer, and cleanses the atmosphere of the poisonous fumes which were spread for a moment by Luther's chorale, or rather by what it represents."

"You will see," he wrote Durand, "what Luther's hymn 'catches' for its impudent intrusion into a *Caprice à la française*. At the end, a modest carillon rings a sort of pre-Marseillaise. Please excuse this anachronism, but it is permissible at a time when the streets' pavements and the trees in the forests are vibrating to this ubiquitous song."

In the third piece Debussy set to music a single line from a poem by Charles d'Orléans he had used before—"*Yver, vous n'estes qu'un vilain.*"

These compositions put an end to a long spell during which he could not "think musically" and Debussy was eternally grateful to Pourville, the little spot that was no longer fashionable nor cosmopolitan, where he had found the tranquillity he needed. "It is, of course, not indispensable that I should write music," he thought, "but it is the only thing I can do more or less well; I humbly regret my state of latent death ... therefore I have been writing like a madman, or like one who has to die next morning." He also felt that it was unnecessary for him to join the ranks of the draft dodgers and dwell on the atrocities that were committed. Far better to react against them, in his own case, by creating, to the best of his ability, "a little of that beauty which the enemy was attacking with such fury." But although he showed no patience with the armchair strategists, he did a bit of his own commenting on the progress of the war. "In my humble opinion," he wrote Durand, who he thought saw the situation "draped in black," "the Austro-*Boches* are shooting their last arrows made of bad wood." He continued:

The atmosphere in Paris, where there is as much optimism as pessimism, where everyone wants his good breakfast, makes us forget, it seems to me, our usual common sense. Let us not forget that France has seen worse things and that she is always "the most beautiful realm under the skies"—and this despite the jealous desire of the rest of Europe, except for our allies (?), to destroy her.

Since you accept our moral resurrection ... speaking of this, did not our supposed disintegration come from that wave of foreigners who deluge Paris with their various horrors, finding there an opportunity to accomplish something with more freedom than in their own country? The soul of a Frenchman will always remain clear and heroic...the dominant virtues have many ways of expressing themselves.

Once more, if you accept our *tournure* and our cohesion, why do you lose faith in all the wills that are tending toward the same goal?

It will be hard, long, pitiless...but for us, the men in the cities, let us forget our anguish and work for that beauty which people instinctively need, even more now since they have suffered so much.

Forgive me, my dear Jacques, all these phrases, that are only, after all, "words, words, words..." as Prince Hamlet, the brother of our neurasthenia, used to say. If they make you smile, they will disperse, for a moment, the sinister clouds where your present anguish reposes.

But two weeks later Debussy confided to Durand that he also had his moments of anxiety about the war. He was afraid to open a newspaper, which said nothing anyway and only, according to its slant about the events, speculated to catch the readers' attention. Debussy was frightened of falling back into the same state of mind he had been in in Paris. "Speaking of the Russians," he said, "I think we have forgotten that they were at one time our most treacherous enemies and today perfectly simply they are doing it all over again with the Germans—who have not yet burned Moscow!" Perhaps Debussy was not sure of his interpretation of Russian strategy, for shortly afterwards he wrote Durand:

We have failed, probably, to notice that the Grand Duke Nicholas is too *grand* [Grand Duke Nicholas was commander-in-chief of the Russian armies and a very tall man]. This man does not look enough at his feet, where his armies fall to pieces.... He sees Petrograd, Moscow, perhaps even the capital of Tibet—I forget the name of it ...is it Lhassa?

And now people are talking about Japanese intervention. Why not the inhabitants of Mars while we are at it? All this can only give more reason for arrogance to the *Boches*, who don't need it. And [turning his attention to the politicians in his own country] what a terrible arrangement to square our accounts afterwards! Why are so many invited to eat a cake not yet baked? Monsieur de La Fontaine wrote a beautiful fable on this subject, but this happened when France had wisdom for the whole of Europe. As for the secret session of the deputies, those are ideas worthy of a concierge. Monsieur Viviani speaks very well, but his eloquence is pure dilettantism. These opinions, coming from me, have no importance, yet it is annoying to realize how little politicians change and how the number of imbeciles multiplies.

To speak of the Germans (put on your gas mask), I don't know how to "turn" them. Perhaps time will do it. You may say it might do the same to us. In this case I think that we are better off and, without "bluffing" as they do, we have economic and moral reasons to see an acceptable end of it. For nothing on earth should we worry about the others, nor should we spoil such a tremendous effort and leave it without recompense. There, everything is an X; Russia wants Constantinople, England is against it. For us only peanuts—Alsace and Lorraine.

But Debussy left no doubt as to how he felt about the Germans. "While I was in Dieppe I saw Monsieur X, who came on furlough. He is a skeptic and declares that he has not seen a single *Boche*, and compares their existence to that of a rat. On the other hand, the son of my wife's maid came to see his mother, and has an entirely different attitude, I assure you. Here is a real Frenchman and a real soldier. Here is one who does not talk of stopping the war, who has *seen* the *Boche's* face and wishes, at least, to wipe it off the earth. He says all this in simple words, but very vividly, and like a Japanese, he smiles."

Debussy said he was sorry not to have a chance to join up in the struggle. He would have been only a nuisance with his little miseries of a sedentary man, but he was going to play his part and make his contribution, he insisted: "I want to work not for myself, but to give a proof, small as it may be, that not thirty million *Boches* can destroy French thought, even having tried to degrade it, before annihilating it. I am thinking of the French youth stupidly ruined by these merchants of '*Kultur*,' of which we have lost forever what should have brought glory to our country. What I am composing will be a secret homage to them—a dedication is superfluous."

Debussy was completing his piano and cello sonata. When it was ready for publication he dedicated it to Madame Debussy, but on the title page under his own name he wrote *Musicien français* as if to assert once more that he knew no nobler title, no expression of a greater pride.

The cello sonata, on which he worked from the end of July to the first part of August, was the first of six sonatas Debussy planned to write for different combinations of instruments. It was his first answer to the question he posed to himself: "Into whose arms will the future of French music fall? The young Russian school is offering us theirs; in my opinion they have become as little Russian as possible. Stravinsky himself dangerously leans toward Schönberg; otherwise it is, nonetheless, the most marvelous orchestral mechanism of our time. Well then, where is French music? Where are our old clavecinists who had so much true music? They had the secret of gracefulness and emotion without epilepsy, which we have negated like ungrateful children. . . ."

His sonata surprised musicians by its resemblance to the French sonatas of the seventeenth and eighteenth centuries and its un-Beethoven character, although Debussy maintained that "the proportions and the form of the sonata were almost classical in the true sense of the word." Those who expected to find the traditional solemn atmosphere were disconcerted by the "sarcastic, almost facetious" mood of this latest Debussy opus. It was reported that originally Debussy intended to call it *Pierre fâché avec la lune* and had planned to portray characters from an old Italian comedy.

Six weeks later (from the end of September to the beginning of October) Debussy had written with similar ease and speed the second sonata—for flute, viola and harp. At first he thought of using oboe, but eventually substituted viola because of the more somber coloring produced by the blending of the instruments. "It is terribly sad," Debussy said, "and I don't know whether one ought to laugh or cry at it. Perhaps both."

Besides these works, during that summer he composed twelve *Études,* two books each containing six—"a thousand different ways of treating pianists according to their desserts. . . . They are not always particularly entertaining, but they are at times very ingenious," Debussy said. Each study was to solve some technical problem and he realized the difficulty of their execution. "They will terrify your fingers," he wrote Durand, to whom he commented on his work as he progressed. "You may be sure that mine sometimes halt at certain passages. I have to stop and catch my breath as after a stiff climb.... Truly, the music soars to the summit of execution. Some fine records will be established." And he could not refrain from a facetious quip: "The *Études* will be a useful warning to pianists not to take up the profession unless they have remarkable hands."

But he was not concerned only with the technical problems of the studies. "I am sure you will agree with me," he said, "that there is no need to render the technique more depressing for the sake of making a serious impression; a touch of charm has never spoiled anything. Chopin proved that, and he makes my attempt seem very presumptuous, as I am well aware. I am not 'sufficiently' dead to be safe from the comparisons that will inevitably be made to my disadvantage by my contemporaries—colleagues and others. ..." and Debussy added that his *Études* conceal their severe technical aspect beneath flowers of harmony—"you can't catch flies with vinegar." He explained further that some of them were special experiments in sonorities "with effects you have never heard before, despite the fact that your ears are inured to all sorts of strange sounds."

Debussy felt that this work was an important contribution to the literature as well as to pedagogy. He omitted exact tempi indications, at first because he did not have a metronome with him, and on second thought "because they are good only for one measure, like roses during one morning."

When the work was ready for publication, Debussy wrote a preface stressing his point of view in regard to fingering: "The fingering is intentionally omitted in these *Études*. It is obvious that the same fingering cannot suit differently shaped hands. The modern method of writing several fingerings over one another is supposed to solve the difficulty, but it results only in confusion.... It makes the music look like a queer sum in arithmetic in which the fingers, by some inexplicable phenomenon, have to be multiplied by one another.... Our old masters—I mean *our own* admirable clavecinists—never indicated the fingering, no doubt because they had confidence in the ingenuity of their contemporary performers. It would be unseemly to distrust the skill of our modern virtuosi. To sum up: the absence of fingering provides excellent practice, it abolishes the spirit of contradiction which prompts us to avoid the composer's fingering, and proves the truth of the old saying: 'If you want a thing done well, do it yourself.'"

Debussy was meticulous in his choice of format, color, paper, etc., for publication of the *Études,* and also for a while could not decide to whom he should dedicate it: Chopin or Couperin. "I have an equal respect for these two composers, both so admirably intuitive." Finally he chose Chopin.

As for the Bach sonatas, Debussy again begged Durand to be patient and give him more time for his own work. "The Muse who you think presently lives within me has taught me not to trust her fidelity and I would rather hold her than run after her." There were days when he forgot about meals, and nights without rest. "It certainly is a strange existence—that of an artist."

"Ouf!" he sighed with relief when on September 30, at midnight, he wrote into his manuscript the last note of the *Études*— "the most meticulous Japanese engraving is child's play next to the *graphique* of certain pages." But it was a good work, he said. He was satisfied with it.

He had had a good summer, but it was drawing to a close. It was raining in Pourville and getting cold. Debussy hated to return to Paris—"If I had a lot of money, I would immediately buy *Mon Coin* if only as recompense for having found there the opportunity and capacity to think and work. When I remember the inactivity of the last year, I feel cold shivers in my back and I am afraid to go back to Paris to find there that 'workshop of nothing' that my working room had become...." He said that he was "decidedly made for a life under a clear sky, among the discreet trees. The big cities frighten me, there you have too often to shake treacherous hands. This does not come either from disgust or misanthropy, but from a desire to save what is left of myself."

Paris, he said, was a prison—one was free to think, but "even the walls have terrible ears.... To find sympathy there, this is, frankly speaking, wishing for the moon. I wouldn't know what to do with it anyway—just think of all the calumnious journalists who try to extract your plans before you have a chance to realize them. ...."

"Adieu, oh sea, adieu tranquillity! ... The fatal hour of departure is approaching!" Debussy said. "I am going to work up to the last minute, like Andrea Chénier, who wrote poetry before he walked up to the scaffold. While this comparison is macabre, there is a bit of truth in it." The curtains were taken down, his things were being packed. "As cats do, I feel depressed at the sight of a suitcase," Debussy brooded as he watched the preparations for departure.

On October 12 the Debussys arrived in Paris. Good news waited him there. Monsieur Thorailler, the representative of the Société des Auteurs et Compositeurs dramatique de France in Russia, had arranged a performance of *Pelléas et Mélisande* in Moscow. But Debussy was pessimistic about it. "I know the attitude of Frenchmen in Russia. They believe what they are told, noticing only later the deaf irony so peculiar to the Russians. Let's not forget the contempt with which the Russians treat a Frenchman when they have no immediate need of him." He felt better about it, however, when Bakst forwarded to him a review of the performance. Debussy was pleased that Karathygin, an eminent critic—"not in the least Debussyst"—announced nevertheless right at the beginning of his article that "the production of *Pelléas* marks an important date in the history of musical culture in Russia."

Upon his return to Paris Debussy intended to continue working on his plan for the six sonatas—the third was to be for piano and violin, the fourth, for oboe, horn, and clavecin. He was full of energy and enthusiasm for the work he had accomplished during the summer, but he had hardly settled in his home when suddenly his health took a bad turn. An immediate operation was considered imperative. "Tomorrow I'll be operated on," Debussy wrote to Durand. "The short notice left me no time to send out invitations; next time I'll try to think of it." Debussy suffered agonies. The

cancer of the rectum had rapidly progressed and it was decided that
evacuations would have to be made through the side.

True to his words that like André Chénier he would compose
up to the last moment, Debussy wrote, in the forty-eight hours preceding his operation, the poem and music for a short song, *Noël*.
It is one of the most touching expressions of a great patriot. He
wrote two versions of it: one for solo voice with piano accompaniment and another for children's two-part chorus.

> *Nous n'avons plus de maison!*
> *Les ennemis ont tout pris,*
> *Jusqu'à notre petit lit!*
> *Ils ont brûlé l'école et notre maître aussi.*
> *Ils ont brûlé l'église et monsieur Jésus Christ!*
> *Et le vieux pauvre qui n'a pas pu s'en aller!*

"I still have so much to say," Debussy told Dr. Pasteur Valléry-
Radot, a great Debussy enthusiast and a friend of the family.
"There are still so many musical things that have not been realized.
For instance, the voice. It seems to me it has not been given its
'true place.'"

Debussy was thinking of composing *L'Ode à la France*, a cantata
for soprano solo, chorus and orchestra. Laloy was going to write
the poem.

CHAPTER XXIV

CLAUDE DEBUSSY, *MUSICIEN FRANÇAIS*

"THE MOST TERRIBLE things have happened, the gravity of which my precious sick one does not suspect (I hope)...." Madame Claude Debussy wrote Dr. Valléry-Radot on January 31, 1916. "He is getting better, but it is going to be a long, very long time for him. Above all, when you come (because you are coming, aren't you?) don't show your anxiety for his state or for what he might say to you. Please forgive me for saying all these incoherent things —I have been living in such anguish during these past two months! I was promised they would help him with his pain. I don't dare to write more, everything I say worries me. He is better and slowly regains his strength. I make him sleep a little in the afternoon, but after four o'clock you could come to see him—it will make him so happy! As soon as he can start working a little time will be less long for him, but first he must not suffer so...."

Valléry-Radot found Debussy had lost weight, he looked tired, his eyes were sad. He spoke little. Radot had a feeling that death was near. Debussy had to remain in bed. He was getting radium treatments and injections of morphine. He felt like a living corpse. He wished he could work. He thought again of Poe's "The Fall of the House of Usher." "I suffer like the damned," he said, and the only work he could do was to read the proofs of his *Études*.

"These drugs are shrouded in mystery and I am asked to be patient ... Lord! How can I? After sixty days of various tortures." In February and in March he was again told to have patience. In April there was some talk about organizing a concert tour in the

United States. He was to go with Arthur Hartmann, the violinist, and Debussy said he would write a violin sonata for them to play, but he added, "I don't dare to decide anything at present. My friends could always 'organize' a nice funeral...." In May and in June he was told again to be patient. "Alors! Oh! Alors!" Debussy exclaimed quoting Golaud from *Pelléas*. It would be better to tell him, he said, if his illness was incurable. "Claude Debussy without writing music has no reason to exist," he said. "I have no hobbies. I have not been taught anything except music. ... This is endurable only on one condition—to compose a great deal; but to keep tapping a brain that sounds hollow is ungrateful." In July he felt a little better, not well enough "to sing the song of victory," but well enough to tell Durand that he was not going to remain at the orders of an illness that had become a bit too autocratic. "We'll see; if I have to go soon, at least I want to do my duty."

After Debussy was permitted to get up, a few friends would come to visit him: Paul Dukas, Stravinsky, Godet, Laloy and Durand. They did their best to distract him, but they could not avoid speaking of war. Debussy said he could no longer understand it—"I know it is difficult to put an end to it, but this sort of warrior's nonchalance is something very irritating. When will this hatred come to an end? And is it only the hatred? When will we cease to trust the destiny of the people to men who consider human beings as a means for their profit?" From his bedroom he could see the fortifications. Never before had they appeared to him so ugly, he said, "and the blue uniforms, the Joffre blue, was the most false color one could find."

Thinking of his own illness, Debussy often wondered whether it was worth fighting it "for so little in life." The monotony of his existence was such that he did not feel like speaking about it. He watched days go by, minute by minute. He would go to bed, yet he knew that nine times out of ten he would not be able to sleep and he fervently hoped that the following day "could be kinder" to him. But there was no change. His illness, "this faithful servant of death," chose him as a field for experiments. God knows why, he said. He tried to work, only to prove to himself that in his state he should do nothing. And he wondered how long it would last.

Chouchou and Madame Debussy had whooping cough and their doctor advised a change of air. "It is extraordinary how little knowledge these men have of people's lives," Debussy thought. "They come, disarrange your apartment, order you vacations, when very often you have hardly enough to keep you from starving." Indeed, Debussy's financial situation was beyond repair. Durand's firm was still paying his monthly allowance, a mere "drop in the bucket," but his illness—doctors, hospital bills, and expensive drugs—had swallowed what was left of Madame Debussy's own income. Debussy was more than aware of it, yet since he realized there was nothing he could do to improve their financial situation, he agreed for Chouchou's and Madame Debussy's sake to go away for a while. "This house has a curious resemblance to the house of Usher...," Debussy reflected, "except that I don't suffer from a mental disorder like Roderick Usher. However, we have in common the hypersensitivity...." Everything and everybody was getting on his nerves. Sometimes his life seemed to him like the worst nightmare, but he controlled himself and blamed his "fate."

Without knowing what to take with him, or how long they were going to be away, not having any practical sense of packing, hating "departures" in principle, Debussy found himself on the way out of Paris, a long twelve-hour train journey which seemed never to end. There was no more reason to come to Le Moulleau-Arcachon than to go to Singapore, he said when they reached their destination, and if it were not for the ocean, the pine trees and the fresh air, he would have insisted on leaving before they unpacked their bags, so unhappy was he at the hotel which, according to him, was a model of discomfort. There were too many pianos in the hotel and in the neighborhood. "One of them tried *Danseuses de Delphes* [Debussy Prelude] but continued with a much better performance of Tchaikovsky's *Romance*. And across the street a young girl"—Debussy swore he did not know her and certainly never had done her the slightest harm—"plays César Franck most of the afternoon. Oh, Lord!" he exclaimed. "When you have the sea, when you have the sight of a sunset that would make you weep... ! If I were the sun, I would go down somewhere else...."

Debussy complained all the time—he had lost pleasure in traveling, hated leaving his home, had difficulty in getting used to the change of climate, the temperature, the strong winds, as well as to living in an hotel, "in a numbered box, where even the walls were hostile." He wished they had gone to Pourville, to *Mon Coin*. It was all his fault, he said—he was a sick, old man who had enriched his collection of manias (some of them unreasonable, he admitted), such as, for instance, a hatred for the small tables in hotels, no more than seventy-five centimeters long. "You will see," he threatened, "that I will get nothing worthwhile from this voyage, except the regret of ever undertaking it."

Debussy had been in Arcachon before, but a long time ago, when he was taken there with the rest of her entourage by Madame von Meck. It was the beginning of his career, of his life. Now he had come to the end of both. Was it worth it? What was left of it? he mused. D'Annunzio had stayed in Arcachon while they were working on *Le Martyre de Saint Sébastien*. "D'Annunzio left unforgettable memories in these parts—they are still talking about his dogs and his clothes..." and Debussy smiled sarcastically.

His depression was further aggravated by a visit from a man who may have been a well-known musician, since on publication of Debussy's letter reporting it Durand deemed it necessary to substitute an X for his name. Or he may have been "nobody" in the musical world. Whoever he was, his general remarks and some specific criticism caused Debussy not only to regret for a while that he had ever written a sonata, but to doubt his knowledge of this form of composition. "Of course there are bad musicians everywhere," Debussy tried to excuse his guest's opinion. It only explained to him, he said, the frequent incomprehension with which his music had been received. "Without dramatizing it more than is necessary, it is terrifying," he complained. "Why wasn't I taught how to polish eyeglasses? I should never have imagined I could earn my daily bread with my music—it would be a false calculation, I would go so far as to say dishonest! Unfortunately, it's too late, alas, to face this sad truth."

This incident, he said, had greatly upset him, it was fraught with all sorts of consequences, he was losing faith in his own compositions. Actually Debussy was too strong to yield to his doubts. Much as he disliked the three weeks at Arcachon, it was there, while taking a walk on the Cap Férrat, that he was inspired with an idea for the finale of his violin sonata. "Only the first two parts won't have anything to do with it," he warned. "And as I know myself, I am not going to force them to suffer from a disagreeable neighborhood." The sonata had no relation to the one he had sketched out once, some twenty years previously, for Ysaÿe. It was going to be the third in the series of six he began in *Mon Coin* at Pourville.

But upon his return to Paris in December his doctors (there were three) told him again to be patient, to be careful and not overdo. They said it was the morphine that was upsetting him. "No," he thought, "there is something really broken in this curious mechanism that was once my brain. Whose fault is it? Perhaps it is because of the miserable war that is losing every day a little bit of its grandeur. It was silly enough to have faith in the Bulgarians. And anything would have been better than the Greeks. These people have been lying for a long time. And their King George resembles a pencil merchant. Naturally, the storytellers grow like weeds. Every morning someone nominates his own generalissimo. It is as if you were a hunchback and you kept changing your tailor, each time hoping that the new one will know how to disguise your hump. We have no sense for war, despite Napoleon. Anyway, Napoleon was a gambler who did not know when to stop—that is, a true gambler! And besides, we don't care."

A Danish newspaper posed him a question: "Did the World War diminish or augment your faith in eternal peace in the future?"— "Now how do you like this 'neutral'?" Debussy asked. "Why ask questions which cannot be answered as long as men are alive? Of course, we have very intelligent people who can write as many variations on 'this annoying theme' as there are pebbles on the shore, but I happen never to have liked 'variations.' It is a way of getting a lot out of very little; sometimes it's a form of vengeance, and less often the poor theme revolts with disgust against the travesties obstinately imposed on her."

To forget the daily news during the long nights he tossed in his bed without rest, Debussy read G. K. Chesterton's "Napoleon of Notting Hill," which had nothing to do with Napoleon, he said, and tried to understand the French *Code Civil*, where paragraphs "danced a savage rondo, some of them acquitting you, others condemning."

"I continue this life of waiting—the life in a waiting room at the station, I could say, because I am the poor traveler who is waiting for a train that will never come," Debussy said with resignation.

To distract him, Durand arranged a private performance of his sonata for flute, viola and harp. With the same old Debussy-the-critic's eye, he noticed that the young woman who played the harp resembled one of these musical priestesses one sees on the Egyptian graves "stubbornly in profile," nor had he overlooked her shapely figure. On another occasion, at a charity performance, he accompanied *Le Noël des Enfants qui n'ont plus de maisons*. This took place at the house of a bourgeois, "where they usually have hearts of stone. My dear, they cried so that I wondered whether I should have apologized," Debussy said.

At about this time Rouché asked him to write an extended lyric-drama for *Saint Sebastian*, using all the music already composed. Debussy turned to Godet for advice. "What do you think?" he asked. "I don't know any more." He was afraid to make any plans. If he had any, he said, they eventually landed in his wastepaper basket—the cemetery of his dreams.

There still was one subject that did inspire him—it was *L'Ode à la France*, the cantata he had been discussing with Laloy. Laloy said he had seen Debussy many a time when he was worried and depressed, but somehow he always managed to get over it; a new idea for a composition, a scheme for a new theatrical project would stimulate his interest. But he never saw Debussy so "beaten" as during the hard battles at Verdun and on the river Somme. Debussy spoke of nothing but the suffering of his country. Violence was odious to him, Laloy repeated Peter's words. The war became an obsession. Laloy even believed that the state of Debussy's health was affected by it—"It may not have been the cause of his illness, but it certainly accelerated its sudden progress, which was quiescent until then."

The mere discussion of *L'Ode à la France* seemed to calm Debussy. The main role in the cantata was to be given to Jeanne d'Arc —"as a symbol of suffering France, a victim sacrificed to appease an unjust fate and save future generations." Laloy brought Debussy *La Ballade de la pitié du royaume de France*—the beginning of the ode—and they talked over the plans for the following parts. Unfortunately, Laloy was in the War Information Service and as the war progressed did not have much free time. When, a year later, he wanted Debussy to see the rest of the manuscript the composer was too ill. They did not speak of it.[1]

Meanwhile Debussy took up "The Fall of the House of Usher" again and this time wrote what he considered the final version of the libretto. After nine years of work, he destroyed all the sketches he had made and the music he had written, and only a few pages of the libretto remain. They give a vague idea of what kind of music Debussy intended for Poe's story:

One hears from afar the voice of Lady Madeline, who sings about the haunted castle. At the end of her song, she walks across the back of the stage.

RODERICK USHER: Madeline! Madeline! Was anyone here? Who was it? No! It is that horrible desire, always the same, which I have been expecting to come true for so long. Oh! You old stones, you dull stones, you gray walls, you have weighed on my childhood so that I could never escape a single thought that was gloomy and drab. My soul must have your color. My thoughts oppress my heart as you oppress my eyes. What a mysterious power you must have, you who have taken everyone I have loved, one after the other, without anyone escap-

---

[1] In 1928 Choudens, the publisher, asked Marius-François Gaillard (with Mme. Debussy's authorization) to orchestrate the sketches left by Debussy. *L'Ode à la France* was given at the new Salle Pleyel on April 2, 1928 and was regretted by musicians who found it unworthy of Debussy, although Laloy maintained it had a close resemblance to *Le Martyre de Saint Sebastien.*

ing you! Why do I always return to find you even more gnawed by the harsh teeth of old time? Ah! you know it well, I cannot leave you. You know that soon you will take my sweet Madeline, my beloved sister, the only one who despite your shadow sometimes could smile, and leave me, frail and desperate, the last of the ancient race of Ushers....

* * *

Can you not understand me? It was not in vain that all these of my race suffered and loved in this house. Through them, the extraordinary and dominating soul of the stones slowly developed and I, the last of the race, could only obey. Where would I find the strength to struggle against the mute but horrible force, which for centuries seems to have directed the destiny of my family and made me whatever I am? (*To his friend*) Come... look at that large gap in the wall which stretches out and is lost in the fatal waters of a stagnant pool. This gap is growing every day, and is like a wound that I feel is going to take my reason and my life. It is also through this gap that this horror, this hideous phantom comes every night to see me. A day will come when nothing will protect me in this uneven combat, not even you, my poor Madeline, poor sister so tenderly loved. I will die of this gap ... I will die in this combat... I will die because of the House of Usher's past. (*He sobs in desperation.*)

* * *

Do you not hear? Yes, I hear! I have been hearing it for a few minutes.... Oh, have mercy on the miserable unfortunate that I am! He has locked her alive in the vault, I know it! I tell you that I know it, I tell you that I am sure of it. A few minutes ago I heard her feeble movements in the vault... Ah! Ah! the death rattle of a dragon, the noise of a buckler. Ah! ah! ah! say, perhaps, it is the grating of the door—the iron door.... (*He lifts himself on his hands, his words are cut off by hysterical laughter*) There, do you see? Don't you see her in the copper vestibule? Don't you see her poor little hands bleeding? Her dress is covered with blood! She cannot walk any more. Oh! Oh! Roderick... the one whom you loved so much—isn't she coming here soon, isn't she going to reproach me? She is going up the stairs... I hear her steps, I hear the horrible beating of her heart.... (*He yells the last words as if he were dying*) Insane! Insane! I tell you—she is now behind the door!

At this moment, as if her voice had attained all the power of magic, the large antique panels to which Roderick Usher was pointing slowly opens. At the same time a violent gust of wind blows the door wide open. Lady Madeline appears, her white dress covered with blood. For a few moments she remains trembling and indecisive, then with a plaintive scream she falls into her brother's arms (he has moved toward her), and in her last agony pulls him down to the floor.

The horrified friend runs away. The storm is raging. Suddenly, the full moon, red like blood, bursts forth, the walls fall apart. Only the deep, stagnant pool remains visible which will soon silently close in on the ruins of the House of Usher.

After Debussy had sent the libretto to Durand he never spoke of "The Fall of the House of Usher" again. I will leave it to psychiatrists to draw a conclusion from Debussy's constant preoccupation with Poe's story and to answer the question: was it guilt complex resulting from his behavior toward Lily?

The winter months of 1916-1917 were hard for the French. "This life where one must struggle for a piece of sugar, or music paper, not to mention one's daily bread, demands stronger nerves than mine," Debussy said. He suffered from a cold caught while getting coal for the house and he begged Durand to help him obtain some wood and perhaps a little more coal. Still, he worked on his violin sonata. By the middle of February the first two movements were completed; the third gave him unusual trouble. "That terrible first version of the finale, the 'Neapolitan one,' savored too much of the surrounding atmosphere of anxiety," he kept repeating, and during the following three months he was rewriting it. Had it not been for Durand urging him to complete the work and send it to him for publication, Debussy most probably would have given it up.

"In future beware of works that seem to have been planned under a clear blue sky, often they have stagnated in the gloom of a morose brain," he told Godet. "Thus, the finale of this sonata goes through a curious development to join in a game on a simple theme which turns back on itself, like a serpent biting its own tail."

Finally, after many delays, Debussy turned the manuscript over to his publisher. When a month later he received the printed copy of the sonata, he congratulated Durand on his speed and efficiency. "Let the *Boches* publishers show us their latest works!" Debussy proudly exclaimed, with defiance. But to Godet he confided his true feeling—"Your enthusiasm for the sonata is going to receive, I am afraid, a cold shower when the 'object' is in your hands. Believe me, to keep you in this spirit, it would be better if you never saw it. You might as well know, my trusted friend, that this sonata was written to appease my publisher, who was at my heels. You, who know how to read between the lines, will see the traces of that Devil of Perversity who pushes us to choose ideas that should be left alone.... This sonata will be interesting only from one point of view, purely documentary, and as an example of what a sick man could have written during the war. And now, enough about the sonata."

On May 5, 1917, at the Salle Gaveau, Debussy played it with Gaston Poulet for the first time in public. If the audience behaved with exceptional respect and the critics with restraint, it was because they felt they were present at a human tragedy.

While a few pretended that Debussy seemed better than they had expected, his appearance shocked the audience. He looked gaunt and his ashen face had an absent-minded, weary expression. The flame of fever did not glitter in his eyes, there was no bitterness in his smile but rather the utter weariness of suffering, with now and again spasms of anguish. Having seated himself at the piano, he looked at the audience with dull eyes from under flickering eyelids, like one who seeks to see without being seen.

During the intermission in hushed voices it was said that Debussy's confused air was caused by his shame at showing how he suffered. It was also said that he had even allowed his disease to develop by concealing the symptoms, and this secretiveness was attributed to that desire for perfection which was inseparable from his art.

This was the last time Debussy ever played in Paris. "There are some ruins that should be hidden; and although I am old, I cannot expect people to feel any historical thrill on seeing the ruin that I have become," he said later.

But ill as he was, work was Debussy's only salvation. He organized a concert for the wounded soldiers, promised to take part at the reopening of the Société Nationale de Musique, discussed plans for concert tours in Switzerland and England, and in June, after a performance of *Shylock,* he told Firmen Gémier, the actor, of his "old dream," to write music for *As You Like It.* Gémier was interested, and on the following day sent Debussy a man who would do the translation and work with him on the play. Debussy patiently listened and then explained that for him *As You Like It* for a long time had been united with the name of Toulet.

Toulet was still sick. He was living in Guéthary, a small village in the Pyrenées, near St. Jean-de-Luz. Except for occasional letters from Madame Debussy, he had lost contact with the composer. A month before, in May, Debussy had written him: "I have revisited the suffocating Bar de la Paix and the crowded Weber, the places marked by your presence in letters of fire (yes, sir). And yet, there is nothing left of the good old time; the people are even more ugly —one even misses the 'undesirables' of the past.... And you are no longer there—the indisputable truth—and I don't see anyone who could take your place. You probably know of the obscure punishment from which I have suffered for the last two years and a half. Rest assured I am not going to darken the beauty of your horizon by a story where the grotesque is mixed with the horrible in the most painfully exact proportions. If the war did not touch me physically it has demolished me morally: I am lost and my means don't let me offer an honest recompense. Perhaps we'll see each other when it is more *quiet* [in English in the original]. Among my wishes I have one—to see you ... to write you is insufficient."

Toulet had heard of the operation, but he knew nothing of the nature of the illness when in June he received Debussy's letter asking him if he was still interested in collaborating on *As You Like It.* "Aside from this," Debussy wrote, "there is a war, as you know. My health has reduced me, I regret to say, to the role of a spectator, similar to the one that people in the theater usually refer to with: 'I would not have played this role in that way!' "

Toulet had mislaid his old manuscript; he was willing to cooperate, but he was afraid of Gémier's "theatrical intentions."—"I rather think that, like Antoine, he is afflicted with *'chexpyrite'* [1] and will insist on a strictly literal translation—word for word."

"Like poor Mélisande, 'I don't do what I wish to do,' which is indeed the greatest punishment," Debussy wrote again, anxious lest Toulet would refuse. "You imagine Gémier to be too much of a disciple of Shakespeare. If only you knew the translation of *The Merchant of Venice* you would be reassured. All Gémier wants is to use his gifts as a producer and to make his crowds move about. *As You Like It* will not be of much use to him for this. But he'll find some way of doing what he wants, you may be sure. If necessary he'll make the theater attendants act or have the people in the stalls go and change places with those in the balcony. But without any pointless jokes, I believe you could do *As You Like It*." And in his concern for Toulet's cooperation, Debussy decided to spend the summer near him at St. Jean-de-Luz. Less than a month later, in the first days of July, he wrote Toulet: "To make our correspondence easier, we have come to your part of the country."

Debussy was enchanted with the house they had rented—"It is Basque, with a 'pergola,' as in Paul Bourget's novels," he said, "and has a view of the mountains, soft and without pretensions to becoming famous, a small garden and a biblical calm—an extraordinary silence, as Maeterlinck would say." The house belonged to A. L. Nicol, a British Colonel who was at the front; his wife was in London. Debussy was amused by the English atmosphere of the estabment, so English that he expected "to meet S. Pickwick, Esq. descending the stairs." The walls were covered with pictures of Zululand, views of Christiania, terrifying rifles that fortunately did not go off, and an assortment of family portraits, probably painted by someone from the Nicol family. Among them one particularly haunted Debussy—a portrait of an old man, very good looking but very severe. "One feels that it was not easy to get along with him,"

---

[1] Toulet's pun on Shakespeare's name.

Debussy said. "When I am late in the morning he assumes an air even more severe, as if to reproach me for my nonchalance."

But there was no view of the sea. One had to walk for a quarter of an hour to reach the beach, which like all the beaches was "full of people who could have been less ugly," Debussy remarked. "Not far away, at Guéthary, is Toulet, the famous humorist, an obstinate alcoholic with a face resembling a sunset by Van Dongen. All this would work itself out if it were not for 'me,' who is completely destroyed. Up to now nothing is changed...

> *Les morts*
> *C'est discret*
> *Ça dort*
> *Bien au frais*."

Debussy wrote again to Toulet and reminded him not to worry about Gémier, and to feel free in his treatment of the play: "As regards music, Gémier is a bit of an Antoine who 'did not give a damn about that sort of thing.' And as that charming actor used to say, it costs a lot of money and no one pays any attention to it. Even though we don't share his views, we must manage to do it at the least possible cost. It is contrary to my usual habits, but there is no use in being too smart... I am too anxious to write this music not to be willing to make some sacrifices....."

But nothing came of the project. Both men were too ill to work. "Toulet is dead and alive at the same time," Madame Debussy said. "We see him often, but his nervousness tires *Le Maître*, who is happy with the silence he enjoys here."

"There are mornings when the effort of dressing seems like one of the twelve labors of Hercules," Debussy complained. "I long for anything to happen that would save me the trouble, even a revolution or an earthquake. Without being unduly pessimistic I may say that my life is a hard one, for I have to fight against both disease and myself... I feel I am a nuisance to everyone. Lord, do people think it is any fun for me? If they are looking for someone to conduct the Music of the Spheres, I think I am perfectly fitted for that *high office*. Let's not talk about me."

Days, weeks and months dragged on. Debussy was not sure that if they had stayed in Paris he would not have felt just as well, perhaps better. He would wake up tired and annoyed before he knew what the day was like. He could not bring himself to do anything; even reading was a chore, and he would leave a book after glancing through a single page. Sometimes he took a ride in the country, but if he passed Toulet's house he would not call on him, he did not feel like seeing anyone. He said he had a new idea—to write a series of short concertos, like the series of sonatas, for piano and certain combinations of instruments. He wished he were at *Mon Coin* in Pourville, he wished for the summer months of 1915. He remembered how at the end of that summer he did not have enough music paper, "just like Russia without ammunition," [1] how he took his *Twelve Études* and the Sonata to Durand. He could plainly see that afternoon when he came into Durand's office in the Place de la Madeleine. He was playing the *Études*. It was so hot he had to take off his jacket. Durand was pleased. "I felt as though I had conquered and was back on my horse.... What has happened since?" Debussy pondered. He did not dare to think. He was two years older. "This is not exactly going to help my future ... I must, I absolutely must find the way out, to wipe away this sort of sweat that seems to crush my brain, because otherwise I will take a walk in another world."

Two events late in September of that summer gave him pleasure. Gaston Poulet came for a concert in St. Jean-de-Luz and they again played Debussy's sonata. After the intermezzo the audience called for an encore, but Debussy refused out of respect for the unity of the composition. If they were to repeat, he explained, they would have to play the whole sonata. And at two concerts of the Société Charles Bordes, Francis Planté, the famous pianist, played the Toccata from *Pour le Piano*, *Reflets dans l'eau* and *Mouvement*. Planté came to ask Debussy's advice and it pleased him. And then they talked about musicians in Paris—"What else is there?" Debussy asked.

---

[1] Russia had suffered her worst defeat on the German front in 1915 because of lack of ammunition.

He wished someone would explain to him what was going on in Russia—there were rumors of Russia signing a separate peace treaty with Germany. "These people have a strange sense of responsibility! Of course we always hear of 'mysterious Russia!'" Debussy grumbled. "If mystery means stupidity, I agree with you. The truth is that the country is absurdly large—they need two 'presidents' at least. The telephone may bring the ears together, but not necessarily the hearts. Do you blame them if 'the Petrogradians' don't always agree with the 'Moscovians'? With these strong words, I will go to bed and try to sleep . . . to sleep! It is to die a little. . . ."

The three long months "passed in the suffocating atmosphere of an eiderdown without leaving anything behind. If I were young," Debussy said, "I would write it down in my accounts under credit and debit and not speak about it. Alas! this is not my case. The sight of the suitcases will soon reappear . . . so melancholy . . . this time even more melancholy, when I have nothing to bring with me . . . not even the Basque songs. Bordes has probably collected them all. The Basques now love only false music, the kind that makes Negroes and nervous little children cry."

In October the Debussys returned to Paris. It was a cold autumn and Debussy was advised to remain in the house "to avoid a relapse," and later on, in bed. "Always in bed, in bed!" he said in desperation. "well then, let's correspond," he wrote Durand, and gave his instructions for a performance of *La Boîte à joujoux* he was anxious to see produced, because, he repeated, it was conceived in the true French spirit. He had managed to make a transcription for cello and piano of Bach's sonatas for *viola de gamba* and clavecin, and in his last letters to Toulet he spoke again of *As You Like It*.

"I work in a void and exhaust my strength on schemes which only increase my despair. Never before have I felt so weary of this pursuit of the unattainable . . ." Debussy complained. "Is this to be the end of me—of my constant desire to go forward, that meant more to me than bread and wine?"

"You are my only friend, alias Roderick Usher," he wrote Godet in his last letter. "Don't be angry with me if I am not going to speak any more about my plans... Music has completely abandoned me. If there is nothing to cry about, at least it is a little ridiculous. But it is not my fault and I have never forced anyone to love me—if music is badly served by me, it should address itself elsewhere...."

And when Alfred Bruneau came to see him, he showed him a few sheets of music paper covered with his handwriting. "Look at it," he said. "I can't compose any more."

During the following five months Debussy suffered terrible agonies of pain. He never left his bed. In January 1918 he showed signs of improvement. "For the first time in almost two months, this morning *Le Maître* traced a few lines on a piece of paper," Madame Debussy reported to Valléry-Radot. But these were the last in his handwriting.

When the German final offensive started with an intensive bombardment of Paris, Debussy was too weak to be taken down into their cellar for shelter. On March 24 Valléry-Radot came to see him. Debussy's eyes had a faraway look, his hands shook. He smiled as if awaking from a dream and said a few affectionate words. Then a haze enveloped his brain. He died on the following day at ten o'clock in the evening. Madame Debussy held his hand. Valléry-Radot closed his eyes as she withdrew from the bedside.

Debussy had wished to be buried at the Passy cemetery which he thought less sad than others in Paris. He would be there among the trees and the birds, he used to say. Chouchou outlived her father by one year. She died in 1919 of diphtheria. Madame Debussy died in 1934. All three rest at Passy.

But in 1918 the Debussys did not have a vault there and the remains of the composer were temporarily interred at Père Lachaise. Paris was under bombardment by Big Bertha. Many lives were lost and the crescendo of German fury was in its irresponsible, wild progress. It culminated in killing and maiming the men, women and children who, to the accompaniment of the choir that was once a source of Debussy's inspiration, prayed at the Saint Gervais church.

The Paris newspapers, curtailed because of the war, carried no obituary notice, and only a small group followed the coffin on the

long trek from the Square de Bois de Boulogne to the cemetery.
The long avenues were deserted except for army trucks rolling
along the boulevards toward the front.

As the procession turned into the narrow streets near Montmartre
a thin rain began to fall. A few curious shopkeepers came out to
watch the cortège go by. Women left their chores and stood silent
on the sidewalk while the boys ran to the coffin to read the inscrip-
tions on the wreaths. "It seems he was a musician," the women said
as they took the boys by the hand and walked them home.

A FOOTNOTE ON DEBUSSY'S "GABY"

By VICTOR SEROFF

Every student of Debussy's life has been interested in learning more about Gabrielle Dupont, "Gaby" as she was called, with whom the composer spent ten years. At the time when most biographies of Debussy were written there was so little information available that no one knew where she came from or where she went once their love-affair terminated. Alfred Cortot, the pianist, claimed once to have seen her working as an usherette in a theatre at Rouen. He was wrong. Gaby never lived in Rouen, never worked as an usherette in a theatre. The story, however, gave an erroneous conception of her later life.

After my biography of Debussy was published in a French translation, it apparently reached M. Henri Pellerin, the president of a society for the conservation of historical monuments and sites, who lives in Orbec-sur-Auge in Normandy. It induced him to write a lengthy article in "Le Pays d'Auge" about someone he personally had known well, and whose life belongs to the history of French music. Now, thanks to M. Pellerin, we have the answers to many questions about Gaby, filling in the details without which her portrait was incomplete.

No one among Debussy's friends ever mentioned where Debussy met her. The gossips claimed that he had picked her up in some frivolous place on one of his casual visits there. But that was not true. Gaby was born on June 11, 1866, at Lisieux in Normandy, of a middle-class bourgeois family. Her father Auguste-Edmond Dupont, also born in Lisieux, came from a family which in the sixteenth and seventeenth centuries gave France a number of students of law, landowners, and members of the clergy. He himself worked as a foreman in a textile factory. Tall, pleasant, and intelligent, he was well liked by the local community, although he was not regarded as a model of virtue. When Gaby grew up, they said, she resembled her father.

Her mother Henriette-Aimée, born Duchené, was a year younger than her husband. She was a good-looking woman, but local snobs considered her background inferior to that of Auguste and her intellectual horizon rather limited. Gaby had a sister Blanche, a year younger, whom she loved very much. Both girls worked at Lisieux: Blanche as a sales-girl in a shoe store and Gaby as a seamstress. But Gaby was beautiful, a coquette, and loved pretty clothes on others and even more on herself. She felt that Lisieux was too provincial.

At first, when she spoke about it, her parents were against her departure, but when she became of age they let her go to Paris. It was not long before she was noticed in the cafés she frequented after work, and she became the mistress of a young aristocrat, the Count of Villeneuve. This was her first love affair. It lasted only as long as such passions usually do. A year later, disappointed in her first experience and still looking for the *grand amour*, she met Debussy. She was twenty-two and he was four years older.

Gaby was in the prime of her beauty. She was blonde (actually a bleached *chataine Claire*). She had already then a strongly pronounced personality, accentuated by the way she carried herself — holding herself straight and often tossing her head back, which gave her a rather haughty appearance. But it was her eyes that caught everyone's attention — blue-green, "eyes of steel," as Debussy said, and "deep as the sea."

355

Gaby moved into Debussy's room on the third floor of an old dilapidated house at 42 rue de Londres at the foot of Montmartre, and, during the following ten years she kept a roof over their heads on their meagre earnings. In my book I have given as detailed an account of their life together as was then possible, but now I must add one episode which led Debussy to compose "Jardin sous la pluie."

Gaby loved Paris and yet she welcomed every opportunity to go to the country to visit her parents and her sister, who had married Jules Riffaut, a mechanical engineer, a widower with three children. They lived not far away from Lisieux in Orbec-en-Auge. There was, however, one obstacle to these visits. Jules Riffaut did not approve of Gaby's way of life in Paris and refused to receive "her lover" in his home. Blanche had a different temperament from her sister and a "different point of view" — her home, husband, and children meant everything to her — still, she loved Gaby and the two sisters met secretly while Debussy strolled along the streets of Orbec and examined the sights of the little town.

The fact that Debussy's and Gaby's relationship continued for seven years did not soften Monsieur Riffaut's attitude. Thus, on one of their visits to Orbec in 1895, Debussy sat for some time in a garden waiting for Gaby. He was particularly struck by the perfume of a yew-tree which the gardener was trimming. This, Gaby explained later, was why he used the theme from an old popular song "Nous n'irons plus au bois, les lauriers sont coupés." It began to rain just as Gaby came to fetch him and they returned to the hotel where they spent the night. Before going to bed Debussy made a few notes on a piece of paper — these were the seeds of "Jardin sous la pluie," one of his most-played piano pieces.

Because not much was known about Gaby, and because Debussy later spoke of her in a patronizing way, it has generally been assumed that she never was his intellectual equal. Actually, Gaby was remarkably intelligent and well read, with a keen appreciation and taste in music and painting. Debussy often consulted her about his works and while she may not have been able to advise him, he paid close attention to her reactions. She spoke of this to her family and her friends, and to M. Pellerin when she was reminiscing. She spoke of this simply, without bragging. If there were reasons for Debussy's complaints against Gaby (actually none have been recorded) Gaby, too, had much that was not to her liking. Debussy did not seem to mind living in artistic disorder, worrying very little about the slim chances of improving their financial situation. Gaby, a girl from Normandy (people in Normandy are supposed to be practical), wanted to have an orderly home, at least. Their Bohemian existence, with its constant lack of money, lost its original charm. It needed a philosophical attitude and a sense of humor which they seemed less and less to have been able to muster. But life in the garret on the rue de Londres, at times hell and at times heaven, still held her captive. Gaby was willing to bear it and to carry on, for she was deeply in love with Debussy. When, however, his philandering became more than an occasional sidestepping (these she forgave him, because he claimed they "did not count") — when he contemplated, not for the first time, marrying someone else — then even Gaby's patience came to an end.

One such incident almost drove her to suicide. While she was convalescing, her unhappiness was further aggravated by the sudden death of her father and worry over her mother's future. Gaby made several trips to install her mother in a small house she rented for her at Orbec. Debussy believed that these occupations would distract her and make her forget his latest escapade and forgive him once again, but Gaby had made up her mind. Although she returned and they continued to live under the same roof, they lived like strangers and Gaby was only biding her time for an opportunity to leave for good.

Perhaps just to appease her feminine pride, her wounded ego, she had a love affair with a painter. His name remains unknown, except for the initials V. M. The affair did not last long, but she kept the painting he gave her for the rest of her life. Gaby was waiting for someone who could offer her a better life and not "more of the same."

The opportunity offered itself when a wealthy South American banker, an amateur poet, called on Debussy and asked him to write some incidental music for his play "La Fille de Pasiphaé." Blond, bald, and with a long moustache, Count B. wished to be known in artistic circles simply as Monsieur Victor (hence René Peter's reference to him by the initial V.,) but in trying to persuade Debussy to collaborate on his play he did not fail to mention his financial resources. Debussy was not interested and declined the offer. Brandishing his manuscript like a whip Count B. shouted: "Monsieur, I am offering you half my glory!" — "Keep it all," Debussy advised the Count and saw him to the door.

Gaby happened to be present at this scene and she noticed that the banker liked her. Later she managed to meet him again. When she finally made her decision, she came back to get her things from the apartment. This time there were no tears. Debussy was in love with Lily Texier, a friend of Gaby, whom he married a few days later, and Gaby did not feel she was abandoning him to a lonely life. Parting with her, Debussy gave her the original manuscript of "L'Après-midi d'un Faune" with the following inscription: "A ma chère et très bonne petite Gaby, la sûre affection de son devoué Claude Debussy."

In a sumptuous apartment on the Avenue Niel, rented for her by her lover Count B., Gaby lived in the luxury and splendor she had been craving. Costly jewels, cupboards filled with elegant dresses, a carriage at her door, and servants — these were merely the necessary accessions for her new life. On the arm of the Count she moved in high society, giving parties, attending receptions at the Ministry of Foreign Affairs, going to the races and night-clubs and traveling abroad·as far as Cuba, where the Count had a part of his fortune. Gaby seems to have adapted herself to this life with the same ease as she had when she shared Debussy's on the rue de Londres. Of her old friends she saw no one except her sister and brother-in-law — they often came to stay with her. This time M. Riffaut objected neither to Gaby's mode of life, nor to her lover. Was she happy at last? Probably not. As the years went by she shared her charms with more than one man whose name could be found in the Paris social register. Eventually she had to think about her old age. In 1910 she bought a large house at Orbec, not far away from the garden that had inspired "Jardin sous la pluie."

Then came the war of 1914, and the Russian Revolution, which wiped out all of Gaby's savings, invested in Russian bonds. Shortly afterwards she moved to her house where her sister's family joined her. But the monotonous life in the provincial little town bored her, and whenever she found an occasion she returned to Paris to see her friends. Then her trips to the capital became less frequent. She remained in Orbec, seeing no one, reading and reminiscing about the old Bohemian days.

During all these years she followed Debussy's life through the newspapers. She read about the controversy over the first performance of "Pelléas," which he had composed with Gaby practically sitting at his elbow. At that time she was pleasantly surprised to receive from him a luxurious copy of the opera as a "testimony" of their past, so near and yet already so far. It was Debussy's last communication with her. Later, she read about Lily Texier's attempt at suicide, Debussy's marriage to Madame Bardac, his new home at 12 Square de Boise de Boulogne, his illness, and his death in 1918.

After ten years in Orbec Gaby finally decided she must have a change. Also, she needed money. Madame Valette, an old friend from Gaby's fashionable past, told her about Monsieur Colaneri, a doctor of medicine, at Forge-Neuve in Dordogne. The doctor was a widower and lived alone with his daughter. He was looking for a governess, someone "serious, conscientious, and honest."

Gaby arrived at Forge-Neuve "silent, distinguished, a little precious, but smiling" as the doctor described her. But later on, when she became used to her new environment, she was less shy. Of all the episodes in her past she preferred to talk about Debussy. "Why did you leave him?" the doctor asked. — "Because we had terrible quarrels on account of money. I know I was wrong to leave him, but I was young. It was terrible always to be without any money, never to be able to go out, to have fun. I knew a rich man . . . . he has died also, and now I am poor and alone."

She took wonderful care of the doctor and his daughter, but could remain with them only a few months because it tired her to climb the stairs.

Once again she returned to Orbec to her hermit's life. Only on rare occasions, such as, for instance, when her niece Elisabeth Riffaut was making her first communion and the family and their relatives gathered for the festive event, did Gaby feel she had to join them — she appeared in one of her resplendent dresses. Carrying her head proudly under a large black straw hat, *la belle Gaby*, as the people of the little town called her, looked as if she had stepped out of one of Toulouse-Lautrec's canvases. She belonged to *l'epoque brilliante* and she lived in her past. The town people knew that Gaby wanted to be left alone.

During the Second World War Gaby was saddened by the death of her sister in 1943, and during the German occupation she suffered particularly from the lack of tobacco. She was a tobacco addict. The cigarettes generously given her by her family and friends were not sufficient. Often she was seen at night, dressed in an old over-coat with a gray knitted cap on her head scurrying along the walls of the houses looking for cigarette-butts. She did not care if any one saw her. While the battle for the liberation of France was on, Gaby was evacuated along with the aged from the hospital at Orbec to the Chateau de Familly. There she remained from June till September (1944). Gaby was seventy-eight years old and seemed not to realize the gravity of the situation. When she returned home she looked like a ghost. A few months later she had an accident. She fell and broke her hip. Pneumonia developed, and Gaby died on May 12, 1945.

INDEX